Casualty of War

Number Eighteen
Eastern European Studies
Stjepan Meštrović, Series Editor

Series Editorial Board
Norman Cigar
Bronislaw Misztal
Sabrina Ramet
Vladimir Shlapentokh
Keith Tester

Casualty of War

A CHILDHOOD REMEMBERED

By *Luisa Lang Owen*
Foreword by Charles M. Barber

For Charlie
with gratitude
and affection

Luisa Lang Owen

Texas A&M University Press
College Station

The paper used in this book meets the minimum requirements of the American
National Standard for Permanence of Paper for Printed Library Materials, z39.48-1984.
Binding materials have been chosen for durability.

Library of Congress Cataloging-in-Publication Data

Owen, Luisa Lang, 1935–
    Casualty of war : a childhood remembered / by Luisa Lang Owen ; foreword by
    Charles M. Barber.— 1st ed.
       p. cm — (Eastern European studies ; no. 18)
    ISBN 1–58544–212–7 (alk. paper)
      1. Owen, Luisa Lang 1935– 2. Germans—Yugoslavia. 3. Genocide—
Yugoslavia. 4. Yugoslavia—History—1945–1980. I. Title.
  II. Eastern European studies (College Station, Tex.) ; no. 18.
  DR1305.095A3   2003
  949.702—dc21   2002006713

To the memory of my parents, Barbara Schüsler Lang, and Johann Lang

and

In commemoration of survivors and those who did not live.

Contents

Illustrations

Maps

Foreword

Concentration camps are no place for a young girl—nor for any human being, naturally. But a girl like Luisa Lang, caught up in the machinery of hatred so common to the genocidal conflicts of the twentieth century, somehow evokes our poignant horror even more than other victims. Numb and indifferent as the unaffected may become to the mass slaughter of adults, the grisly fate of a child challenges our callousness and dares us not to let at least some sorrow and compassion break through.

Unlike many less fortunate children in the aftermath of World War II, Luisa Lang survived, but she was never separated from the experiences that became her memoir. Few would have reason to doubt its authenticity. Sympathy is another matter, perhaps. Luisa is German; well, more or less German. She spoke the language from childhood. But she also spoke Serbo-Croatian. She was *Volksdeutsch* (ethnic German), a *Donauschwabe* (Danube Swabian), a German-Hungarian—take your pick. She was, at any rate, not the sort of German whom Germans brought up in Bismarck's or Kaiser Wilhelm's Germany and recognized as "authentically" German. These latter called themselves *Reichsdeutsche* (national or imperial Germans), and looked down their noses at Volksdeutsche, the way big-city society matrons and their banker husbands might disregard "country bumpkin cousins" in the United States.[1] And the Nazis, despite their proclamations of solidarity with all German-speaking peoples, actively discriminated against Volksdeutsche, both individually and collectively. When drunken guards of Reserve Police Battalion 101 went looking for a Pole to kill on New Year's eve but killed an ethnic German by mistake, they simply covered it up by switching identity cards with one of their Polish victims.[2] On a larger scale, the male Danube Swabians of Yugoslavia of military age were drafted en masse into the Waffen SS, not only because it suited Himmler's purposes but also because they were ineligible to enter the Wehrmacht, which was for "national Germans only."[3] For some of those who survived and chose to emigrate to the United States, this act, totally beyond their control, proved to be a permanent burden.

In 1944, unfortunately for Luisa Lang, the crimes committed by Hitler's national Germany in the name of Germans everywhere, whether they approved or not, were avenged in kind once the Third Reich began to disintegrate. Amidst the bloodletting that Yugoslavs were all too willing to inflict on one another, there was little room for the Red Army or Tito's partisans to accept the humanity of the Švabe or Danube Swabians. Hitler's genocidal imperialism had simply been too awful for tolerance to rear its inconvenient head.

Luisa Lang was luckier than many, however. Although she too was "guilty by reason of race," a condition she could not avoid, she and her fellow Danube Swabians were the targets of random revenge and ethnic cleansing rather than systematic extermination. On a scale of relative horror, this was a break. Luisa thus did not become one of the more than thirty thousand children who died in Yugoslav captivity, or one of the estimated 2 million Volksdeutsche killed in the *Vertreibung* (Expulsion), the ethnic cleansing of the Germans from Eastern and east-central Europe.

Luisa's captors also did something quite unusual for bitter partisans. They allowed her the power, albeit briefly, to break through to them in a poignant way. Luisa Lang could sing one Serbian folk song—"Jedno dete malo"—sweetly, and the more it was requested by the partisans around their campfires, the harder it became for her tormentors to hate her, at least in these pithy moments.[4] That Luisa Lang should know both German and Serbo-Croatian folksongs from her childhood is an example of what made the 2 million Donauschwaben unique among the Volksdeutsche of Eastern Europe. The musicality that stretched beyond language and cultural boundaries had been a hallmark of these German-speaking settlers of the middle Danube for close to three hundred years. In a discussion of one of their poets, Nickolaus Lenau, Agnes Vardy quotes a saying attributed to Metternich that Lenau was "a Hungarian poet who sang in German."[5] The Danube Swabians living in Yugoslavia, Romania, and Hungary were, in fact, descendants of pioneers who settled there in the seventeenth and eighteenth centuries in the wake of Habsburg military victories against the Turks.[6]

The expulsion of ethnic Germans from Eastern Europe and Russia was a traumatic event involving the lives of some 14–16 million people at the end of World War II. It did not occur in isolation, however. It was part of a collective rage against Germans channeled by governments in Eastern European countries that had suffered under Wehrmacht depredation and Nazi imperial rule. Although some Reichs- and Volksdeutsche had been enthusiastic supporters of the Nazis, some had been sympathetic, and many had been resigned to Hitler's reign, most of the ethnic German refugees had had no culpable connection with Wehrmacht and Nazi actions. They were wives, children, and elders, left in the path of the Red Army and partisans as the Wehrmacht and SS divisions retreated toward a crumbling Third Reich. Their fate is not generally known to the American people. It was also not well known to the American experts at the Potsdam Conference in July–August, 1945. As Robert Murphy, special envoy to Presidents Roosevelt and Truman, reports: "There is no doubt that many of us in the West were indifferent, or actually uninformed and casual about the flight of these millions of Germans."[7]

At the onset of the flight and expulsion (October, 1944–January, 1945), roughly 600,000 Hungarian Danube Swabians lived south and west of Budapest along the Danube, although some scattered settlements could be found in all corners of the country.[8] Some 585,000 Romanian Danube Swabians lived primarily in the Banat and Sathmar, with some intermingled with the Transylvanian Saxons. Because the Transylvanian Saxons settled in the twelfth century A.D., they are usually treated separately. They were mostly Lutheran, while the Danube Swabians were, for the most part, Roman Catholic. Nevertheless, the Saxon experiences in the Vertreibung often paralleled those of the Danube Swabians in the Banat and those of the Volksdeutsche in the rest of Eastern Europe.[9] About 510,000 Yugoslavian Danube Swabians lived primarily in the northeast sector of Yugoslavia called the Vojvodina, broken down regionally into the Banat, Bačka/Baranja, and Srem.[10] Definitive numbers before and after the expulsion may not appear for a long time, if ever.[11]

Luisa Lang's people were the descendants of farmers and skilled workers who were the economic backbone of their respective areas. Recruited originally for their agricultural skills, they had flourished under the policies of the Habsburgs. Danube Swabians had thus lived in their respective villages since as early as the late seventeenth century in relative peace with their Magyar, Slavic, and Romanian neighbors, under a German-speaking emperor, until nineteenth-century nationalism, World War I, and the Treaty of Trianon put them on the cultural defensive. In 1920 most of the Donauschwaben were anxious to prove themselves good citizens of Hungary, Romania, or Yugoslavia, while hanging onto their German language and customs, but this was not an easy task. When a linguistics professor in Budapest, Jakob Bleyer, coined the term "Danube Swabian" in 1922, he could not imagine the larger events of the Nazi disaster that would sweep away his *Landsleute*. He was concerned, instead, with the smaller but still nasty effects of the Treaty of Trianon and Magyar nationalism, as his fellow former Hungarian-Germans reacted to Romanian and Yugoslav (primarily

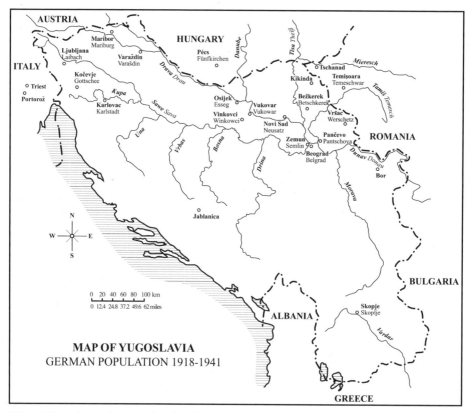

AUSTRIA

HUNGARY

ITALY

Maribor
Mariburg

Ljubljana
Laibach

Varaždin
Varašdin

Pécs
Fünfkirchen

Kočevje
Gottschee

Triest

Portorož

Karlovac
Karlstadt

Kupa

Drava Drau

Save Sava

Una

Vrbas

Bosna

Drina

Osijek
Esseg

Vinkovci
Winkowci

Vukovar
Vukowar

Novi Sad
Neusatz

Danube

Tisa Theiß

Tschanad

Kikinda

Temișoara
Temeschwar

Bežkerek
Betschkerek

Vršac
Werschetz

Mieresch

Tamiš Temesch

ROMANIA

Zemun
Semlin

Pančevo
Pantschova

Beograd
Belgrad

Danav Donau

Bor

Morava

Jablanica

N
W — E
S

0 20 40 60 80 100 km
0 12.4 24.8 37.2 49.6 62 miles

MAP OF YUGOSLAVIA
GERMAN POPULATION 1918-1941

BULGARIA

ALBANIA

Skopje
Skoplje

Vardar

GREECE

Map 1. Yugoslavia, showing the distribution of its German population, 1918–41. After a map in *Verbrechen an den Deutschen in Jugoslawien 1944–1948* (Munich: Donauschwäbische Kulturstiftung—Stiftung des privaten Rechts, München 1998).

Serbian) nationalism. Although Bleyer's efforts in post-Trianon Hungary and those of like-minded moderate conservatives, such as Kaspar Muth and Andreas Nagelbach in Romania and Father Adam Berenz in Yugoslavia, have gone unheralded, they have not gone unrecorded. In addition to numerous Heimatbücher, oral testimonies, and secondary works, there is the substantial collection of materials known as the Ostdokumentation at the Bundesarchiv in Koblenz. Although they have shown up in at least one partial study of the Danube Swabians, these rich materials have yet to be tapped in sufficient depth to yield the full story.[12] Until such documents are used with regularity as sources by Anglophone historians, monographs and general studies of the Danube Swabians and Volksdeutsche will continue to reflect the anti-German stereotypes that have bedeviled German-Americans since World War I.

The Ostdokumentation/Jugoslawien/Rumänien/Ungarn is organized by author, region, and village. These documents include reports of local political and military authorities and eyewitness depositions concerning the SS, the Prinz Eugen Division, flight, internment, and expulsion. There also is an entire section of questionnaires sent out by the Bundesarchiv in the late 1950s to former Danube Swabian officials. The virtue of these documents is that they give a glimpse into the thought processes of the "acted-upon," rather than simply those of the "actors"—the movers and shakers of Nazi policy, whose viewpoints come out so clearly in sources at the U.S. National Archives, at Bonn, at the Berlin Document Center, and in SS materials in Koblenz. To ignore the Ostdokumentation is to ignore the voices of those for whom the Nazi leadership may have had great plans but who were not consulted as to what those plans might be.

When one peruses the Ostdokumentation, it becomes rather clear that the vast majority of Danube Swabians during Hitler's reign in Eastern Europe fall into the category of bystander rather than murderer, victim, or,

Map 2. Vojvodina, with distribution of the ethnic minority shaded; Serbo-Croat and German names are given for places mentioned in the book. Major death camps are indicated by solid circles and double asterisks. Enlargement based on Map 1.

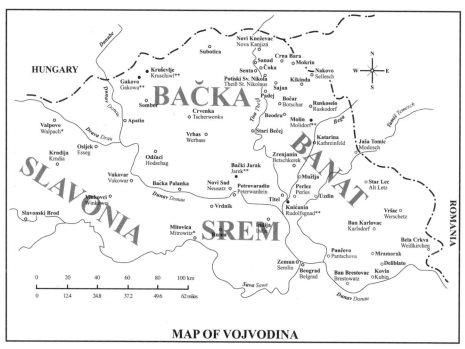

MAP OF VOJVODINA

least likely of all, hero. This large bystander category is defined by Cynthia Ozick in her prologue to Gay Block and Malka Drucker's *Rescuers: Portraits of Moral Courage in the Holocaust:* "Three 'participant' categories of the Holocaust are commonly named: murderers, victims, bystanders. . . . Probably it is hardest of all to imagine ourselves victims. . . . But what of the bystanders?: They were not the criminals, after all. . . . A bystander is like you and me, the ordinary human article—what normal man or woman or adolescent runs to commit public atrocities. . . . A hero—like a murderer— is an exception, . . . a kind of social freak . . . Taken collectively, . . . the bystanders are culpable. But taking human beings 'collectively' is precisely what we are obliged not to do."[13]

After the fall of 1944, the Donauschwaben are no longer bystanders to the Holocaust but victims of ethnic cleansing. Their voices can be found among other Volksdeutsche in the eight volumes of testimony published by West Germany's Ministry for Expellees, Refugees, and War Victims in 1956 (in German) and 1961 (in English).[14] The first three volumes are devoted to Reichsdeutsche, destroyed and driven out of territories east of the Oder/ Neisse boundary that became incorporated into Poland and the Soviet Union. Volumes 4 and 5 deal with Donauschwaben and other Volksdeutsche ethnically cleansed from Hungary and Romania. Volumes 6 and 7 concern the removal of Sudeten Germans from Czechoslovakia. Volume 8 chronicles the fate of the Donauschwaben in Yugoslavia.[15]

It was in Yugoslavia that the fate of the Danube Swabians was most catastrophic. On November 21, 1944, the legal basis for proceedings against the Swabians was laid down at Jajce (Bosnia) by the Antifascist Council of the Yugoslav Peoples' Liberation (AVNOJ). All persons of German descent in Yugoslavia, regardless of previous political affiliation or anti-Nazi activity, lost their citizen and civilian rights. Second, all possessions, movable and immovable, of all persons of German descent were henceforth considered as confiscated by the state. Third, persons of German descent could neither claim or practice any privileges (rights) nor apply to courts of justice or to state institutions for their personal or legal protection. The only legal exceptions to this were Danube Swabians who were children from a marriage with one parent of Slav, Hungarian, Romanian, Macedonian, Italian, Gypsy, or any other but German descent or those who had married someone who was not German.[16]

Besides initial slaughters, legal proscriptions, and mass deportations, which numbered as many as forty thousand for 1944, each district had its slave work camp housing Swabians who were able to work.[17] Those who could not work were put into concentration camps: "Their inmates were old people but, above all, children. Those children who through the deportation became orphans peopled those death mills by the thousands and were mercilessly ground into death. Whoever in those concentration camps could work offered to; if he was accepted he had the rations of the slave work camps. Those who did not succeed to get those rations—and children almost never did—was [sic] cruelly starved to death in a short time."[18]

Two of the best secondary treatments of the general expulsion are by Geza Paikert, *The German Exodus: A Selective Study on the Post–World War II Expulsion of German Populations and Its Effects*, published in 1962, and *The Danube Swabians: German Populations in Hungary, Romania and Yugoslavia and Hitler's Impact on their Patterns*, published in 1967.[19] Also, in 1987, the Land government of Baden-Württemberg opened up the Institut für Donauschwäbische Geschichte und Landeskunde in Tübingen, a likely source of continuing research in this area. Examples of expellee memoirs published in English are quite numerous. They include Elizabeth B. Walter, *Barefoot in the Rubble*; Eve Eckert Kœhler, *Seven Susannahs, Daughters of the Danube*; Traudie Müller Wlossak, as told to Margaret Farnan, *The Whip: My Homecoming*; Maria Schnur, *Unforgettable Years*; Michael Nagelbach, *Heil and Farewell*, and Elvera Ziebart Reuer, as told to Marjorie Knittel, *The Last Bridge*.[20] Also, most of the Danube Swabian Heimatbücher for each of the former home towns have a chapter on the expulsion at the end of each local history.[21]

What is needed, besides thorough consultation of these ample resources, is a greater attempt by students of twentieth-century German history, American history, and German-American history to make a differentiation between the politics of warmaking in World Wars I and II and its counterpart—the politics of revenge in the postwar periods. In addition, there needs to be a better focused search for historical accuracy among the documents and voices of the less powerful, and for its counterpart, simple justice. Nowhere is this issue more dramatically demonstrated than in legal cases involving American Danube Swabians and the U.S. Office of Special Investigations (OSI). According to information from documents in at least two deportation cases in United States District Court, Northern District of Ohio, Eastern Division, the United States Department of Justice has engaged in suppression of evidence that would have exonerated Danube Swabians accused of violating visa regulations as members of the proscribed Waffen SS.[22] In a letter of November 1, 1995, to Eve Eckert Kœhler, Joseph McGuinness of Cleveland, attorney for the defendants, described the process by which the OSI prosecution suppressed information vital to a proper defense. The documents showed that the U.S. State Department, on August 20, 1951, had revised the collective condemnation of Nuremberg to exclude any enlisted man in the Waffen SS, Prinz Eugen Division, below the rank of major.[23] Although the OSI was briefly brought up short in the 1990s by this courageous lawyer, and a few stalwart federal judges, such a process against people who came to this country secure in the faith that they would be fairly treated reeks of the odor of McCarthyism.[24]

Despite its uniqueness, Luisa Lang's story shares some common threads with those of her predecessors. She is trying to exorcize the devilish nightmares of her experience by committing them to paper. That is a traditional approach for any victim of wartime horror. But as a Danube Swabian, as a Volksdeutsche, she writes in the face of a powerful stereotype. She and other Danube Swabian memoirists know that they were victims, but they live in an America that refuses to accept such a role for them. When Elsa Walter tried to tell her story in a high school English essay, her teacher handed it back with "This is not true!" written in red across it.[25] The refighting of World War II, almost every year since 1945, by Hollywood, by journalists, and by popular historians, has produced a mindset that is loath to accept the idea of Germans as victims. Luisa Lang Owen's fellow Americans are led to believe at their local movie houses, newsstands, and bookstores that her people could not possibly have been mere bystanders during World War II—and certainly not victims. Only the role of perpetrator is available for the ethnic German in the mind's eye of American popular culture and media, despite the fact that close to one quarter of the American population, in the twentieth century (52 million in 1988) is of German descent.[26] Victimhood for Germans, Reichsdeutsche or Volksdeutsche, therefore, is not part of the script. Unfortunately for Luisa, she did not grow up in a script. She grew up in Knićanin—Rudolfsgnad—a concentration camp.

None of the material I have mentioned, however, has quite the power to match Luisa's story. Documentations of the Vertreibung may shock us with their brutalities and sadness to the point of paralysis, but they do not move us in quite the same way as this simple and painful story, told by a child through the adult, a story that refused to die out in the aging process. Because of her special linguistic and singing talent as a child, and her determination not to forget, Luisa becomes a powerful voice for the voiceless Donauschwaben of her generation.

No child ever "has it coming," no matter what the crimes of the parents. And if the family members have committed no crimes—what then? Guilty by reason of ethnicity? Simple questions to ask, but difficult ones to be borne in mind by Americans when the victims are German speaking. To ignore these questions is to accept the ideology of collective guilt, thus drowning out both common sense and common decency. In reading Luisa's story, it becomes apparent that the Austrian/German Adolf Hitler was actually more foreign to these Donauschwaben than the Serbian King Peter. Few of us in the post–World War II world can grasp such a commonplace for the Danube Swabians, unless we read a speaker for her people like Luisa Lang Owen. This poignant and bittersweet tale of her survival in Yugoslavia and emigration to the United States allows us a glance at the power of charm over brutality, when it is allowed to emerge, however fortuitously, and however rare such golden moments might be.

—Charles M. Barber

Notes

1. William C. Sherman and Playford V. Thorson, eds., *Plains Folk: North Dakota's Ethnic History* (Fargo: North Dakota Institute for Regional Studies, 1988), 120–21.

2. Christopher Browning, *Ordinary Men: Reserve Police Battalion 101 and the Final Solution in Poland* (New York: Harper Perennial, 1993), 41

3. Robert Lewis Koehl, *The Black Corps: The Structure and Power Struggles of the Nazi SS* (Madison: University of Wisconsin Press), 207.

4. "A little child"—who lost her mother, looked for her everywhere in the world, and would not go home to her stepmother.

5. Agnes Huszar Vardy, *A Study in Austrian Romanticism: Hungarian Influences in Lenau's Poetry*, Program in East European and Slavic Studies, no. 6 (Buffalo, N.Y.: State University College at Buffalo, 1974), 27, 122.

6. For descriptions of the victories of Prince Eugene of Savoy and the Danube Swabian settlement that followed, see R. W. Seton-Watson, *Racial Problems in Hungary* (New York: Howard Fertig, 1908); Count Paul Teleki, *The Evolution of Hungary and Its Place in European History* (1922; reprint Béla Király, ed., Gulf Breeze, Fla.: Academic International Press, 1975), 80–86; C. A. MacCartney, *Hungary, A Short History* (Chicago: Aldine Publishing Company, 1962), 116–19. An interesting map of the major Danube Swabian migrations in the eighteenth century can be found in Kinder and Hilgemann, *The Anchor Atlas of World History*, vol. 1 (New York: Doubleday, 1974), 286.

7. Alfred M. deZayas, *Nemesis at Potsdam: The Anglo-Americans and the Expulsion of the Germans* (London: Routledge and Kegan Paul, 1977), xv.

8. Alfred M. deZayas, "The Legality of Mass Population Transfers: The German Experience 1945–48," *East European Quarterly* 12, no. 1, p. 8; see also maps in A. Burkardt, "Zur Volksbiologie des ungarländischen Deutschtums in der Nachkriegszeit," *Sonderdruck aus Deutsches Archiv für Landes- und Volksforschung* (S. Hirzel, Leipzig), L. Jahrgang, Heft 3, July–August 1937.

9. DeZayas, "Legality," 8.

10. DeZayas, "Legality," 8; see also maps in Leopold Egger, *Das Vermögen und*

die Vermögensverluste der Deutschen in Jugoslavien (Sindelfingen: Landsmannschaft der Donauschwaben), 1983.

11. The figures for the notes 8–10 were compiled by Alfred deZayas from West German sources (Statistisches Bundesamt, *die Deutschen Vertreibungs— Verluste*, Kirchlicher Suchdienst, *Gesamterhebung*, and *Brockhaus Enzyklopädie*). They represent a point between higher estimates of Anton Tafferner, a Danube Swabian contributor to the Südostdeutsches Archiv, Munich, and lower estimates of the official statistical organs in Hungary, Romania, and Yugoslavia. For other estimates see Steven Kertesz, "The Expulsion of the Germans from Hungary: A Study in Postwar Diplomacy," *Review of Politics*, 1953, pp. 179–208; Joseph Schechtman, *Postwar Population Transfers in Europe, 1945–1955* (Philadelphia: University of Pennsylvania Press, 1962), chap. 11; Egger, *Das Vermögen*, 13–18; and "Expellees and Refugees of German Ethnic Origin," *Report of a Special Subcommittee of the Committee on the Judiciary, House of Representatives, Washington D.C.*, March 24, 1950, 87 pp.

12. Anthony Komjathy and Rebecca Stockwell, *German Minorities and the Third Reich: Ethnic Germans of East Central Europe between the Wars* (New York: Holmes and Meier, 1980).

13. Cynthia Ozick, prologue, in Gay Block and Malka Drucker, *Rescuers: Portraits of Moral Courage in the Holocaust* (New York: Homes and Meier, 1992), xi–xvi.

14. *Dokumentation der Vertreibung der Deutschen aus Ost-Mitteleuropa*, (8 vols.) *Vertreibung I: Östlich der Oder/Neiße 1; Vertreibung I: Östlich der Oder/Neiße 2; Vertreibung I: Östlich der Oder/Neiße 3; Vertreibung II: Ungarn; Vertreibung III: Rumænien, Vertreibung IV: Tschechoslowakei 1; Vertreibung IV: Tschechoslowakei 2; Vertreibung V: Jugoslavien* (Bonn: Bundesministerium fuer Vertriebene, Flüchtlinge und Kriegsgeschädigte, 1956); English edition, *Documents on the Expulsion of the Germans from Eastern-Central Europe* (Bonn: Federal Ministry for Expellees, Refugees, and War Victims, 1961).

15. Ibid.

16. Ostdokumentation (OSTDOK) 16/Jugoslavien (Jug.), Bundesarchiv, 5400 Koblenz [Karthause], Potsdamer Str. 1, Postfach 320, #25, 5–6; see also Sepp Janko, *Weg und Ende der deutschen Volksgruppe in Jugoslawien* (Graz-Stuttgart: Leopold Stocker Verlag, 1982), 303.

17. Ostdokumentation, 6–7. In the Banat they were located at Werschetz (Vršac), Gross-Betschkerek (Veliki Bečkerek), Gross-Kikinda (Velika-Kikinda), and Pančevo. In the Bačka they were located at Neusatz (Novisad), Palanka (Bačka Palanka), Hodschak (Odžaci), Werbass (Novi Vrbas), Apatin, Sombor, and Subotica as well as Semlin (Zemun), Mitrovica, and Esseg (Jetfal/Osijek).

18. Ibid., 8.

19. Geza Paikert, *The German Exodus: A Selective Study on the Post–World War II Expulsion of German Populations and Its Effects*, (The Hague: Martinus Nijhoff, 1962), and *The Danube Swabians: German Populations in Hungary*,

Rumania and Yugoslavia and Hitler's Impact on their Patterns (The Hague: Martinus Nijhoff, 1967.

20. Elizabeth B. Walter, *Barefoot in the Rubble* (Palatine, Ill.: Pannonia Press, 1997), 265 pp.; Eve Eckert Kœhler, *Seven Susannahs, Daughters of the Danube* (Milwaukee: Danube Swabian Society, 1976); Traudie Müller Wlossak, as told to Margaret Farnan, *The Whip: My Homecoming* (Canberra, Australia: Golden Leaf Publishers, 1982); Maria Schnur, *Unforgettable Years* (Chicago: Bollman Publications, 1983); Michael Nagelbach, *Heil and Farewell: A Life in Romania, 1913–1946* (Chicago: Adams Press, 1986); Elvera Ziebart Reuer, as told to Marjorie Knittel, *The Last Bridge* (Aberdeen, S.D.: North Plains Press, 1984). *Seven Susannahs* received an honorable mention from the Council for Wisconsin Writers as one of the best nonfiction books of 1976 by a Wisconsin writer.

21. Other sources in English and German include: C. A. Macartney, *Hungary and Her Successors, The Treaty of Trianon and Its Consequences, 1919–1937* (New York: Oxford University Press, 1937); Anton Scherer, *Donauschwäbische Bibliographie, 1935–1955: Das Schrifttum über die Donauschwaben in Ungarn, Rumänien, Jugoslawien und Bulgarien sowie—nach 1945—in Deutschland, Österreich, Frankreich, USA, Canada, Argentinien und Brasilien* (München: Verlag des Südostdeutschen Kulturwerks, 1966), 407 pp.; Johann Weidlein, *Pannonica: Ausgewählte Abhandlungen und Aufsätze zur Sprach-und Geschichtsforschung der Donauschwaben und der Madjaren* (Schorndorf, Federal Republic of Germany: Im Selbstverlag des Verfassers, 1979), 424 pp.; *Der Prozess gegen Dr. Franz Anton Basch* (Schorndorf: Im Selbstverlag des Verfassers, 1956), 17 pp.; Johann Wüscht, *Population Losses in Yugoslavia during World War II, 1941–1945* (Bonn: Edition Atlantic-Forum, 1963); *Die Ereignisse in Syrmien, 1941–1944* (Kehl am Rhein: Im Selbstverlag, 1975); *Die magyarische Okkupation der Batschka, 1941–1944* (Kehl: author's ed., 1975); *Beitrag zur Geschichte der Deutschen in Jugoslawien* (Kehl: author's ed., 1966), and *Ursachen und Hintergründe des Schicksals der Deutschen in Jugoslawien* (Kehl: author's ed., 1966); and the story of Adam Berenz in Michael Merkl, ed., *Weitblick eines Donauschwaben: Widerstand gegen national-sozialistische Einflüsse unter den Donauschwaben Jugoslawiens und Ungarns 1935–1944* (Dieterskirch: author's ed., 1968).

22. Mark Rollenhagen, "Finding Truth about German Guard Consumes Lawyer," *Cleveland Plain Dealer,* January 12, 1997; "United States of America, Plaintiff, vs. George Lindert, Defendant," *In the United States District Court Northern District of Ohio Eastern Division,* Case No. 4:92 CV 1365, Judge Ann Aldrich, September 6, 1995; and "United States of America, Plaintiff, vs. Algimantas Dailide, Defendant," *In the United States District Court Northern District of Ohio Eastern Division,* Case No. 1:94 CV 2499, Judge Paul R. Matia, Filer Jan. 2, 1997, 1:58 P.M.

23. Document #1: L'Heureux, Chief, Visa Division, Department of State, Washington, October 2, 1951; Document #2: Mr. Robert J. Corkery, Coor-

dinator, Mr. Edward M. O'Connor, Acting Chairman, "Action by the Commission on Proposals Concerning the Revised Inimical List of June 21, 1951"; Document #3: "Interoffice Memorandum," U.S. Displaced Persons Commission Headquarters, Frankfurt, "To: All Senior Officers— Instruction Memo N. 242 From: Robert J. Corkery, Coordinator for Europe Date: 12 Nov. L95L Subject: Modification of Revised Inimical List dated 21 June 1951 (Waffen SS)," 1.

24. Mark Rollenhagen, "Finding Truth."
25. Walter, *Barefoot in the Rubble,* dust jacket
26. J. Richly, ed., *Adressbuch Deutsch-Amerikanischer Vereine und Gesellschaften in den USA* (Chicago: US-Directory, 1. Auflage, 1988), 14, 15.

Preface

I started this book in response to revisiting Rudolfsgnad, Knićanin, as a private account to express my experiences, to bring them to clarity. Events that happened in the former Yugoslavia soon after sharpened my intent. Despite the public outrage about atrocities witnessed at the end of World War II (1945), those that happened in the Vojvodina in 1945–48 went virtually unnoticed, and now, after fifty years, there is not even a footnote in the news, anywhere, linking the new horrors with past atrocities practiced by the same government to eliminate its ethnic German minority. This telling neglect now doing away with us publicly provoked a public response; instead of a memoir for my grandchildren, I became more determined to see it as a published book.

Before the first chapter of the manuscript was in the computer, a document arrived—a deposition my grandfather, Johann Schüssler, had given in 1951 about his experiences in Yugoslavia in 1945–48—with not even a letter to explain its arrival. I later found out it had been sent through my aunt Elisabeth Martin by Nora Kendl, whose husband was with us in the concentration camps. I took this as encouragement to complete a collective account; and a whole community of survivors, the larger village, showed interest and gave their support.

About my memory: as an artist, I have always relied on sense impressions, the felt quality of things. Thinking on this level is easy for me. The texture of a doll's dress remembered may recall other details—the width of its hem, its color, its puffed sleeves. Such remembering is not altogether unlike an anthropological dig, where small shards convey the larger object. Some things I remembered while writing; writing the first chapters was like revisiting my home. Memories of our pantry, perhaps its dark smell, recalled other details. Groping though the sensuous images, I would "see" the shelves and "discover" the oilcloth with which they were covered. The circular walker, remembered, which I would have experienced before I was one, could be verified; I could ask my mother about it. The image of the cage-carrying birds on the horizon in Knićanin was verified, years later, by my aunt, who was one of the women coming home from the woods at dusk; though she did not see the image, she knew when I described it what I had seen. But the liquid blue of tetka Mila's eyes cannot be verified, and not just because she is dead; even if the color were well described, it is uncertain if anyone would imagine the same blue as I do, and it is impossible to determine how close these blues are to the color her eyes actually were. Looking for the true color of memory, its absolute accuracy, is like looking for the color of a painting as it was when the artist painted it, centuries ago. To the experience of the painting, the search for its "true" color is irrelevant. Memories, like sensuous images, are not verifiable like facts. As experience expressed, they can, however, be known. The act of recalling my experiences was a celebratory act, and the best of my memory was offered to clarify the larger event, the experience in common.

Acknowledgments

Thanks go first to my mother, whose strength and resourcefulness helped us to survive, and to my father, whose goodness continues to inspire; to my son Erik for his wisdom and generous heart; to him and his wife, Deirdre, for providing the pen and the motivation, and to my grandchildren, Marina and Oona, who brought with them the world of the child.

To the memory of my friend Anna Bramanti Gregor, whose grace and affection recalled the feeling of belonging, my lasting gratitude. Thanks go to my friend Elizabeth Reischl for her understanding and belief in the work, for many readings, wise suggestions, and good discussions over lunch. Without her continued support I would not have had the courage to persevere; I hope she knows how grateful I am.

I am indebted to my relatives, the larger village, for confirming my account of their experiences; to Rose and Josef Schüssler and especially to Elisabeth Martin for providing dates and verifications; to Walter and Werner Lang, Johann Martin, and Josef Schuessler for their support; and to Josef Marschang, Robert Kiss, Zita Forrai, Ervin and Eta Kis, and Vladimir Berger for checking my Serbo-Croatian, Hungarian, and village dialect.

I extend my gratitude to first readers Sada Ashby and Ann Guthrie, for their insight and encouragement, and to others who read the work—Anna Bellisari, Andrée Bognár, Suzanne Clauser, Nick Crome, John Ferguson, Richard Freeman, Mary McIver, Elisabeth Schüssler Fiorenza, Charles Funderburk, Erna and Josef Schuessler, Suzy Sebastian, Michael Trapp, and Burga Voudris—for their support. Special thanks go to Ralph Keyes for his invaluable advice, and to Rosemarie Friz for her generous help.

Many thanks to April Holten and Joyce Thomas for assistance with the computer; to Elizabeth at OMS Photography, Doug Snyder, Nancy Koehler, and Frances Cooper for their help; and to my colleagues at the College of Education and Human Services at Wright State University for their support.

To friends Frank and Vera Berger, Dorothy Drake, Wilma Focht, Walter and Rosemarie Friz, Elisabeth Jung, Angela Kemper, Horst and Maria Klemm, Maria Rendl, Vivian Varney, Pat White, Erdmute Yakovski, and Yolie and Berger Mayne for leading the cheering section, thank-you.

I am grateful to all who are mentioned in this book, especially to the humanity of Mila Zorić; I honor her memory with my life.

Profound gratitude goes to Stjepan Meštrović for his support; and to James Sadkovich for his wisdom and guidance in transforming the memoir into a book and for making everything easy.

Casualty of War

Introduction

Florence is dry-cleaning its art,
the Botticellis are bleating
claiming the right pallor, dead on the mark.
Cleansed of all poetic past, expunged of all experience,
free of all those gazes, of all those eyes
that layered them with glazes love and time bestowed.
Cleansed. They stiffen estranged boasting their name.

And haven't I seen the solemn-faced comings and goings
at Santa Maria del Carmine,
hovering over Masaccio, intensive care encased,
entrusted to restorers; an army of resuscitators,
redeeming it, those bastard saviors,
restoring it to everlasting life, not letting it die,
those sons of bitches. Why?

And on the picture screen, live, in living color,
I see myself in telling faces, telling of others,
thousands, not fifty years ago.
Time has not changed these faces;
we know what they are saying;
we don't need to hover to discover the virgin color of their truth.
Why not worry about their death impending?

Who are they, these truth-sayers;
is any one among them nameless?
Is what they say not clear at its source?
Twentieth-century-truth-bestowed,
is what they mean less in need of a poetic eye?
Why not worry about such losses, hovering over our darkness,
restoring sight to a mauled Masaccio?

The train moves, almost imperceptibly, leaving the station Santa Maria Novella; scenes of Florence slide against the glass. The man at the window is reading a book. I am going home. My anticipation accelerates to the shift and glide, the lunge of buildings quickening. I am going home. Brash voices, words spoken in English, laughter out in the hall, converge at the open door in breathless banter over nearly missing the train, teasing and polite regrets to the young man who got stuck on the train escorting his two female companions. Oblivious to everything but their own excitement, they seem to overlook that the plush seats of the compartment are all taken, and their luggage now gets hoisted over our heads with careless ease and as if no one were present. The older woman—slim, of average height, golden skinned, the shock of blond hair cropped to a boyish bob, crisped in khaki designer casual from her knitted silk tee-shirt down to her initialed glove-leather shoes with metallic piping, her steely eyes raking the back of our seats—tells the man next to me and the other across the aisle to move. Her brusque words enunciated slowly, aiming to ensure understanding, shrill to no avail, and finally, exasperated but self-assured, she says: "These seats were reserved for me; you will have to move." The men, looking at her questioning, stay seated. A barrage of reprimand concerning propriety and frugality, softened to sound like advice—"You should have made reservations"—is tossed at the accused. "I can't believe anyone would travel without making reservations," she quips, looking to her companions in the hall, who, immersed in conversation and giving no indication that they have heard anything she has said, inform her they are leaving for the dining car. The two men speak to each other over her gesturing hands, and the man at the window looks up from his book, interjecting words spoken softly, with even cadence, which have the appropriate effect. She now sits next to me facing the empty seat, restlessly shifting in hers, glancing past me, fidgeting, looking for something in her handbag.

The woman across from me sits tall, motionless, her sturdy hands resting in her lap, her look fixed on something distant. She and the man sitting beside her, though they do not speak or glance at each other, look like they belong. Alike in dress and demeanor, both showing simplicity and care, they carry the village with them. Their worn shoes, endowed with identity, lovingly polished, express the life they lead, and their clothes tell of closeted care, lavished pampering received as things that belong and are intended to last forever. Their faces open like an offering to everything around them; everything goes through them like through an open door. They, like their things, are still, receptive. Their integrity is familiar—looking at them, I feel at home.

The woman next to me is fidgeting; from where she sits there is no view to the village. The world revolves in front of her door; her glove-leather encased feet leave no cast of their past. Free of identity, her shoes boast only initials. She now gets up and leaves.

In Munich they called me the American. Even Frau Kemper in whose flat I took a room and who, like me, is a Donauschwabe from Banat, would refer to me as the American. I once asked about her home, the name of her village. "Nakovo," she said, reluctantly, "you would not know about it." And how surprised she was that I could describe not just the village but her very house.

The American woman returns to the compartment, carrying a Coke. She stands in the doorway with her offering—would anyone like a Coke? She waits, searching our faces. Expressionless, together in disbelief, we move our heads, individually, indicating no. Only the sound of the moving train razes our silence. The man at the window keeps to his book. "It's cold—are you sure you don't want it? Here, take it. I got an extra by mistake. The machine—" Astonished, she quits for a moment, only to continue exasperated, "I can't believe anyone would refuse a cold Coke, and in this heat." Not having said a word, I cannot bring myself to say anything now. Frustrated not being understood, she becomes more aggressive, trying to make us understand by show-and-tell: "See, I am going to throw it away," she says, and pointing to the container in the hall, she goes through a pantomime to make her intent clear. Our passive eyes follow. "Well," she says, giving up, lowering the bottle into the encasement, "imagine, refusing a Coke!" Later, when her daughter returns, they chat about the details of an upcoming event, discussing invitations, attire, food, unencumbered by our presence, flaunting their talk, impersonal as a TV broadcast, interrupting it now and then with sliding glances to the window. Suddenly she announces, with the enthusiasm of a discovery, "Doesn't she look just like Maria?" and leaning toward me she says, haltingly but loudly, as if I were hard of hearing: "You look like our distant relative Maria, who lives in Rome." "Mother, she doesn't understand you," the daughter interrupts. "She does look like her, don't you think? So quaint." The man at the window is smiling into his book.

I am going home! My cousin Johann and his wife Lisel are waiting for me in Triest. We will spend some time in Porto Rož; they have rented a place with a view of the ocean.

And the streets of Triest already remind me of home. The sun-warmed air chants the scented breath of that beloved piece of earth. Home. Outdoor cafés boast familiar food—*burek* (a salted pastry). We inhale it to the afternoon-sun's welcoming. It is evening when we arrive at the house on the hill in Porto Rož. The boys, Michael and Alexander, have just come back from the beach.

Pristine white walls look down to the blue. The light at play with sea and sky delights; the scented air invigorates. "It's a beautiful spot, Johann; we must come here often," I inhale a sigh taking in the view. "The owners of the house have invited us this evening. We must tell them that we are leaving for the weekend, leaving the boys," Johann says, showing his usual concern. The boys are sixteen and fourteen and eager for us to leave.

With the house built into the hill, the owners living above and our rooms hugging the hill below, our paths never cross. We now meet the captain and his wife; she is American. They lived in San Francisco for six years, but her husband was continually homesick and they had to return. Living here for years, does she miss home, we ask? But she goes for visits, though not lately. She has not been well, and the supervision of her daughter, now nineteen, keeps her here and busy, she laughs, looking at her husband, betraying concern. I speak to them in English now; it is a relief to abandon oneself to fluid speech instead of clutching at words to say what one means and miss, losing oneself in the bargain.

"We, too, have come home," I blurt out suddenly. "We are from Yugoslavia," I say, looking at the captain to gauge his approval. "We are Germans from Vojvodina—*Mi smo švabe is Banata.*" I look to see, but he does not flinch, he only nods. I catch myself telling about the village, the artesian well water, the sweetest drink on earth, wooing him with all that is dear to us as if I needed his permission to go home, as if I needed his approval, his forgiveness that I am still alive. I want him to know that I will not take much time, that I will be here only for a little while. I want him to think well of me. This is only the tone of my tune; the wording is measured and cautious, the rhythm fluid, and since my English is better than his, I am somewhat confident that I can please. And after a while, I say what I am afraid to say: "We were in a concentration camp, Johann and I, when we were children. Here, in Yugoslavia, in Vojvodina, from January, 1945, to March, 1948. After the war." He looks unaffected, as if he did not know about these things, but I know that look, and we understand each other. "Oh," he says, his face impenetrable, and his wife's vociferous astonishments flesh out a hasty surprise. "Yes, it is true, but it was long ago—more than forty years have passed. And, still, after more than forty years we are homesick," I laugh, reaching for humor. We think of going back home to Banat—as soon as tomorrow morning. We are leaving the boys, just for a few days; they are very responsible. All this we tell them, but we keep to ourselves the one thing we would not dare tell anyone here: we will stop on our way, to find the camp, the place where we were put to die.

· · ·

The yellow Mercedes is speeding down the highway with all its windows open. We pass Rijeka at sunrise. "Karlovac!" Johann shouts later; the sound, buffeted by hot winds, gropes to reach me in the back seat. The land is under a siege of heat. It is the summer of 1987. Still, burnished greens greet us on hills, in forests, on meadows—and what do I see? Houses, imports from a modern Germany, marring the landscape. Adding my judgment to the unflattering addition, I shout, "What are these foreign houses doing here in the heart of the homeland? Who invited them?" "Gastarbeiter," (guest workers) Lisel shouts back, taking my comment seriously. "Many of them working in Germany buy the plans, build them. They have a right to improve their lives," she adds good-naturedly. The map in her lap makes a flapping sound; strands of my hair tickle my face as I lean forward to listen. The land is lovely; the style of such houses seems ill fitting here, I explain, looking at the hills skirting Bosnia. The glare on the road mirrors the heat in solid sheets. We stop to fill the tank and get something to drink. The car sizzles; its top is scorching to the touch. "Anything hot from the griddle, anyone? Eggs, pancakes, perhaps *palačinke* (crepes)?" Johann clowns. "Or fried brains, perhaps yours?" we tease him back, unkindly. We cannot wait to get moving again, to be fanned by hot air. Bosanski Brod, Slavonski Brod— signs passing. "Somewhere ahead we will have to turn north if we still want to find the place," Johann says, looking about as if we were under surveil- lance. "Do you think we'll be able to find what we came for?" he queries, glancing back at me. "Do we still want to go?" Lisel looks at him exasper- ated. "Really, Johann, we didn't come all this way for you to change your mind now." I am quite happy in the back seat and say nothing.

The noise of air rushing in covers my voice as I softly sing, to some tune unknown, the first line of a nursery rhyme: "*Mei Kroßvater had me a Karte kaft,*" I sing over and over again, weaving melodious variations of plaintive sounds—words like ribbons, trailing. The wind hovers to take them in, to keep them secret. "My grandfather bought me a garden," I sing in our dia- lect, adding in English, "and it was the pride of the land!" I look out on the heat-hazed plain, caressing it with my song. In front Johann and Lisel are having a conversation. "Look," he says, "there is Osijek." Far in the dis- tance I see a steeple rising above a dense gather of buildings. "Perhaps it is Vukovar," Lisel corrects, looking at the map. "I am sure it's Osijek," Johann insists, shouting to the back, "Do you want to stop in Osijek, Luisa?" Lisel protests: "If we want to find what we came to see, we ought to get there before dark." She is our navigator and keeps us on track.

We are no longer on the highway; we have taken a dust-covered road skirting the shallow bluffs of the Fruška Gora. Johann sees a monument not far off the road: "We should investigate; it may be the place we have come to see." At first I think he is kidding and only wants to stop for a rest. "Perhaps they built a monument for our dead," he says, looking like the little boy I once knew. I sadden to think I have come on this errand with a fool, I tell him, stepping into the heat-demented air. "No, no, it could very well be; lots of people have relatives who died here. Perhaps they paid . . . Let's go and see; it's only a little walk. It will do us good to stretch our legs." "You're deranged," I gibe at him, watching him dash for the site, and I follow Lisel into the tall corn. When Johann returns from his quest disappointed, I greet him with heaping handfuls of warm powdered dust from the road. I drag my feet through it, running along the cornfield. "Let's take a bath in it, Johann," I shout, smiling. He smiles back and takes his turn in the corn.

Back on the road, we make a few wrong turns and end up in a village. Perhaps there is an artesian well. We find a pump instead. The water is cool and sweet; must be the real thing. Refreshed, we loiter around an iron railing enclosing a spacious green with a chapel at the back. I remember standing here before . . . I finger the wrought iron, memories burning under my touch, inhaling sighs. I think this is Bačka Palanka. I have been here before to see Seppi; I look at the buildings, which then were an orphanage. I am quiet and very nervous.

We follow the road to Novi Sad and take a secondary road to Titel. It is already late afternoon when we arrive. "Where to?" Johann says curtly; he, too, is quiet. I tell him to stay close to the river and keep a lookout for a bridge. With no view of the river and no bridge in sight, we stop. "Let's ask someone," I suggest, "preferably a young person—someone who does not connect the place with a concentration camp." Lisel is still looking at the map, convinced we have come to the wrong place. "Knićanin is not on the map; see for yourself, across from Titel, nothing." A glance at the map shows Titel marked on the wrong side of the river. We see a young man walking up the street. We will ask him. The young man is moving slowly, carrying something he holds with both hands; I wait for him at the curb. "Is there a place called Knićanin close by?" I ask in my best accentless Serbo-Croatian. "Yes," he says looking at me quizzically, "but you won't find it unless I show you the way. It's not very far, but hard to find. I am going that way anyway." A ride in the Mercedes seems a fair exchange, and he takes his place beside me in the back seat. It is then I notice that the young man is carrying a large piece of lean, red meat in brown paper wrapping, the raw flesh looming out of his hands. I have seen such meat, such packaging, before. "Yes, Knićanin, I used to visit a family there, but it was years ago. We want to see if—" He interrupts brusquely: "What is the name of the family?" Perhaps it is only my paranoia that tinges the tone of his voice with the past. I quickly say, "Zorić," tetka Mila's family name. I could have said any name, but here, so close to the place of terror, I fall victim to old habits. He does not know them. "Perhaps they no longer live here, but being so close . . ." I can't seem to stop making up lies to excuse our being here. The young man gives directions and asks questions about the car, looking reverently about its interior as if he were in a cathedral. Before the bridge he asks to be let out. "On the other side of the bridge," he says pointing, clutching the piece of meat in one hand, "don't follow the road, but go immediately to the left, under the overpass; there are no signs, but that is Knićanin." We thank him and he waves us on.

"True, we would never have found it," Johann says, passing through what to me seems like a tunnel. A somber sepia tone washes over me and I am stunned to silence by its light. Distance disappears; everything is close and like an open wound. The houses are isolated, no walls encircle them, no fences. The gardens are open. A woman sitting on the grass, playing with a small child, vanishes behind the slide of houses passing. Johann wants to know where to turn to find "our" house. "If we go along this street, we will get to tetka Mila's house—stop in the center of the village; I will orient myself there. It will give us a starting point," I tell him, nervously looking about. We creep along; ours is the only car on the road. The houses on both sides of the wide street giving no clue, we stop where the street dead-ends into a field of tall grasses. "We will be less conspicuous here than in the center of the village," Johann remarks, and we get out of the car. I know where I am. I look down the field, squinting. "This is where the dead were taken. We are standing at the foot of their grave. I know the death-wagon's path, you can count on it," I hear myself saying. "There is nothing here," Johann whispers, "only a wasted field." "Looks abandoned and a bit spooky," Lisel says, "but so does the rest of the village." I think of my grandmother, whose grave it is, and I say nothing. A remnant of a weathered board boasting rusted nails bulges out of the dust to console the injury of disbelief. "I would dig them up bone by bone with my bare hands, even now, if it would help to bring their grave to recognition—I would!" I hear my anger talking. Johann looks at me startled. "Look at it," he says in a consoling voice, "it's only a field of grass." I don't think of saying the obvious: so many dead had to be dumped somewhere—why not here where I know they are?

On our way back down the street, we stop the car and get out in front of what used to be tetka Mila's house. Wrapped around the corner, windows facing the side street, the house is empty now, its windows broken. I stretch to look inside. The large rooms I remember have been partitioned into small ones, all looking violated, forlorn. Johann is afraid our looking about will attract attention and calls me away from the window. There is a park across the street; tall evergreens pierce the eye with color. "This is where the bombed-out church used to be," I tell them (we are talking in hushed tones). Lisel, still not convinced we are in the right place, looks at me disbelieving. "Those trees are tall; they had to have been here forty years ago. Are you sure this is the right place? There are no facilities here, no signs of a concentration camp." What does she know about us, I think unkindly. Facilities? Consider the economy of simply letting people starve to death, I want to tell her, but I only fuel my anger with her words. A wagon loaded with hay moves into the periphery of my vision. The man walking behind it, carrying a pitchfork over his shoulder, looks at us one-eyed, grinning from afar, eyeing the yellow Mercedes. When he comes closer I call to him; we would like to ask him something. I do not look at Johann; I know he is aghast. The man greets us in German, baring golden teeth, and without waiting for our question says, pointing his pitchfork, "The cemetery is that way." He is pointing to the cemetery of the village before it was a concentration camp. We comment on his speaking German. He worked in Germany for many years, he woos in broken accent: *"Ich gerne in Daitschlant—Daitschlant gut leben; scheene Madel, gute Auto,"* he points to the yellow Mercedes. "We only stopped for water; is there a well nearby?" I interrupt. He points to the pump in front of the park (where it always was). Has he lived in this village long, I query? He answers "yes" in a roundabout way. "Was this always a park?" I ask, looking at the green, telling him how beautiful it is. "No, not always. There used to be a church here but it was kaput, bombed-out long ago." I feel vindicated. "Why are these big buildings abandoned; why are they not used?" I point to the houses around us where the seat of power used to be. "No good," he says shaking his head. "People don't like living in them; no good, no good," he repeats and walks on. The bleakness of the place, the deceptive questioning, the spectral appearance of the man with the gilded grin, his ghoulish grimace, fill me with revulsion, loathing. I don't know where to direct my rage; I notice that I am digging my fingers into the palm of my left hand. My gaze runs amuck; I look around as if I had to swallow all, and then—I don't believe my eyes—I see the sunken house, the cellar, the place of punishment. It, like the abandoned buildings around us, has kept its earthen tone; turned to stone! A monument in reverse, I think; all the houses of the camp seem to be inhabited and the places of power stand in ruin.

I stand at the entry gate to tetka Mila's house. The door seems smaller, and the wide board across its base over which I had clambered long ago stops me from entering now. It seems, in raising a step to cross it, my body remembers the little girl I once was, standing here as if I had left her. And the earth trembles within me to affirm—the little girl, this place. No senti-ment, no sorrow; only a sober realization. My thoughts race to catch up to the undeniable truth my flesh already understands, offering stammering rationalizations: it is true, this place exists on earth, not just in my mind as a story; it really happened. I really am this girl. I really am! All denial falls away in front of this door; the earth knows; the earth does not deny. And as if something is returned to me, I feel affirmed, strong, abundant, generous even with my rage. When Johann asks me to find the house we shared with forty others, I tell him with savage candor, "You want to know where our house is? Fix your eyes on that field. There is our house. Never forget it!"

The yellow Mercedes passes the place of the Komandno Mesto, now stripped of its enclosing walls, buildings razed, a more recent two-story import squatting among tall grasses where the offices used to be. We make a left turn and I scan the left side of the street. I think that is it: a house facing sideways, four windows to the street. Johann dares a picture. There are no people on the street. In one of the fenceless gardens a mother and her small child are sitting in the grass. An image to console, a parting grace, a live memorial.

And the yellow Mercedes slips through the hole in the embankment, marking time. No one is saying anything. We stop at my relatives in Mužlja; Johann and Lisel will go on to theirs in Subotica. It is difficult to talk, and the greeting relatives notice. "We have been to Rudolfsgnad—Knićanin," I stammer. "We wanted to . . ." (I am clutching my hands, right hand digging into left palm). Johann tries to help me out with words, but no one needs an explanation. The circle in the side yard is closed at eight, all of us silent. I know it is still hot enough not to shiver, but I feel naked in my sleeveless tee-shirt. Someone is wiping tears. It looks and feels like a wake. There are no prayers. Eta hands me a blue and white short-sleeved sweater. Johann and Lisel leave. It is a long way to Subotica; they will not get there till dark.

All night at Lisi néni's house I toss and turn. I want to go back . . . to find the house . . . to walk over that field. Why did I not go inside tetka Mila's house? Why did I not think of looking for Smiljka's place? Why did we not roam around the village? I want to go back without that conspicuous yellow car . . . I want to spend time . . . I will ask Ervin to take me there, to drop me off and let me stay a day. Or I will take a taxi. I will take the train. I'll walk. And all the time I feel the tremor, the earth shaking, the gesture of the little girl waiting within. And in the morning, seeing me so distraught, Lisi néni tells me, "You shouldn't have gone there, Lujzikam—it was a mistake to go there. How many sleepless nights did I spend crying, knowing my old par-ents were there starving to death, and I, here, a stone's throw away, not able to help them. You have to put it out of your mind. Never go back there

A house in Rudolfsgnad, home to some forty people from 1945 to 1948. *Photo by* Ervin Kis, 1993

again!" The familiar voice, even wordless, has a way of comforting. I smile. But later in the afternoon when Sosa, Lisi néni's Serb neighbor, comes to see me, I still have to tell, to explain my wretched looks, my being upset: "I went to Knićanin, yesterday . . ." She pretends she did not hear me and talks about the weather. And when I repeat "Knićanin, the concentration camp," she looks daggers at me for mentioning it—for repeating it to make her listen, for my having been there in the first place—and continues talking about the weather.

• • •

On our drive back, no one speaks. I sit in the back seat and look out at the land passing. I am saying good-bye. I will never come here again, no matter how homesick I get, I promise myself and the desolate grasses of that field. Standing at the site of the grave intended to be my own, still having to pretend to others it is nothing, still having to deny myself in front of them, having to agree with them that nothing happened, is something I will no longer do. I will not stand on our grave pretending it is a mole hole. As one among the thousands discarded there, left to die, I cannot deny the deed, and I will not be an accomplice to the lie. To come here is to keep doing away with myself, to play into the lie. "Only the lie has to be done away with—not the liars," I hear myself saying out loud, and the winds over Bosnia rush to shroud my words. Johann shouts, "Did you say something back there?" I wail back, "I will never come home again till you find a monument in those tall grasses."

We stop at a rest stop and before we even get out of the car, three boys, aged perhaps ten or eleven, converge on us, throwing themselves on the hood, peering through the windshield, their brash voices insistent; they want to wash our car for *Deutschmarks*. The suddenness of the approach, the brusque attitude, the brassy gaze startles us, and before Johann can say anything, I hear my own voice shrill, "Don't touch it—get away from the car!" The tone chills. Johann is taken aback. "They are only children," he offers, but his voice has a tinge of reprimand. Lisel is quiet. We do not want our car washed, he tells them, we are in a hurry, but he gives them money. They leave, yelling, "*daitsch-mark, daitsch-mark.*" Later, I listen to Lisel talking about her grandmother—how after her husband of only a year was killed in the First World War, she hated all French people—and I lean back into my seat looking out the window, the wind on my face. She means well. But she does not know, and I will never be able to tell her, or anyone, that hating these people would be like hating myself, for they and this land are a part of the beginning of things; they are part of who I am, part of my perception and my understanding. They are my home. If I hated them, what would be left me of my love?

The sun shines into my room in Porto Rož. A look down to the flash of blue sparks the white walls gleaming with sunlight; the clatter of dishes shrills, telling of breakfast. In the kitchen I hear Johann talking to his sons about Knićanin. "You can see immediately on entering the village that something happened there—and the withered field, if you look down it carefully . . ."

• • •

In 1992 images span the television screen: the faces familiar, hollow eyes staring, looks evading. Bodies, skin over bones, skeletal ribcages behind barbed wire—live on the screen, all easily put aside with the flick of a finger. I stare. Images of men, mostly, of specific ages, the familiar numbers mentioned on the news. But I remember women and children of all ages and old men. Still, it is the same game, starting anew.

"Never again!" said those who witnessed such atrocities at the end of the war in 1945. Only I did not hear them then. For me the game had already begun, again. I was nine and a half when it started, and I was there till the end in 1948. I was there with the many thousands living and dead. We were patient; we waited—waited for someone to intervene, to save us, even though we never heard them promise they would. We had faith . . .

I know the graves that do not exist and where they are. The uncounted dead—victims of ethnic cleansing practiced on the German-speaking minority in Yugoslavia, ending a way of life for more than half a million people—the children who died waiting, waiting so patiently to live, tell their story against the dark.

CHAPTER I

Sacred Ground

THERE WAS A SOUR CHERRY TREE in my grandfather's garden. I remember him picking clusters of ripe cherries out of the polished dark green foliage, just for me. The brightest, the ones that seemed to be filled with light, looking almost transparent, he would hang carefully in pairs on both my ears, whispering solemnly: "I give you the jewels of the land, your heritage; be worthy of it." This was our sacred ritual. We did not speak further. I looked up at him, squinting into the sun, and in his approving glances I felt the sunshine and I could not distinguish the blue of his eyes from the sky above him. Quietly I took his large hand and walked slowly beside him. I carried the heaviness of our treasure. I held my head erect and imagined the bright transparent glow of our heirloom shining like a light about me. I glanced with reverence to the ground before me. As we walked, I tried to keep my head very still so as not to disturb the light. The soft rich scent of the ground followed us as we walked, my grandfather and I, out of the garden.

The ground was sacred in my grandfather's garden, but not only there—it was so in the village, in the fields, in the vineyards, and beyond as far as I knew. Everything on that ground was itself, mysterious and significant, gifted with the power to express the individual quality of its spirit. Everyone—people, animals, plants as well as things—participated in intimate communion with the ground. It seemed as though all things received their identity in this communion. Even the air was a solid entity that spoke in scents of the ground. Woven out of a myriad essences, past and present, it filled every breath with remembered existence. Everyone spoke this language of the land, and everything was in fluid conversation. Ordinary sounds were audible aspects of this communication. Silence itself could speak. One was part of the mystery and understood. And all things were known, familiar and open like one's own house; one could go in and out of everything and feel at home.

I knew every tree in my grandfather's garden. The blue plum tree was like any other of its kind, small and scraggly with angular branches and a gray scaly trunk with dried drips of honey-colored sap encrusted in its bark, which gave it the appearance of being neglected. The texture of this chewy sap was as distasteful to me as it looked, but the neighborhood children taught me to respect its flavor as part of the ritual of growing up. The plums themselves, except for their color, were a disappointment to me even when I found them halved and sugared in dumplings that my mother made. I liked them better cooked beyond recognition into a thick dark paste that, though it looked much like the stuff I saw being put on axles of wagon wheels, tasted delicious spread on bread. The best effort of plums, I thought, went into something my grandfather cooked. It took a very long time and required a great deal of vigilance, but in the end the plums themselves altogether disappeared. This transformation, the change into a clear colorless liquid, was magical and produced the most remarkable fragrance, better smelling than any of my mother's perfumes, which she kept in closed little bottles in her bedroom. My grandfather called this brew *Schnaps* or *šljivovica*, interchangeably. I liked its second name. It seemed more loyal to the plum. Because I liked its fragrance so much, I could detect its presence anywhere in the house. No matter how cleverly my grandmother would hide the bottle, I knew how to help my grandfather find it. This pleased him and earned me his respect at a very early age.

Our plum tree not only had a collective identity; it was itself and not interchangeable with any other tree of its kind. It was something larger than its name or anything one could say about it. Like every tree in the garden, that which it was could not fit into a name. Because everyone knew this, no one questioned it or needed it explained. The sweet cherry tree in our neighbor's garden made this very clear. Although it was the same kind of tree as one of ours, it was itself and had, one might say, its own attitude. This tree stood firmly on the ground. Its branches opened like an embrace, revealing a huge canopy of flickering greens from which hung, in grand profusion, uncountable red cherries; its opulence obscured the sky. Standing under this tree, looking up, one was aware of an overwhelming generosity. Our sweet cherry, on the other hand, showed itself pinched and proud. Its clusters of large fleshy red cherries looked almost artificial and seemed withheld rather than offered. Polished in form and color, this tree gave a lesson in arrogance and taught humility instead. I did not like picking its cherries, out of respect for myself.

The sweet apple tree, vibrant with light green foliage aflutter over the small and even lighter green fruit, had a way of looking and smelling like goodness, and sometimes, something about it would remind me of my grandmother and cause me to think about our family. It would make me feel sad at such times and it could even make me cry.

The apricot tree seemed most sophisticated, and the exotic fruit with its delicately aromatic orange fruit flesh was exquisitely balanced with the robust edible kernel encased in a hard almond-shaped nut that had to be broken with the aid of a stone. But the tree with the most fragrant fruit, a taste so special it could not be fully recalled from season to season, the peach, seemed transient, offering its rare pleasure just for a time, a pleasure that could not be detained, that disappeared even from memory. I often tried to recall its goodness, but it was too complicated for me to imagine. Until it returned the following year, I could only remember it by its name.

The mulberry tree in my grandfather's back yard was as permanent as the ground itself. It had the appearance of a giant structure that had been standing forever and no longer had a need to distinguish itself as being anything. It grew beyond identity and personality and was simply present. In winter it had a somewhat malevolent appearance and one could get frightened by it on moonlit nights. In summer it was covered with playful leaves that seemed to have a life of their own. The large black berries, not intended for anyone, fell to the ground and covered it, lying there in their sweetness for everyone. Grown into its surroundings, this tree could not be anything but impartial.

The sour cherry tree, with its pleasantly rounded shape and low-hanging branches, was partial to the ground. It was, more than any other tree in the garden, in harmony with the surroundings and looked inconspicuous. Despite its vibrant colors seen against the stark white wall of the neighbor's house, its bright red cherries sparkling in deep green foliage, it was not easily noticed; it attended to the ground and was absorbed by it. Forgetting itself, it reflected this intimate communion, as if it were essential to its own image to make the ground invisible in itself, to be one with the ground, to belong to it.

Some trees did not know how to belong. Through no fault of their own, they were misplaced. Some inattentive persons, who liked their image or some other aspect of them, brought them from a faraway place where, no doubt, they knew how to belong. Despite the care and affection lavished on such trees by their owners, they always looked unloved. Such were the trees across the street from my grandfather's house, at Stein's. They had a very fancy name, which I loved saying. They came all the way from America. My grandfather said they were distant relatives of the acacia trees we had in our village. I could see the similarity of their flower clusters and leaf structure, and the fact that they had thorns. For me this similarity only pointed out more poignantly how much like visitors they were. These fancy trees with light purple flowers and very delicate foliage, beautiful though they were, seemed too frail for these surroundings. With their thin trunks bound against wooden poles to give them stability, they appeared dressed up and posed, propped for picture taking, instead of growing into the ground. I thought everyone could see their unfortunate displacement for the terrible mistake I thought it was, and I could not understand why their misfortune was so blatantly exposed. I could not look at these trees without wanting to cover them, to shield them, and would often cover my eyes instead.

The acacia indigenous to the surroundings were tall, slender trees with strong trunks. They carried their foliage and white flower clusters, together with their thorns, high above the ground, into the sky. They lined the streets of our village; standing in front of the houses to which they belonged, their rough bark painted white far beyond where I could reach, they looked domesticated. They were part of our lives. Around them children would play games until late in the evening, and under them people would sit on benches and talk late into the night. We would speak into the darkness and everything would listen, and the conversation would grow softer and more intermittent with long silences as the night went on. At times like these everyone was acutely present, and together we were securely cradled into the dark. Sitting in someone's warm lap, listening to the conversation, the darkness and the night air blending with the sound of voices, I was aware of a feeling I could not name, which felt like belonging. I wanted this feeling never to end. Sometimes the sound of words would accompany me into a half slumber where, disassociated from their meaning, they became comfort and reassurance and the sweetest way to fall asleep.

That the trees took part in these nightly gatherings was clear to me especially at parting; when everyone had gone, their presence remained with its sweet assurance. Left to themselves, outside, they could be heard rustling about as we, inside, were going to sleep. And they were there each morning, ready for play. Some children could shinny up their slender trunks, but no one would climb into their thorny branches. The older children knew how to get sprigs of the sweet-smelling flowers out of these branches, from the ground. With long hollow reeds, ends cut into a prong, they reached and twisted the tender growth and brought it down. Everyone but the trees loved this trick. The children ate the white parts of the flowers immediately. The taste of this stolen delicacy brought out of the sky was like nothing on earth. Sometimes even my mother would resort to this trick, and out of the petals from many flowers, she would make a small salad with sweetened vinegar and water, just for me. It was a delicacy for children only, she explained. I thought it was truly a taste of heaven.

The acacia trees were tolerant. They were our friends. One could hold them tightly and cry quietly into their bark when one felt hurt. They would hide one's face behind their trunks when one was shy. And they knew wonderful games like hide and seek, and *tapša lapša ko moj drug?*—a game like red-light/green-light, to the chant of "clippity clappity, who is my friend?" The acacia trees were present at all occasions and in all seasons. Their white flower clusters wove a veil of sweetest fragrance over the village and made it look like a bride in spring. The familiar rustle of their sensitive foliage was part of the sound of summer. Autumn winds played mellow wood sounds through their trunks, sounds that accompanied us into our houses and made them seem warmer and safer. And their exposed branches cut the winter sky into familiar pieces. Outside the village the acacia stood alone or in isolated clumps, marking the wide, flat landscape, giving it scale, offering shelter and shade. Against high skies, on the curved horizon, they appeared like solitary travelers, giving the land its special image.

• • •

In the beginning it seemed to me that all things came into existence with my own being, that there was nothing before I was; everything was new and I filled all things with my own special power. Sometimes this power could surprise, as happened to me with the moon.

Late one night, when I was very young, my parents were walking home from a visit with friends who lived on the same street, far from our house, at the other end of the village. The acacia trees lining the street stood in pairs in front of the houses, like giant guards, holding their leafless branches stiffly into the winter sky. The sky responded by tossing their shadows silently before them. It was moonlight. The air was cold but I was bundled up snugly, sitting securely around my father's neck. All was quiet. The village was wrapped in darkness, sleeping. Nothing moved, and in this stillness, I was floating above my parents' heads and they where gliding below without a sound. Only an occasional barking dog in the distance and the changing shadows of the passing trees moving gently, with a dancelike motion, seemed to tie us to the ground. There were no footsteps to be heard; they were swallowed up by the deep silence in which everything only listened. I noticed the sky high above us making a domed ceiling of stars over the village, which now seemed small, huddled in its darkness. I saw the moon and kept looking at it. It seemed the moon and I were invisibly connected; we were gliding together, so to speak. We were doing a little dance. I was delighted. Made bold by this collaboration, I decided to test the moon's response to me. I moved my head, holding it this way and that, and the moon would follow, whatever I did. For a long time I danced with the moon and we kept this up in mutual delight, so it seemed. At some point, however, the moon became animated beyond my expectation, and I got a little frightened of it. I said quietly, disturbing the silence, "The moon is following us." "So he is," my father said, looking up as he continued walking silently beside my mother, and the earth and the village seemed all of one piece.

The earth was at home in the village. The wide unpaved streets that separated long straight lines of houses facing each other were like ribbons of earth ironed smooth by the steel rims of wagon wheels and the heat of the sun. Summer traffic ground them into a soft warm powder, ankle-deep, so friendly to bare feet. And summer showers transformed them into a playground to match in material abundance the rich imagination of children. We made things to play with and devised games to play. Balls of mud were pinched into potlike forms with straight walls; thrown, inverted, against the brick sidewalk, each pot would make a large sound and at the same time leave a great eruption in its base. It was a serious game. We spat into each pot for good luck in making the largest sound, the most impressive eruption; we did this not for the sake of competing with each another but rather for the sake of the pot, that it might shatter, breaking into the fullest possible sound.

In rainy weather mud was unavoidable in our village. One could follow the brick sidewalks next to the houses to wherever one wanted to go, but crossing the wide streets took some navigation. The mud with its sucking sounds could easily remove a shoe, and it stubbornly clung to one's clothes. One had to be careful of its prankish wiles. I sometimes talked to it or to myself just to keep my wits about me. I would pull my pant leg up and step carefully into the mud with one foot, lower the pant leg, and then proceed similarly with the other foot. I continued this rhythmic motion, lifting one pant leg up while letting the other down, and putting action into words, I sang: "*Gaće gore, gaće dole,*" giving myself a verbal cue, chanting, "Pants up, pants down." I practiced this little ritual on my way home from Grandmother Korek's house when I was very young, and it was observed by the storekeeper across the street, who would remind me of it, mimicking the gestures and words, to tease me when I was much older.

The ground was grass-covered only outside the village, past the Big Water, in a meadow we called *Hutwaat*, where ducks and geese were taken during the day by the older children of the family, and in fields where pigs and cows were herded early each morning to graze all day, and where sheep and cattle stayed all summer long. In the village, the ground was exposed; it was the background of our every day and the base on which everything stood. Even our houses, their thick walls, and the walls that enclosed yards and gardens were made of earth. Earthen floors brought the ground itself inside. Here, in our rooms, it tinged even our dreams with its rich color.

• • •

I first thought the village was made up of my family and the people and houses I knew. My earliest memory was of my mother—more precisely, of my mother's hand. It was as if, suddenly, there existed something other, separate from myself, a hand beautifully shaped with tapered fingers, belonging to my mother. This realization gave me a new identity. It also made me sad, and it filled me with longing. Later, when I could already walk, I would recall this first feeling any time I saw an article of my mother's clothing or discovered things that belonged to her.

Some early memories were predominantly sensuous: the feel of warm water rolling over me at regular intervals, waiting for it in anticipation, listening to the soft wooden sounds of the tub; the smell of my father's skin and the reassuring sound of his voice; the milky green color of furniture; a circular walker with two wooden rings, one encircling me under my armpits, not allowing me to sit down, the other making a wide circle around my feet, connecting me to a seamless motion over the surface of a yellow ceramic floor with hexagonal tiles.

In the beginning I identified people by their particular scent. Such orientation was comforting; it provided security without the need for much verification, and it was safe from rejection as well. Once taken in by a smell, one could feel at home in it. Lisi néni, who lived across the street, had a pungent smell that I liked very much. She came to our house daily and I liked being held in her lap and being carried off by her, for long stays at her house, which seemed plain and dark inside compared to ours. I called her husband Jebegači, when I could not say Jakob bácsi. This always made him smile and caused others to laugh. Lisi néni's mother, Nancsi Omami, lived in the room at the end of the house. She wore black clothes, like my grandmother, and had an acrid odor that I did not like so much. Sometimes she showed, with looks and sounds, that she found fault with me; she would even scold me. Lisi néni had a girl of her own, Rosi, who, I thought, was mean. She would come to the blanket where Lisi néni had put me and would tickle me mercilessly; I would fall on my back, and she would not let me get up. Though I could not stop laughing, I had an overwhelming urge to stop her. I never grew to like this girl, and she did not mind. But I liked Lisi néni and the rest of the family, the house with the plain pointed gable, and the garden with the large walnut tree; they were part of my earliest experiences as a member of the village.

The house of my great grandmother was only a house away from Lisi néni's. It was a small yellow house with a rounded gable; it looked pleasant and inviting. Inside it smelled of anise. I would visit her by myself and she would always give me things to eat. I would sit on a footstool in front of a backless chair, which was my table. Hot cornmeal mush spooned into cold milk tasted good, especially in cold weather. Eating it at her house made it special any time. We sometimes had gingerbread and anise tea with honey. She knew how to make tea from many things, even from rose hips. It was always warm and quiet in her house, and one could hear a wood fire burning and the mellow measured ticking of a wall clock. In spring we would pick strawberries from her garden and dunk them, washed, into the sugar bowl before eating them. And she would give me sweet wood to chew. She was the mother of my grandmother Korek, and my father was the eldest of her grandchildren. She was very fond of him. When he was a boy, she told me, she bought him the bicycle on which he took me for rides. Standing on a small table were many pictures of her other children and grandchildren who lived in America, where she herself had been several times. I did not know any of these people. They were my father's aunts, uncles, and cousins, she explained, and she told me all their names. To me they all looked very remote, alike in their attire and their expression. One picture larger than the rest, of a young man all dressed in white, playing an accordion, smiling, showing lots of teeth, epitomized the expression on faces in the pictures from America. This picture of a favorite grandson, Albert, was responsible for my long held opinion that in America everyone was always smiling and all men dressed in white. I was not quite four when she, my *Altkroßmotter*, died. I don't remember seeing her ill or mourning for her; I only remember feeling her absence and often recalling for myself the strong sweet smell of anise.

I did not know about death. But even before my Altkroßmotter died, I had often heard about it. I knew death brought about change. I saw how Laci, the little boy at Högyis, shrank into himself after his mother died. I often saw them together on the street in front of their house. He was lively and inquisitive and she spoke with a weeping voice. When she died he grew pale, became shy, and stayed inside. His sister, Kató, who had a large birthmark over one eye, which made her look kind, suddenly seemed older and sadder. Only their beautiful sister, Juci, remained unchanged and appeared hard because of it. The little house, between Lisi néni's and Altkroßmotter's, looked vacant and turned in on itself.

People talked about the dead. And often we knew them as well as the living. Mama Tijana always spoke of her daughter. I knew the dark-haired Jelena who died at sixteen when I was almost three. They said her death had to do with tending roses. The familiar image of mama Tijana—a large woman dressed in black, holding a stick upright under one arm, spinning the bound

Altkroßmotter's house, photographed in 1960. *Courtesy* families Werner and Walter Lang

fleece on it with one hand and with the other twirling a spindle very fast, to wind the evenly spun yarn, walking and talking and only periodically looking down at the work while taking a breath—remained forever connected with the memory of her daughter.

Even the people I had not known before they died were still talked about in connection with the living. Sofija, tetka Mara's half sister, whose fall from a window ledge when she was an infant had hurt her spine and caused her to grow up small and disfigured, was often talked about in relation to her exceptionally beautiful mother, who had died long ago, when Sofija was very young. The memory of the beautiful mother still clung to the willful, sickly daughter and was like a reflection in her. I remember Sofija leaning out of the window in the big yellow house that directly faced Altkroßmotter's. She would sometimes smile and say something to me as I walked by. The smiles she gave were more like grimaces. She had a terrible temper, which commanded respect and the attention of everyone in the household. They said she was always in pain. One day, she deliberately set fire to the straw stack while she was sitting in it. She wanted to die, they said. (Sofija died when she was only thirty. I was then already four.) Once, when I was visiting, Sofija took me up to the big house and into the front room. There, on the wall facing the windows, in a massive gold frame, and larger then Sofija herself, hung the portrait of her mother. The huge dimly lit room with the unfamiliar scent of musk seemed like an exotic church in a faraway land, a place one had to be worthy to enter. The two of us stood silently beside each other. The gesture with which she conveyed that this was her mother was compelling, complete in itself without any words. A feeling of reverence for Sofija overshadowed the admiration I felt for the beauty in the picture. Her simple utterance recalled the painful sweetness of recognizing my separateness, the feeling of missing my own mother. It was as if I had seen Sofija for the first time, in a sacred place, in front of the dimly lit picture of her mother.

• • •

We lived on the summer side of the street. This only meant that the houses there kept their shadows away from the street to let the sunshine onto it. I remember our house changing when I was five. Deep ditches were dug, into which the wide walls of my father's blacksmith shop were sunk and out of which they emerged, turning the house sideways, giving it three instead of two windows and huge, twin wooden doors that closed in the middle. Its new facade was a tinted maroon stucco. Inside things kept their places. Three rooms in a row all opened into each other. The front room was bright only when the wooden shutters on the inside were open. When the shutters were closed, there was nothing in this room but darkness, and it could become a most frightening place when the only door out, the door into my room, was closed as well. This was my parents' room. Their almost life-sized, tinted portraits hung, oval-framed, above their wide bed. I thought my mother looked beautiful in these warm brown and rose tones. My father looked much thinner and darker than he really was. A disk-shaped light fixture, hanging low, flaunted its cool opalescence. The satin comforter, its crisp white cover buttoned on in such a way as to expose a square of tufted yellow satin at the center, only slightly covered the two stacks of large pillows with embroidered white flowers and my mother's monogram. The bed was usually covered up by a heavy, floral tapestry that closely matched in color and texture the upholstery on the ottoman and chairs. Two night stands, their contents concealed behind small doors, boasted of heavy medical books with intriguing illustrations: images of rashes, oozing sores, grotesque aspects of disfiguring diseases, each covered up by a page of translucent tissue that softened their effect with small crackling sounds.

A piece of furniture we called *Schpigltisch* filled the span between the two windows. The drawers on each side of its large oval mirror secreted powders in boxes, creams in little jars, books with pictures, as well as treasures like rings, beads and lockets, and my father's pocket watch. Its ledges showed photographs under glass, bird-shaped salt stone sculptures (one of

My mother, Barbara Schüssler, at nineteen, Senta, 1929.

First portrait with my parents, 1936.

them, a swan with its head under its wing, made my mother cry when it broke), small bottles containing mists of floral fragrances, and vases with fragile, dried ornamental grasses, which sounded, when touched, much like their natural color, a delicate whisper of silver and gold. The soft light falling through lace curtains examined each treasure discreetly, and the mirror kept its secrets and reflected only the contents of the room and the upholstered bench before it.

Two massive wardrobes, so tall they almost touched the ceiling, held all we possessed of clothes and linen, and out of them emerged new and forgotten treasures. My mother would show me the many nets and laces she had made, and all the monogrammed linens of her dowry that my grandmother, with Grandfather's help, had embroidered while the two of them were in America. That which must have taken years to accomplish now lay pressed and tightly folded, and all this effort procured the sweet smell of lavender that tinged the bed linen and pillowcases on which we slept. Summer dresses that a long winter made one forget one had emerged like a sweet surprise, making one feel glad having them anew. This was also the home of important documents, which were placed in a green suede envelope-like briefcase and tucked between folded linens and laces, shirts and pillowcases.

A small oval table with two elegant armchairs found a place against the stenciled wall—a lush green field with leaves of lighter green outlined in gold. The floor made mellow wood sounds softened by woven runners. This room always seemed cool and everything in it was important; it was the room that kept our treasures. We called it the front room. It was our best room and the one we offered to our guests. The door to it was often closed.

My room was much smaller and had an earthen floor painted yellow ocher. Long strips of woven rugs laid next to each other obscured most of its color and muffled the sound of the ground. A window looking into the neighbor's yard was densely curtained with laces. A picture of a beautiful angel leading a little girl over a bridge hung above my bed; my mother said it was the guardian angel—all children had one, and mine perhaps looked like the one in the picture. I was puzzled. My bed cover, richly layered with lace netting and organza ruffles over a light rose satin, was the most decorative aspect of the room. At night I covered myself with the downs that were under it during the day, while it lay folded on the bench in front of the mirror, glistening softly on moonlight nights. It was a bright room and the furniture was a pale whey-green. A slender wood-burning stove with a silver stovepipe heated the room in winter. In summer my doll, Griseltis, stood on top of it, held up by her funnel skirt. I liked sleeping with my head at the foot end of the bed, facing the window; below it sat my beautiful doll Nora attended by two white toy poodles. All my dolls and the doll carriage were in this room. Some dolls were ornamental and stood about only to be admired. I did not play with them. They looked so awkward and uncomfortable; they did not like to be touched. Often, lying in my bed, concentrating on the ceiling, I could invert the room. Looking at the ceiling as if it were the floor, walking about it unrestricted, gave me a different point of view and everything else a new identity.

One winter my father hung my swing, from outside, into the doorway of my room. It was a beautiful swing, hung on four instead of two ropes, enclosed on all sides by pale wooden dowels and large, light blue beads. The thought of being able to swing from one room into the other was exciting. Swinging itself, inside or out, was not a pleasant experience; I would get a sick feeling from it and would need to get off very quickly. Once on the ground, I would forget how it felt and try again. But the same sick feeling would come back, all by itself.

The back room was dark and cool in summer and bright and warm in winter. It had the only door to the outside. A double door: the inside door was half glass, and the one on the outside was wooden. Between them was a generous space; a place to play. This room had many such places. Behind the wall-oven was the most private, and under the table, with the long table-cloth, could become the most secluded. The backless chairs, called *Hockedl*, when inverted, became a house, a wagon, or anything else one wanted them to be. The ceramic floor of yellow hexagonal tile, covered by a braided-grass rug, cushioned our walk to whispering sounds. The window, like that in my room, looked into the neighbor's yard, but it was so high one could only see the sky and was not a window for looking out; even my mother had to stand on a stool to open it, which she sometimes did when tetka Katica, our neighbor, knocked on it, calling: "Vavika."

The wall-oven that kept the house warm in winter was a large rectangular protrusion, bulging a bit at the middle. Attached to the back wall and almost as high as the ceiling, it stood away from the wall that held the window, leaving a warm space between them. High above, where I could not reach, was a small door into which my mother put pots of food for slow cooking. There was no door from this room to the summer kitchen; there was only a window, which my mother converted into a wall closet with glass doors. There she kept the beautiful floral china, its cups and plates and soup tureens, and the Japanese tea service, a wedding present from the Čurićs, which we rarely used. The cups were so thin one could almost see through them, and the painted images of bridges and Japanese ladies with parasols were so delicate one was afraid to breathe in front of them.

My mother often changed the appearance of this room by moving the furniture about. She did not seem to mind; perhaps she did not consider that something was lost by such changes and that one had to have time to get to know the room in its new arrangement. These changes were difficult for me and I always showed my displeasure. I did not mind, however, when in winter the black cooking stove from the summer kitchen and a wooden chest that served as a washstand, with the large white-enameled washbowl we called *Lawor*, were moved in. This change filled the room with wonderful sounds and smells and made it even better. The two large cerulean blue enameled water cans were then placed near the door, where they looked almost ornamental. They contained the drinking water from the artesian well at the corner of our street, where it flowed (from an iron pipe) like a silver ribbon. Everyone in our street fetched water there. It was a long way to carry things so heavy, but my mother used a bowed wooden bar with prongs at each end on which she hung the lidded cans and so carried both on one shoulder. We called this utensil *obranica* (it was a carrying yoke). When I was a little older, I would carry one of these cans, half full, from the well by myself. But I had to put it down many times along the way, and I had to be careful not to let the can be tipped by the ground. The deep lid, inverted, was like a mug; the water tasted sweetest drinking from it, and I could drink almost to the bottom.

Drinking water from the artesian well was a memorable pleasure. I would often prolong my thirst just to be able to look forward to this, and I could always determine the exact point of satiation and not drink past it. Artesian water was sweet, cold in summer and in winter pleasantly tepid. It flowed from deep within the earth, day and night, interrupted only by cupped hands and the mouths of water cans. When it filled to overflowing the large cement trough from which horses drank, it followed, almost unnoticed, the rills and ditches of our street, losing some of its crystalline clarity, and gathered into a body of water outside the village. There it became part of what we called *Kroßwasser*, Big Water.

We, like everyone in the village, had a well in our yard, but the water there was bitter by comparison; it had a metallic taste. We never drank it. Only the animals did. Well-water, as we called it to distinguish it from the water we drank, was hard, and we did not bathe or wash our clothes with it. It was sometimes used in cooking and other preparations. My father kept it in the barrel where he dunked the glowing iron he had pounded into horseshoes or plow shares. This made the water sizzle, and the steam from it smelled much like its taste. We carried well-water in watering cans to plants and flowers in the garden. It also was used to settle the dust and to cool down the streets and yards in summer. In the early evening, women sprayed down the street in front of their houses with ritual-like concentration, swinging their watering can with one arm, the other arm slightly extended for balance, and with wide, measured movements laid sprays of lyrical lilting lines onto the smoothly swept ground. They continued this twofold dance—walking backward, keeping time with the graceful flowing line that followed them, leaving a pattern of their movement on the ground—until the space in front of their houses was full of the dancing design. Such patterns greeted one in the evening all over the village, adding their soothing order to the end of the day, and the cool familiar fragrance spoke of an anointed earth.

Our well was the most prominent structure in our front yard, looking quaint amid flower beds and vegetable garden. The huge, bright green, gathered-up leaves of the horseradishes grew tall around its square enclosure. Mounted under the roof canopy of the well, a round beam turned with the aid of a crank would lower the chain with the bucket and pull it up; it seemed like a big toy. The well itself was round, its shaft bricked in. The water glistened darkly from depths below. Ever since I was tall enough to see over its encasement, I did not look down the narrow shaft without feeling a particular horror. That there were sometimes frogs in the well added disgust to this horror. But the quaint outward appearance of the well continued to belie the terror it held, and one got used to its double image.

Only a small slit, a window in the neighbor's pantry, squinted in on our front yard like a bad eye and watched the vegetable garden below it. Our open hallway, sheltered by a dense cover of climbing ivy, looked across flower beds of tall summer chrysanthemums, multicolored velvet pansies, red geraniums, violets—asserting privacy to house and yard.

The summer kitchen, an addition to the house, had its own roof, and its shallow attic was accessed by a movable ladder. I could climb this ladder to the top when I was three, but getting down would require urgent calls for my mother. Here, at the end of the house, where the brick walk continued into the back yard, a wire fence with a gate that latched separated front from back yard and kept the chickens out of the flower and vegetable gardens.

The window of the summer kitchen, with its single pane of glass to the outside, had a ledge the width of a wall; it was the perfect stage for the small dolls I made myself. They were no larger then three inches and looked more like crosses to anyone else. To me they were complete, perfect in themselves. I made them from the old broom, cutting out sections of its reed handle. It was a soft, pulpy reed with a polished pale yellow surface. By making a slit a third way down the cut section of reed, I could easily slide in a narrow sliver from its polished skin to serve as arms. I imagined their faces. They had clothes for all occasions, which I cut from scraps of material: brightly colored silks and floral cottons for dresses and small-checked woolens for coats. On the wide stage of the window ledge in the summer kitchen, these dolls acted out in intricate variation all I knew and could imagine of social interaction, adding the rich detail, their own personalities, to my experience.

On rainy days I watched the storm scatter the chickens under the young corn, where they stood still for long periods, drawing their necks into their wings, anticipating the fall of raindrops from leaves above. I felt sorry for them, and I sometimes tried to chase them into the chicken coop before the rain started, but they made a game of it and would not go, even when I cried. My mother said I need not worry—they knew how to take care of themselves. So I watched them through the rain-covered window pane and learned to let them be. During heavy storms she would say, "God is scolding," as if to ask me to listen for the thunder. I liked the large noises and the surprise of the lightning. I did not understand why she asked me, at such times, not to play by the window.

The summer kitchen was an easy place to be. The door was usually open and the doorway was covered by a long linen cloth that billowed gently; it was hung there partly to keep the room cooler inside and as a precaution, a warning for inquisitive flies. Once inside, long, sticky, amber ribbons hanging from the low ceiling were waiting to catch them. Everything in this kitchen was simple. The walls were a pale yellow covered with minute, randomly spaced brown dots that my mother had flung on them, on purpose, using paint on a hand broom. The earth floor had a patina and texture from the many washes with a mixture of water and dehydrated cow dung. This application made a pattern of the wide, softly rounded strokes the length of my mother's arm and gave the floor the clean smell of hay.

Everything was open and exposed in the summer kitchen. The enormous built-in black iron kettle in the corner was used for big jobs, when fires were lit under it with straw, dried corncobs, roots of cornstalks, or the dried long stalks of sunflowers. Such kettles were used not just for boiling water but also for cooking fruits and vegetables into jams and preserves. Lard was rendered, bedclothes and linens were boiled, and soap was cooked in them. Sometimes people would borrow our kettle; lifted out by its handles, it left a large round hole in its square housing. On the wall next to the kettle housing, a hinged tin door concealed the opening to the oven that heated our back room and in which we baked our bread. Here in the summer kitchen, the other side of the same wall closet that displayed our good china in the back room held stacks of heavy white ironstone dishes we used every day. Its plain painted doors concealed all it contained, denying any resemblance to its interior glass facade. The large table in the middle of the floor, the backless chairs, and the bed in the far corner were all of the same simple construction. The brass scale and the mortar, both looking noticeably more sophisticated than their surroundings, adorned an open shelf with red enameled pans among the blue. Two embroidered wall cloths with appropriate phrases in Gothic script, praising cleanliness and good cooking, hung tacked above the washstand and the stove.

A small mirror hanging at a slant reflected in bits and pieces the events that had fallen into it here in the summer kitchen. The awkward silence of an evening left alone with Péter, my father's apprentice, who seemed grown-up at fourteen when I was five, dimly reflected on it's slippery surface: I shyly showing off two foil-wrapped chocolate chickens I had received for Easter; he quietly watching. The silver hen, sitting on a basket of multi-colored eggs, was a miniature replica of the real hen brooding in the corner next to the washstand. The rooster, foiled in robin's-egg blue, paraded over the red-checkered tablecloth, conscious of being watched. The persuasion that it was chocolate and something to eat led to a bold action, a sweet taste, and a quiet tearful disappointment. The silvery rustle of the hollow form meant the toy was gone. I wanted to be brave and tried not to cry. In the corner, the hen shifted her position and turned her head from side to side as if to get a better look at the cause of my dismay. Soon the chicks would hatch and move about in soft yellow clusters following their mother, taking shelter under her, making the pleasant noises of reassured comfort. Perhaps the mirror would lift up one of their gestures and keep it. Later, when they started getting feathers among the down, they would be outside and on their own, waiting for the transformation. As sleek young hens and roosters with glossy plumage, they would strut about the back yard. Some would find their way back, and their image would appear again, raised up from the floor of the summer kitchen onto the silvery surface of the mirror.

We had lots of chickens. I liked watching them. A game I devised for myself was to assess their personality from their appearance and action. Another such game was to pair animals. With chickens this was easy; male and female turkeys fit the same model. Ducks and geese made a convincing pair until I observed two geese chasing a duck away from their goslings. Cows and horses were a match according to stable wisdom until I saw donkeys, mules, and oxen, when the whole scheme became complicated and confusing, but I went on relentlessly correcting and repairing. My observations of animals led me to form definite opinions. I noticed, for instance, that when released to the back yard, the hens that had been with chicks for a long time showed excessive fondness for the rooster's attention. They would repeatedly lie down in front of him in submission. This would confuse the rooster; it made the elaborate dance he did around all the hens unnecessary. It was amusing to see the rooster looking surprised, awkward, and somewhat annoyed—first lessons of the back yard.

On Sunday mornings I would watch my mother catching chickens in the yard; sometimes I would help her by holding my arms stiffly in front of me, to keep them cornered. She was quick and always caught just the one she wanted. Usually it was a young rooster; we had too many of them, she said. If it was one I particularly liked, she would choose another, until next time. With her arm at her side she carried it carefully, her hand around its legs. It, hanging upside down, bent up, trying to peck her. On the floor of the summer kitchen, its wings fluttered against the ground. The simple economy of movement proceeded like a dance. Everything had meaning, and nothing was wasted. She held the chicken's feet pinned down only by the ball of one foot; the other she placed on its folded wings. She shielded its entire head in one hand, making sure its eyes were closed, and then turned its long neck up. Holding the knife in the other hand, she carefully plucked some feathers from its neck as if it required a cosmetic procedure. One gliding stroke of the knife and the bowl of the wide-rimmed ironstone plate filled with bright red blood. All of this was done skillfully, with precision and the concentration and reverence required of a sacred ritual. I would watch my mother and learn. Such learning was a bodily acquisition and wholly unlike knowledge acquired by instruction. One saw and intuited each action and it became one's own. These ritual-like activities transformed the preparation of a meal into a rich sequence of experiences and made it an important event. The summer kitchen was a place where such events culminated, where all activities integrated, and only the mirror reflected the countless separate images.

Sundays were especially pleasant at our house. My father was home. He would play the accordion, and my mother and I would dance. He always closed his eyes when he played, to concentrate on making the sounds. He had taught himself to play; he said this as if it were an apology. He was always smiling as he played. His smile seemed to be an underlying aspect of all his expressions; it was a sign of his pleasant disposition. I equated my father's smile with his goodness and associated both with the smell of his skin. When my mother or I was ill, the darkness of his eyes seemed to color his entire face, and the underlying smile in it looked betrayed. He did not often play with me, even when he was home. He had a serious nature. But he was attentive and would call me his *Menschl*, his sweetheart, and he said it so softly that I sometimes felt I did not know what to do—it made me so happy. He carried me around and talked to me, but we did not know how to play with each other. For me, his affection was evident just in his presence, and our Sundays were filled with special pleasures. The Sunday meal with its many courses—clear soup with delicate dumplings or finely sliced lacy noodles, cooked meat with fruit or herb sauces, fried or roast meat, perhaps *Wiener Schnitzl*, creamed vegetables in countless variations, fresh salads in spring and summer, desserts from the simple to the exotic—was followed by a nap in the cool of the back room. Buying *sladoled* (ice cream) and soda water, eating cold yogurt from earthen jars or a watermelon drawn from the well, bicycle rides accompanied by a self-conscious hardly audible whistling, outings to soccer games, and the sweet presence of my father are Sunday memories.

And other days were memorable too. My mother was always doing something important, and I was allowed to practice my version of everything she did. Peeling potatoes, making noodles, stirring egg yolks and sugar till they were creamy when she was baking cakes, and later licking the bowl clean were activities that needed practicing. When she baked bread, she made me a miniature of the large, round loaves, and when she baked *Schtrudl*, I helped to pull the dough till it looked transparent draped over the tablecloth, reaching halfway to the floor; she taught me how to trim the edges of the pliant dough, and I watched as she filled and rolled and placed the strudel into baking pans, making her every gesture my own. I watched her build exotic desserts and delicate pastries: *madártej*, also called *Schneenockl*, white mounds of sweet meringue cooked in milk, floating in a yellow vanilla sauce; *Crempite* and *Schaampite*, a delicate, flaky, powder-sugared pastry, one with vanilla filling, the other filled with sweet meringue; *Schaamrolle*, cream-horns, an architectural feat; many layered tortes—all took a lot of patience. One had to be careful not to get in the way; when things went wrong, she could become very irritable, even cross. Usually there were remnants to sample, leftover filling and cut-off bits of pastry, all tasting delicious.

Visits from my grandparents, Nancsi Omami, Lisi néni, Altkroßmotter (while she was alive) and tetka Mara, my mother's best friend, were an integral part of the day. That my mother continued whatever she was doing was not only acceptable but appropriate, since they liked taking part in what was going on. All visits were welcome, and our visitors were an extension of our family.

And all belonged, as the beginning of things, firmly rooted to the ground.

CHAPTER 2

Extended Family

VISITS TO TETKA Mara's house enlarged my notion of home. Only the small white house with the pointed gable, the Hallais' house, separated our houses from each other. She and my mother were inseparable. She was about my mother's age but still unmarried. She could never marry because of her condition, I heard some say; she had unpleasant breath. I was confused; since I knew everyone by their scent, I was surprised that something so essential could be separated, spoken about as a condition. The scent of her breath, I thought, suited her pleasant deep voice, her dark hair and eyes. I thought tetka Mara was very pretty. Her younger sister Lina had yellow eyes and was considered beautiful. To me she seemed haughty, aloof. She married and moved to the other end of the village. Her husband, Slavko, who looked small beside her only because of her carriage and attitude, seemed to adore her. Duško, their brother, was tall, lean, and unpredictable—sometimes friendly but often sullen and even rude. Mama Smiljka, a small woman, talked to herself, which seemed perfectly reasonable, since no one else paid much attention to what she had to say. Whenever she talked to others, there was a smile in her voice as if she had long ago accepted that she was not easily heard; it was her way of letting them know she did not mind. She was always there, part of the background, cooking and working; an essential aspect of the household. I often thought that tetka Mara seemed more like the woman of the house. She, like her father, Braca, was self-assured, even-tempered, well-disposed. Tetka Mara was educated, my mother said, and to her that was something of special value. That their friendship was based on genuine affection was very clear to me. There was contentment and ease in all they did together. They talked about everything and did needlework and

35

made laces. They sewed and knitted and laughed, and sometimes they even pulled pranks on passers-by. In the comfort of their companionship, I was left to myself and liked it.

The Mulićs had a large house and a huge yard. They owned much land, my father said. I remember the rooms of the big house as spacious, with wood floors and high ceilings. One felt very small in these rooms; even the furniture seemed isolated in them. Closed up, like a sanctuary open for special occasions only, their sounds and scents amplified, resonating darkly, these rooms seemed mysterious, exotic. Luscious animal skins, woolen fabrics, tapestries, and *ćilims* (kilim rugs) removed them far from the familiar. In one of the back rooms there were looms on which tetka Mara wove fine homespun wool cloth for the wide-legged trousers that Braca wore summer and winter. She wove hemp and linen cloths that were made into towels and bed linen. There were spinning wheels, tools for carding wool, and frames on which laces were made. Behind the house were huge stables for cows and horses, barns with wagons, carriages, and even a large sled. A generous open corridor with square pillars flanked the house with shade of ivy vine. Below it grew roses and dahlias. Brightly colored glass balls, held up on wooden sticks, peeked over the tops of flowers, their mirrored surfaces picking up the rustic disorder of the yard beyond the shallow fence, they carried its reflection unwillingly; their ornamental effect lost in this setting, they looked disappointed and became unattractive. The yard had pigs and goats roaming; chickens, guinea-hens, turkeys, ducks, and geese running about everywhere. Only the little chicks were confined under loosely constructed wicker tents, to prevent them from getting lost. There were several cats about, and rats as well; large ones, with unappealing tails. And always, there was a smell of grain among the bustling animal life in Mulić's yard.

A moplike red dog usually lay where the middle of the large wooden gate met the ground imperfectly. With just an ear and its snout exposed to the street, there it would go unnoticed until it growled fiercely, startling passers-by. It had a prankish nature and it was unpredictable; once it even bit Duško. Some days it was nowhere to be seen. Deep in the back yard, perhaps chained, it made no noise at all. Never knowing its whereabouts, I was always cautious; opening the door in the big gate just a crack, ready to pull it shut, I would call, *"Oće kera?"*—will the dog bite? Such request for those inside to assure that the dog would not bite always brought a response and safe passage.

Most of the time we visited in the summer house. The orchard beside it was full of plum trees. One of them was a beautiful yellow plum with fruit the size of large cherries; a perfect match of color and taste. One had to be careful, however, when looking for these luscious plums in the tall grasses,

With my mother in front of tetka Mara's flower garden, 1938.

for the Mulić's sometimes used this orchard when it seemed too far to walk deep into the back yard all the way to the outhouse.

The summer house was used all year round. Mama Smiljka and Braca even slept there. An icon in a gilded frame of Sveti Sava, their patron saint, hung on the wall. Below it, a large wooden bench covered with wool pelts

Extended Family

to cushion its seat, a table, and two chairs aside completed the simple altar-like setting. A bed of yellow wood elaborately carved and covered with a ćilim, a three-legged wicker bread basket taller than I, a spinning wheel, pale green-enameled water cans, and earthen jugs with nippled handles are things I remember being in the summer house.

I remember the taste of *kisela čorba*, sour soup; slabs of bread dough slashed in the center and fried like doughnuts; wonderful sheep cheese, scraped out of a wooden barrel with a spoon, and *kiselo mleko*, yogurt made of sheep's milk. There was *ajvar*, a roasted pepper salad; eggplant; lamb; *lepinje*, a flat bread topped with sour cream; *česnica*, phyllo dough with raisins and nuts, drenched with honey, and cut into small diamond-shaped pieces. All were new experiences for me. I remember eating suckling pig. I had never seen a small pig baked whole, its skin glazed caramel to taste chewy, sticky, sweet. There was heavy red wine in tall glasses during a feast that was both eloquent and intimate. Unlike our festivities with their lighthearted civility, this was serious, sensuous, ceremonial; a ritual intent to revitalize an older instinct: reflected in this opulent feast was a sense of mortality. The layers of tastes, sounds, and scents converged in the deep jewel-like glow of the dark red wine to reveal the fatal generosity, the tribal secret. Only the cold yellow glint in Lina's eyes reminded me that I was, after all, just a guest here, an outsider. The occasion for this feast could not have been Christmas—that room would have been strewn with straw in honor of the Christ child born in a stable. It must have been the feast day of their patron saint.

Tetka Mara, like some of our other neighbors, was Serb Orthodox, my mother said, and we were Catholic. To me the distinction meant an adventure. Once, at Easter, tetka Mara took us to their church. From the outside, except for the shape of its dome, this church looked much like ours. Inside it was dark in comparison; candlelight illuminating it darkly, its space appeared mysterious. The rich interior, the lament-like chanting of the priest, "*Gospode pomiluj*" (Lord have mercy), which seemed a request for affection rather than a plea for forgiveness—all reflected a somber, unaccustomed, spiritual tone. The priest swung the incense with quick, energetic strokes, and he lay down prostrate facing the earth to kiss the ground. For communion, spoonfuls of wheat kernels, cooked in honey, were placed in our cupped hands and we ate them with our fingers. The taste of honey, the faint smell of heavy red wine, the glowing ember and scent of incense converged in the ruby glow of the cup with the sacred fire on the table-like altar. In this church everything was grounded, glowing, pointing to the ground. Our church seemed lighter, more ethereal, and everything in it pointed up. Separated from us, our priest spoke to us from above the ground. Here the priest walked among us. This was an intimate space and the glow of its light was a somber dark red.

Sometimes we would go visiting with the Mulić's, riding in the fancy carriage, traveling far away into the country. I remember one of these visits to a *Sallasch*, a farm surrounded by fields with no other houses in sight. It was summer. The solitary house afloat in a sea of fields, its interior all simple elegance—Persian rugs and domestic ćilims; tall, dark-haired ladies in pale summer dresses moving gracefully about; open doors to the flat landscape, the summer breeze floating through the rooms bringing fragrances of field flowers, the smell of sun inside.

In winter Braca often took me with them on sled rides. Everyone wore fleece-lined, brightly decorated suede coats; even I was wrapped in one of them. They wore boots and fur hats. The jingle of bells, gleaming silver around horses' necks, a large gliding motion, smiles, and my luxurious attire made such occasions into exotic adventures.

The frequent contact with tetka Mara brought with it countless riches even without any particular intent on her part. I remember the beautiful gold ring with the large rectangular topaz that Braca bought for her when Lina got married. Its fine color was reminiscent of her sister's eyes and the succulent yellow plums in their orchard. The look in tetka Mara's eyes when she first showed us this ring enlarged my wisdom; it obliquely recalled the rows and rows of golden *dukats* she kept in a lidded box, strands identical to those that Lina always wore around her handsome neck. Not just a rich variety of sensations but feelings, and such complicated notions as friendship and trust, were brought to my awareness in tetka Mara's presence before I knew names for them. I remember forever the familial look from her dark brown eyes; I recognized it later in those I trusted. It was a legacy from my early childhood. And, on her daily visits, tetka Mara brought with her the riches of her language. Because I learned it simultaneously with mine, this gift went unnoticed.

• • •

Our neighbors, the Hallais, spoke only Hungarian and I was convinced I understood. Except for greetings and some polite niceties, I did not have occasion to speak much Hungarian. The Hallais often came to our house in the evenings. We listened to Rádió Budapest but mostly we listened to stories told. Jani bácsi knew how to tell a story well, and even if one did not know why everyone laughed at the end, it was riveting just to listen, and the ensuing laughter was contagious. Jani bácsi was outgoing, witty, jovial. His wife, Örzse néni, seemed serious in comparison. She, like her husband, had clear, bright blue eyes. Seeing them next to each other, sitting tall on the wagon coming home from the fields, I often noticed how good-looking they both were and how clear it was that they belonged together. Their two grown-up daughters, less favored by nature, inherited only the beautiful blue color of their eyes. Maris, the elder, was kind but rueful; in her voice there was always some hint of complaint. Her sister Bözse had a loud brassy voice that suited her brazen demeanor. It was a voice that knew how to speak aggressively and how to talk back. When she was scolded, she would not cry—she only bellowed defiance; her voice would shatter if it had to utter a submission. If she said anything to me, it was to tease me, mimicking my pleadings to my mother when I got spanked. We did not like each other and that seemed worth knowing. That she was cunning I learned only later when Péter, our apprentice, lived with us. Because she wanted his attention, she would often pretend some interest in me.

I did not often visit the Hallais by myself. They had a black dog that guarded the house well. Everyone who tried to enter was screened by his ferocious barking and striking display; this dog would hurl himself against the gate, threatening calamity. He would quickly be silenced with a reprimand from Kata néni, Jani bácsi's mother, when my parents and I visited on winter evenings. There were stories to tell and usually some work was being done, like *kukruzriwle* (corn shelling), which I too knew how to do. At times sewing, mending, and needlework accompanied conversations about work and about interesting experiences, one's own and other people's.

The rooms of Hallai's house were small and in pristine order. The walls were unadorned except for two large pictures, versions of Mary and Jesus, hanging above the two single beds. These beds, unlike ours, had long slender legs and were piled up as high as the headboard with down comforters, stacked evenly, covered with a bright paisley spread, the soft folded downs showing at the foot end, flush up to the very top. Identical in height and appearance and as straight as a board on top, these beds exhibited the skill and neatness of the household. It must have required faith to build these beds each day; they seemed to express the gesture of a prayer. The earthen floor, painted a bright yellow under each piece of furniture—the long legs of beds and chests of drawers revealing the cheerful squares and rectangles on which they seemed to float—danced a lively pattern and made the white walls sing. The wall clock with the colorful floral face ticked away quietly, while the weights attached to brass chains moved continually away from each other. The Hallai house had its own perfect measure and the wholesome sweet scent of fresh milk.

I remember an unfortunate incident that occurred on one of these visits. I had taken interest in Örzse néni's sewing basket and discovered a box of buttons. To me the form and shape of every button suggested a distinct personality. I paired them off and made up stories about them. I became fond of these buttons and told my mother I wanted to take some of them home. She, of course, told me they would have to stay. I fully expected that my admiration of them entitled me to have them, and I eventually approached Kata néni in the kitchen. I showed her the button I liked most and she said I could have it. But Bözse protested, and that was that. I carried this button around all night, and when it was time to go home I slipped it, unseen, under the elastic of my bloomers. As I was undressing for bed, my mother caught me groping for this prize button. Yes, yes, I know, I cannot keep it, I cried, but must I really take it back and apologize? And what about the vicious dog? I kept thinking I would not be able to do what she asked. But the next morning I went, alone, to give back the button. I was very afraid; I did not want to feel ashamed. Because it was a hard thing to do, once I had done it, I expected to get the button as a reward. But that did not happen. Örzse néni, somewhat surprised by the whole thing, took the button and that was that. I felt disappointed, shamed.

In early fall when the Hallais brought the corn home from our fields, it was dumped into our front yard, immediately behind the gate. In the evening we sat around this huge pile of corn with neighbors and friends; the corn was husked to a flow of jokes and stories, while I played in the enormous pile of rustling corn husks, jumping about, lying buried under or nestled in, looking at the stars. The corn was put into large baskets and carried off to the corn bin. It upset me when I was younger that the Hallais took much of it home with them. I cried to see the pile of corn husks go. Later my mother explained that the Hallais worked our fields for half their yield; they planted our wheat and corn and did the harvesting; half of what they grew on our land was rightly theirs. My father had a trade, she said, and no time to work in the fields.

• • •

Especially in summer, the rhythmic sounds from the blacksmith shop could be heard all over the village. Integrated in our nightly gathering, they became part of its familiar resonance. Late at night, long after everyone had gone, my mother and I were waiting inside, listing for the hammers to stop. The farmers needed the plow shares in the morning, she would say. I felt snug sitting in her lap, listening to stories told in the dark, about her many adventures when she was small, and I would fall asleep before my father came home. In the morning when I got up, my father's presence was there in the sounds of faraway hammers.

Until I was almost five, my father worked in Grandfather Korek's blacksmith shop, in the street behind ours. I would often go to see him there with my mother, and even at three I could find my way there by myself. I would walk past tetka Mara's house and past many houses up to the artesian well at the corner, where I would turn into the side street, sometimes holding onto the corner of the house itself, to make sure I did it right. I would always rush past this corner to avoid the man who lived in the house, and in my hurry, I would sometimes brush up against the nettles growing along the wooden fence that enclosed his yard. Where they stung, it would feel hot like fire. Ritter Vedde Hans, if he saw me, would whisk me up and toss me high above him. He was very tall! Sometimes he would give me many kisses before he would let me down. I would laugh, but I did not like this game. When I saw him I would try to engage him in conversation, as a diversion, to avoid being picked up. Somehow he knew this and would delight in surprising me, doing it anyway. The dread that he might appear would leave me by the time I reached the baker's house. Sometimes I would rest there on the wooden bench before going on to the next corner. Hansi bácsi would often be outside his store and the silvery sounds of his voice could make me think of the candies I had seen in a large tin inside. I would cross the street, pass the butcher shop, and the second house, the one with the fancy green iron gate, was where my grandmother Korek lived. It was a large house, facing sideways, with three windows and a door to the blacksmith shop. In this house were rooms I did not know; they were always dark—not mysterious, just sheltered from the light. My aunt Lisa, who was much younger than my father, would sometimes take me to one of these rooms and show me treasures, which she carefully removed from dresser drawers: a variety of intricately beaded purses, exquisite necklaces, lace collars, and pale leather gloves, most of them things Altkroßmotter had brought home from America. The dim light and the brief exposure increased the volume of these treasures, and they reappeared in countless variations in my imagination. I liked my aunt; I thought she was very pretty and pleasant to be with. But the things she showed me were somehow telling that nothing in my grandmother's house belonged to me. Not one among the many things kept in the *Schängl*, the little cabinet in the kitchen—the many balls, the dominos, the puzzle blocks with the blistered pictures of barnyard animals, things no one but I played with—not one was mine, not even the yellow teddy bear, Mazko. I never felt at home. I seemed to be a visitor in Grandmother Korek's house.

My grandmother Korek was lovely and round. Her dark hair, pulled away from her face, was neatly tucked into a small braided bun at the nape of her neck. I liked her face. It was open and flat like a plate; her dark eyes looked kindly and had a gesture of solace in them. When I came to see her, she would always offer me things to eat; often it was *Rahmprot*, sour cream on soft white bread. She could make a ritual of the simplest thing, and she did everything slowly. We would visit in the kitchen while my aunt and her apprentice, Magda, were sewing in the next room. My aunt was a seamstress and my uncle, Niklos, was a tailor. They shared the long rectangular

My father's family: Standing are my father Johann Lang (left), his brother Nikolaus Lang, and Johann Korek (Grandfather Korek's son), with their sister Lisa seated between Grandmother and Grandfather Korek, 1928.

room with the many windows. The floor there was always littered with threads and small pieces of material. I could gather up the ones I liked and they would let me keep them. Uncle Niklos, whom I called Pat because he was also my godfather, had a deep breathy voice that I liked very much. I would watch him and his apprentice Jani cutting and pressing, and they would playfully tease me, sometimes without looking up from their work. I would see the ladies who came to try on unfinished dresses that had to be pinned on them with so many pins it often required my aunt to hold some pins in her mouth. The sound from the sewing room, a continuous quick click-clacking punctuated by conversation and laughter, seemed far away here in the kitchen, where its muted resonance became the reassuring background of the visits with my grandmother.

The kitchen was a light and pleasant space with a slow pace and sleeping cats. I always sat on the ottoman under the window to face an array of well-spaced porcelain mugs displayed on the shelves of an open wall cupboard; they were there to be looked at only. The sunlight coming through the window played on their smooth, satiny surfaces and made them shine. Their shapes, full-bellied like a pitcher, made them look opulent. They shared a

Tanti Lisa, Elisabeth Korek, age twelve, in Potiski Sveti Nikola, 1934. *Courtesy* Elisabeth Martin

subtle similarity in color and design, and their variations intrigued: some had satiny finishes candy-striped in pastel colors, delicate pink and gold, and others, similarly striped, were pale turquoise and silver, lavender and bronze; some shone opalescent, others looked milky. I would never tire looking at them.

Often my grandmother would tell me stories of things that happened long ago, while I quietly watched her darn wool stockings. She would sing songs for me that I had never heard and I would please her by learning them quickly. Later, she would take me by the hand and we would walk to the stable, the cats following. I would watch her milk the cow. Relli, their black-and-white-spotted dog, chained in the backyard, would wag his tail. Back in the kitchen, Grandmother would take from the shelf one of those wonderful mugs, which she never used, and would pour into it the fresh foaming milk, for me to drink. I could hardly believe it the first time it happened, and it became our ritual, our own private communion. I would sit at the kitchen table, facing the cupboard, with both hands around the belly of the mug, looking down its silken hollow, the milk folding around me warm and sweet.

My grandmother had a pleasant mellow voice. When she sang it seemed as if she were talking. Most of her songs were sad. One of them, especially, made an impression on me. It was a long ballad about hunger and death in which a child repeatedly asked her mother for bread: *"Mutter, Mutter es hungert mich, gib mir Brot sonst sterbe ich"* was the repeated refrain. But the request was deferred; the child was asked to wait until the bread was baked. It took the whole cycle of planting, harvesting, and milling of wheat to make the bread, and when all was done, the child was dead. It was an ending I had not expected. I had my grandmother repeat the song again and again as if something in it, something incomprehensible, had to be clarified or some error corrected. I hoped for an intervention that would prevent the unwanted ending, but it was always the same. Somewhere in the retelling, the tragic feeling made itself clear. With each telling, at the exact moment when I understood, I started to cry and my grandmother would smile good-naturedly, and eventually she would refuse my request to repeat the song just one more time.

Because my grandmother liked teaching me things, I would show her the things I had learned on my own. I once showed her how I could whistle. I thought she would be pleased, but she said instead that Mary, the Mother of God, cries when girls whistle. I was confused. But secretly I thought it was just one more thing confirming my previous conviction that this Mary was not as good as she could be. The pictures of Mary and Jesus were always framed alike and hung as a pair. Having seen variations of them, I often thought that they were wrongly paired. I liked Jesus. And I stopped whistling only to please my grandmother.

Grandfather Korek was very stern. He intimidated everyone, even my father. He was tall and stiff, with wrinkles across his brow that appeared insincere, unearned. They were there because he deliberately pulled up his forehead to raise himself above everyone to whom he spoke. Even with his eyes wide open, he seemed to look down on everything. He made it clear that he admired only the smart and clever and talked as if he were one among them. He had a way of looking important. He liked dressing well, showing good taste, and was a bit vain, I thought. It was one of his more likable qualities. In his house, as in his conversations, it was clear that his opinions were not to be opposed. He rarely acknowledged my presence, and nothing I did seemed to have the power to please him. When, on occasion, my grandmother pointed out to him how quickly I learned the songs she taught me, he would dismiss it with a wave of his hand. At such times I would feel ashamed. Whenever I visited in the blacksmith shop, he was annoyed, as if he begrudged me my father's attention. The kisses we gave, brushed by the familiar scent of my father's skin and the flavor of soot and salt, were given and taken quickly, and our conversation was restricted in Grandfather Korek's presence.

Sometimes I played in the yard, close to the blacksmith shop, among wagon wheels and sawhorses standing about. Once, I mounted one of these horses and, pretending it was a real horse, proceeded to ride it. As I continued this imaginary play, bouncing, shouting the appropriate encouragement to the horse below me, the horse, to my great surprise, became animated and we not only rode—we flew. It seemed quite unbelievable, and after dismounting, I had to test this newfound power again, on another of the sawhorses, to see if it too could fly. And again we flew. In the midst of this wondrous play, Grandfather's face suddenly appeared close up, red, and all contorted. He screamed so loud I could not focus on what he was saying. It took some time to understand: I was to get down. I was never to do that again. His wrath reduced the wonderful power to shame. I did not cry. I was sad for myself and for the abandoned horses that could fly.

I often pondered the things that Grandmother Korek told me about God and the Devil. I used to feel sorry for the Devil. No one liked him. I thought this to be the cause of his devilment. The obvious solution, it seemed to me, was for someone to like the Devil. Perhaps because I never liked Grandfather Korek, it was easy for me to equate his behavior with devilment. Having seen his angry face, I knew my assumption that somebody could like the Devil was obviously incorrect.

Grandfather Korek did not have a garden and no tree grew in his yard.

• • •

Across the street, in the middle of the long row of houses, stood the house of my Schüssler grandparents. My grandmother said it used to be the largest house in the village when her mother was a child. Now there were many larger houses around it. Its rounded yellow gable reflected with affection everything that was familiar inside. The main entrance, a door in the facade, faced the kitchen door across a long open corridor, but I always entered by the door in the wooden gate. Wilson, Grandfather's dog, hardly ever barked and often would not even notice my arrival. I was at home here and did not need announcing. The apricot tree beside the weathered well and the line of trees behind it filled the wide rectangular space along the wall of the Lochs' house. This orchard perfectly matched the house itself in width and length, and the space between them, the front yard, was always swept clean as if it were the floor of a room. A lattice fence separated house and orchard from the animals in the back yard.

The stable was a continuation of the house. There was a large bed by the window; a crib and the straw below it marked off the space for the cow and horses. Wooden steps led up to the attic through a large door in the ceiling. I often went up there with my grandfather to fetch smoked meat from the chamber around the chimney. Mounds of grain were stored on the attic floor. Some trunks stood about, looking discarded. Two small openings in the gable offered a look to the street and into yards below. At the opposite end of the attic, a narrow door opened a hall-like space across the width of the attic. There were nests for hens to lay their eggs and perches for chickens to sleep. I would help my grandmother gather eggs, but I did not like the smell of this space. For a long time it was a mystery to me how the chickens got into the attic. Below, in the eaves of the stable, nesting swallows could be observed more closely. Their fleet elegance, the beauty of their nests, were an ornamental aspect of the stable.

In the attached open shed, its roof slanting so low that one could climb its scalloped tiles with ease, my grandfather kept his wagon. The harnesses—boasting a rich array of silver rings, leather straps and patches—hung next to the stable door. The large kettle was housed in one corner of the shed. Strips of wood nailed against the wall, in lattice fashion, lead to a square hole in the gable—the passage by which the chickens got in and out of the attic. Watching their hesitant flight down, one wondered why they kept climbing up. Habit, my grandfather said. I liked playing in this shed, especially when it was raining. The smell of rain, the hush behind the sound of its fall, infused the joy of uninterrupted play with a sense of the extraordinary—of playing outside in the rain and at the same time being in a sheltered space, cut off from everything by the shaft of its fall.

There were pigs in pens, but ducks, geese, and chickens freely roamed, restricted only by the fenced-in garden where, among the fruit trees, my grandmother had planted vegetables. And the entire back yard was under the spell and protection of the mulberry tree, which was much taller than any house around.

Inside the house everything was familiar. The rooms opened into each other and nothing in them was hidden. The dark furniture—beds with slender posts, chests and wardrobes of the same elegant simplicity—had always been there; only the bentwood chairs, a gramophone, and the *Kachlofe* (a rectangular shaft of glazed tile, replacing the wall-oven) were newer additions in these rooms. The large portraits of my mother's grandparents, in heavy gilded frames, reminded us that this had been their house, and we knew it had belonged to their parents before them. My mother often told me about her grandfather; how much he loved music and how he sometimes cried when he listened to it. She told how he asked the lady doctor to give him a shot to help him die, and how she obliged out of kindness and respect for his suffering. Sometimes, when we listened to the gramophone, I felt as if I knew him.

I knew from my mother's stories that she and my father had lived in the front room of my grandparents' house when they were first married. I knew

My mother's family: Seated in front are Barbara and her brother Josef, in front of their sister Magdalena and their maternal grandparents, Karl and Barbara Brandmayer; their parents Johann and Barbara Schüssler (far left and right) were added to the photo in America, ca. 1915.

that my sister, Else, was born and died there. I saw no picture of her any-where, but my mother told me about her, repeating the words she could say. She was only ten months old when she died, my mother said, looking faraway as if she meant to reach the grave that we often visited. She told, in detail, how my sister got whooping cough and how ill she was before she died. They put a golden locket and some of my mother's rings in the small casket with her, and my uncle Seppi brought down the ancestral chest that we had in our family since time began, and they put her casket into it to keep her safe in the ground. Her soul was an angel now, my mother some-times added. I did not like to see her look so pale and distant, and I did not like to see her cry. But I did not think of these stories when I visited at my grandparents' house, where all the rooms were friendly.

In the room where my grandparents slept, above their beds, hung their large mahogany-framed portraits. My grandfather had dark hair then and a handlebar mustache. My grandmother was beautiful. Heavy, raven hair framed her face. Large almond-shaped dark eyes under rounded brows, a well-shaped nose, full lips, and beautiful skin made hers the most perfect face I had ever seen. The pale blue blouse with high neck and puffed sleeves she had bought in America, where the picture was made. She was always embarrassed to admit that this was her portrait. Although I never compared her with this image, I thought my grandmother was beautiful still. She was tall and slender and, I thought, graceful, even to the appearance of her hands; her fingers, bent at the joints, were twisted, and she sometimes had to use her arms to pick things up. She was not self-conscious about her hands; only about her teeth. She would shyly cover her mouth with one hand, when she thought of it. I never really noticed her lack of teeth. She wore black clothes—long skirts and long-sleeved blouses, a black kerchief tied under her chin—like all the other ladies her age. I recall an image of her standing tall and lithe, somewhere out in the field, with her arms raised and folded behind her head, walking as if on a breeze, talking to my grandfather across an open space. Perhaps it was in the melon field in summer. The image is all awash with light and carries with it the warmth of summer sun.

Sun shining through the window, the large oven with the bench around it, the cupboard with the dishes where Grandfather kept the Schnaps, the massive table under which I played, and the smell of Grandmother's cooking made the kitchen warm, inviting. The back of the kitchen was a private space, much darker, with a feeling of its own. At the far end of this space, between the bed and the pantry door, Kroßmotter, my great grandmother, would usually be sitting. Seen from the front of the room, the place where she sat seemed far away, and her image made a distinct impression on me. She did not speak. In her dark clothes and kerchief, her body erect, her legs crossed, her hands held in her lap, she sat there for long periods of time. She seemed immobile except for the rhythmic swinging of her leg, as if her leg, on its own, were measuring out time. She herself looked timeless. Her face was lined and weathered, leather-like. She looked like a deity. Immovable. Impartial. Her eyes glistened like mica in her earthen face, and they would light up when she would get something she wanted. Usually it was *Schpeck* (bacon) she asked for, and sometimes it was water. She would groan to get attention—it was a rhythmic not a complaining groan. I remember my mother once asking me to give her a cup of water; I remember myself being very small. The way from the door to the end of the room seemed long. Slowly I made my way, half in dread, half in reverence, and always watching the level of the water so as not to spill it from the cup. It was an enameled mug, white inside and out, with a green lip and handle and a cluster of red cherries with two green leaves stenciled on it. I knew this cup;

I drank from it myself many times. It had a chip in the bottom. I watched myself coming closer and stretched my arm out, carefully, holding the cup at arm's length. She took it eagerly, with both hands, and drank with soft gulping sounds. She smiled, handing me the empty cup. I remember running around the room being glad. Sometimes I would see her outside, sitting in the shade, the dog under her foot enjoying the unintended strokes; I often thought of her and the mulberry tree as being somehow alike.

When our Kroßmotter died, the kitchen remained the same. My grandparents now slept in the bed by the pantry. It was wide enough for me to sleep with them as well. There, in total darkness, in the space between my grandparents, wrapped in the quieting sound of their voices, the familiar smell of their skin, I was aware of an affection as clearly present as the scent of the bed linen and the warmth under the downs. My grandparents did not pray. But from what I knew of prayer, being together and safe from harm was what one prayed for, and that I experienced being with them.

In winter we would sit around the warm oven and my grandfather would tell stories. He had no patience with fairy tales and would make up stories of his own. They were one of a kind and could never be repeated exactly; it took me some time to notice that these stories were never quite the same. But that was part of my grandfather's charm; when he played, he could allow for many possibilities. If I questioned him about these variations, he would hide a smile under his mustache, and keeping an otherwise serious demeanor, he would affirm, without hesitation, that the latest version was as true as any before it; the truth was in the telling. My grandmother would sit and mend and be amused. Grandfather could make things sound very interesting. Even curses. He would make curses naming Jesus, Mary, and Joseph together with Maria Theresa, Constantinople, Turkey, Slavonia, Bačka, and Banat—and everything that's round should tumble after, he would add at the end. The declamations were often so long and so entertaining one forgot they were intended to be curses, and we would laugh. My grandfather was the only grown-up I knew who took play seriously.

He would often talk about the time spent in America, about the ice cream factory where he worked, the procedure of making ice cream (described in detail), the huge quantity of ingredients it took, how it was sold in containers the size of a brick, and how he would bring home such bricks to eat all year round. I imagined how great it would be to eat a whole brick of ice cream. I knew the taste of ice cream. It was a summer pleasure. My father would buy it for me from the man who pushed the cart with the round silver lids. He only came on Sundays, when the weather was hot. With little bell sounds he would announce his presence on the street, repeatedly calling out: "Sladoled, sladoled." I would get some in a cone.

Often, Grandfather would take me to Hansi bácsi's store just to buy me chocolate. This could happen any day of the week. He always held my hand as we walked, and he engaged me in important conversation. I thought he was the most worldly man. I felt proud walking beside him. Although he would have none of the chocolate we bought, he would watch me eat it, sharing my pleasure, delighting in my enjoyment. He approved of pleasure. Pleasure was an important aspect of life, he would say, and one should take care not to avoid it. He also allowed me to participate in things he liked. I watched him roll his cigarettes with concentration; he showed me how it was done. It was not just a matter of skill, he would say—one had to put one's heart into it. He showed me how he stoked his pipe and always asked for my cooperation in lighting up. For this he produced a pouch from one of his pockets and removed from it a brown flint stone, a yellow cottonlike substance, and a small steel bar. In this ritual the stone was carefully covered by just so much of the cotton and held just so. Struck against the steel bar, it produced a spark. All this he did, with great precision, himself. I was asked to watch and blow at just the right moment to help ignite the cottony substance. The little flame produced a smell of its own and brought great satisfaction to my grandfather, and all of it gave me a feeling of accomplishment.

Sometimes, my grandfather would take me down into the cellar to help him get wine. There the light, like the walls and the floor, was earth-colored, and the air was damp and had the scent of wine barrels and wet sand. My grandfather would lift me up to the top of the largest barrel, and I would straddle it, sitting straight, my head almost touching the ceiling. It was clearly a task just for me. I examined the hole in the middle of the barrel, but I could not see—only smell—its contents. Grandfather showed me the hollow gourd with the long neck and large belly. It had two small holes, one at each end. One could tell this gourd was used many times; its paleness was only a reminder of the yellow color it once was. We lowered the long narrow neck into the barrel. With the gourd in place, I was told to suck the hole on the belly of the gourd; I would soon see some magic. It gave my grandfather great pleasure to see me put my best efforts into this task. I would suck and, at times, I would have to rest. He would then place his finger on the hole until I was ready to try again. He would watch me carefully. Surprised by a mouthful of wine, I would stop, astonished. My grandfather would notice and tell me to swallow. It tasted sour but, as always, it was good. The gourd was then cleverly removed and while its content flowed into the waiting bottles, I watched from the top of the barrel.

Everything I did with Grandfather seemed important. He allowed me to help with all he did, and he was very helpful to me as well. With great deliberation and much ceremony he gave names to all my dolls, names I had never heard before. Dolls that were plain had to have exotic names, like Griseltis, Appolonia, Aurelia, and all names had to be chosen with special care; they had to fit. He was clever with names. He named all his dogs after important people. Wilson, the black dog he presently had, was named after a president of the United States. Though my grandfather was not interested in politics, he would know how to talk about it. He was, rather, a peacemaker, and he knew what was fair. He would always intervene when my mother thought to punish me. He would remove the slender switch that she kept across the lintel of the door. He would break it and throw it away. Of course, that would only make her more angry when she needed it and did not find it there. Since her idea of being good and my notion of what that entailed did not usually coincide, she used it often and would always get another. Even so, Grandfather's intervention gave an edge to my defiance and it was comforting to know I had an ally when he was not there to protect me. It took the sting out of that switch.

My grandfather could be funny when he did not even intend to be. When he got sick with a headache or a cold, for instance, he would go to bed and moan, repeating over and over, "Oh, dear children, dear, dear children, now Grandfather has to die." No one laughed outright, but everyone thought it was very funny. During bad storms he would simply go to bed, cover his head, and emerge from under the downs when all was over. But he could also laugh at himself and he knew how not to take himself too seriously. On occasion, he would get really mad. I remember the time he locked himself out of the house; how he ranted and raved that he could not find the key, and that no one was home to let him in, out of the rain. But he was standing in the shelter of the hallway, I reminded him. Yes, like a beggar in front of his own door, and in the rain, he added defiantly, making a dramatic gesture toward the sky. At such times he would fiercely curse mother, God, and country in great detail and in Hungarian. In the midst of his raging, I would detect the smile that I often saw him hiding under his mustache. I would quietly watch and be amused. To me there was no one more interesting than my grandfather.

In my grandfather's house I was at home. Everything in it was part of what I knew about myself and in it I knew how to belong.

My mother's brother, my Seppi Onkl, also lived in this house, and later his family lived in it as well. Before he was married, he would come to our house often. I remember him taking me on long rides on my father's bicycle. Sitting in the little metal seat in front, I would sometimes start singing and I would listen to my voice vibrate as we rode along. He would pretend to be annoyed. At first this made me sad, but I soon learned that it was just a game. When I would forget and sing again, he would again ask me to stop, just to continue the game. He had a smile like Grandfather's, and bright blue eyes that smiled as well. Sometimes he was a bit of a prankster. In winter, he would take me for rides in the beautiful green sled that my father made for me, a miniature of a fancy sled. All bundled up in my winter clothes, a woolen shawl across my mouth and nose, my hands tucked in a little fur muff, and wrapped up to my waist in a blanket, I would sit calling, "Faster, faster!" He would look back at me as if to see whether I was ready for what was about to happen. Then he would go very fast and, with a quick jerking motion, dump me out of the sled. After the initial surprise, I would lie there quietly in the snow, unable to move, waiting to be picked up. He seemed amused by my lack of initiative and would tell my mother later that had he not picked me up, I would still be peacefully lying there in the snow, waiting.

CHAPTER 3

The Larger Village

HE VILLAGE BECAME LARGER as I grew older. The people I passed on the street were a familiar aspect of the village. We recognized each other with the appropriate greetings. Sometimes our greetings did not sound the same, but we knew they corresponded. I greeted everyone in their own language, with *Kisstihant, Kezitcsókolom, Ljubimruke*. It was a greeting that children used and it meant "I kiss your hands." It was not a promise or an expression of intent but a declaration of esteem. There were greetings appropriate for the time of day, and some invoked blessings from God. I heard and knew all of them in German, Hungarian, Serb, and Slovak. Our individual greetings were the reaffirming acknowledgment we gave each other in respectful recognition.

Everyone in our village was accounted for; we knew where everyone lived. Sometimes it seemed that the facades of houses bore a striking resemblance to the people who lived inside; it was an expression of the integral unity of people and things. Everyone and everything in our village was essential; nothing could have been left out, and all belonged to our notion of home. Our ethnicity, expressed by our name, our language, the way we dressed and kept our houses, the way we worshiped and celebrated, gave us a separate social identity. But we were nevertheless integrated and inseparably grounded in a common experience. The life we shared made us kin among strangers. Recognizable to each other, we would forever remain for each other the bearers of that particular intimacy—home.

In our village there were no strangers. People we did not know were guests of those we knew. Often they were relatives from neighboring villages, and sometimes they were just friends. Because we saw no need for such distinction, we used the same word; *Freint*, we said, to mean both. Sometimes our guests came from faraway places with fascinating names: Arad, Tschanad, Betschkerek, Botschar, Temeschwar, and Vukovar. All came bringing the excitement of the unfamiliar and enriched our imagination. We were pleased and proud to have guests and showed them off to our neighbors and friends.

Kirweih was a yearly event for which relatives from neighboring villages came to visit. It was the anniversary of the consecration of our church, Saint Katherine's Day, the twenty-fifth of November. Both the German- and Hungarian-speaking Catholics shared this holiday, each with their own separate celebration. In some villages this event lasted three days, but we made do with two. In tents around the church, there were things to see and toys and candies to buy. The pale gingerbread figures displayed in neat rows—dolls, slippers, hearts, hares, horses—all promised to be delicious. But their colorful decorations, decals with angelic faces, mirrors, and sentimental verses made them keepsakes for everyone. Occasionally one would see a headless horse in the hands of a small child. I would carry my gingerbread doll securely, recalling the minute pinholes of its airy texture under the parchment-like surface, remembering its delicate flavor. Its sweet smell would often tempt me, but I would save my gingerbread doll with the mirror on its chest as long as I possibly could.

Feasts from morning to night were linked into one continuous celebration. In the evening there was dancing at the inn we called Habag. There, the young men and girls in their festive attire were observed and their dancing was admired by those too young or too old to dance themselves. Everyone was noticed. My shyness was exacerbated by the exposure to so many people. Preoccupied with my own feelings, I was too busy to be observant. The harsh brassy sound of the music close by and the noisy chatter when the music stopped were continuous irritants. For me, the long sleepy walk home, in the chill of night, was the more appealing aspect of that part of the *Kirweih*.

I was intrigued by the visiting relatives. My cousins from Mokrin, a village near the Rumanian border, came with their parents by wagon and stayed at our grandparents' house. They were the children of my mother's sister Leni. I called her Kodl, because she was my godmother. I liked hearing her voice, the way she said certain words, and especially her laughter. She had married at eighteen. The man who became her husband had seen her only once, which in itself was not uncommon, since marriages were often arranged and involved people from different villages. In her case, it was her own decision that led her to marry. Everyone in the village knew the story. The boy she loved and intended to marry had once publicly humili-

Village musicians, Grandfather with his violin (back row, center), 1920s.

ated her. He ignored her at a dance, in front of everyone, and danced only with his partner from dancing school, showing off his newly acquired skills. His vanity and bad manners had to be repaid, and soon afterward she married and moved away. I never liked this story. The romantic stories I made up playing with my dolls and buttons always had a happy ending. I never had them marry quickly. They married after a long trial, preferably just before they died, and only because they loved each other. The choice to marry was always the end of the story, and to keep the story alive, marriage had to be delayed as long as possible. When my buttons finally married, I called it a happy ending. It was difficult to see the happy ending in my Kodl's story, but I admired her resolve. There was nothing telling of regret in her demeanor now, only a subtle strength that knew how to endure any decision. Her husband, Franz, whom I called Pat (Godfather, a courtesy title given to the husband of one's godmother), was pleasant enough, though a bit boastful. I remember him talking with Grandfather about the harvest and color of tobacco, and something about that memory helps me recall the image of a rotund man with a round, ruddy face, a breathless voice, and an asthmatic cough.

My cousin Jozsi was four years older than I. I remember watching him carve intricate designs with his pocket knife on sticks he cut from tree branches. He brought with him a long leather whip, and he knew how to swing it skillfully in circles, cracking it into sharp shotlike sounds. I did not like the closeness of the whistling whip. He seemed to notice and would bring it even closer. Sometimes his facial expressions revealed the prankster in him. He was not interested in playing with me, but he wanted to be noticed. He impressed everyone with his sensitivity to sounds, his interest in music. At an early age, he could play the most intricate tunes on the little harmonica that Grandfather bought him in a Kirweih tent. And he would listen for hours to the gramophone, mesmerized by the music from *The Flying Dutchman*. His robust appearance, his bizarre sense of humor, and his aptitude to annoy all belied his sensitivity. When he played his harmonica, when he listened to music, he had the power to amaze. Though he did not invite my affection, he had my respect.

Perwi, his sister, was ten years older than I, and I thought she was beautiful. Her hair was raven, and she had large dark eyes and full lips. The look in her eyes, informed with a wisdom that made her seem not to require a mother, held something solitary, fleeting; a reflection complete, filled with itself. She was perfect, I thought. That I should be related to her, that we shared the same grandparents, was almost too much for me to realize. I remember the Kirweih when she visited us by herself. Sitting in bed in our front room, under the portraits of my parents, she seemed the richest of our treasures. I admired her not just for her beauty but also for her ability to work hard at home and in the fields. She was not used to being pampered, she said, but she seemed to enjoy the attention we paid her and promised to return and stay with us longer. I did not know then that she would never come again. The following summer, we visited her in the hospital in Kikinda. She looked pale and weak, lying in a white wrought-iron bed in a room that smelled of disease. A burst appendix; peritonitis, they said. She said she wanted to get well. She was only seventeen. The look that made her seem more like a mother and no one's child was even more exposed and fitting. By then it was war in our country, and the boy whom she loved and intended to marry was a soldier. They did not tell her about the news they received that he was missing in action. They buried her in her wedding dress. We did not go to the funeral because my mother was very ill.

My father's cousins, the Langs from Sanad and the Gerhardts from Hidjosch, both predominantly Serb villages, came to visit by train. The relatives from Sajan spoke only Hungarian. Though they had last names like Brunner and Becker, in a village with no German schools and no other German-speaking people, they no longer spoke their mother tongue. Some married Hungarians, and their children did not even understand German. They would tell, half in jest, about their grandfather Lang's concern to protect the family identity; how it caused him to search among the German population in nearby villages for marriage partners for his sons and daughters. Even though he succeeded, and his five children—among them Grandfather Lang, my father's father, who died in the Great War—all married into German families, still half of his grandchildren now spoke no German at all. We laughed. Because we all spoke Hungarian, it did not seem important. There was a time, my mother later explained to me, when German schools were prohibited, and Hungarian was the official language. German-speaking people were pressured to change their names and to become Hungarian. No one liked this, but some found it necessary to comply in order to get the education and position they wanted. Some people in our village called Laub changed their name to Lázár and considered themselves to be Hungarian, even though everyone knew them to be the same. They changed their identity and with it their relationship to the ethnic group of which they had been a part. To be Hungarian was not in itself objectionable, my mother explained, but to be forced into denying or changing one's identity was unacceptable. It made most people more determined to affirm their ethnicity, even if this meant being in a position of disadvantage socially. It is not a matter of choice who one is, she would say, but a matter of integrity. It is, she would add with great conviction, a matter of social justice to respect everyone for who they are. My mother was uninhibited when it came to expressing her opinions on matters of fairness and equality. When she perceived an injustice, she spared no one's feelings, nor did she allow anyone to intimidate her in putting matters right.

Perhaps it was a concern for the preservation of our identity that drove her to teach me to read German when I was only three. I remember sitting on a footstool, using a backless chair for a table, looking at a book of Gothic letters; a first reader. The letters had names and I was to remember them and learn to recognize their linear configurations. My mother was leaning over me and asking, first gently, for the name of each letter. One by one I knew them till we came to a page I had not remembered well enough. She insisted and then demanded that I give the appropriate answer. I looked intently but I could not determine what the spiked line she pointed to had to do with the recognizable images of boots and stockings, and they gave no clue to name the hooklike configuration. My thoughts raced and clashed with the sharp, agitated sounds of my mother's voice. I repeated, I did not know what letter it was. She was not very patient. I wanted to remember, but her insistence just made things worse. Suddenly, I became very quiet inside myself as she raged on. It became clear to me that there was nothing in my power, and I was convinced that there was no clue on the page in front of me that would help me give her what she wanted. I was disappointed in my mother. I expected her to know that I could not possibly do what she asked. And, for the first time, I dared to think that my mother was not smart. I was ashamed of my mother. This made me feel very bad and I cried. When I was old enough to go to school, the Gothic alphabet my mother taught me was replaced by Latin letters.

My first experience at school. I was five. The teacher and the children spoke only Serbo-Croatian, which in itself was insignificant to me since I spoke it fluently myself. I remember, instead, the distressing experience of being overlooked, of not really being seen. The teacher, a young woman with dark hair and a nervous disposition, did not really look at any of us. It was as if she had something in mind to which our presence was just an interference. We moved around randomly, looking for recognition. We did not have time or opportunity to be with each other, to notice who we were individually. In our attempt to give meaning to this gathering, to do something together, we made a noisy crowd. Preoccupied with my own feelings, I glanced helplessly about. Everywhere around me, in the eyes of the other children, I saw the same searching, questioning look. Our fragile attempts at being acknowledged passed unnoticed. Why did she not want to know us? Why did she pass over us without allowing for mutual recognition? We filled the room making a small unit, moving perpetually about her orbit. Shrill sounds, in words that told what and what not to do, enforced the order of the place. Another young woman, engaged in conversation with the teacher, looked equally absent. Someone standing close to me, a little girl, seemed distressed. She had wet her pants, and her stockings clung to her, cold and tired. In her face, I recognized something familiar, reminding me of shame and rage. A feeling of compassion overwhelmed me. She looked at me and almost smiled. Later the teacher's helper took her away, and I heard her soft whimpering, listening to it as if it were my own. I will not go to school, I said that day to my mother and repeated it again, crying, orbiting around her, to keep away the sting of the switch. As an apology for my defiant assertion, she wanted me to say: "I will like going to school." Though it hurt to say it, I finally did. Quietly I repeated it to myself, listening to the words being fragmented by uncontrollable leftover sobbing.

At six, Kindergarten seemed a better place; by then I had learned what to expect. We often played games in the garden and learned new songs to sing. I knew all the children. We were all German-speaking. Our teacher had very curly blonde hair and pale blue eyes, and her face was friendly and covered with freckles. I don't remember looking for acknowledgment. I recall, instead, how my whey-green enameled drinking cup with its light gray pebbled interior looked among the others, and how it seemed to reflect my own identity.

My mother put great value on being educated. She perceived it to be synonymous with personal power—being strong and at the mercy of no one. She was determined that I should receive a good education. I always knew that my mother would have wanted me to be more assertive. But I was more like my father. She felt frustrated by his inability to stand up to Grandfather Korek, his stepfather, and she would have liked him to have been stronger. I often heard her argue her opinions, pointing out her concerns about matters he did not handle well. I heard these subtle accusations of my father and it always made me feel sad. They would often not talk to each other after such confrontations, and I felt uneasy, afraid. I tried to hasten their reconciliation by saying something clever and funny, to make them laugh. When I succeeded, I felt glad, but very tired.

My mother was assertive, direct, outspoken. We were not perfectly matched in temperament. I was shy. She had certain expectations of what I should be like that were never quite clear to me, and she spared no effort to shape my behavior accordingly. I was very stubborn; I would give in to her demands only after she wore down my resistance. Often she had to resort to the use of the supple switch. It did not hurt; it only stung. But it humiliated. I did not like her power over me. I obeyed her demands, but I never allowed her to change my mind. Sometimes I would express my frustration by telling her outright, "Just you wait, when I get big and you are small, I will give it all back to you." She had nothing against such outbursts and seemed amused rather than enraged by them. Because it was easier to obey her than to defy her deliberately, I was usually quite accommodating. She, however, was difficult to please. She wanted me to be good, and that, too, I challenged—not because I did not want to be good but because I realized that being good was not something I clearly knew how to do; it seemed to entail something different in every situation. "I would like to be good, but I do not know how," I told her when I was three. I was tired of getting spanked and still getting it wrong, I explained. She laughed, but I was serious. In her quest for perfect behavior, my mother would not always punish or scold. Sometimes she would praise me to get me to do what she wanted, and I would be overwhelmed by such attention. Beside myself with joy, I would do all she asked.

• • •

In summer I went barefoot. I wore the short-sleeved dresses I had forgotten I had and new ones that my mother made for me. I liked how the cloth felt stretched across my chest, how the skirts twirled around me when I turned, and how my arms filled the circular bands that held in the puffed sleeves. Looking in the mirror, admiring the dresses, I could sometimes remove myself from the reflection and think of it as a doll, and I would watch my motions as if they belonged to this doll that could move. It was a game I liked playing, but I took great care that myself and this reflection did not drift apart too far and were safely united again. A sense of wholeness and well-being was part of these summer dresses; they made me feel new to myself and glad.

I played hopscotch with the girls across the street, with Kristina, Mira, and their cousin Lina Markov. We tossed shards bearing elegant designs in deep colored glazes, pieces of plates and pottery that we had found buried in the ground. Remnants of the Turks, someone said, gravely. These shards, from the distant past, brought their mute wisdom to our games. We admired their beauty, weighing their worth with the full measure of our affection. We tossed them, skipped across and picked them up, always attentive to their motion in flight, the gravity of their fall, and the sound they made against the ground. There were many games we played on quiet summer days, when the village was left to us children and those who did not work in the fields. Mostly we played on the street, but often we went to each other's houses to play in the yard. In playing with others, I had to learn that my wishes and my perceptions of things were not always regarded as being important, and that some games evolved contrary to expectations and a certain adaptability was necessary to survive the unforeseen consequences.

I remember, in particular, two such games, both initiated in Markov's yard. I was six years old. Mira and Kristina were nine and eleven, and their brother Branko was only four. Lina, their cousin, was ten, and tetka Katica's niece Ljubica, who had lived with them since the age of two, was twelve. She was talking to the older girls about a game she knew that had to be played in pairs. I did not understand the game; they were secretive about its rules, whispering and looking very serious. They had paired me off with Branko, who always smiled sweetly, perhaps to compensate for the chronic problem with his nose. Thick, greenish mucus running in two lines, falling just short of his mouth and being sniffed up at intervals, making a most unpleasant sound, rendered that smile ineffectual. I knew I would not like this game as soon as they paired me with Branko. We were to hide with our partners in the closed shed, where the hay was kept, and to wait for further instructions. There was plenty of space in the shed, mounds of hay to hide in, and I did not see the others, though I heard them. The instructions that followed surprised me. I was not about to take my clothes off—that I decided immediately. I was thinking of how I was going to get away. To leave would be courageous, but it would mean having to endure their teasing and perhaps being excluded from future games. I looked at Branko, who was trying to take off something he wore. I remember helping him, being very careful not to get near his nose. Suddenly, I heard my own voice saying the obvious: "My mother is calling me, did you hear?" They had not been listening, but they all knew they would have to leave if their mother was calling. At home, I was still curious about this game and I asked my mother about it. She only said that I did the right thing telling her about this, and that I should not allow anyone to persuade me to play games I did not understand or like. I was pleased. But the next time I wanted to play with the girls across the street, they ignored me and called me a traitor. At first I thought they were angry because I had left and spoiled their game, but it was much more serious. It seemed our mothers had a talk over this game, and theirs punished them for playing it. For a long time, they did not play with me, and I always felt I had done something wrong.

Later, when I was eight, we were playing outside when Branko and some other boys discovered a source of frogs and decided to chase them; the girls were also participating. It was a game made worse for me because I had an aversion to frogs. In our village frogs were everywhere; they would turn up unexpectedly in the most unlikely places, darting out of nowhere in front of one. Their appearance provoked instant revulsion; a feeling only frogs could inspire. Caught in this game, I had to be cautious not to let anyone notice that I was horrified. For fear of getting one of those frogs tossed at me, or worse, slipped under my clothes, I tried making my way out of the yard, carefully, slyly feigning amusement as I watched the frogs being caught and confined, and my caution kept me there just long enough to witness something quite unexpected: the killing and cutting up of the frogs. I was totally surprised by this turn of events, and the attending horror gave me the necessary courage to hasten my exit. But the bizarre images, the apparent fervor with which the slaughter was executed, and the sounds connected with this execution remained with me and became associated with betrayal and Markov's yard.

• • •

In summer people left the village hours before dawn so that the early morning light might find them at their destination ready to work. The wagons returned late in the evening, bringing the smell of hay with them and raising the dust on the road. As presents for us children, they brought back remnants of the bread they had taken with them, tightly knotted in checkered cloths. Left in the shade of wagons all day, it had absorbed the smell of fields under summer sun. We loved its sweet flavor. We called it *Haseprot*, rabbits' bread, named after the rabbits there. It was our share of labor done.

At harvest, the wagons came back from the fields moving slowly, swaying stacks of wheat towering high above them. The people sitting atop seemed an apparition on these high-rising structures that looked too fragile to have been climbed, but they were an essential aspect of the arrangement and not just there for the ride home. With skill and precision, they would fork down the sheaves, tossing them onto the waiting pitch forks below, and those on the ground would stack them again into a solid structure in their back yard. Later the threshing machine would come, and its crew of men and women would work all day under the noise of the engine that overwhelmed all conversation close by. They would convert the golden sheaves into sacks of grain and stack the remaining straw back into a solid structure, undiminished by their labor. This crew fetched and carried, and their gestures seemed mimelike, their words rendered mute by the giant sound screen, the noise of the threshing machine. Colorful kerchiefs tied in back covered their heads. They wiped the dust and sweat from their faces with blue paisley handkerchiefs. They drank a lot of water. The smell of goulash initiated a needed respite from the noise. The next day the threshing machine would be at someone else's house, and children would run again to watch.

Though the fields were far from the village, all activities in the village pertained to and were governed by them. Even who married whom was said to have something to do with the fields. Though I did not quite understand, I knew that the land one owned was of great value and important to the life of the village. Land was alive and forever, I heard them say; compared to it, a house was a dead thing. Most people worked the fields, and those who did not had professions that supported the work in them. Some people had more land than others, but everyone lived by its value. Field work was hard, people would say, but it never sounded like a complaint. It seemed more like an affirmation of its value, a measure of worth. As children we were often present and took part working in the fields. The seriousness of people at work, the rhythmic pace of the work itself, the visual expanse of earth and sky, the exposure to sun and wind, and the continuous vitality of the ground itself, was all part of the collective experience. Isolated by long distances and far from the village, we were united by the work in common. Seeing people at work in the fields, I often thought I heard sounds that reminded me of the sing-song vespers I heard in church. It was the song of the fields. Watching the summer breeze move through endless wheat fields, lifting their golden sound into high skies, was the poetry that moved our heart to recognize its own affection. Sitting on the wagon next to my grandfather, passing the people as they walked home at dusk, our reciprocal smile and the nod of our greeting seemed like a mutual benediction.

My grandparents often took me with them to their fields. I sat between them and sometimes held the reins, shouting appropriate remarks to the

horses to encourage them. Lencsi and Basa knew the way. Our trips took us
to various fields. Near the river Theiss, a few kilometers from the village,
my grandparents had a field of watermelons. Long stretches of dark green
bulges dotting the ground as far as the eye could see all had to be examined,
turned, and pampered to make them grow even larger. Some were probed
with a flick of a finger, others received a knock of the knuckle, and the
sounds discerned related their condition and state of maturity. The largest
had outgrown the delicate vine and were ready to be severed from the life
source. The melon field was a continuous birthing place; one had to be
there when their time came. Living, roofless, roomlike structures—squares
outlined by a row of densely planted sunflowers grown tall—received the
ripe fruit and kept the sun away from them. Empty, this floral architecture
seemed a fitting place for transient spirits, spirits of the field.

There were cantaloupes in this field as well as cucumbers, tomatoes and
peppers, peas and string beans, onions and garlic, and rows of poppies we
called *Maak;* I helped in their nurture and harvesting. Towering sunflowers
around the base of the small hut, built for overnight stays and to shelter us
from sudden storms, enlarged the shade available in the treeless field. There
we would take a rest and eat our lunch: cantaloupe and bread, and often
ripe tomatoes and peppers, warm off the vine, young onions and garlic; we
ate these with bacon and bread. The water we drank, we brought from
home. Sometimes, when my help was not needed, I would sit at the edge of
the field making wreaths from the wild flowers there—daisies and corn-
flowers, purple larkspur and pale buttercups, red poppies and shepherd's
purse in delicate lavender, pink, and pale gold. I learned to make dolls from
poppy flowers by gently turning them inside out. Their crowned heads and
their silken gowns of bright red, trimmed at the neck in black, made them
look regal. The wide expanse of breathing fields warmed by the summer
sun brought essential messages from even the most hidden grasses; essences
woven together with those of growing grain from fields beyond laid their
scented tapestries onto the ground. The buzzing sound of flies, the lull of
grasses, grasshoppers darting in and out, kept time with the larger movement of the sun above the wide horizon. In the distance, the solitary well
etched its distinct diagonal into the enormous sky, and nearby horses were
chewing hay, their large heads leaning into the belly of the wagon, showing
their teeth amid grinding sounds, snorting, swishing their tails rhythmically at intervals. An inaudible breeze, conducting the warmth of the sun,
moved the grasses to sing in whispers. My grandparents far afield, distances
apart, gently bending toward the ground, looking small, and I sitting among
my scarlet kings and queens, feeling smaller still, we belonged and were
part of the music, the song of the fields.

Often we would stay overnight. My grandfather would ride away to the well to water the horses. Sometimes I would ride with him, seated in front of him on Lencsi, and Basa would walk beside us. With the sun low on the curved horizon, we would cross the wide plain in measured paces, looking over the expanse of land and sky before us. My grandmother would cook on a low iron tripod over an open fire and we would eat from metal plates, sitting on the ground, quietly talking till dark. Sometimes it felt as if this were our only home and we, part of a nomadic tribe, kept our transient treasures in fragile floral dwellings while we ourselves slept under open skies, on the ground.

We would wake early in the morning to find the melons under the dew; pearls, I thought, and used my finger to draw faces and make designs on them. A flick of the finger and a discerning sound; if it rang like a bell, it needed the sun, and if it had a full-bellied sound, its day had come. This had to be determined before the sun came up. Touched by the sun, my grand-mother said, they all would sound full and some would belie their true condition. We assessed and determined and carried the ripe fruit into the floral chambers, away from the sun. And another day would begin, new and unlike any other. Later, on our way back to the village, we would visit Basa bácsi, their friend, who lived nearby on a *tanya*, an isolated farm, a *Sallasch*. Basa bácsi, a small chubby man with a pink face and a friendly disposition, and his wife, a feminine version of himself, were both pleasantly talkative, and together their laughter made one full sound that I associated with ripe watermelons. They often invited us to stay for supper, and we would visit, speaking Hungarian, and drive home at dusk. On the way home, Grand-father would promise to take me to the melon market in town, someday.

The vineyard was closer and east of the village. We would often stay there at night. We would sleep in the little hut, all three of us in a narrow bed. We called these overnight stays *weingartehiede* (vineyard-watching). I wondered why it needed watching. We had to watch it grow, my grand-father said. I did not understand how we could do that in the dark. When we blew out the lantern late at night, it was the darkest dark and so quiet that nothing seemed to exist besides our breathing, the comfort of familiar scents, and the convincing presence of our touch. "Listen to the vineyard growing," my grandfather whispered. My grandfather knew everything. And it was sweet to fall asleep while the vineyard grew.

In fall, when the grapes were ripe, the whole extended family helped in cutting them off the vines. There was such a variety of grapes: large, round, dark-blue Oxeyes; long, whey-green Goat's-tits; and some with fancy names like Schtanschiller, Burgunder, Riesling, and Mascharka. Most of the grapes were the kind for making wine, but some were table grapes, kept for eating;

Grandfather (standing, third from left) in a party tending the vineyard, 1890s.

one variety smelled like sweet perfume. Hung in the attic, table grapes would stay fresh till the first freeze. Half the fun of this harvest was finding the hidden treasure in the opulent foliage, and of course, I had to try them all before putting them with the others in huge wicker baskets. The full baskets were loaded on the wagon and taken home. Before the first wagonload left the vineyard, I already had a stomachache.

In Grandfather's yard the baskets were emptied into a large press, mounted on a wagon. The juice seeping through trickled along a trough to flow into the open barrel below, from where it was carried, in buckets, to the prepared barrels in the cellar. Everyone liked drinking the fresh foamy juice we called *Moscht*. We celebrated the end of the day with a feast. Days later I would see my grandfather fuss with the barrels, taking samples to check on the various stages of the wine, and at each stage, he would perform the appropriate ritual to perfect what I thought needed no improving. At each stage, some of it had to be consumed to celebrate its perfection before the next metamorphosis. I liked the wine best still sweet but with a certain sting. Often my mother would give me some to drink at mealtime; she said it would make my cheeks rosy. Later, when the wine was tart and dry, she gave me only very little of it, on special occasions. Rumor had it, she would say, that too much wine caused children to become dull. Everyone drank wine, and it seemed to last no matter how often we drank it; at every gathering and celebration, it was present, undiminished.

On Sunday afternoons the older men took turns playing cards at each other's houses; I saw them at my grandfather's house, quiet, drinking with great seriousness. At such times they did not like to be interrupted. Wine was for all occasions, for contemplation and celebration, and it had a sacramental function as well. When Hallai Maris married, a barrel of it languored in the shade of the acacia trees in the front yard of the bridegroom's house. It was a hot day, and though the tables were set up to catch the afternoon shadow of the neighbor's house, everything on them was in danger of wilting. My mother had been busy for days baking some of the cakes, among them a nine-layer cake with chocolate filling. Candy-glazed, it looked much like a drum and was, I thought, appropriately called *dobos (dob* being a drum in Hungarian); it alone took two days to make. Such desserts had to be kept cool to prevent them from melting, and it was an accomplishment just to do that. After the cheese and the apple Schtrudl, and the traditional meal, which included goulash, these sweets were brought out in astonishing profusion and disappeared in due time. But the wine kept its steady flow amid the plaintive sound of *cigányzene* (Gypsy music) till early morning, lending its sacramental seal to the wedding feast.

There were many harvests in our village, and not all of them had to do with the fields directly. The *disznótor* (we also called it *Schweinschlacht*) was a harvesting of sorts in early December, when the fattened pigs were butchered. All year round they were fed, with corn mostly, and now they in turn would provide us with food. Various tools and instruments needed for the task—large knives and gadgets—were laid out the night before and looked important. Uncles and aunts, cousins and grandparents, the whole extended family took part in this event. Early in the morning, before it got light, there was a lot of noise in the house, which, together with my anticipation of the day, kept me from sleeping. Water was boiling in the kettle in the summer kitchen and the men prepared themselves for the cold outside by drinking a glass of šljivovica; they said it was to keep them from freezing. Out in the back yard they made preparations, and I watched them in the half light as they let the pigs out of the sty. Two of the men cornered each pig, which seemed easy, since the pigs were too fat to run. I heard my father call me away; he said he needed me inside. Out of the corner of my eye, I saw the men falling over our pigs and I heard strange unpleasant sounds, squeals and gargles that made me listen to the quiet after. I was glad my father was not among the men in the back yard.

The activities that followed were so engaging they took my attention away from the plight of the pigs. I watched with curiosity as the men, using heavy chains, lowered the body of each pig into the scalding water that filled the long wooden tub we called *Mulder*. With the help of these chains, they rolled the pigs from one side to the other. Old spoons with edges worn thin and razor sharp were then used to scrape the bristles from the scalded skin. I remember being startled at this point, seeing the pigs naked in the *Mulder*. Without the bristles, their skin bore an uncanny resemblance to human skin. It was a surrealistic image, this strange bath, and the attending feeling was momentarily disturbing. Clean shaven, the pigs were hung on the prepared scaffolding where, gutted and with their heads removed, they received their meatlike appearance and were redeemed.

I admired the skill and agility of all involved in what seemed to be one continuous, coordinated action. I was allowed to watch, but I was not to get in the way. Balloons! The cleaned bladders, pumped up with air and tied to strings, were given to me to play with. I was eager to show them to the children across the street. But rather than playing, I preferred staying close by, watching the assorted tasks as they progressed throughout the day. Inside, my grandmother was cleaning the small intestines, scraping them, from the outside, with a blunt knife down a diagonal wooden board till they where almost transparent. She let me try my hand at it. We scraped and washed them repeatedly and rinsed them in cold water, until they were perfect as casing for the sausages that were to be made in the afternoon. The kettle was boiling again, and soon appetizers, bits of liver and meats, were sprinkled with salt and tasted. At noon my mother's goulash received glowing praise; it had the distinctive savor, the taste expected once a year, unequaled and delicious. As a courtesy, we sent fresh goulash to our neighbors, and they in turn reciprocated when they had their disznótor.

Delicious smells tinged the air throughout the day, spreading over the village to become forever a flavor of winter. By afternoon the large sides of bacon and hams as big as wagon wheels, I heard them say, had been salted and placed into barrels to cure. The remaining bacon was cut into small pieces and rendered to lard in the kettle. Later the fried bite-sized bacon bits were removed and offered, salted, for tasting. Meat that had been cooked in the kettle earlier was now being prepared for the various sausages. Mounds of garlic, paprika, and pepper were ready, waiting to be added for spice. Fresh meat was being ground and spiced for the sausages we called *Protwirscht*. It was a kind of magic watching the ground meat push through the sausage press, appearing in long round rolls curling up on the table. Even Grandfather Korek seemed almost playful, admirable for his agility with the sausage press. Some sausages, like the *Protwirscht*, were thin, the fresh ground meat showing through the transparent encasing; others, like the liver sausages, encased in the large intestines, were fat, opaque. The head cheese, a curious gelatinous sausage, was encased in the stomach and pressed, flattened, with weights. Some sausages were hung in the smokehouse. Later all would appear in our pantry, and some of the meat and lard had to last the entire year. The whole event concluded with a cleanup by early evening and was celebrated with a grand feast, starting with a special soup, followed by roasts, fried sausages served with sauces, pickled peppers and green tomatoes, sweet fruit preserves, good bread, and plenty of wine to drink. Such a feast seemed like a thanksgiving; a closure to a good year, and at the same time an act of faith, a preparation for the year to come.

• • •

Memories of Christmas recall the miraculous. I remember coming into a dark room, seeing a tree so tall it reached up to the ceiling. Its branches, holding glowing candles, glistened with candies wrapped in shimmering colored foils delicately fringed with pastel tassels. Nuts and figs and *Poxendl* (the glossy seed pods of carob) hung suspended, appearing golden, twirling in the candlelight. That there should be such a tree at all, that it should appear by itself, conferred upon it supernatural power and inspired belief in the divine. The scent of miraculous sweets, exotic fruit, oranges, the fragrance of evergreen, candles burning—a meld to rival the sacred smell of incense—recalled the hushed reverence of church. A doll smiled, suspended in an eternal space. Nothing but the miraculous moment existed. The ethereal taste of candies from this tree continued to affirm that it was indeed something holy; this tree and the presents around it were gifts brought by *Krischkindl (Christkindl)*, the Christ child. I remember wooden shoes lined with fur, just my size; a pink bedroom set, complete in every detail, with beds large enough for my doll Nora; and I remember my parents and grandparents watching.

Later in the evening, winged angels came with Mary and Joseph bringing the Krischkindl to our house. They were all dressed looking much like the statues in our church and were the size of tall children. They sang songs and said important things, but I got as far away from them as possible. Sitting on my bed, I watched through the open door. I had many questions when they left; I tried to give the event some reality. One of the angels, I told my mother, looked exactly like Hilda. I often visited at Hilda's house. She lived in the house next to my grandfather's, and their garden with the enormous cherry tree was directly behind our back yard. I remembered having seen a framed photograph of a little girl dressed like a bride, lying in a coffin. Hilda, who was much older than I, told me it was a picture of her sister who died and who now was an angel in heaven. Surely the beautiful angel that came to our house this night was Hilda's sister, I said to my mother; I must go and tell Hilda. My mother smiled.

Christmas lasted till New Year's, and the new year seemed a continuation rather than a new beginning. There were many holidays after Christmas. On Three Kings' Day, our priest came to our house and wrote on top of our door frame—right below the hidden switch—with much ceremony, in intricate letters: Gaspar, Melchior, Balthasar; the names of the Three Kings. When he left, the house was filled with the smell of incense. The letters written with white chalk would remain with us throughout the year, reminding us of our blessing. On this day it was customary to bake doughnuts with coins hidden in them. Those who found a coin got to keep it and received the honor of being called a king. Children would go begging, asking for coins outright. From house to house they went, chanting: *"Ich pin a klane Keenich, kipt me ned so wenich, loßt mich ned so lang to schtehn, ich muß um a Häisl weide kehn,"* explaining their doing in rhyme: declaring themselves little kings, they wanted lots of money, quickly, before going on.

Many of our celebrations had something to do with saints. The days of the calendar were filled with their names: Anna, Katharina, Barbara, Elisabeth, Karl, Joseph, Johann, and all the other names one could never have thought of without them. Every one of them had a day that was especially their own, and people in the village who had been given that name celebrated their collective nameday; individual birthdays were not celebrated. On Barbara, the day of the saint, our Kroßmotter, my grandmother, my mother, my cousin Perwi, and all the other women named Barbara were acknowledged and wished well. Unless a name was most uncommon, there were many others with whom one celebrated one's nameday.

Sometimes two saints shared the same day. Saints Peter and Paul had such a day set aside for them. Large fires were made in the village that night. Apples were thrown in to roast and retrieved to eat, and people would leap across the flames. We chanted a rhyme: *"Pede un Paul, tie Äppl sein faul, tie Piere sein sieß, tie Krotte huppse uf fier Fieß."* It referred to summer days, when apples were rotting, pears were sweet, and frogs were hopping on four feet. It was not something one needed to understand; it required participation only. The fires, the daring jumps, the fragrance and flavor of roasted apples on a summer evening needed no other meaning.

There even was an All Saints' Day. My grandfather once told me that it was a precautionary measure against having any saint offended, excluded. By some careless oversight, their name may not have gotten into the calendar. So on that day, people went to church to celebrate all of them. The day after, on All Souls' Day, we burned candles in our windows for the dead and visited our relatives in the cemetery. There I would get a little nervous and would smooth my hair and pull up my socks before getting near the graves of my great grandparents. Remembering impressions of them, I would stand there anticipating their approval of me.

• • •

I knew a lot about our village before I went to school. I would have been able to explain its physical configuration for others to find their way. The village was laid out like a grid with three long streets running parallel to each other and five shorter streets crossing them. The first long street we called *Kroßkass*, meaning big or grand street. A short street, merging with it, we called *Barakass* (*bara* being Serb for pond). The second and third streets were called *Zwatkass* and *Tritkass*, respectively. A single row of houses facing meadows and the cemetery was called *Anschicht*, implying its incompleteness. The streets running crosswise we called *Kreizkass*, and we referred to them by number. The official names of streets, written on small metal plates attached to the gable of each house, were ignored even by the postman. Under the number 25 on our house, in black letters, was the name of our street, honoring the heroic Serb Czar: Cara Dušana ulica.

The large sign above the door of the railroad station, showing the name of our village, Potiski Sveti Nikola, in Cyrillic and Latin letters, identified it to those passing by as Saint Nicholas on the river Theiss. Its Hungarian name was Tiszaszentmiklós and its German translation Theiß Sankt Nikolaus. We called it Klan-Niklos, Small Nicholas (carelessly we left out the saint), and as such it made reference to some other time when it and its namesake, Groß Sankt Nikolaus, Big Saint Nicholas, now in Rumania, were both part of the Austro-Hungarian Empire and needed such distinction. The stretch from the railroad station to the east end of town was, my father said, one kilometer long; a tiring walk, especially on hot summer days. From the station to the center of the village, most of the houses belonged to Serbs. The Slovaks and the Gypsies lived in houses at the northwestern end of the village. The Hungarians, Germans, and Jews lived predominantly on the east end. But in general the ethnic groups were well integrated throughout, with the wealthiest people living in the *Kroßkass* and near the center of the village. Among the large houses and other buildings there—the schoolhouses, the apothecary, the doctor's house, the municipal building—were stores displaying their wares in their windows, with names above: Beinhauer, the dry goods store, and Bata, the shoe store—the name itself could recall the smell of new rubber boots. Three church steeples rose above our village. The Catholic and the Serb Orthodox churches were in the center of the village, only a block apart. The space around them was used for weekly markets and special events. The Slovaks' Evangelical church was at the west end. An ordinary house on the first side street, close to the Catholic Church, was the Lutheran prayer house. There was no synagogue in our village.

Throughout the village, craftsmen—shoemakers, tailors, potters, wagon and furniture makers, weavers, carders, and rope makers—worked and sold their wares from their houses, and one knew about them without their having a sign above the door. Butcher shops and bakeries, stores, and inns often had glass doors to the street but no other sign to identify them. There were four blacksmith shops in the village. My father's was the newest and had a wooden sign over its door with large letters: Johann Lang, Schmiede.

Past the Kroßwasser at the edge of the village, an estate dating from the 1720s, owned in the past by various landed gentry, was now jointly owned by three families. It was referred to by its old name, Herrschaftsgut or Kaschtell, and consisted of a stately building behind an impressive brick wall. The most picturesque building, however, was a windmill near a small pond at the other end of town. There were two other mills in the village, one driven by steam, and a lumber mill. Three artesian wells, conveniently located in the center and at each end of the village, supplied the drinking water. The River Theiss, not visible from our village, was one kilometer west of the train station.

It was known that almost five thousand people lived in our village and that the majority of them were Serbs and Hungarians in equal number. About five hundred Germans, less than two hundred Slovaks, five Jewish families, and four families of Gypsies made up the rest of the population. Such information seemed unimportant to most, but there were people who liked knowing such things and had them memorized. Everyone knew that the wealth of the village, in land and property, was unequally divided and that the wealthiest farmers were Germans and Serbs and a few Hungarians. The richest merchants in our village were Jewish. The poor of every ethnic group worked for wages as field hands and servants and lived in small houses of their own.

The most colorful people, flamboyant in dress and manner, remote from the rest of us by custom, the Gypsies, represented the exotic in our village. Dark and handsome, fluent in speech and extravagant in gesture, they beamed confidence and had an air of mystery about them. Some had a trade; others traded horses, read palms, and told fortunes. Their appearance in the village attracted attention, and meeting them on the street signified good luck. But the most dramatic figure in our village was the Orthodox priest. Tall and bearded, dressed in black, wearing a tall black headdress, he walked about the village with an entourage of Serb children following to kiss his hand. Our priests and teachers, the doctor and the lady pharmacist, the educated in general, earned special respect. The wealthy farmers and merchants cultivated a relationship with them and all enjoyed their distinction from the rest of the population. The professionals were next in this hierarchy. In spite of all these divisions the general citizenry, including the smallest farmers and those without land, developed a robust sense of equality and a healthy self-affirmation; living in the village one knew these things from experience.

The official language of the country was Serbo-Croatian, but not everyone in our village spoke this language. Only very few Hungarians spoke it; most spoke only their own language. The Jewish people of our village always spoke Hungarian, but they knew Serbo-Croatian. While many Germans spoke both languages (most knew Hungarian), only very few others spoke German. With Slovaks it was similar. The Serbs in our village spoke no other language but their own. The most-listened-to person, the drummer, who recited the news and informed the village about official business in a shouting voice at street corners, first in Serbo-Croatian and then in Hungarian, was understood by most everyone. In conversations with people from different ethnic groups one accommodated according to the language skills of others. Simple words and gestures expressed our shared experiences quite well even among those who did not speak each other's language.

Going to school was mandatory up to the sixth grade, and everyone now received an education in their own language. Children whose parents could afford it went on to higher education in nearby cities and towns. Others who were apprenticed to master craftsmen to learn a trade, like my father, and those who went to nearby towns as cooks, nannies, and servants, like my mother, had to be grown-up at thirteen. All young men, regardless of their ethnicity, were subject to military duty to serve our country and our king. I had seen the many letters my father had written to my mother before they were married, when he was a soldier. They were tucked away with the important papers between linens and laces in the safety of the front room.

My mother often talked about her experiences in Senta, a town about ten kilometers north of our village, on the other side of the Theiss, where she had worked for eight years before she married. At thirteen she took care of the three Fekete children (Irén, Olga, and Mátyó), working in the household of Orthodox Jews. Later she worked for the family of the district veterinarian, Dr. Čurič, taking care of their little girl Tatjana, being cook and maid as well as nanny. She felt like a member of the family, she said, and she learned a lot about life outside the village. It was her education. On weekends she would walk home mostly to see my father, who became her boyfriend when she was fourteen. I could imagine her walking along the river dam and through the fields, her yellow parasol dancing above her, shielding her face from the sun. In the village this parasol, and she in her city clothes, made quite an impression, she said, and she was criticized by those within our ethnic group who were slow to accept change. But my mother would

My father serving in the Yugoslav army (second from left), 1931.

do just as she liked. Her education in town supported the attitude that she had developed long before she left the village. Her family was liberal, less confined by class distinctions than some. Her grandfather, who had great influence on her, supported her strong convictions about such things as equality, liberty, and justice—which, she explained to me, had something to do with not being impressed by status, not being confined by a conventional attitude, and being fair to everyone, feeling inferior to none. My mother revealed her feelings regarding social restrictions, and by telling me about them, she made me aware of some things I did not experience myself.

Gossip was an aspect of the village; it was part of the social structure. Within the ethnic group, especially, people were aware of the doings of others and measured them against an unwritten code of behavior. It seemed to me that people liked talking about others doing things they did not think well of, which implied that for the sake of good gossip, transgressions were desirable. Gossip allowed for such feeling as chattiness, envy, greed—feelings no one would like to admit having—and released them in good company. At its best, gossip was good entertainment. Professional gossips were well known, and gossip, like frogs, was impossible to avoid in our village.

The more aggressive and independent, like my mother, who spent no effort to win the approval of others, were likely to be gossiped about. Having the first radio in the village was perceived as outrageous. Gossip had it that the rich German farmers disapproved of their money being used for such extravagance. My mother would be amused and would reply to bearers of such gossip, enunciating slowly, as if she were correcting the faulty sentence structure of a child: "Not their money," she would say, "but my husband's work, our work, bought the radio." Some people found no charm in my mother's assertiveness. Her candor would sometimes embarrass me. Even when I was very little, I was aware how my mother's attitude affected some people in the village. My wearing a dark blue ski-suit received a critical comment from a German lady passing us on the street. We knew each other, but the little girl at her side seemed not to recognize me in my new attire and asked, "Grandmother, who is that little girl?" "That is not a little girl," the lady quipped, "that is a fool!" Clearly, this was intended for my mother to hear. Such critical comments were exercised as rights and were means to control the values and attitudes of those within the ethnic group to preserve the order of the social structure. Control of this kind was not practiced on members of other ethnic groups, for obvious reasons. The independence my mother's behavior exemplified was looked down upon and interpreted as betrayal: it abandoned the order that gave the existing social structure its meaning. Though my mother was strong enough to do what she thought was right, the criticism and the implicit lack of support were things of which she was acutely aware. When I experienced the hostility of others toward my mother, I often misunderstood its cause. I thought it was because she was so outspoken, and it made me uncomfortable whenever she spoke her mind. I became convinced that being shy was, after all, more expedient in getting along with people, and that pleasing people was necessary if one wished to be liked.

As a little girl, I felt liked by many people in the village. Our Serb neighbors showed their approval openly as soon as I could speak. They were pleased with me for speaking their language. Some asked me questions just to test me, and they gave me many opportunities to know them. Due to the inherent social distance, Serb and Hungarian neighbors and friends offered acceptance on individual merit. Some of our German neighbors, acting much like relatives, judged us according to family values. And, indeed, most of the German-speaking people in our village were interrelated.

The affection one received in the village was varied and had different sources. I, as an only child, was at the same time one among many children of the village; I was aware of belonging to many others outside my immediate family. Being recognized by everyone within the German ethnic group as one of its members meant the entire village knew of my existence and considered me one of their own. Yet even with such popular approval, one did not always feel equally liked.

Mother with Tatjana Čurič in Senta, 1929.

My best friend Anna, a distant cousin related to me from both sides, was always liked better by some of our mutual relatives. She was pale and sickly; next to her I seemed robust, brash, even bold. Being compared to others, I realized, I became something different, and I learned to recognize myself in this continuous becoming. Though I would clearly see my changing self as an aspect of my relation to others, I was often quick to become insecure and very jealous when others were being preferred over me. I liked Anna; she was good and very pious. I was always careful, when playing with her, not to offend or injure her in any way, because her crying

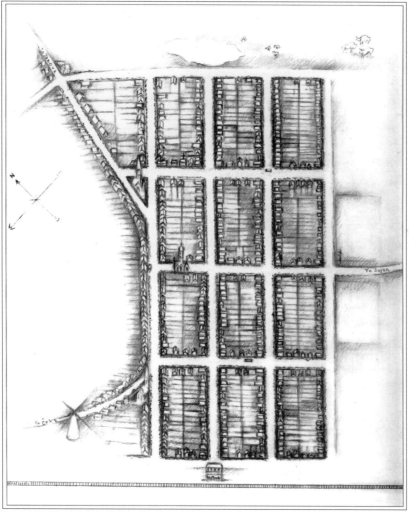

Mental map of our village, Potiski Sveti Nikola/Theiß Sankt Nikolaus/ Tiszasentmiklós.

could arouse much sympathy. I tried not to let it show when she got special attention and I felt ignored. Once, when my mother casually commented that Anna was taller than I, I was quick to reply that it did not matter, adding, "But I have a bigger head." I really did not know why I said that. It made my mother laugh.

In general, the larger village I came to know was tolerant; it provided for a rich variety of individual differences and it accepted all manner of excess and eccentricity. Every virtue and vice, every personality and character was affirmed as part of the variety of being. Physical appearances, with the quirky exception of red hair, were appreciated for their own sake. Though gossip was abundant and overt criticism was practiced, as everyone's business was one's own, there was something larger present in the village that overshadowed individual shortcomings, differences in custom, religious belief, ethnic fervor. It was the ability of its members to empathize, to take the individual gestures of others as if they were their own. The stories told about people of the village, living and dead, attested to this ability. These stories, which vivified individual personalities, were also telling of the clarity and affection with which they were perceived. Everyone liked the telling of these stories. No one tired of them. They were expressions of the affection the village felt for itself.

CHAPTER 4

Changes, Love, and War

B ECAUSE I DID NOT like change, I noticed all changes more acutely. I noticed that my grandparents' house changed when Seppi Onkl married. A cradle was placed at the foot end of the bed in the kitchen, and I remember rocking my cousin Seppi with such vigor that he rolled from side to side in it; to stop him from crying, I said. I was being too rough, Grandmother scolded. I was hurt by her criticism, but I knew I had been rough on purpose. How did he get here, I wondered, and why? His presence changed the space of the house and brought it under new restrictions. And he would be there, sitting on a blanket on the floor of our summer kitchen when I got home from school, looking incredibly cute. I would let him play with the little red leather bag in which I carried my snacks: dried fruit, bread and sugar cubes meant to be eaten together, which I always ate bread-first, saving the sugar for last. I showed Seppi how the zipper opened and closed, and a slice of dried apple, left uneaten, found its way into his mouth. Suddenly, he was choking. Panic stricken, my mother whisked him up and went running through the house as if rescuing him from a fire and I ran screaming after. He was turning blue. She stopped and reached down his throat with such intensity it sent the piece of apple flying out. By this miracle, Seppi was restored to us and I had suddenly acquired a brother.

There were changes in Grandmother Korek's house as well. My Pat, Niklos, married my friend Anna's grown-up sister Lisa, whom I now called Kodl, and they moved into Altkroßmotter's house. Tanti Lisa, eloped and struck a blow to Grandfather Korek's pride. The whole family was called on to quiet his rage. He walked about the house red-faced, shouting how he would kill them both, how he would disinherit her, and how she would get

Seppi standing on a *Hockedl*, 1943.

nothing, not even her own clothes. I thought of the dark rooms with the drawers full of beaded purses and all the beautiful dresses, remaining forever under the spell of his anger. The steady voice of my grandmother intruded, and another blow fell. Lisa had taken her clothes and all that belonged to her. She had outwitted him. Nightly her things had left the darkened rooms through an open window, and she had lived with the secret of empty dressers and drawers, waiting for the right time to leave herself. It was Kirweih when she left. She walked out of the church and vanished in broad daylight. He who was so strict and so controlling had no power over her. He had forbidden her even to talk with the boy she loved; he would never have allowed them to marry. Now he raged, betrayed. My parents interceded on my aunt's behalf: "They are in love," they said, "nothing can be done about that." In time my aunt and her new husband were forgiven. The very handsome young man I now called Jani Onkl was soft spoken and gentle, and in his presence I sometimes felt shyly flirtatious. My cousin Johann was at home in Grandfather Korek's house, and all the toys—the dominos and puzzle blocks, and the yellow Mazko, things I only played with—belonged to him, and Grandfather Korek looked pleased whenever Johann learned something new.

Some changes were transformations and did not seem to be the cause of anyone's action. Such happened, as if by magic, in front of the apothecary. The apothecary was itself a place of charm, with its potent odor and the many white jars with gold trimmed labels on shelves lining the walls up to the ceiling. Whenever one entered, the lady pharmacist, gaunt and serious, forgiving of the interruption, emerged graciously from the back rooms. Her appearance behind the counter with the ornate golden scales matched in full measure the immaculate order of the place. The gilded lacelike stencil on the glass of its stately double door identified the apothecary, from the outside, as a place of significance.

It was spring and the weather was warm enough to wear my coat unbuttoned. The large house on the corner extended its familiar look like an invitation. Its low-pitched reed roof was enhanced by the intricate basketry of the huge nest on its chimney, to which storks returned faithfully each spring, teaching constancy within the passage of time. I crossed the street languorously onto Kroßkass, walking toward Kindergarten. Below the steps of the apothecary, recalling the gilded-bell sounds that opened its doors, I noticed a boy coming toward me. A strange anticipation filled the space between us, and a feeling for which I had no name and nothing to compare with suddenly came into existence. I took hold of the moving image to keep my balance, but filled with light, it was difficult to focus. The boy with golden hair was blue-eyed, his face familiar, and his whole appearance complete, like a puzzle solved. I think I smiled at him. Walking past him, I felt the sidewalk move beneath me while I seemed to be standing still. I tried to turn around to take another look, and it seemed I was upside down, floating.

The new feeling would not be contained; it spilled over everything within my perception and everything was glowing in its light. Nothing would ever be the same. I could hardly wait to tell my mother. She listened attentively. What I felt might be love, she said. She fell in love with my father when she was twelve. I was only seven.

I kept this feeling secreted like a treasure, and examined it often to assure myself of its presence. And each time I saw a boy with blonde hair, I quickened with anticipation. I smiled at all blond boys and was disappointed, confused; the expected feeling was not present. Like a treasure lost, the feeling remembered acquired a certain sadness. Only later, when I went to school and saw all the blond boys gathered in one room, was the joy restored. Authentic and constant, it was attached to the appearance of one boy only, whose name was Horst.

• • •

People were talking in hushed voices. War was mentioned and one could sense the tension building. Neighbors would crowd into our back room every evening to hear the news. Huddled around the radio, they would listen intently and leave with sad faces. There had been discussions about war for sometime now, and names like Churchill, Hitler, Ribbentropp, names of people we did not know, were repeated on the radio. News of war disturbed people. Soon, they feared, the war on the radio would come to our country. A pact with Germany consoled some, but others criticized and opposed it: "*Bolje rat nego pakt*" (better war than the pact), they shouted; they would rather have war. But the people I saw were clearly afraid of war. They talked of terrible things they had witnessed during the Great War. War was an internal upheaval; I could tell by listening and watching what the anticipation of war did to people in the village. I soon noticed that people changed and became distant; some were unfriendly. They did not smile and they greeted grudgingly. Instead of being themselves, they suddenly became Serb, German, Hungarian, Slovak, Jew, and Gypsy. Forgetting themselves, they put on a bold face, the mask of generality, Grandfather said; they were getting ready for something terrible. Sometimes it seemed to me that people wore this mask to hide the terrible that had already happened— the loss of themselves.

There were tensions between the ethnic groups. People talked about it in ways I did not understand. The Serbs, anticipating a German invasion or a war with Germany, now mistrusted the German-speaking minority in our

Horst crossing Kroßkass, Theiß Sankt Nikolaus, 1941. *Courtesy* Maria and Horst Klemm

country; the German minority, in turn, were afraid of the Serbs as well as of the impending war. I heard these discussions, but I learned more by watching people's faces as they passed each other on the street, looking suspiciously, avoiding each other's eyes.

The pact was broken, we heard on the radio, and our country prepared for war. At first only the Serb men of the village were called in for military duty. Later my father and all the other German men were summoned, but in less than a week my father was back again, working in the blacksmith shop with Péter. Our young king, Peter II, fled to England, I heard people say, and his soldiers, not knowing what to do without him, came home. I knew it was a bad thing for us to be abandoned by our king, but I was glad to have my father home again. I do not remember German soldiers marching into our village; they simply appeared, and I noticed them from time to time. That this invasion brought many changes, I noticed more.

It was dusk and I was sitting on the ottoman in the front room. The windows were unshuttered and a soft light filtered through the lace curtains. The children continued playing outside without me. My parents had called me in; they had something important to tell me. They prefaced it by saying that there would be a change of which I needed to be informed. I did not remember ever having been approached so cautiously by my parents. It made me anxious. Something was going to be asked of me, I thought, something very unpleasant. Perhaps the goat my mother bought for its milk, and which I treated like a pet, had to be given up, sacrificed. In the diminishing light, the room lost its color and everything in it became a meld of earthen monochrome. I waited. They said that from now on the German-speaking people in our village would have to greet everyone on the street by raising their hand to say *Heil Hitler.* I had seen the soldiers do this, and as their greeting I had nothing against it. But I could not imagine myself facing people in this position. "Why can't I go on greeting people as I always did?" I pleaded. "Surely, one greeting is equal to another, and I would like to keep my own." I always fought things that were forced on me, but this was different. There seemed to be a threat in this proposal. The recent tensions that caused some to whisper in groups and others to be distant seemed to converge and were contained in this coercion. I began to understand; this was no trivial request. "Must I greet everyone, even our Serb and Hungarian neighbors this way?" A quiet affirmation followed. I imagined myself making this gesture in front of particular people, and I was convinced I could not do what was asked of me; the discomfort attending the imagined performance was painful enough. I started to cry. "I will cross the street if I see people coming toward me to avoid any greeting from now on," I added defiantly, to excuse my tears. My mother said nothing. I was only being informed, my father consoled. Fear and a vague apprehension were present in our small gathering, foreboding events to come. As Wagner Vedde Hans later bluntly put it, using a play on the word *heil*, taking it to mean weep, "Mark my words, there will be cause to weep." Though the new greeting came to be used by some people, it was not enforced as the only greeting, and I never had to use it at all. Even so, its introduction was my private initiation into the war.

An all-inclusive disquiet, unease, dis-ease lingered in the village; like a stranger among us, it had our attention. I knew enough about fear to recognize it. My mother often fell ill quite suddenly. A quiet desolation transformed the house at such times and I felt the emptiness inside me. I took this emptiness with me everywhere, even to play. Sometimes I would wake up at night and see my grandmother sitting on the bed next to my mother, putting cold compresses on her chest, and my father standing by, looking worried. Often the doctor was there as well. I was filled with the fear that would keep inside me and would take hold of me when I least expected it; playing somewhere, I would suddenly have to go home to see my mother, even when she was not ill.

The new fear was less defined. Its shadow hung over the village, and one would be reminded of it in various ways. It showed itself in a carelessly drawn star on the walls of some houses, which seemed disfigured by this. It appeared with the bands some people wore on their sleeves; some were black, some yellow, others red, like those worn by soldiers. All seemed to me like bands of mourning and had the smell and flavor of this fear. Later, on my way home from Kindergarten, I saw it in a tangle of furniture sitting forlorn in front of the apothecary, and in the long line of people pushing to go inside. Such images nourished this fear and gave the village a broken look. A sick feeling and an insistent yearning for a time before I knew this fear followed me about, weighing me down, spoiling my notion of home.

At home my parents talked about the scene in front of the apothecary. The Jewish people of our village, among them the lady pharmacist, had been taken away at night, some time ago, they explained. Now their property was being auctioned off. My mother said she could not imagine anyone buying such things, and that doing so was worse than stealing. Those who participated in such purchases were criticized openly by others who did not; they received my mother's full contempt. Taking even a needle from such estates would be a reminder of the larger crime, she said, and she was sure that even the smallest of things would carry a curse with it. My father spoke softly and looked sad. The seriousness with which the subject was discussed made me aware that I had seen something very grave and that I had been rightly disturbed by it. This made me even more afraid.

Those who were Jewish among us had not been separated from us in the past. Now they were spoken about in hushed voices as if they had met with an unnatural disaster. Instead of an explanation, there was secrecy, mistrust, and that vague oppressive feeling of dis-ease. The missing faces confirmed the assault against our village. But the gestures of those missed were still part of us. Irma, the little girl who lived in the Kroßkass, was no longer there. I often saw her playing in front of her house with her little brother. We used to greet each other, shyly, in Hungarian. I was not aware that she was anything other than herself. Her empty house, turned inward, like all the other abandoned houses, bore a reflection of the missing. But such houses were no longer part of anyone's home, and not even the carelessly drawn star could claim them. Like accusing monuments to the violence that diminished us, they recalled the lost integrity of our village.

• • •

The oppressive feeling attending my parents' arguments washed over me as I stepped into the house, and as always, it nullified everything I might have been feeling before. Usually such arguments were about my father's business, but now that he was working at home, away from Grandfather Korek, such arguments were rare. I listened. My mother was talking mostly; there was a whip in her voice that lashed and stung and she drove a point home with words that had a complaining as well as an accusing tone. My father would have to go to war, he said. She was disbelieving. "It is not a matter of choice," I heard him say, "it is the law." "The law," she repeated condescendingly. "Just wait and see, the rich will stay home. None of those who support this political venture are going to war themselves. They will stay home!" She mentioned Emil's father. Emil was my age; we went to Kindergarten together. His father was a very rich man and a spokesman of sorts for the German-speaking population of our village. "Hubert," she said, "will surely stay home." My father had a way of making her even more angry by defending the accused, saying that the order came from afar: the *Prinz Eugen Division*, a division of German-speaking men, was being formed to serve within the country along with the other domestic forces, Serb and Croat, to defend it from the Communists. "It isn't our war!" she interrupted. He never got angry, but his tone was defensive now, and he told her again that every able-bodied German man within a certain age range was being drafted and had to go or be shot as a deserter. Suddenly my fear grew into panic. I could not fully comprehend what I was hearing. My mother said, very calmly, "Let them shoot you. They are sending you to war to be shot, so what is the difference? If all of you would refuse to go," she added, "they would not shoot you all!" For a long time nothing was said. I was afraid to move. I sat on my bed and stared before me, repeating to myself inaudibly: *my father has to go to war, my father has to go to war,* and it felt like a plea for some intervention, like a prayer for peace. I heard my mother say in a somber tone, "Promise me, if any one of them gets to stay home, you will come home, immediately." Everything was quiet in the front room. My father's voice emerged, calm and subdued. He was concerned about his apprentice; Péter needed six more months to finish; it was important for him to be able to do so. I heard my mother's weepy voice consent: Péter could work alone—her father would help—and she would set him free after his time.

I do not remember the actual day my father had to leave. It was the spring before I went to school, in 1942. Later, when I had learned to write, I remember writing him letters, having to start over and over again because I had made many mistakes.

School was a large white room with a high ceiling and four long windows that looked inward. Horst, the boy with the golden hair, was there and all the other German children up to sixth grade. Our teacher was serious, exacting. We called him Herr Lehrer (Mr. Teacher) and always paid attention when he spoke. We sat two by two in two long rows, a wide space separating the boys from the girls. I sat in the second row with Else. She could read everything much faster than I, and she could write flawless letters to her father. Anna sat in front of me. She often had nosebleeds and would have to tilt her head back, leaning it on my desk. Sometimes her father, who was much older than mine and did not have to go to war, would come to take her home. Emil, whose father was still at home just as my mother had predicted, sat in the boys' front row, across the space that divided us. Horst sat with the older boys; he was in fourth grade. When he was absent, I felt disappointed. Once he got hit with a wooden shoe in a scuffle with Hungarian boys and his nose was broken. He was absent for a long time and people talked about him being a bleeder; they said he might die. The thought of him dying was inconceivable; I cried about it when I was alone. I tried not to show how much I liked this boy, but the other children knew it, and sometimes even grown-ups would tease me about it. Occasionally, when our teacher would read to us, we would be allowed to sit wherever we wished, and Horst would choose to sit beside me. I could not stop smiling. But this feeling of love was demanding and sometimes uncomfortable. Often I would be too shy to take a breath in Horst's presence, which made breathing as well as being with him difficult.

I remember getting punished in school, not by our teacher but by the new priest. I had noticed, with some regret, that he was not as handsome, but I did not know that he was not as kind as our own Polen Pfarrer, our priest with the beautiful voice, who left us to go to a predominantly Hungarian village. The new priest came to school once a week to teach us the

Family portrait before my father was drafted, 1942.

catechism, the commandments, and about being good. On one of those occasions he asked who among us had not gone to church last Sunday. My intention to be good, and my concern to show that I had paid attention to previous lessons, prompted me to tell the truth. Without hesitation, I raised my hand. I expected his approval. He asked those who raised their hand to come forward. I thought we would be praised for telling the truth, but as we approached the desk, I had some apprehensions. Watching the others, I still could not believe that I was really going to be punished. I stretched out my arms in front of me, palms up as he asked, and with one clean sweep, the cane cut the air between us. Stunned by the pain, I felt the second blow slice my palm with the same stunning surprise. On the way back to my seat, my chin was trembling so much I had to cover my mouth to conceal my shame, my disappointment. I could not reconcile such punishment with my telling the truth. Telling the truth was being good, I thought; the pain in my hands caused me to regret it. It occurred to me that if I had lied, I would not have been punished. So in addition to feeling wronged, I also felt foolish. I was convinced that being good was something unreasonable, and wanting to be good, for the moment, lost its appeal.

Surprisingly, my mother took offense when I told her about being punished. Later, gossip had it, she went to the priest to protest. She pointed out an inconsistency to him: her husband, a soldier, was being instructed under threat of punishment not to go to church, while her child was being punished for not going to church. In any case, he was not to punish me at all. If my behavior needed correcting, she was to be informed. She would do the disciplining of her own child. I was proud of my mother. My confusion about what being good entailed remained. Still, I went to first communion dressed like a bride in a long white dress we borrowed. My mother had cut my hair and I did not like myself as well without my long tresses. Vain and pouting, I went to receive communion and the Eucharist got stuck to the roof of my mouth, and even pushed by my tongue, it would not be swallowed.

My greatest accomplishments in school were on stage. No one could have predicted this, since I was shy. In the little play in first grade, Anna was chosen to play Snow White and I was to be the stepmother. I came home crying. But my grandfather said it was a challenge. Anyone who was pale and dark-haired could be Snow White, he said, but playing the stepmother required talent. I was not convinced, but I stopped crying. Later, at a public occasion, on a real stage in the Habag Haus, I was among the children chosen to recite a poem. Though anxious to the last minute, not believing I could do it, I looked into the crowd of people, soldiers among them, and spoke to the dark, sitting on my fear like on a horse. I spoke the words of a father written to his child: an explanation for his absence, a regret that there was war, a promise of peace. The poem was affectionate and consoling in tone and I imagined my own father talking to me. I received great applause. And even Vedde Matz, the *Birgermeister* (*Bürgermeister*, mayor), who had not been on friendly terms with my mother, swallowed his pride and shook her hand, praising my performance. Later there were plays in which I had the leading role. I liked being a princess, moving about on stage in a long silken-blue gown. Except for the promise to marry Niklos, a boy with dark hair who played the prince, I said my lines convincingly. But the achievements at school were less important in light of the events that intruded to disrupt our way of life.

There were strangers in our village now, not just soldiers in uniform but civilians as well: people who took refuge here for reasons I did not understand. Our neighbors, čika Milan and tetka Katica, had guests, a man and a woman, who stayed for more than a year and never left Markov's house. Perhaps no one else knew about them. We visited with them frequently and my mother lent them my father's accordion, which the lady knew how to play. They seemed to busy themselves with books and charts, and the door to their room was always closed. No one explained why they were there. Ljubica was curious about them and would encourage us to look through

First Communion, 1943.

the keyhole. Later the young man called me into the room and instructed me in a firm voice that it was rude to listen at doors and look through keyholes; he said it did not suit me. I was embarrassed and tried to say something in my defense, but my voice choked up fighting back tears. I was not like the other girls, he continued, trying to console me; but once criticized, it was hard to value anything good he might have to say about me. The lady added her praises, saying how beautifully I sang and how quickly I had learned "Jedno dete malo" (A little child), a very long song I had heard her sing only once. Would I like her to play it again, she asked, reaching for my father's accordion? No, I shook my head, trying to smile, but she played it anyway, and the door was opened on my hurt feelings, which took refuge in forced joviality, and the familiar sounds of the accordion only added to the painful experience.

People fleeing the bombings of Belgrade had come to the village and stayed. The baker's grandchildren, two boys older than I, were in Belgrade when the bombs fell; they said they were not afraid of bombs. I showed them our bomb shelter; everyone had to dig one before the occupation. Ours was in the back yard and looked like an open grave. We had to use it only once. The sound of church bells, followed by the drone of many planes, made us run to it for cover. We huddled in the shadow of the oppressive noise, helpless, trapped by its horror, expecting to die. We looked up only briefly to see the sky covered with planes; dread kept our eyes lowered. The terror of bombing and the sick feeling attending it stayed with us long after planes stopped flying over our village.

The war changed everything. My father's blacksmith shop seemed changed, though everything in it was still in the same places: the large bellows that nourished the flame needed to heat the iron red hot, the oversized hammers that I could not lift, the three anvils mounted on round wooden bases, the long press-bench and all the tools and vices needed, the large barrel with water to cool the iron. The bed for the apprentice, which Péter never used because he was afraid of heights, still hung suspended above the door. Without my father, the shop seemed empty and looked unlike itself. For the time Péter worked, with Grandfather's help, under my mother's management, the blacksmith shop still seemed to belong to us. But people did not bring much work. The interruptions in the village were affecting the work in the fields as well. Everything was rationed, even the nails for shoeing horses. Rations were often restricted to preferred customers. I clearly remember an incident pertaining to such rationing. The Birgermeister himself delivered our allotment of horseshoe nails. He brought them directly to my mother with the precise order: "These are to be used only for shoeing German horses." I could tell that she did not like being ordered about by this arrogant man. She had known him all her life; he was almost old enough to be her father. She took her time to reply. In a quiet respectful tone, loud enough for me to hear, she said, "Vedde Matz, I have never seen a German horse nor a horse of any other nationality. Though I have seen many horses, you are the biggest horse I have ever seen." In common parlance, she called him a horse's ass. She went on explaining to him in the same detached, quiet tone that everyone, without exception, who brought a horse to our blacksmith shop would be taken care of till the nails were gone; of that he could be sure. Visibly shaken by her candor, he threatened that she should be careful, but he left the nails. She walked him to the door, and that was that. Within a day everyone knew of my mother's rudeness and Päsl Liss, the Birgermeister's wife, wrote my father a long letter of complaint that later entertained us when he came home on leave.

The only good part about my father's absence was the anticipation and the actual event of his homecoming. Everything I loved about him renewed itself on such occasions. The memory of him showed itself unworthy in comparison, and I was surprised each time, delighted in his presence. But my father could not stay long and could not come home often. Sometimes news of him was brought to us by fellow soldiers home on leave. On one such visit we were told of my father being drunk once and kissing every soldier in sight. No one had ever seen him drunk, not even my mother. But she liked the kissing part and surprised him when he next came home with a barrel of wine she made herself.

My mother was often ill and traveled about seeking help from different doctors. Sometimes she would take me along. Though being in new places, seeing new things was exciting, all experiences were burdened by the awareness of war.

I once saw the war. The lady in whose house we stayed took us atop a hill of vineyards on the outskirts of Werschetz/Vršac, to show us the war, she said. She pointed to a distant hill and we took turns looking through binoculars. I could see nothing looking through them. The war I saw from where we stood—wooded hills dotted with little puffs of smoke above the tree line, popping sounds accompanied by a distant rumble—did not match the feeling of war I carried inside me. The internal upheaval that tinged with terror all I experienced was a more desolate landscape; the war she showed us was not at all like the war I feared. "Maybe your father is there," the lady said, and I took another look, anxious to find him. "Partisans are everywhere; there is no place safe from them anywhere," she said as we passed an empty hut. But we did not see any Partisans on our way back to town.

• • •

Grandmother Korek was never ill. She died suddenly in spring when I was eight. On my way to school I had seen something hanging on the door in the green iron gate; I could not be sure if it was a wreath with black ribbons trailing. I kept on walking. The teacher sent me home when I arrived; did I not know my grandmother had died, he asked? It must be a mistake, I thought. She only had a cold when I last saw her. I did not want to believe it; I did not want it to be true. Later I saw her lying in the coffin in one of the darkened rooms. Her eyes were closed. She looked distant, less like herself. Her round open face kept its familiar look like an offered plate; it helped me recall the look of solace that her eyes had always given. Outside, in the treeless yard, we stood about the black coffin while the priest said things and led us into prayer. My father was not with us. I felt my mother's hands on my shoulders and the sun touching my face. I could hear the quiet crying in voices about me. Everyone looked serious, removed into their sadness. I looked up at my mother and felt reassured. I wanted to but I could not cry.

A lid was placed on the coffin. The sound of the hammers surprised me. The coffin was being nailed shut. I did not want this to be so. I hoped for some intervention. The sound of crying was getting louder, but the beat of falling hammers insisted on the irrevocable: my grandmother was being nailed into the closed coffin. I was unable to cry.

At the site of the grave with the others, I watched the casket being lowered into the ground. We each picked up a clod of earth, and one by one we threw them into the open grave. I, too, approached the edge of the grave and looked down the sunken hollow. It seemed a long distance, and the piece of earth I threw reached the coffin breaking into a sound I could not have anticipated. Its expansive hollow had full import. It was like a solution. Everything was dissolved in this sound. It redeemed hammer and nails and the thought of my grandmother shut within a coffin in an open grave. This sound was large. It encompassed everything comprehensible, refined it, and reduced it to clarity. Clear, whole, and hollow, full only with itself, it resounded: Nothing. This large sound from my grandmother's grave remained with me; I could recall its clarity years later and listen. I thought of it as the gift of parting, and I often recalled with it the silken hollow of warm milk, the sweetness of our secret communion.

In the fall of 1943, my mother was away for a long time. She had gone to Szeged, Hungary, and I stayed at my grandparents' house. While she was away, we received news that Seppi Onkl was missing in action. At night I slept with Tanti Rosi and listened to her crying without letting her know I was awake. She gave me a bracelet my uncle had given her, but I did not wear it. My arms were too small for it. During the day everyone talked in hushed tones as if someone inside lay dying. A week later news arrived that they had found my mother's illness and had operated immediately, and my grandfather left to see her.

Late one evening, standing in line to fetch water at the artesian well, I overheard two Hungarian women behind me talking in whispers about the misfortune that had befallen my grandparents: "Their son is missing in action, probably killed, and now their daughter is dying." I tried to pretend I did not hear what was being said. I waited to fill Grandmother's tin water can and never looked up from the ground. Away from the well, I started running with my heavy load, water splashing out, making my stockings wet. I was too scared to cry; I only moaned. I confronted Grandmother with accusations, but she assured me that no one was deceiving me; my mother was not dying but getting well. I wanted to believe her, but not until Grandfather came home was I truly reassured. He had seen my mother. He had seen the angular amber-colored stone, the size of a large marble, that they had removed from her bile duct, and the surgeon, a master of his art, assured her recovery. Grandfather did not tell her that my uncle was missing; he wanted to spare her for a while, he said, and Grandmother quietly cried.

We all thought my uncle was dead. I was kneeling at the edge of the open door to the cellar, looking down, watching my aunt doing something below—she was always cleaning now, to keep herself from going mad, she said—when I heard shouting on the street, a woman's voice frantically calling my aunt's name, *Rosi, Rosi*. Breathless, disheveled, looking spooked, the woman appeared in the yard crying: "He is coming! He is coming! Seppi, your husband, is coming." My aunt looked at her in disbelief. Someone had seen him at the station, the woman said, and she was last in running to relay the news. My aunt did not move. Dazed, her black eyes reflecting mistrust, she balked— "a cruel joke," she quipped. The lady assured us she had seen him coming in the distance. My aunt moved reluctantly, rising slowly from the cellar. Out on the street we stood rooted to the ground. The figure in the distance kept moving toward us. The lady continued talking, but we no longer listened. My aunt started running and I with her. She ran so fast I could not follow, and I stopped when I saw two figures merging far ahead of me.

My uncle had returned from the dead. He looked gaunt, weary. He had spent more than a month in captivity and had endured torture. His stories, told to those who came to see him, about his capture by Partisans and how he had escaped, were often repeated. People came in disbelief to be convinced it was really he who had come back. There was a solemnity to these gatherings; people listened intently. Of the many stories, one was most vivid. After my uncle had been starved for several days, they had put him in a small, overheated room and brought him a large portion of cooked meat smothered with salt; the flesh of dead prisoners, they told him, and forced him to eat it. Later he got thirsty, which was part of the torture, and they refused to give him water. Every time I heard this story, I had to drink lots of water. There were funny stories as well. He made everyone laugh when he described his experiences being escorted through villages dressed in only a remnant of what used to be trousers. He was barefoot over the whole duration of the thirty-eight days of his captivity. He told how he made his escape by knocking out the guard, who was lighting a cigarette, and how he ran into the night and kept on running. He described, in great detail, how he approached a house at the edge of a village and how he felt, peering through a window, seeing the familiar religious image, a picture of the Virgin Mary. The people were Croat farmers, Catholics.

Seppi Onkl's return was like a miracle to us, but he seemed detached and sad. When he was not telling his stories, he kept to himself. We had to be quiet around the house to let him rest. The doctor and even the priest visited him behind closed doors. At a certain time, each afternoon, my uncle would cry out and keep crying for a long time. I never heard such a cry before. This particular cry was so large, it spread over the house and occupied it. I asked Tanti Rosi what the crying was about. She said my uncle's feet, frostbitten and badly bruised, were hurting. I listened to this cry intently, and though I could not understand its meaning, I knew it was too large to be about aching feet. A cry so inconsolable would match a fall down to the core of the earth.

My mother came home pale and weak but with assurance that she would finally be well. She had her own stories to tell, and neighbors and friends were willing listeners. She showed the stone to our village doctor, who had sometimes made light of her illness, even mocking her about always being ill and never dying. It gave her some satisfaction to remind him of twelve years of medical incompetence.

Our blacksmith shop had been rented by a young Slovak blacksmith for some time, and now his sister, Zuska, came to stay with us while my mother was convalescing. Zuska was thirteen and learning to be a maid. I was especially glad that she still liked to play. Sometimes our antics caused trouble. Using my mother's creams and spilling her favorite perfume got us each a serious scolding. But when Zuska inadvertently left heavy pillows on the basket in which the newly hatched turkeys were sleeping, killing all but one of them, my mother, though visibly upset, consoled Zuska instead of scolding her. I was less forgiving, but I tried not to let it show. Together we nursed the lone survivor, following my mother's instructions, giving him caster oil with a tiny spoon, and he lived to be a grand tom, strutting about the yard gobbling ferociously when anyone came through the gate, acting more like a dog than a turkey.

Now our yard was often filled with strangers. The German soldiers used the blacksmith shop whenever they needed it to shoe horses and to repair machinery; at times, six or more were working in the shop alongside Zuska's brother, who did his own work. All of these soldiers seemed pleasant. Some were shy. Most of them were very young. The tallest, the one I thought most kind because he always smiled at me, was only seventeen. They called him Heinz. I once saw him reading a letter behind our straw stack, crying. Later his friends told us that the bad news was about his family in Germany: they had all been killed by bombs.

Long letters came from my father from somewhere in Bosnia. My mother's joy expressed itself in large tips to the mailman. My father could not get leave to come home now, but he assured us he was safe. He was lucky; he was shoeing horses and only had to use his gun once, to shoot an unfortunate lame horse. That he wanted to come home, that he missed us, he repeated throughout the letters in various ways. We would read these letters many times and I would inhale the scent of the paper to feel my father's presence. Nightly I would say the same small prayer before I went to sleep: Heavenly father let us all stay well, let the war soon be over, and let my father soon come home. Much later, long after the war, after I had forgotten how to pray, that little three-part plea would surprise me in times of severe panic by saying itself over and over again: *"Himml-Tati pittscheen loß uns alli ksunt, taß te Kriech pal ans Ent kehd, un taß te Tati pal haamkummt."*

The unhealthy atmosphere in the village continued, and the threat of Partisans hidden in the cornfields extended the realm of dis-ease. Some people were suspected of helping the Partisans, and several Serb men were arrested. Even our neighbor, čika Milan, was away for a time, imprisoned in Čoka. Weekly, Ljubica would be sent to take him food; sometimes she borrowed my father's bicycle for these trips. Once, instead of taking the food to čika Milan, she ate everything herself, she admitted, and got a terrible beating for it from tetka Katica. Later, Grandfather's help was needed to get čika Milan released. Their gardens, divided only by an earthen wall, made them neighbors, and the makeshift gate that allowed us and my grandparents to go back and forth to each other's houses through čika Milan's yard and garden was cited as evidence when Grandfather had to swear to the authorities that he knew čika Milan was not involved in any subversive activities. Most people helped each other out of difficulties, but a few used the opportunity to throw suspicion on people with whom they had a disagreement in the past. A man and his wife, strangers, who rented a room in the baker's house, were arrested because the baker was convinced they were

Partisans. He was afraid of them and afraid of incriminating himself by not reporting them. People were guarded and careful; they did not know whom to trust. Two drunken soldiers on leave killed a Serb man because they suspected him of being the lover of a German woman whose husband, away at war, was their friend. It was the one killing that took place within our village during the German occupation. Everyone was horrified by this crime. The two men involved were known to be irresponsible fools, but people were cautious and kept their opinions to themselves. Most people tried to keep to the natural order of things, as the work in the fields demanded, but a foreign force intent on dismantling the order of our way of life made itself at home in the village. Though this force was bred among us, it seemed foreign to us because it obscured our notion of home. It was our common enemy, the destroyer of our village.

Amid this general upheaval a sense of community developed among women in our village; a matriarchy; a last sanctuary. The women whose husbands were away rallied around Kowi Anna néni (Mundloch Anna). Strong and stately, she gave the appearance of being rooted like a tree. In the somber timbre of her voice, the slow cadence of her speech pattern, our dialect, rich like the soil of our fields, retained its integrity even when she was speaking with soldiers, making intercessions for us, matching their perfect German, every word, with the mellow cadence of our native tongue, not altering a syllable to compromise its lovely sounds, unfurling it like the banner of our home that it was. Anna néni was unencumbered by petty frailty or personal interest; her judgment was impartial. Her house was open to everyone and her garden reflected the sweet order of our way of life. There, among the hazelnut trees and raspberry bushes, where I shared the ripe red berries with the turtles on the ground, the promise of our anointed earth renewed itself for the last time. It was the summer of 1944.

In fall the worst happened. The ethnic Germans were advised to flee. Long lines of covered wagons were coming through our village to cross the Theiss at Senta. The German-speaking Romanians, women, children, old people, were fleeing. They had been traveling for some time. Their wagons were mud covered and their wet clothes clung to them, coated with mud. Solemn, closed into their journey, they seemed removed, unreachable. Like sleepwalkers, they moved through our village oblivious to us in our houses. They were part of something larger and no longer felt any kinship with us. Sealed off by their fate, they were more open to the weather than to us.

It rained and rained and would not stop. No one was willing to understand that we too would have to leave. How could we believe something so foreign to us? It was inconceivable, this ill-advised intentional separation from our own existence. We could not imagine such dissolution; we could not abandon our home. Our leaving could be considered only as a temporary flight from danger. No one could imagine leaving forever, and some could not imagine leaving at all.

Why should anyone leave? Our neighbors urged us to stay; they were sure that we could take care of each other. The Russians were coming and the Partisans were waiting to take their revenge, some said. The German-speaking population was at risk not just because they had been involved in the fight against Partisans, as were the Serb Četnici, the Croat Ustaši, the Hungarian Honvédek, but because they were of German descent. No one had a reasonable explanation for that. Most of us had survived the war so far; why should we flee another occupation, we who harmed no one? Especially the old and those without anyone in the war, why should they leave? Those guilty of any wrongdoing should go. There were others among us who urged that an evacuation was expedient, necessary. People were not officially informed about the dangers they would face by staying, though rumors were abundant. Most people knew only that they did not want to leave home, and this made them discredit all warnings. The fear, the uncertainty of going, perhaps into harm's way, made some ignore the danger of staying. There was no outside leadership that advised people about or assisted them with this proposed evacuation, just the local self-appointed advisors and the resolve of individuals who structured the proceedings.

Preparations were made in the village to provide wagons for everyone. Before school was dismissed altogether, I knew the children whose families were leaving; Horst was among them. For that reason I, too, wanted to go. It was my grandmother who was opposed to our leaving the village. In spite of the many messages from Seppi Onkl urging them to leave, she pleaded with my mother not to go, and I remember contradicting her with my own pleas. I had some notion that the German military had taken my father with them when they left our country, and I wanted us to go and find him. "If we don't go, we will never see my father," I said, adding my concern. It was the first time I heard my grandmother say anything unkind. "Shut up, you little snot-nose," she said, scolding, "you don't know anything!"

The attempts to prepare for this leaving were chaotic. My mother would sort things and put some into sacks and containers. Some things would have to stay. There was no time for indecision and long leave-taking; we could not take everything. The house had lost all semblance of order; every room was ravaged. The outside facade, behind closed shutters, tried to deny things that were going on inside. With the help of Lisi néni, our only turkey—our pet gobbler, which my mother could not bear to kill—was roasted and preserved in lard within a metal container. Other foodstuff was prepared, wrapped, and packaged.

My mother's ambivalence grew as preparations proceeded. The wagon allotted to us belonged to Emil's father, the man she associated with betrayal. She was not setting foot on this wagon, on principle. Anna néni pointed out that the wagon no longer belonged to anyone; all wagons furnished for our evacuation were common property. But even her counsel did not influence my mother's stubborn pride, and when no other wagon was offered her, she held onto her opinions and gave in to pressures to stay. We were not going, she declared; my grandparents, Tanti Rosi, and little Seppi should go without us. Grandfather delayed preparing the wagon for his own reasons. Lisi néni offered to take the two of us with their wagon. But when my mother saw that Grandfather did not have the ill-fated wagon ready, she declined; she did not want to leave her parents behind. The planned departure was hastened by the arrival of the Russians in Betschkerek, and overnight the wagons were readied to leave the village. In the confusion no one notified my mother till the morning, and there was no time for other decisions or further arrangements, no time for the necessary preparations that were left undone. Almost grudgingly we said good-bye at Lisi néni's. Our leave-taking, charged with sorrow and disbelief, was burdened by a nagging feeling of being abandoned. The wagons gathered at the Habag Haus and left without us in pouring rain one hour before noon. My mother and I did not go to see them leave the village.

It rained continuously the day the wagons left, as it had for weeks and as it would for weeks thereafter. The streets were heavy with mud and difficult to navigate. The sky was invisible. A gray light hovered close to the ground. The village was bereft. More than half of the German-speaking population was no longer with us; their houses, like coffins closed, were empty reminders. Our front gate now opened to the ghostlike appearance of Lisi néni's house across the street.

In our house a feeling of gloom made itself known amid the empty pieces of furniture, their contents sacked, and they, standing amid the sacks containing their treasures looking forlorn and discarded, as things without worth, things we would have left behind. Cold turkey lay unappetizing on heavy white plates; the carcass, surrounded by grease in the large tin, took on the appearance of an unworthy sacrifice and was a dead corpse rather than meat to eat. I cried a lot, but my grandmother looked relieved, and somehow her contentment comforted. I consoled myself with thoughts that the wagons would come back when all was over, that their departure was not a parting forever; it was only an evacuation out of harm's way. For those who had decided to stay and weather the storm, this parting just meant time and waiting. But however matters were rationalized, an emptiness hovered and crept among us like dense fog and our intensified anxieties would not be dispelled. We were abandoned. An oppressive feeling made a place for itself inside me and I carried it with me like a lodestone, and everything around me gathered to confirm an inconsolable loss. I imagined, at times, what it might be like being on a covered wagon with the others, in pouring rain, going over the Theiss on the ferry, going to faraway places looking for my father—and I felt abandoned again, betrayed.

The day after the wagons left, the Lochs came back to have their wagon fixed. Hilda's mother offered to take Tanti Rosi and Seppi with them. And the Lochs left for the second time, alone. Another wagon came back. Karcsi bácsi, who had deserted, found his wife and daughter at the crossing and came back with them, to stay.

At night the rumble of cannons grew louder, more constant. Cracks appeared in several windowpanes in the summer kitchen. The sound of rattling glass and the chatter of our own teeth kept us awake, shaking in bed. My mother developed severe stomach cramps from nervousness and would get up often. I would follow, too scared to stay in bed without her. Afraid to go to the outhouse, we kept a bed pan between the double doors. There we would hover and cry together in the dark.

The sound of heavy guns, becoming ever louder, seemed less threatening in the gray light of day; the violated image of the village took our attention away from the sound of guns. The village had registered a serious blow, the effects of which could already be felt everywhere. There were some who, preoccupied with self-interest, may not have recognized the change for the disaster it was. Some Serbs, glad about recent events for immediate good reason, seemed oblivious to the devastation. The destruction of the integrity of the village was nevertheless real and far reaching and would continue to affect all. The physical village as well as the fields would soon reflect it. The facades of abandoned houses already foretold the future of those remaining in the shadow of this loss. The village, our beautiful village, bore its loss in silent rage, the new assault against it adding to the others. We who mourned the loss of its friends and our own lived with this quiet rage and felt diminished. Within days, the Russians entered the village.

CHAPTER 5

Move into Darkness

THE VILLAGE SHRANK and turned in on itself. Irrevocably altered, it hid behind its familiar facade. The streets seemed to lead nowhere. We confined ourselves to our houses and those of our immediate neighbors. I did not go to school, and my visits to Grandfather's house were now made exclusively through čika Milan's yard, through the break in the wall that divided their gardens. I used this shortcut with caution, always keeping one eye out for tetka Katica's bad-tempered short-legged rooster, who would charge out of a crowd of docile hens and assorted domestic fowl in chase of a fleeing foe. I was familiar with the strategic maneuver by which he defended his domain. He would lunge into the air with acrobatic agility, propelled by quick flaps and sputters. Suspended in midair, poised for a frontal attack—bristling plumage a blaze of burnt umber, claws spread eagle-like, beak pointed in a dart-for-the-eyes gesture—he would convince even the boldest grown-up that he meant business. Crisp shrieks, scolding cackles, and sounds of beating wings accompanied the flashy show, making it a magnificent spectacle to watch from the safety of our back yard. But when he chased me, I ran as fast as I could to reach the makeshift gate that patched the hole in the wall to Grandfather's garden.

Trips to the artesian well for water and running to listen to the drummer at the corner were my only outings. I no longer played with the children across the street, and we seldom had visitors. Tetka Mara's visits had been diminishing for some time, and now they were short and incidental. Often she only came to borrow things she needed, like our red-enameled pan with the pebbled interior. Though she kept her pleasant ways, she seemed remote and guarded. My mother interpreted this as a protective device to divert attention from their friendship. Tetka Mara's visits to Markovs, on the other hand, steadily increased, which according to my mother was a measure of protection as well. It was obvious now that Ilija Markov had been supporting the Partisans during the German occupation with money he collected from Serb farmers. Especially the rich farmers dared not refuse him, and they needed his endorsement now.

Ilija Markov, the father of the children across the street, was a tall man with disheveled reddish blond hair, a ruddy complexion, and freckles on his face and hairless arms. His sheepish grin seemed like an apology for his strong lumbering body and made him appear inept, awkward, shy. But this was only a deceptive device of his cunning nature, a sort of camouflage, betrayed by the foxlike movements of his eyes. Later he would come to show his cunning openly, offering my mother protection in return for special favors. She, being alone, needed the help of a man, he argued. I did not understand what his proposition entailed. I was aware, however, that his visit was unpleasant, that my mother shamed him. "My husband has been gone for two years now; I was alone all this time and now you come with your offer when my hands are tied and my back is against the wall," she accused, and called him a coward. He left red-faced with his head hanging, looking down.

The Russian troops came through our village on the sixth of October, 1944, at nine in the morning, and the local Serbs, under the leadership of Partisans, took possession of village government. The Serbs celebrated hosting the Russian liberators, toasting them with enough šljivovica to float the entire village, its familiar scent wafting illusions of dispelled danger. The Russian soldiers drank the potent brew like water. Within three days of their arrival there were two deaths in our village. A Russian soldier, celebrated by his many Serb hosts, drank too much and was poisoned by alcohol. His hosts then took him to a Hungarian house and left him there to die, with the intent to incriminate the man whose house it was, against whom they had a grudge. The Hungarian man was beaten to death in retribution by the Serbs the following day.

The Russians I saw at tetka Katica's house were friendly and not at all frightening. Treated like celebrities and hailed as heroes for liberating us, for freeing our country from German occupation, they were the guests of honor on many occasions. One of the soldiers observed, jokingly, that judging from the general plenty we had, it seemed more appropriate that we should come to Russia to liberate them. We laughed. Tetka Katica expressed her joy in the recent turn of events, praising Communism, citing its virtues, which according to her were equality for all, no strife, no greed, no need for money. Freedom. "The communist government in our country will assure freedom for all," she proclaimed, gravely, as if she were mouthing an oracle. Her proclamation was cause for another toast, and reasons to celebrate grew stronger with each drink.

At first, having the Russians in our village seemed much like the previous occupation—tolerable. But soon there were rapes occurring at night. People were talking among themselves, whispering. I knew that rape meant forcible violation by the word we used, and from the way it was whispered I sensed that it was something shaming and that it brought about disgrace. My father's cousin, Kädi, who lived three houses away from Grandfather's, was raped by six soldiers. They came to her house in the middle of the night and Kädi's father and mother, Vedde Fritz and Päsl Mari, could do nothing to prevent their forceful intrusion, and nothing to help Kädi. People looked embarrassed and ashamed when they talked about rape, and some women cried and were afraid. A young Hungarian woman was assaulted by so many soldiers she had to be taken to the doctor. The rape of a seventy-two-year-old German woman convinced everyone that no woman was safe. Women felt uneasy at night in their own houses and took to sleeping in hiding.

Our neighbors, the Hallai girls, Bözse and Maris, approached my mother to hide with them. They also asked the Högyis across the street, Kató and Juci, who brought along their brother Laci. No one could be told about this, not even my aunts. Tanti Rosi made her own arrangement and even we did not know, till much later, that she slept in the shallow attic above the pigsty with Seppi, who, at two, somehow realized that he was not to make a sound. We never asked tetka Mara if she slept at home in her bed, nor did we tell her that we did not. We assumed that the Serbs had less to fear since none of them were among the women raped. To expect our Serb friends to hide us was unwise, my mother said. We could not endanger or trust anyone in this matter. It was understood that our old way of communicating, when our village was whole and in touch with itself, was no longer appropriate.

Nightly we selected new hiding places. One night our little group picked a place in our yard. It was the old bomb shelter now cleverly hidden under the haystack. No one would ever look for us there, we agreed. I dreaded the unpleasant feeling of having to slide into a dark hole, feet first, not knowing what else was in it. Kató and my mother went first, and Laci and I were lowered and carefully received in the darkness below. We made room for the others, getting as far away from the opening in the hay as the space allowed. I clutched my mother, never letting go. Once we were all in, we noticed that five women and two children had standing room only and crouching made it a much tighter fit. The dark in this space was impenetrable. I could not help thinking that there might be frogs about. The air

My mother and I with Tanti Rosi holding Seppi, summer, 1943.

was damp and heavy and it became increasingly hard to breathe. Though I was in my mother's lap, the undefined space around us frightened me. I felt swallowed up. I wanted out and said so. "We are going to suffocate in this hole," I warned, using a prophetic tone, hoping to scare them, but everyone was hushing me up. Settled in and quiet, not convinced that I could endure from moment to moment, I tried not to think of the long night. Suddenly, small sounds from all directions were converging on us. The space inside the hole got smaller as we tried to defend ourselves, fending off the persistent inhabitants. Our perfect hiding place had already been claimed by hordes of mosquitoes; they were attacking us, defending their space. Allies, I thought, gratefully. The decision to evacuate was unanimous, reached without discussion.

Relieved and vindicated, I tried to assert my will further. I was tired and wanted nothing more than for everyone to go home. I wanted to sleep in my own bed and started fussing, pleading with my mother to abandon the attempt to find another hiding place. I knew rape was something terrible because my mother said if it happened to her she would go insane or kill herself immediately after. It had to be something very bad because my mother never wanted to die. But Kädi hadn't killed herself, and she seemed much the same when I last saw her. "Please let's sleep in our own bed tonight. No one came so far and no one will come, you'll see," I pleaded. My mother was giving in; perhaps she was tired too. We were just about to go inside when Maris suggested hiding in their corn bin and Kató, with her kind maternal ways, convinced my mother to come along. I was pouting.

The Hallais' corn bin, like ours, was a rectangular structure rising above the pigsty, golden corn still on the cob showing through its lattice siding. Perched directly behind the wall that divided our back yards, this *Kotarka* offered a view into our own yard. Once inside, we built a trench in the middle, which made the bin seem fuller from the outside. The corn raised on all sides hid us from view and kept the draft of night air away from us. Sitting in the trench on an incline, though not altogether comfortable, was much more pleasant than being in the dark hole. I must have fallen asleep immediately.

Sometime during the night, I awoke with a start hearing my mother's name called from somewhere in the dark, accompanied by loud pounding-on-wood noises. I recognized čika Milan's voice. I reached instinctively for my mother to wake her to answer. I could not see anything, but I was aware that everyone in the corn bin was awake, listening, pleading to the quiet not to give us away. No one moved. I was frozen in terror. The sounds came from inside our yard. The knocking and the call, "Vavika," were fixed in position, at the wooden door to our back room. At intervals čika Milan repeated this pounding and calling. The familiar voice and the urgency in it tempted to a habitual response. My mother must have felt it too because she put her hand lightly over my mouth. I suddenly understood. For a moment everything stood still and fell out of time. I had visions of being on the other side of that wooden door, as we almost were. I saw my mother screaming, tearing her hair out. Mad. I saw her dead in the coffin, under that wooden pounding. Had my mother and I been at home, she would surely have responded to the familiar voice by opening the door . . . I could have caused my mother to kill herself.

Suspended in a space in which direct comprehension voids mediated thought, in a vast impartial stillness against which events are like stones tossed, falling, I, the child sitting in the darkness, was such an event, falling out of time. The wordless cadence of men talking, somewhere in the void, seemed separated from my comprehension and was only a dissonance to my suspended self. In this stillness, the tense space that my body occupied, my breathing, and the beating of my heart seemed things on their own and not a part of me.

Someone's teeth chattered . . . voices of men talking . . . words spoken in Russian grew clearer before they faded into the night. I saw nothing but darkness before me and I felt only the hollow space inside me.

As soon as it started to get light, we left our hiding place to go back to our houses. One of the women said she would just as soon stay in the corn bin until the Germans came back. We climbed over the fence into our yard and unlocked the wooden door; we entered the house reluctantly. My mother sat on the bed and stared at the floor in front of her. We did not speak. I thought she was angry with me, but I did not ask any questions. The same day Jani bácsi came to tell us he was taking Bözse and Maris to Jazova, to their relatives, and we could go along. Jazova, a predominantly Hungarian village and the home of our apprentice, Péter, was off the path of Russian troops; we would be safe there.

After a week Jani bácsi came for us with his wagon. On the way back to our village there was talk of rape. While we were gone, a Serb woman and her daughter were raped in front of their father and now, Jani bácsi said, the authorities made it known that rape was prohibited and would be punished. The last of the Russians were leaving the village anyway, he added, to reassure us that it was safe to come home again. We were relieved. "There is other news," Jani bácsi said evasively. "The German people are not to leave the village. If they do, their houses, their property, will be confiscated." My stomach knotted. There was a discussion about it being unlawful to take land and property away from citizens. We were no longer under occupation . . . the Russians were only passing through . . . we had rights . . . the war would be over soon and things would get back to normal. Everyone added their thoughts to distract from the obvious. "No one in the village believes that our German people's citizenship will be taken away, that they will lose their rights, their property." If that was part of the news, Jani bácsi, who was a good storyteller, neglected the most important detail. My mother did not seem to be surprised. "It is, most likely, a rumor to frighten people," Jani bácsi asserted reassuringly, but his voice had the tone of consolation. I judged by my mother's face that she was not taken in by it. With her strict profile, pale and marble-like, framed by a deep maroon kerchief, her countenance expressed conviction. Calm and collected, resigned to acceptance, sitting up straight with Jani bácsi at the front of the wagon, facing the road ahead, she was an image of strength.

That our things could be taken from us was made clear the very day the Russians came and the Serb authorities took away our radio. And later things were taken from the German people by Serbs and others. Anyone could plunder and harass us, just for the sake of it. Some did it to repay a wrong they had suffered during the German occupation. Because the offenders were no longer present, the retribution was doled out indiscriminately. Sometimes raids were systematically executed on the entire German ethnic group. At times they were random, with no explanation at all. They always involved humiliation of the victimized, and the boastful gloating of those intoxicated with power. But sometimes a deep sorrow stepped out of the shadows to reveal itself in rage and retribution. Olga, whose mother was German and whose Jewish father and grandmother had been taken away during the German occupation, took part in these raids visited on our houses, though she was barely fifteen. At my grandmother's, she raided the pantry and accused her of having things in it from their store. Starch. My mother had made it from potatoes, in a barrel next to our well, in summer. It had taken so very long to make and it had received such wonderful praise from all the other women who had come to witness the proceedings. But, there, in the dark pantry, it now earned my grandmother a slap in the face and a barrage of verbal abuse—the painful rage of a girl, a child almost, whose father was known by everyone in the village as the kindest of men. It was a time when the village took turns to spit on itself in revulsion.

All livestock was taken away from us. Two policemen, Serb men from our village, came to our house to check if we had fattened pigs or geese. They knew we did not have any cows or horses. My mother led them to the empty pigsty to assure them we had no pigs. "As for the geese, you would have to look for them in the outhouse," she said, bluffing. They laughed and left. Had they looked where she told them, they would have found the two fattened geese she was force-feeding late every evening and early each morning, so quietly that there was no sound at all. Not even our neighbors knew, and not even I standing close by could hear anything except the soft hissing sound of their labored breathing. We had to be very careful now, even sounds and smells could betray us. "Is it my fault they don't listen when I tell them the truth?" my mother teased. We laughed, but my knees were shaking.

Most of the time we were apprehensive. We did not feel safe in our houses. We were often in the yard, airing our vigilance in open spaces; it gave us the illusion that we could escape the inevitable. My mother hardly left the house and yard unless they came to fetch her for some mandatory labor. German women cleaned and cooked in the municipal building now, but most often they worked in the fields. The corn in the fields of those who had fled as well as that of others who had stayed remained unharvested, and this work was now being done by German women and the remaining old men, collectively, under supervision. Sometimes my mother worked in sheds and attics of abandoned houses, sorting rotting harvested onions that stained her hands a brownish red. Her clothes, steeped in the foul odor, would spoil the air throughout our house.

The daily activities that had been part of our domestic life, if they could be done at all, were now done routinely, without interest. Even cooking was an unlikely undertaking in these times; my mother seldom cooked. The fear that had driven us into ourselves was paralyzing; it deadened our desire and our interest. Sometimes the ordinary, the mundane, like an old habit, had the power to move us into a familiar response. The beat of the drum, for instance, could still send me running to hear the news. On one such occasion, I came running back home bringing the news to my mother and, assessing her general disinterestedness, I added: "The drummer announced that from this day on, all mothers must cook!" It made her laugh.

Days moved slowly now, and they too did not belong to us. Occasionally my mother and I would go for an all-day visit to a Hungarian family who lived at the edge of the village, near the cemetery, just for the temporary diversion and relief. But we could not impose on our friends and neighbors. And visiting with other ethnic Germans only exacerbated anxieties; among ourselves, people talked freely about their misgivings, repeating rumors of coming disaster, voicing despair. At night fears intensified and heightened apprehensions of things to come. Sleep was a present for the unaware.

• • •

Late in October, after the Russians had gone from our village, my grandfather and the other German men, except for the very old, were jailed in the municipal building by the officiating Partisans. The men were severely beaten and kept there for three days. Only my grandfather and his brother,

Vedde Niklos, were released without such beatings. It seemed one of the young Partisans, a local man, had a debt to repay; Seppi Onkl had vouched for this man's father, who had been accused of being a Partisan during the German occupation. The release of my grandfather and his brother was explained, officially, by their ages; being over sixty-five, they were the eldest among the men imprisoned. The other men were taken away. We did not know where. Only much later did we hear about their plight, that they were taken to larger jails, some to Kikinda and others to Kanjiža. Some were severely beaten many times; Anna's father had all his teeth knocked out and his ribs broken. Most of the men, my teacher among them, were shot, along with many others from other villages. We eventually learned all this years later, from people who had been with them and survived. No one knew why some were shot and others were only beaten. Indiscriminately, the Partisans shot old and young, rich and poor, farmers, teachers, priests, and even nuns. In some villages women, children, the very old, all were killed. Since no one knew the rules to these proceedings, it was useless to contemplate claiming an exemption.

On the first of November seven of the men they had taken away were brought back to the village to be executed: three Germans and four Hungarians. Among them were Vedde Matz, our Birgermeister; our butcher Vedde Mattheis; and Schlumper Jakob, the carder and rope maker.

Vedde Mattheis was Wilma's grandfather. She sat behind me in school. Once she had to have an operation to remove a tapeworm, which was, I imagined, coiled up inside her, looking hideously disgusting. She looked pale and bloated because of it, and her eyes had the look of pained revulsion. People said she would die, but she got well. I remember her grandfather carrying her, seated around his neck, when she was too weak to walk to the doctor. Vedde Mattheis was tall, big bellied, strong, and his booming voice had a rasp in it. He liked to boast and tease and he accompanied both with robust laughter that matched the generous measure of his barreled chest.

Vedde Schlumper (we called him that because of his profession) was the unfortunate man whose wife betrayed him with a Serb lover during the German occupation. Though he had nothing to do with the death of his wife's lover, the event was now about to claim his own life. One of the Hungarian men was among the accused for having named his mule Stalin long before there were Communists in our village. His having shouted this name coupled with vulgar language to encourage his stubborn mule caused some to object now—not because it was abusive and disrespectful to the mule but because they interpreted it to be politically subversive. Even names could incriminate. I thought of my grandfather—it was lucky he had named his dog Wilson.

Grandfather's brother Vedde Niklos and Päsl Leni, Lisi néni's parents, ca. 1900. *Courtesy* Elisabeth Kis

The seven men were herded through the village barefoot. Severely beaten, they were hardly recognizable to the people who saw them. It was drummed out that they were going to be shot, and everyone in the village was to come to witness it. The place of the shooting was the ditch in front of the Catholic cemetery and the time was four in the afternoon.

That afternoon my mother and I were at home, alone. She locked the gate and we stayed outside in the front yard. The weather was still warm enough to be without coats, in sweaters. We sat crouching against the white-washed wall of Hallai's house to catch the afternoon sun. I was drawing lines on the ground with a stick, as I often did. Though no one else noticed, not even my parents, Grandfather said I was "practically geniused" when it came to drawing. When I was quite small, my mother would draw for me: always the same picture of a woman in profile, in a dress that revealed legs with shapely calves and shoes with high heels; with only one arm showing, puff-sleeved, elbow bent, the woman was carrying a basket. She had been to the butcher, my mother would say, to explain the basket. I admired this drawing and made one like it, adding my own variations, and soon I made more realistic drawings of everything around me. Drawing was the opportunity for me to be good, even to be better than my mother expected, but she did not make a fuss about it, and I took it for granted. I often drew on the ground and on paper when it was available; it was the natural thing for me to do. Now, my making marks on the ground was an extension of my extreme anxiety.

The sun against the stark, whitewashed wall reflected a cold crisp light. Crouching below it recalled images of sickly baby chicks I had seen in spring, seeking the sun with their eyes closed, shivering, making soft peeping sounds, noises of lament: a complaint against their misfortune, and a receptive response, an invocation to the warmth and goodness of the light. My mother said it seemed like Good Friday. I visualized the large draped-in-black crucifix in our church. Bells were ringing. It was an ominous sound of repeated gongs with punctuating pauses. Rather than the continuous playful ding-dong pealing into fluid celebratory sound, this was a droning monotone with intervals pointing toward disaster, measuring out time. At one point my mother whispered prayers. Then all was quiet. Only the domestic doves that lived in the attic above my father's blacksmith shop, flying in and out of the small openings in the gable, added in soft sounds of beating wings, with rhythmic reassurance, their timeless measure to consoling cooing.

Street sounds—latecomers running to catch the show, a scatter of chatting and laughter, betraying a careless haste; a woman's voice yelling to wait up . . .

I had a stomachache and pressed my knees against my chest, my arms wrapped around my legs. I felt something pressing from the inside against my throat. My mother vomited. She got up to wash her mouth at the well. Pacing back and forth, she was saying, as if to herself: "I don't think we can survive this. What shall we do? What will I do?" Sounds of faraway noises interrupted: a distant crowd, a flock of birds, or perhaps there were popping sounds. We stopped listening. My mother knelt down in front of me and held my face with both her hands, tilting it up gently. The sun fell tepid on my face and shoulders. She looked straight into my eyes, solemn, resolved, as if she had found a solution. "Will you promise me to do what I say?" Her voice seemed far away. "Will you do what I ask? Will you do this for me?" she repeated. I could not have imagined what she wanted me to do. "Will you jump into the well with me," she said and it was no longer a question.

I looked at her closely and saw that she was serious, but I felt as if I were in religion class. This must be a test, I thought, to find out if I had learned to be good, obedient. I nodded. "Yes," I said. But I only said it because I knew it was the right thing to say, and I only said the right thing because I did not believe that she intended to do what she said. I could not believe that she would jump into the well. I reassured myself that she would not, but part of me imagined what it would be like on the way down. It was such a narrow and deep well. We would hit its bricked-in shaft and shatter falling. And it was dark down there, and there were frogs. I could imagine being down there dying of terror—the agony of hopeless yearning to be pulled up. Macabre images, the horror I dared imagine, churned up feelings in my stomach. Distracted, I could only hear fragments of what my mother was saying: ". . . there is no place for us to go . . . no place to hide . . . no one to help . . . it is better . . . the only way out." I watched myself getting up and walking slowly, with my hand in hers, toward the well. I wanted to start laughing. I wanted to stop and tell her I was only pretending. Though I could not believe in the reality of our undertaking, I could see at the same time that my mother was serious. I felt capable of acting out what was asked of me, but I could not believe that it would actually happen. I was hoping for some intervention. I looked ahead to the stiff gather of horseradishes around the base of the well, their frayed, brown-edged autumnal foliage showing a bitter-gall green.

My mother stopped abruptly, and turning toward me, she fell down on her knees and with both arms around me, her face against my chest, she sobbed violently, repeating over and over: "Forgive me." I felt stiff, like a doll, in her folded arms. I understood; we were not going to jump in the well. Listening to her weep, I began crying with her. I was too ashamed to weep on my own. I felt I had betrayed my mother, deceived her. I only said I would be her accomplice because I did not believe she would do what she said. I was false, an unworthy witness to her grave intent and undeserving of her apology. Her grief shamed me. I felt a chill and shivered. Street noises of people returning, talking and laughing, were coming closer. Falling footsteps, calls of passers-by to those across the street. The sounds fell like tossed shards, reminiscent of times past. The sun left the space of our front yard. It was getting cold.

Those who saw the shooting talked to others about it. One could not stop them; they had to tell. I heard them and watched the strained expressions flicker over their faces. They had seen something terrible that incriminated them, something that dwelt uneasy on their faces: another man's death, witnessed as a spectacle. It reminded me of the shame that tinged the talk of rape. The smile of disbelief that marks the innocent, scowled on their faces. They had to tell, to bring the ugly image of their witness into fading. Meticulously they described every detail, counting on the pallor of words and the wash of tears, their own and those of others. By each telling, the smell of blood would evaporate over the village. The men had to take off all their clothes, they said, before they were shot. The request to declare their loyalty to a political leader was their last test; their last hope; a last humiliation; a hoax. The men mouthed what their executioners expected to hear. The informed said, *"Živio Tito!"* Confused, some hailed Stalin. Only Vedde Mattheis, the butcher, who lived by the edge of the blade and who never could resist teasing, said, *"Heil Hitler!"* before they shot him. All were left lying in the ditch, their blood spilling together, seeping into the ground at the edge of the cemetery, there at the foot of the missing cross; the life-sized crucifix.

It was said that certain people teased and tormented the men before they were shot and that some spat on the dead corpses lying in the ditch. Those named were people we knew. For three days the bodies lay exposed. It was forbidden to cover or bury them. After three days some of the German men of the village were ordered to dump the bodies into an unmarked grave.

Many in our village had seen the killing; we only heard about it from our own people, those who thought they had to be there because they were told to go. "No one should have gone," my mother said, "unless they were willing to take the place of those being shot." I was embarrassed by this assertion. What my mother said seemed clear enough and right, but I disliked hearing it said in front of those already stricken by what they had seen. It seemed an added assault. But my consoling gestures, like my mother's assertion, went unnoticed. In the face of the horror they had seen, righteous indignation as well as compassion were useless.

• • •

Inside, our house had never regained its former look. It still showed signs of the many packings and unpackings from the time of indecision. In the front room, the disarray was most telling. Feed sacks were standing about half filled with clothes, and others lay empty on the floor. A huddle of giant, thick-skinned white pumpkins, proof of a hefty harvest, squatted obtrusively, looking like surprised visitors in unaccustomed spaces, while the familiar objects stood about unattended, unloved. Gaping doors and drawers to furniture, their contents disturbed and diminished, spoke of neglect. Some things, like the radio, were missing and their accustomed places looked accusingly for them. My mother had started giving things away. The window facing tetka Katica's house, the one in my room, was opened at night, and all the floral china and the tea set—the elegant ladies with parasols on cups that looked too fragile to touch—were pushed through into the darkness outside and received in secret on the other side, for safekeeping. The Hallais received bundles over the wall that divided our back yards. Our brass scale made its appearance there; standing on the wide earthen wall, it glistened darkly, looking important, indispensable, as if its presence, required for secret measuring, weighed the strange nocturnal proceedings. My father's wool coat, his best suit and his pocket watch, embroidered laces and pillow-cases, the can of lard from the pantry, grain from our attic—all left by night, some through the window to tetka Katica, others across the wall to the Hallais, all for safekeeping. Those who received them wanted it kept a secret. We kept their secrets even from each other. My father's accordion, well known in the village, could not be given to anyone. It would be looked for and would incriminate the keeper. Nora, in her diaphanous pale yellow gown of sheerest silk crepe with intricate cording at the yoke, was given to tetka Katica. Ljubica was too old to play with dolls; Nora would be put away for safekeeping. I placed Nora in the black carriage and covered her with the miniature light blue quilt enveloped in its buttoned-on white casing. Her blue glass eyes glistened consoling familiarity. In the dim light of my room, in the corner where no one could see it, I inhaled the scent of celluloid warm from the touch of my lips. I whispered her name like a caress for blissful play lost. "Nora," I said in disbelief watching the carriage hoisted up, and disappear into the dark.

We were disowned and dispossessed. This information was casually read by the drummer at the street corner with other news and given as much importance as the price of eggs. I recall feeling confused, shamed hearing it in the presence of others, and acting as if it did not matter, I looked proud instead.

It was difficult for us to interpret such a pronouncement and harder still to accept its implications. The things we lived with, that belonged and seemed an extension of ourselves, were our life. Without our fields, what would we do? Without the work that gave life meaning, who would we be? Our possessions were not things in themselves; they expressed the love of our labor and the meaning of our life.

First, we could not believe the announcement. Then we started to look at our things with great regard; we felt we had to save them—more out of habit, having taken care of them for so long, than out of foresight to preserve them for future use. Not being able to save ourselves, we tried to save the things meaningful to us. Our things, we said, and laid claim to them in parting. We buried things in our yards and gardens; important papers and photographs, things no one could use or want, took refuge in the earth itself. We bequeathed the proof of our belonging, like our dead, to the receiving ground. Surely the earth we loved would acknowledge our belonging, like our dead, and no one would begrudge us for it.

My mother never asked tetka Mara's advice about political matters concerning us, nor did we approach her to be the keeper of our things. As member of a wealthy Serb family, her position was fragile in these times, my mother said, and we could not involve her; it might cause her trouble.

We kept our feelings of friendship. We would not be deprived of our loyalty, of our trust.

The village government was run by Communists, Partisans, men and women not from our village, but some of the police and officials were village Serbs; some were Slovaks. Zuska's brother was one among them. He approached my mother when she was working in the municipal building, thanking her for her kindness to his sister and to him. He was apologetic about our plight, "You of all people, Vávi néni, and your family did not deserve this," he said. Perhaps he knew what was going to happen to us. My mother could not let it be without saying, "Do you really believe that anyone does deserve the things that have been happening?" He did not answer.

We knew instinctively that not one of the people in the village could save us from what was about to happen. How right we were we would discover only later. It seemed ridiculous to us, though very frightening, that some Serb men, our neighbors, like Ilija and others, came to offer their protection to German women in return for sexual favors. If such agreements were made or if rapes resulted from such offers, no one spoke about them. We only knew about those rejected. We were afraid of the Serbs and of all who were Communists; we knew that any one of them had the power to incriminate, to kill, or to cause us to be killed. But we were just as sure that they did not have the power to save us individually, nor could they collectively save the ethnic Germans of the village.

The oppressive anxiety that separated us from the village occupied us. Publicly disowned by the government of our country, we had no rights. We suffered the injustice without shame. We were not approached with accusations of wrongdoing by anyone and had no cause to feel guilty. We clearly knew, for we were told by those in power, that our fault was simply that we were members of an ethnic group. This was something we could not change, something against which there was no reasonable defense.

Estranged from the village, our fields and livestock confiscated, our livelihood taken away, we lived in our houses, which no longer belonged to us, surrounded by things no longer ours, alien to ourselves. That they begrudged us our existence we should have known. That they intended to kill us they would not say. The problem was not just that they did not want us to have or to be—*they wanted us not to have been*. And rage as they would, no atrocity devised against us could diminish their rage or appease their desire. In their desire they were like children; in their rage they were savage. Because we knew them well, we were afraid. Our fears were well founded. Our endurance, which had served us for centuries, would now further be perfected. We "Švabe," as they called us, were known for hard work and endurance. We would not disappoint.

The decision to stay in the village, made only months before, now seemed a lifetime away. No one could count up the daily terrors since. No one saw them all. Cut off from life as we knew it, events lost their meaning. How excited I had been last spring when my Kodl, Lisa, gave birth to the twins, and Anna and I were going to be the godmothers to Walter and Werner. How disappointed we both were when the priest would not allow it because at eight and a half we were not old enough. Everything about that birth— the wrinkled-up look of the babies (my disapproval of it), the dark visceral smell of the room after birth, the food we took to the house as was the custom—all taught and gave meaning when life was celebrated with others within a social context. Now, late in November, when Tanti Lisa's second child Anna was born, birth seemed a sad occasion. Being born into these times was a misfortune, said those who cared, and they cried. Only Johann responded to the arrival of a sister with conventional wisdom, making us laugh with his expression of jealousy: he wanted to grind her up in the coffee grinder.

Even Christmas had passed unnoticed. Now only death and destiny mattered. No one knew what it would be; when it came we would recognize it.

Early on December 27, my grandmother was at our door. She had Seppi with her. Sometime during the night, they had taken Seppi's mother away. Grandmother was crying. Seppi was clutching her knees, his head buried in her long black skirts, crying bitterly as Grandmother continued to explain. My mother picked him up and kissed him but he continued crying. It was a grown-up cry, like an echo of my grandmother's crying. His dark eyes were filled with a sorrow too large for them to hold and his face assumed a searching look. "They came and took her; they did not say where they were taking her." Every one knew who "they" were. No one needed to ask. We were living among strangers now. Only habit would make us still call them by name. They, too, were diminished, only messengers, no longer themselves. "They said she needed to dress warm and take food and clothes enough for fourteen days." Grandmother kept repeating "Where did they take her?" till it ceased to be a question and became a lament. "We helped her gather her things and watched her being taken away. We watched her leave her child—and we could do nothing about it." Her eyes fixed a vacant look to the far wall of our room. That all German women between the ages of eighteen and thirty-two were taken from our village was pieced together later that day. No one knew anything more.

The new regime worked with numbers, as it had previously, with the men who were taken away. In their efficiency, they were accountable only to numbers. Mothers were taken away from their children. Women with infants were the exception. Someone was always left behind to be grateful.

It gave the proceedings that touch of compassion. Both Lisas, Tanti and Kodl, were still at home. The twins were eight months old. Johann, like Seppi, was already two; but for his sister, now five weeks old, his mother would have been taken away too. I was glad that my mother was past the specified age. She was thirty-four.

No one was watching the weather. It had gotten very cold. Frosted pictures, floral images, roses, appeared on the panes of the small window in the back room. The sunlight glistened through the etched roses and added their fragile riches to those suspended in the lace curtain. Long after my mother heated up the oven to warm the room, the roses would stay, fading slowly during the course of the day. Getting out of bed in the morning teased me with a particular pleasure. I would stick my feet out and, shocked by the cold, I would draw them back quickly to enjoy the double pleasure of escaping the cold and being comforted by voluptuous downs. Reminiscent of sleep, their sweet scent familiar like a lullaby, the downs were a refuge and a shield against the oncoming day. The embracing downs and I, cocooned in them, their soft rustlings whispering enticements to remain forever enveloped, were allies against the cold.

I watched Seppi sleeping, his hair falling softly around his face, his expression like an open door, like an invitation. His presence was a gift that renewed our feeling of belonging, a feeling that seemed to have vanished from the village. During the day we played hide-and-seek and I chased him about the room, pretending he was hard to catch. If my father were home, he would hang the swing into the doorway; Seppi would like that.

But we don't hear from my father any more.

A terrible urgency now makes itself felt, foreshadowing a somber reality, lurching us into the present. The room still looks friendly, and when it smells of my mother's cooking, things seem almost the same. The embroidered cloth on the table where the radio used to stand shows its design without interruption. And there in the cupboard with the glass doors, assorted dishes that displaced the beautiful china mock me with their presence, and I avoid looking in their direction. When I do look, a terrible pain makes itself at home in the pit of my stomach and I stop whatever I am doing. Seppi sometimes cries. He wants to go home to his mother. Diversion is something I have to learn by myself and it is very tedious. I make up stories and often I simply lie, telling Seppi his mother will come home soon and bring him something wonderful to play with. It seems so reasonable I believe it myself. The visits from Grandmother are diversions he likes. Grandfather is too preoccupied now to be playful. When he comes to see us he seems thoughtful and sad. We five make an uneasy unit, comforted by one another.

The ethnic Germans left in our village now are women thirty-three and older, those younger with infants, men over sixty-five, and one invalid; the rest are children. We move about among the others. We recognize and greet others on the street with the appropriate greetings. We talk with each other. We visit but do not leave the village. We go about our business: men and women work under supervision; German children do not go to school; no one goes to church; we do not go to the municipal building without being called. We do not ask questions. We accept these conditions; we want to believe that we still could be part of the village and we are always apprehensive, afraid of losing this hope.

We go to bed with this uncertainty, afraid to fall asleep. Even when I am tired and my eyes are heavy with sleep, I fight it. The stillness outside and the sound of barking dogs in the distance, a sound of reassuring comfort that lulled me to sleep in the past, now is a cause for apprehension. I want to be awake when the terrible, that which everyone fears, happens. And that which I fear most, that they will take away my mother while I am sleeping, continues to keep me awake, listening. Waking up in the mornings, I am surprised I have fallen asleep at all.

The night of the second of January, 1945, I wake with a start. Someone is rapping at the window of our room from tetka Katica's yard. My mother answers, calling out softly in the dark: "Who is it?" A man's voice, not čika Milan's, shouts, addressing my mother: "Get ready, Vavika, it is time to go." I immediately start screaming. My mother quiets me, but I continue shrieking. I am standing at the foot of the bed, below the window, pushing my fists against my screaming mouth. Light from a lantern slices through the dark room and I see the face of a man peering through the frosted panes. The face seems upside down to me—as if the house has sunk into the ground during the night and the man whose face it is has to stoop instead of stretch to look through the window. I look up at the window to address the face: "Please, please, don't take my mother!" Seppi is still sleeping. The two men, let in by my mother, come through the door and I continue pleading, crying, and frantically moving about, clutching my hands, not knowing what to do with them. One of the men is Ilija Markov and the other a younger man who lives in the big house across the street from the butcher shop. His father has many white oxen I recall, calming myself to bring him into recognition. The two men are dressed in heavy coats, wear fur caps, and carry guns. "Please, please don't take my mother away—please. Let me go with my mother!" My pleading seems futile. Not letting my mother out of my sight as she nervously moves about looking for something, I continue my frantic pleading and hear myself screaming as if from far away.

It is the younger man who responds: "You are going with your mother; all of you are leaving." I have to hear it again to believe it. "I can go with my mother?" I ask, imploring in a quiet voice, listening to myself as I would listen to someone else. Immediately I start to thank him over and over again. And I feel an energy too large for my body. I could do any task asked of me. I could pick up the house and carry it by myself if it, too, had to go. I could stretch to reach the ceiling and even the sky. "I can go with my mother," I say over and over again. "I can go with my mother," I continue whispering as I listen to her asking me to dress Seppi and myself. My mother is looking for the keys to the pantry, which always hang on a nail next to the door. Ilija is standing in front of it and steps aside to reveal the empty nail. He stands stiffly about and pretends to look for the keys while his shifty eyes look at everything else. We are to take food for three days and warm clothes, one of the men says. My mother gives me some more clothes and tells me to put as much on myself as I possibly can and to dress Seppi the same way. I can tell she is very nervous. I am slipping on stockings over stockings and a half a dozen bloomers. She is running from one end of the house to the other, grabbing things and stuffing them into a feed sack, a pillowcase. She seems distracted, beside herself, still looking for the keys. Without them we can not get to the food. I see her putting a loaf of bread into a sack, taking the leftover food from the cupboard, and see her run into the front room, while I am stuffing Seppi's little feet into yet another pair of stockings. He is only half awake and it is hard to get his clothes over his head. When he cries I console him. "We are going to your mother," I say with authority and do not know if I am lying. He listens and stops crying. I have enough under-wear on to make it difficult to move.

There is a knock at the window in the front room. Soon, Gerold Anna néni, who lives farther up the street, comes in all bundled up. Her bad eye has the familiar look of regret and her presence gives some structure to the chaotic activity. She helps us get ready. She says that everyone is already at the Habag Haus, waiting for us. Apparently we were forgotten, overlooked. She tells us to take the downs. We are allowed to take two hundred kilos with us. The men may have told us this, but we did not hear it. How are we going to carry it anyway? While the two women are busy getting things together, I put our shoes and coats on, both a tight fit. The two men are standing about watching the proceeding as if they have no part in it. Ilija's ruddy face betrays smugness, and the appeasing smile, which he usually wears to make himself look shy, now gives the appearance of gloating. His attempt to open the pantry door, kicking and pushing on it, looks like a performance. The younger man observes quietly and seems more sincere. "Where could the keys be? They were always hanging there," my mother says, pointing to the nail at the door. But we have no time to keep looking for them; we have to leave. "Take the downs," Anna néni says again, and they are rolled and stuffed into a sack. Seppi, who is sitting on the bed restricted by his many clothes, unable to move, is getting wrapped into one of our large down pillows. All this preparation to leave took less time than anyone could have imagined, and our readiness is largely due to Gerold Anna néni's help. We close the door to our house behind us, leaving it unlocked. The key to the gate is removed from the inside and my mother locks the front gate. "Should we take the key with us?" my mother asks. I don't remember hearing an answer.

Although the men were in tetka Katica's yard to knock at our window, neither tetka Katica nor čika Milan, who must have let them into their yard, came over to our house. The street is empty and the houses are dark. We walk fast to keep ahead of the brisk pace of the men behind us. The snow is not deep but it covers the ground and makes crunching sounds under our feet. My mother carries Seppi and some bundles hang from her arms. I am carrying one of the sacks, dragging it through the snow. Anna néni, whose things are already at the Habag Haus, carries the rest. It is very cold. We move briskly, unencumbered despite our heavy load, the weight of the occasion striking a balance with the weight we carry. "I am going with my mother," I repeat to myself at intervals, and this thought gives me all the energy I need to drag and carry twice my weight. We walk on the empty street barely noticing the houses as we pass them. We are in a cold white heat—in a time funnel, unseeing and unnoticed, directed—in a hurry to get where they are waiting for us. The artesian well at the corner makes its familiar murmuring sounds and sends a delicate spray of steam into the cold night air. I notice a burning sensation between my legs. It feels like sand and burning nettles, alternately, and reminds me of the blisters I get on my heels from new shoes; the bulge of too many bloomers is chafing my thighs. I get a pain in my side from walking too fast and have to stop, for a moment, by the bench at the baker's house. The baker was taken away months ago—perhaps he is dead. I hurry to catch up. The dimly lit street corners reveal the stretch of empty streets. Not a dog is barking. Nothing but the rhythmic cadence of our steps accompanies us, all else disappears behind us.

The scene at the Habag Haus takes me by surprise. A new reality presents itself. The place appears like a small island surrounded by darkness. People are gathered around piled up bundles in separate little groups. Small fires peak with flickering shallow flames to reflect against dark huddles of bundled up people. Clumsy shadows fall on the snow in patches and look like things lost. Wrapped up against the cold, people are unrecognizable, their faces changed by the eerie light, the play of flickering flames. Some people huddle where the light barely reaches. Only men with guns stand around the fires, warming their hands. We find Grandfather and Grandmother among the people outside, but we have to go inside like everyone else before us. I will not leave my mother's side for a moment.

The people inside, mostly men, are carrying guns. Like those outside by the fire, I do not know them; they are Serbs, but they are not from our village. They ask my mother if she has any money and tell her to give it to them. "The keys to the house!" they demand. She left it open, she explains, but the key to the gate is here, and she gropes for it nervously in her coat pockets. They look severe and unfriendly, talking among themselves only. To us their faces are closed. Even when they shout at us about not being here earlier with the others, they do not invite any explanation. They shut us out. The way in which they do not acknowledge our presence feels as if they begrudge us our being here, if not our very existence. In their eyes there is no place that reflects us. It is easy to imagine that they would rip out their own eyes if we were reflected in them. It feels as if we should apologize to them for being here at all, but even that would be provoking. For soon it is clear that in their presence there is no possibility for our being. It is a strange experience, this witnessing of one's own absence; one's annihilation.

Outside, the eerie light spreads a defuse sepia tone over the crowd, making a unit of people and bundles against the bleak night sky. The men with guns hover around flames in the snow. The smoke, rising, hangs suspended against the frozen silence. The ominous stillness of extreme cold separates with luminous clarity from the muffled murmur of the crowd and leaves it isolated. The fear that kept us awake at night for so long is now no longer present. It has taken leave of us, without our knowing it, and we are taken in by our destiny, from which our fear tried to separate us. Now we belong to it. The sound of the crowd, in muffled murmurs, whispers the secret to the night. Shouts to horses and the casual talk and laughter of the men with guns get lost on the night air and are part of the everyday and the usual to which we no longer belong. The shawl wrapped around my neck and face is thickly caked with my frosted breath, and my feet are beginning to feel a familiar numbing. I continue stomping up and down, standing in place, to keep them moving, to get them warm. My hands are freezing in my mittens. The chafing between my legs continues to burn. I have to pee but I do not want to take off all those bloomers and expose myself to the bitter cold.

The people huddled around their bundles are starting to look like them, softly rounded and motionless. Gradually I recognize them, one by one, our relatives and all the others. Some are holding their small children bundled up in pillows and downs. Some move about restlessly, asking questions, and are ignored; no one focuses on their questions. No one knows the answers. Around the fires, the men with guns are readying for some task, taking drinks from a flask, which they pass around among themselves; I recognize the familiar scent of šljivovica, and something about the ritual and the smell of smoke on winter air reminds me of men getting ready for the disznótor, but the present image is incongruous with the rest of the memory. I feel as if we are already far away from the village, some place on a remote island where at any moment a step into the surrounding darkness could cause a fall off the edge of the world.

Uncovered wagons move into the sepia light of our island and line up in front of the Habag Haus. The horses nod their heads impatiently, snorting, puffing their warm breath into the crystal night air. We are told to load our bundles on the wagons, and an anxiety about keeping family members together moves like a shudder through the crowd. Some of the very old have a hard time climbing up on the wagons. People help each other. Under the hush of the harried crowd, the shouts of the men with guns hurrying us, passing signals to each other, the wagons are loaded, and in a short time we are settled among our bundles with our families and neighbors, some sitting and others kneeling or crouching. There are six grown-ups and two children in our wagon; beside our little family unit of five, Grandfather's brother Vedde Niklos, and his wife Päsl Leni, there is Päsl Susi, who has no family.

The wagons start moving slowly through the Kroßkass, the full length of our village: past the church, the school, and the municipal building. The solemn procession through the empty street in the silence of the clear cold night is ours alone. No one is there to take leave from us. Accompanied only by the sounds of the wagons, quietly turned into ourselves, we let the familiar facades pass before us. I know I will remember forever the image of this parting. The wide street echoes the finality, the imposing distance demanded by this parting. It is something large, important, terrible. Three people, standing together, pressed against the dimly lit facade across the street, watch motionless. A voice cries out a name from the moving wagons and a white handkerchief peels away from the collage across the street to become a dove flying toward us, as the wagons turn at the mill, away from the village, into the fields. My mother is using her handkerchief, softly blowing her nose; I know she is crying. I look up at the grown-ups; everyone in our wagon is quietly weeping. They glance at each other and weep. There are no words to this parting. It is sufficient unto itself and understood by everyone. The largeness of it lights their faces, and their own image grows larger with it. It seems as if they are standing up instead of sitting in the wagon; they look tall, enduring. There is no room in them for anything small; they have grown beyond themselves. Their tears are no longer about small things; they are not crying for things left behind, nor are they crying out of fear for their lives. We understand and are each other's witnesses. It is a moment of grace. We know that the life of our people is ending with this parting, and we are its worthy mourners. The spirit of our people is reflected in us and out of the abundance of our love for our home we lift an image of our sorrow high above small things into the clarity beyond the night sky. I listen to the sound of the wagon wheels grinding the powdered snow into the frozen ground. I look down at the tracery of our passage unwinding silver ribbons onto the earth below; a gesture of our passing etches its full heaviness into the ground we love, and the earth reciprocates and unites with us in this moment of grace, in trailing lines of silver ribbons that follow us across the snow.

CHAPTER 6

A World of Countless Separations

THE WAGONS MOVE into the darkness. With no destination and no place to return to, distance becomes a meaningless measure. Time is passing, but we remain in the present now. The sound of moving wagons, breaking the darkness with consoling familiarity, informs that we are. We breathe; we are aware of the vast distance from breath to breath. In the numbing cold, the warmth we give each other lulls to comfort, almost. With their backs toward us, the drivers, men with guns, are cut off from us. They belong to time and space, and we are in the present, among ourselves, alone.

Noises ahead, crisp shouts coalescing with those closer converge and our wagon stops moving. Our curiosity becomes panic when we recognize that there is nothing but darkness to which we have come. "Out!" they shout, meaning us to get off the wagons. *"Hajde, hajde,"* they urge us to hurry. We dismount, and the terror of the new beginning is close at hand. We recognize it in each other's voices. We ask, "Where are we?" We grope for each other, and the familiar voices around us and those in the dark beyond are similarly tinged with the shared terror. What there is left of thinking, we say to each other in questions: "Is everyone here? Do you have Seppi? Do we have all our sacks? The children? Why are we getting down in the middle of nowhere?" We don't expect answers. We keep asking to give our presence some meaning, to give account of our existence. A solitary lament escapes here and there and finds an echo in the crowd ahead. It is a relatively quiet crowd. Its subdued voices carry the terror inward. Only small children are crying out aloud. Some of the very old need help with their belongings; Hansi, the invalid, is being carried. We move in the direction driven, groping past empty wagons and snorting horses, colliding with the slow moving, moving them on, and leaving some behind. Suddenly, a wall appears before us with a gaping wide open mouth. It swallows the people in front of us and we, too, are herded inside.

My eyes accustom to the dark enclosure. People stand in groups facing the enormous door. Grandfather says this is the sheep stall near Čoka; the whispers are spreading among the crowd. The sound of our presence is absorbed by mounds of straw; in one of the corners the straw reaches halfway up the wall of the stable. We wait. The last of the people appear, and the guards block the doorway, talking among themselves, deciding the next move. The infant cry of my cousin Anna is our only voice. They order us away from the center of the stall, and we move farther into the dark interior. Some guards lift their lanterns high above them, and some of us climb the shallow incline of straw, up to its highest part, and lay our bundles down. The five of us are the new unit.

The guards are clearing the center of the stable; they are building a fire. From where I sit, I can see them through the haze of smoke spreading. They shout and laugh and drink from their flasks. Sometimes, when I think I'm getting warmer just looking at the fire, smelling it burn, a cold draft of air from the open door reaches me and makes me shiver down to my frozen toes. I still have to pee. I see the old men stand close to the wall, with their backs toward us, and my grandfather takes me to the farthest, the highest corner of the straw, and with his back toward me, giving me cover, asks me to squat down and pee into the corner. Päsl Liss, sitting in a group downstraw, sees me pulling up my pants and scolds us. The guards seem totally oblivious to our presence; only when any of us goes near the door do they shoo us away. Without looking at us, they shout and point: "Inside!"

No one tells us anything. We watch and wait. No one sleeps. Only when the opened door surprises with a patch of light do we realize it is day. We eat food from our sacks. Grandfather has brought some sausages; he cuts pieces with his *Schnappmesser* (a large switchblade knife) and we eat it with our bread. No one has thought of bringing water.

Later they let us go outside, in groups of twenty at a time. Outside the stable, the assorted crowd, old and young, men, women, and children, expose themselves, squatting, staining the snow, as guards stand by, watching. Robert and his brother Hansi, both a bit older than I, ogle me as I, giving in to my mother's urging, pull down my bloomers and expose my bare bottom.

Somehow my mother has a way of keeping her composure and pride while doing the same. Seeing her gives me the momentary assurance to bear my shame as I squat, with my knees together, hiding the yellow stain. The chafed skin between my legs stings and burns, but the worst is having to stand exposed to the crowd pulling up all those bloomers. The guards are laughing, pointing to Vedde Franz, who—old and rotund, having a hard time trying to get up from a squatting position—exposes a very large pile behind him. Remote, distanced, the guards slide their eyes across the squatting crowd as if observing their herd. Reflected in their vision, we are reduced and returned to the stable as if we had always belonged there. Some people grab handfuls of snow to eat, to quench their thirst. The guards shout disapproval.

The light falls into the night of the stable, and our days are measured by the swing of the massive door. It seems we see the light of many days. Perhaps it is only one. We are waiting, but boredom is not even a recollection. Our existence inhabits us. We tremble in its presence.

They call us down from our perches, away from our bundles. They tell us to line up in front of the door. They hurry us. We try to stay close together, to stand next to our family members, our every movement informed by rumors we have heard about the plight of others, while we were still at home. The hiss of whispers gives way to warnings: "Don't say you are sick or too old to work," people advise, reminding each other that the old and sick of Sanad, promised the return home, were instead shot into a common grave. The sick and old among us take the whispers with them through the uncoiling crowd as it moves into a single line facing the door. A group of newly arrived men with guns rake the line; they do not look at us. They want our names, our year of birth. Some of our names are not to their liking. They torment us with questions, mostly the old men, and curse, shouting abuse of our God: "*Jebem vam Boga švapskog!*" Using the vernacular blasphemy, they are fucking our god! We stand in line, trying to look inconspicuous, to do and be nothing at all, to have no traces of expectation and no visible signs of our terror showing in our faces. We are alert; aware that any utterance or gesture may provoke our inquisitors. Without words, this wisdom is assimilated by the waiting crowd.

Before they let us go back to our bundles, they call out the names of those required for a job outside. This scant information stretches into an opportunity to believe. The crowd listens, and the call of names is answered by isolated cries of small children. My mother's name is among those called. I tremble, and she, closed into her own misgivings, has no time to give me reassurance. The bustle of the dividing crowd adds the solace of impartiality. My mother is leaving with others called. I am forced to accept the terror on my own.

I wait among the others, sitting by our bundles, my eyes fixed to the far corner of the stable. I think of my mother working outside and, to prevent her from freezing, I imagine a cellar below this stable where she now works. Peering into the darkness, I think I see an archway through which I expect her to return. Seppi is sitting, bundled; he moves hardly at all. He has discovered the children sitting like him among the bundles close to us. They gaze at each other, wide-eyed, with mute acceptance. My grandparents are preoccupied, talking in whispers: Grandfather is upset; the attention he receives from one of our captors causes him to worry. Their whispers drift dangerously about, mingling with those of others around us, and Grandfather's secret fear that he will be singled out, made an example of when the guards need amusement, hides in the hissing sounds, reaching for anonymity.

Softly, like a prayer of thanks, the hush of the crowd greets the returning women and makes a unit of us again. I run to my mother. She holds me. I don't hear the sound of the crowd when it changes to loud anxious talk, opposing noises shooing to quiet. I see the incredulous empty eyes watching. I hear the anguished cries of children. I cease to make sense of the sound of words and watch the pantomime of moving mouths, and my senses, left to themselves, mutely reflect the isolated images around me. My mother is reaching into the sacks, looking for something . . . she is taking her clothes. Seppi is crying his grown-up cry. My grandparents are weeping. I don't know if the sounds I am making are my own.

My mother's face, pale, marble-like, her expression set in stone, shows only endurance. Gathered up, flung in the face of adversity, she shines like a flashing sword. She has no time for the vanity of words; everything she says is directly said with her body. Our parting gestures, alive with our feelings for each other, remain wordless, whole, large, terrible.

I walk with my mother down the incline. I refuse to believe that I cannot go with her. I stand before the large door. It opens, and the crowd of women in front of it disappears into the dark. I stand below and see the gaping door fall shut as if from above: a blow—a heavy steel blade fells me with its fall, sealing the doorway, separating me from my mother. Its sound drowns out all others; in it my screaming mouth is rendered soundless. I stand, mute, motionless under its weight. It swallows the space around me . . .

A huge pain fills me. I don't know where I end and it begins. I grope to understand this pain, to make it my own. Repeatedly I recall the savage blow to measure its vastness, to find my way through its desolate landscape. I roam the stable. I approach my relatives and others: "They took my mother away." I say it like an admission. Shamed, I stand before them giving account of my broken state. I search their faces. But no one follows my words to the place of pain. Unable to lead them there, I shrug. I hide my disappointment. I feel alone.

And who could console me in that desolate landscape? Still, I search the preoccupied faces, looking. Sometimes, as if by chance, a look, a cry, a gesture takes me in and I recognize the familiar view, and the place of pain becomes more inhabited and I feel I am among my own.

I discover that I can walk along the periphery of the crowd from one end of the stable to the other. I see the people in various groupings. Most sit motionless, staring. I see the other children. Some are moving about, too. Some venture close to the fire, almost, and are shooed away.

Explored, the stable becomes a new entity—larger, more complex. The memory of the imagined door leading to a basement persists, making the doorless corner into a place of magic. But the stable retains its sinister darkness, affirming the desolation from all sides. Everywhere is the absent look of grown-ups, and the pained, preoccupied look of the very old struggling with discomfort. And everywhere the open faces of children offer their vast wisdom like unexplored planets. Sometimes I see incredible images; some leave me breathless. I recognize—coiled up on himself lying in the straw, shivering with jerking motions, looking almost at home on the floor of the stable, Hansi, the Gerolds' thirty-three-year-old son, who, stricken by an illness when he was a baby, cannot walk or talk. At home, sitting in front of his house in summer, dressed in a long white shirt, his platinum hair and clear blue eyes shining, his smile ethereal, looking as if breezes moved him about, he was the image of light. Now, with his face to the ground, his breathing labored like that of an animal about to give birth, his presence weighty and purposeful, he glows with darkness. His eyes are wide open, and I feel I should kneel before the landscape they reveal. I am almost afraid to touch him—afraid the slightest touch could hurt. I make a motion, barely moving my hand as if to wave and whisper softly his name. His lips quiver, and I imagine the smile that would shatter his face.

While I explore the dark periphery of the stable, Grandfather has another bout with his anxiety. The most recent occasion of humiliation, as guards make some of the men gather the piles of frozen excrement in front of the stable, provides another opportunity for harassment. Grandfather is sitting in the straw; his face, ashen, has taken on a faraway look. My grandmother is uncorking the bottle of šljivovica. I can't be sure of what I am seeing; she is pouring some down Grandfather's chest. The women around us hover over him, obscuring him from view, while Grandmother is reaching under her skirts, tearing one of her petticoats into span-wide ribbons. The small gathering around Grandfather, following orders from Päsl Nancsi, cooperates, and some turn away to divert the attention of curious others. The hushed whispers cancel each other. After a very short time Grandfather emerges unshielded and as if nothing has happened. I see Grandmother stuffing something lumpy into one of our sacks. The participants settle, reminded by Päsl Nancsi that "no one must know." I restrain my curiosity, and later accept Grandmother's assertion: Nothing happened!

At times the guards are restless. They drink and shoot their guns into the air, aiming toward the rafters. They laugh. They peer into the dark of the stable to remind us they know where we are. We look down into the straw so that our open eyes will not provide a target for their amusement. I hear the almost inaudible moaning of Grandfather lying next to me. I put my hand lightly on his arm to console him and to let him know I am here. Some guards leave, others come, and their coming and going has the power to change the atmosphere of the stable. Some tell jokes—I can tell by their laughter. Sometimes they sing loud, bawdy songs, the words getting lost before their meaning reaches us, and the melody, up here, has the sullen sound of a mute contradiction. One of the guards has a guitar. From here on the straw, in our world, it seems out of place, but not there by the fire in theirs. Though we fill the intimate space of one stable, in the vast dividing chasm between us even objects, confused about their identity, would hold their breath in shame.

I can't sleep. It may be morning, or is it afternoon? I have not been watching the door. Since my mother left, I have only been outside once. I hope the guard at the door lets me go out, to pee. I see others moving about in the haze and I make my way down toward the door. By the fire, someone is playing the guitar, softly. The guards are sitting on wooden crates or bundles of straw—I notice their elevated position, and in my imagination they seem fenced off from us, cordoned off, perhaps by a steel rope. They sit and stand around the fire and a few of them sing. The plaintive sounds of an unfamiliar love song cause me to linger. I get very close. I think they notice my presence, but they let me stay to listen. With reciprocal civility, I hear myself saying: "I, too, know a sad song." My voice surprises them, I realize, startled. Caught unaware, they look at me. The voice of a child, my voice, speaking their language with impeccable accent, is out of place here. They look at each other. I wait, frightened. I search their faces. A pinched-faced guard with a preoccupied look and a macabre gilded scowl frightens me most—perhaps he is the one who torments Grandfather. The guard with the large hat motions with quick-gesturing hands: "Come here!" he says, and it seems to me that I have to climb over some physical barrier to get there. I stand before the man with the large hat. "Now," he says, "let's hear what you know. Sing!"

My voice is shaky at first, but as I go on, it gets louder and less breathy. I pay attention to my voice and to the words I sing, and I take no notice of the guards and where I am. It is a long song—I learned it listening to the voice of tetka Katica's guest and the sound of my father's accordion. The song is about a child who laments the loss of her mother. Only when I finish singing do I realize that the guards are quiet. The guard with the hat smiles and says, sounding familiar, "It is true, you do know how to sing!" He lifts me on his lap and, it seems, I am at home in the village again; without reminding me of anyone, he looks familiar, and I am briefly reunited with my former self. Before I leave, they give me money, and I am asked to sing my song again. I sing with a voice informed, looking at their faces.

I scramble up the straw with my heart pounding. I nudge my grandmother to give her the money. "I sang for them," I say to explain. She looks disbelieving, but I can tell she is pleased about the money. She shows it to Grandfather. He seems distant, tired, and I imagine him smiling as I watch Grandmother tuck the money in her bosom. Only when I am lying down again do I remember—I have to pee.

When they want me to sing for them, the guards ask for me. "The-little-girl-that-sings" is the name they give me and, for a very short time, Grandmother's increasing bosom fills her with the confidence to allay Grandfather's apprehensions.

The world of the stable comes to an abrupt end. It is hard to believe that it lasted only three days and nights. They tell us to gather our bundles and wait in front of the door. Päsl Nancsi and her grandchildren, Herta and Hansi (she is less then two and he is almost seven), are now part of our group. Vedde Niklos and Päsl Leni rejoin us.

I am alarmed, beside myself. I have the notion that by leaving this place I am leaving the proximity of my mother. If she is alive, I know she will come here to look for me. Away from this place, I lose her forever. My distress is grave, but no one notices me. The misery of the crowd swallows all individual hardship.

We are on the wagon moving slowly away from the stable. "No . . . no . . . I will not leave!" I shriek and flail and see myself running across the frozen plain, running back to find my mother, but I know I am sitting on the wagon, crying. I cry so loud my throat is beginning to hurt. My continuous crying annoys everyone on the wagon, and Grandfather tells the disgruntled drivers (men with guns) that I am crying for my mother, while he tries to quiet me. For a short time I am quiet, watching the road roll out from under our wagon toward the next. I watch the horses behind us parting the air with their steamy breath. I listen to the creaking wagon. The world around us is frozen-still. And, suddenly, my cry falls into the icy air and shatters like broken glass. Except for short intervals, my crying cannot be stopped. Without a house or a hut to hear it, with only the isolated acacia trees giving it direction, my crying roams the prairie, searching for my mother. I listen to the clatter of wagons hacking it into pieces and lose track of it, momentarily, in the heave of my sobbing, and when exhaustion prompts me to forget, it still pours forth in loud lamenting wails that fade into soft weeping and revive again. My chest hurts from sobbing, and my trailing cries want to lull me to sleep. I long to rest; but when I stop crying, I lose the only access to my mother left to me. I try to cry quietly, out of consideration for the others, but lament is impartial and demands its own velocity. In this private world of feeling, intrusions from outside, consoling and scolding, reason and threat, are only static, disturbing noises that separate me from my mother. A guard appears on horseback. Crisp orders that sound like accusations are shouted into our wagon. "The child is crying for her mother," the driver shouts back to answer, and Grandfather repeats it to the guard, carefully, so it may not be misunderstood as an assertion in our defense. My grandfather is charged with keeping me quiet. "The crying is spooking some horses up front," the guard informs the driver and leaves. I bury my face in the bundle next to me to muffle the sound of my weeping and continue it. Exhaustion gives way to delirium and my crying becomes an intercession, an offering to God, bargaining for the return of my mother. As such, it cannot be abandoned.

It is still dark when we arrive. We are in a house, in a long room with straw on the floor. All of us in this room are lying down next to each other, in two long rows, along the walls. Not all of us are here—where are the others? Are there other rooms like this one? Why were we brought to this place? These are questions people ask each other, but they don't expect answers. The guards pass the open door to our room frequently and their bawdy chatting and laughter from somewhere in the remote interior is a presence among us.

I can't sleep; I have a toothache. Grandmother is convinced it is the ef-fect of my long crying; I still sob involuntarily. "The cold air can aggravate a sensitive tooth," she says, but it does not sound as if she is scolding, think-ing I brought it on myself; the way she says it, it sounds more like a regret. Grandfather gives me the bottle of šljivovica; he tells me to take a sip and hold it toward the direction of the tooth that hurts, without swallowing. It will numb the pain, he promises. I hold the fragrant brew till its burning sting stuns the pain, and, long after the liquid in my mouth becomes tepid, I swallow. Shielding my face with the downs to keep away the draft coming from the door, I try to sleep.

This room is only a place of transition. The next day, they come for us with the same information: Time to go. "Hajde; hajde." The familiar anxiety moves through the room as we hurriedly gather our belongings and those who gather around us, fearing separation. We are surprised this time; there are no wagons waiting.

Herded into a village street, we walk along rows of abandoned houses. We and our bundles are to be their new inhabitants, we assess, as those in front of us are being housed. We occupy an empty room. The floor is covered with straw. The guards leave it to us to mark out our own territory in it. There is another room in this house. The owners, Germans, live in it with their kin. We wonder if they have any furniture in their room. Päsl Leni says she saw a bed through the opening door. The people there seldom speak to us. They resent the intrusion into their house and, holding onto the notion of ownership, jealously guard the few possessions left them. They tolerate us because they must; they do not blame us.

Although there are no guards in the immediate vicinity of house and yard, their presence is always expected. We are told to keep to our rooms and leave our assigned housing only for purposes determined by them.

Eleven people inhabit our small room: a family in each corner. This division would go unnoticed in a room filled with straw where it not for Päsl Nancsi's insistence on a strawless path from the door through the middle of the room, with everyone keeping to their own corner, "to preserve a semblance of order," she says. The room is unheated; we continue to sleep in our clothes. We eat food from our sacks and learn to drink the metallic-tasting water from the well in the yard; some insist on melted snow.

At first we are relieved, grateful for the comfort of the new housing; it gives rise to new hopes. Some say we are being resettled. Some disagree; they think we will soon go home. No one knows. We only know our desires. No one tells us anything. When we remove the layers of clothing and fold them into our sacks, we show that we expect to stay. I wear only one pair of bloomers at a time, now. The chafing between my legs has gotten infected and I have nasty looking black blood-blisters that startle and worry me enough to tell my grandmother. Unlike my mother, who would have wanted to have a look, she doesn't ask to see. When Grandfather removes his shirt to change it, I see the white bands of petticoat-ribbons wound, crossing his chest. I ask about them, but there is no answer. When the guards come to get Grandfather, we worry all day, but he comes back in the evening, and like some of the others, he is taken to work every day. Sometimes Grandfather gets bread at work and saves it to bring to us. But mostly he brings his anxiety, looking solemn, brooding.

All day the cold and the imposed confinement keep us in our rooms, with short runs to the outhouse. Messages from our kin come to us during the day only when a look to the street reveals no one in sight and someone dares to dart across the space from one house to another. In the evening, people who see each other at work bring news of the others. At night we feel more exposed to hidden danger and never venture out of our houses.

In a very short time, our room is a house divided. The quest for external order is disrupted by internal strife. Subtle insinuations follow as food disappears from sacks that are attended all day. Accusations are tossed about. Goodwill among us is fragile, and passive animosity becomes open aggression. My uncombed-for-days hair, my felted braids, are noticed and receive a vigorous brushing and rebraiding from Päsl Nancsi, because Grandmother's crippled fingers and my unskilled hands, at nine, cannot manage. Later the state of my hair earns accusations of neglect. The noise of the children irritates the tired and disgruntled. Seppi runs around, distributing the straw to where it should not be. Hansi leaves the room to run about in the yard too frequently, bringing the cold inside, according to Vedde Niklos. Others suggest that I should be more helpful to my grandmother without having to be told what to do. Grandfather is accused of self-absorption, neglecting the needed discipline that would keep the unruly Seppi sitting quietly. And, while others snore within appropriate volume, Grandfather's snoring is deemed too loud. Grandfather does not take well to criticism. Päsl Nancsi, concerned about keeping order, gets into an argument with him, and the secret under the bind of white petticoat-ribbons around Grandfather's chest is carelessly exposed by a surge of angry words. Päsl Nancsi accuses Grandfather of faking suicide. Plunging the switchblade knife into his chest—getting it stuck in his breast bone, deliberately missing his heart—was according to her just a quest for attention. Later they don't talk to each other, which has only one advantage: she no longer offers to comb my hair. Grandmother is forever the peacemaker; her voice carries the kindness of consoling smiles. Good-natured and tolerant, she never participates in any arguments and never raises her voice. She spends her energy in condoling whisperings to Grandfather at night, but during the day her tired smiles betray a worried preoccupation.

While some in our room are only irritable, Grandfather is irritable and depressed. When he comes home in the evenings, I deliberately play with Seppi to keep him from running about irritating others and causing Grandfather to lose his temper. I get very tired guarding against a potential domestic disturbance, but my anxiety about it makes the divisive distractions seem necessary. I play with Seppi—I laugh and tell stories in a whispering voice, and I giggle and tickle in moderation. I watch Grandfather's face, measure the mood of the room, and play my deceptive diversions to them.

At night our room is pitch dark. There is no electricity. The various breathy rhythms of all of us sleeping are punctuated by snoring from the four corners of the room. Vedde Niklos's loud gasps for air between sequenced snorting and blowing, completed by a flutter of Päsl Leni's appropriately spaced *put-puts*, sound like the workings of a steam engine. Each corner adds to the sound melange. Even Päsl Nancsi, though she would deny it, snores a regiment of well-spaced vibrations that traverse the room in an orderly fashion. When Grandfather snores loudest, I give his shoulder a soft push and he sleeps on soundlessly. I wonder if others, too, have trouble sleeping. Sometimes I hear murmured words and strain to hear Grandmother's voice protesting something. A paralyzing quiet grips me: I can't be sure, but I think I hear the words *rope* and *hanging*. Grandfather wants to make an end to his misery. Grandmother's pleas not to harm himself sound like a threat to his intent. When he leaves the room, she follows. I shiver and wait.

Every night I place my arm on Grandfather's shoulder while he sleeps, his back toward me. I sleep, but when he moves, I wake, listening; I notice his every move. I follow him outside on frostbitten toes. I squat and wait as he relieves himself. I look to the stars, longing to sleep.

The guards come and go. They appear any time—day or night—to inspect, to count, to give orders, or for no reason apparent to us. During one of these inspections, someone in our room dares to mention food: "We have no bread for the children." One of the women guards answers as if to acknowledge an oversight: "Bread!" she shouts in compliance, and, turning to the guards behind her, adds sarcastically, "Why not also give them milk and honey!" They laugh among themselves. Days after, we are suspicious when they announce that all children under six will get a cup of milk daily.

A container I did not know we had goes with me to the milk line. I see Tanti Lisa and my Kodl Lisa among others from our village. Some I do not know; I surmise they are the Germans from Crna Bara. Ladles of milk from a tall container are poured into the various containers held as the women watch, jealously guarding every drop that it may not spill or be left in the passing ladle. A German woman, not from our village, is doing the ladling, and a guard checks each portion received against a paper list. In the far corner of the room, a group of guards are talking among themselves. Some look familiar. When it is my turn, the guard tells the lady something and she measures out two portions of milk into my container. The women behind me protest. "There is only one child in their family eligible for milk," I hear one of my relatives saying. "She is too old to get milk. There are others who are younger, who need it more . . ." The murmuring crowd seems to agree. I am confused. I repeat my age as proof for their assertion, as my defense. I say: "I did not come to get milk for myself." The man who caused the commotion hushes the crowd. I notice that he, unlike the others, is looking at us while he speaks. The tone is crisp and the information clear: "It is by my authority that this milk is given. If it causes problems, the right to milk, for anyone, can easily be taken away." The line behind me is hushed. Only the guards in the far corner continue their conversation uninterrupted. My shame turns into guilt. I am unable to move, to reach for the container, to grasp it, to carry it past the crowd. I stare bewildered before me. A big hat emerges out of the gather of guards and the man approaching notices me: "The-little-girl-that-sings," he says, and in the brief exchange between us, I regain my mobility. I reach for the container with the milk, looking at the man who gave it. I say nothing, and I can tell by the way he looks at me that nothing is the right thing to say. The man in the large hat commends my singing, and the guard at the table adds, affirming, "And her crying has the power to spook horses!" I am surprised and become shy and ill at ease. I am asked to come back tomorrow and stay to sing.

Grandmother, glad for the additional milk, scolds me into going for it the next day, and so it is that I get to know the man called Teza, who is the Komandant here. Memories of the place where I go to get milk are overshadowed by this fragile acquaintance. Images revive and are obscured in his name. I am there—singing, accompanied by a guitar, in conversation, feeling admonished, my chin quivering—when he tells me, away from the others, "You don't have to sing each time they ask you." I only later understand the support intended. I learn to trust the man I call čika Teza. And one day he surprises me with news: My mother works in a place called Jato, near Čoka. He will take me to see her, he says, and I am beside myself with joy. Grandfather says not to count on it. But I do.

Nightly, with my hand lightly on Grandfather's arm, I imagine being on my way to see my mother. I am all wrapped up in a fleece-lined coat and čika Teza is wearing one of Mulić's brightly embroidered shepherd's coats that reaches over his boots down to the ground. We ride on a sled pulled by beautiful horses. We glide over the frozen plain accompanied by the music of belled harnesses. We ride through the mysterious dark woods with howling wolves lurking close by. But our good fortune, our guardian angels, perhaps even the hand of God, and the clever driving skill of čika Teza save us from disaster. We ride through all obstacles and, at the end of our journey, my mother is waiting. The bliss of our reunion keeps me smiling through the countless variations of journeys over frozen landscapes, and when Grandfather's loud snoring interrupts occasionally, I squeeze his arm, ever so gently, and continue on my way. During the day, I can hardly contain my anticipation. Grandmother warns against too much joy; it often invites disappointment and the jealousy of others. Others don't know about this, I think, but, trying to be modest, I limit the variations of voyages to my mother the following night.

I wait, dressed in my coat, and watch the windows frame the falling snow. As the gray light dims, my spirits sink. A brisk wind is howling around the house and the cold from outside is seeping through the walls. Now the room is dark, and everyone is lying down for the night. Herta has a nasty cough. Earlier today, Vedde Niklos produced a spoonful of honey from a lidded tin, without removing it from his food sack, making its appearance seem all the more magical. Its amber glow conjured up memories of bee-hives in a summer garden, eating honey from a honeycomb, as we watched Herta swallow. Now Herta is comforted by the sounds of her grandmother's voice, cooing her to sleep. The rest of us are quiet. The all-day wait, believing čika Teza would come, is now given up to disappointment—all day I kept my coat on, waiting, telling others, out of pride, I am wearing it because I am cold. Grandfather's consoling explanation that it is too danger-ous for anyone to go out in these blizzard-like conditions only intensified my expectations. Now I cultivate my disappointment in the dark.

Suddenly, the sound of footsteps; boots stomping in the entry; a flash of light at the door. The feelings of mistrust dispelled, I sit up. Čika Teza's presence deepens the silence in our room. He stoops to whisper, so that only I can hear, and I listen as my disappointment grows to gather up the image of a frozen sea. He tells me that he is on his way to Čoka. He will go to see my mother, but he cannot take me with him. I know my eyes cannot conceal what I feel, but I cover my quivering chin. He asks me what he should say to my mother. I cannot make words and try to smile behind my concealing hand. He says the words for me and I nod. Tears fall down my cheeks without a sound from me. His whispering voice is firm, gentle; I listen to its soothing breath to keep the pain in my chest from smothering me. When he is gone, I weep quietly into the downs. I follow the mournful howling of the wind into the storm outside, and with closed eyes, I see the bright floral garlands of a fleece-lined shepherd's coat fading in the blowing snow.

Sweet messages from my mother! And a secret I must promise to keep: my mother, as well as the other women, will soon be reunited with us. I give my promise, in good faith, but my excitement is checked. I try to appear glad, so as not to seem ungrateful, so as not to betray my doubt.

Orders to ready for departure surprise us; it is February 14, 1944. With our belongings bundled, we wait in our room. We talk only sparingly. Some-one mentions those left behind: five people from our village have died in Crna Bara, among them Vedde Fritz, my father's uncle. Only those who were unable to dig a hole in the frozen ground to dispose of the dead, know their common grave. It remains a secret whispered. We listen—the rumble of slow-moving wagons is our cue to go outside. We see the wagons coming down the street, and suddenly the crowd of people in front of the houses becomes unruly. Some run toward the approaching wagons. There are people on the wagons, waving. Some jump down to meet those running. My heart is pounding. I know the women are back. My mother is on one of those wagons. My joy leaps toward the miracle that is about to happen; I cannot hold it. I float in it. I see my mother . . .

• • •

Together in the moving wagon, we sometimes weep out of gratitude. I don't mind the cold. I look at my mother's face, reassured, unable to hide my pleasure, and trying not to provoke envy, I look away. The flat, frozen plain, white as far as the eye can see, is still. Impartial. The sky, opaque like milk-glass, breaks into occasional flurries. The convoy of wagons is longer now; the Germans from Crna Bara are with us. Sometimes the wagons stop for a short time. Čika Teza comes to our wagon and offers me a drink from his flask. He is on horseback and has to lean into the wagon to hand it down to me. I feel awkward, shy, exalted. "Coffee—only for big girls," he says, as if to excuse that he does not offer it to Seppi. I take it and drink a sip, and he nudges me to take more. I barely taste its milky sweetness, I am so over-whelmed by the offering. I notice how handsome he looks on his horse.

It is night when our wagons reach the edge of a larger village. Lights at street corners and houses lit from within make us know we have come a very long way. We are close to the Romanian border, Grandfather says; the village might be Sellesch, a predominantly German village. Later we hear the guards call it by its other name: Nakovo.

We occupy the empty strawless rooms of a large building. We sit on our bundles; some sleep. Guards are milling about through the night. In the morning we are lined up, waiting. Whispers are passed on that we are being housed with the Germans in the village. We have relatives in this village. Anna, the younger daughter of my father's cousin, married to a Hungarian, comes to claim us. My mother, Seppi, and I are to live with her family; my grandparents are assigned to the widow Hubert, of Nakovo.

I see čika Teza again. He motions me aside from the waiting crowd. He is going back home, he says, and wants to say good-bye. A nod to my mother and I walk with him around the building. He seems taller to me now and is looking very thin. His dark hair is uncovered—he carries his fur cap and his gloves under his arm. The long knitted scarf around his neck hangs down to reach the hem of his coat. There is something serious in his dark eyes, weighing down the look they give, but his voice has the familiar weighty kindness. He says, quietly, "I am not the Komandant here, but I have friends among the men who came with us. They will be staying. I have told them to look out for you." I feel the familiar anxiety and my disappointment grows as I watch him mount his horse. "Will you be coming back some day?" I ask slowly, but my voice gets weepy and I cover my mouth. He shakes his head. No. "Perhaps, some day," he says, but it does not sound like a promise. I see him riding over the frozen plain and it becomes a wide dividing river between us whose treacherous surface has to be crossed before the thaw. I see him turn around, standing still over the frozen deep. He waves. I hold my hand high above my head to wave back and keep it raised long after the image of a horse and rider, enveloped by the milky light, pales against the enormous stretch of winter sky.

● ● ●

Elli's house is warm. She has toys and friends who come to play with her. She speaks Hungarian. Elli is my age. Her grandmother and her aunt, Maris, also live in Elli's house. They and Elli's mother speak German with us. Elli's father is shy and hardly ever speaks.

Living in the elevated world of furniture feels awkward, embarrassing. Having once left behind beds, tables and chairs, dressers and drawers, their very presence is a reproach. I move cautiously around furniture, out of respect. But sometimes a room full of furniture can provoke a quiet rage— one feels slighted by the preferential treatment it receives, being sheltered and cared for. Its privileged presence intimidates, and I walk around each chair, grudgingly, aware of its superiority. Resentful and proud, I dare to think I prefer empty rooms with a place on the straw.

Our relatives are soft-spoken, modest, and very kind. They share their house with us, and we whisper our experiences to them, sitting around the table at dusk. My mother talks about the time away from us, when she worked in Čoka; how, by coincidence, out of a room full of bed linen being cut into garments, her sister Leni's pillowcases—the ones embroidered and monogrammed by my grandparents while they were in America—fell into her hands, and how cutting into them brought home the painful realization that we would never go home again. Elli's mother speaks consolingly, protesting the notion. "Some nights the Partisans would wake us, order us to line up before them. They would take aim at us, randomly, and then shoot to the ceiling instead. Some women would faint. They would continue this ghastly game and, as if they were giving us back our lives, they would send us to our places. Such jokes where repeated with variations," and she adds how Esti néni, a woman from our village, when ordered to line up, kept sitting in the straw, smoothing the downs over her lap, as if she had to calm them, and with all the time left in the world, would placidly say, in Hungarian, "*Hát . . . ez . . . mégis . . . csak . . . borzasztó!*" My mother mimics Esti néni's quiet exasperation, in voice and gesture: "Well . . . this is . . . really . . . just . . . terrible," making us laugh. "In the stable next to us, were six captured Hungarian soldiers, *honvedék*. Nightly their screams would keep us awake. In the morning we would see them escorted to work, beaten, some hardly able to walk, and at night—the worst were the nights—we would listen to their screams again. Till, one night, disturbing no one's sleep, the cries ceased . . ." Elli's father does not like to hear such talk. "The walls have ears," he fears. We understand. My mother now entertains them, reading their fortunes, laying cards (the way tetka Katica taught her), counting in Serbian: "*deset, jedanaest, dvanaest, trinaest* (ten, eleven, twelve, thirteen)."

Our people work in the fields, some tend the animals, others cook in the soup kitchen. My mother works in the kitchen with Esti néni, preparing the food the Partisans eat, but like everyone else, she gets food from the soup kitchen. We are told to use the streets only to go to work and to fetch our rations. Once a day I go for our rations; I carry our soup in a lidded can. Potato, pea, carrot, and cabbage soups are alternate fare, and I hear some complain when we get the same soup twice in a row. Others complain that the people they live with begrudge them space in their houses and even accuse them of bringing trouble their way. But the local Germans had trouble before we came. Their young women were taken away. Some of their men were shot in the village, others taken to Kikinda, where, "naked and bound with barbed wire, they were slain like pigs, shoved into a ditch, covered up together—the wounded with the dead." I hear this whispered by Elli's grandmother across the darkened room, late one night, when I pretend to be asleep. Elli's grandmother lived in Kikinda at the time. As the widow of a Hungarian man she was free, considered Hungarian.

We are guests at Elli's house. I try not to get used to the new feeling of safety; I am aware this feeling could disappear overnight.

I awake to piercing screams from within the room. Thrashing and thumping—sounds of a struggle—terrifying noises in the dark. Against the dim light framed by the kitchen door, I see Elli's grandmother wrestle with someone on the floor. The bed across the room is empty. Elli's mother and mine are standing over the contorted figure on the floor. It is Maris! Foam is coming from her mouth through the slit where a wooden spoon is wedged between her teeth. Terror is everywhere. It cannot be avoided.

In her quiet way, Elli makes me feel she would like it better if I were not living at her house. I hear her talking with her friend one day; at first they whisper it among themselves, but later they say it loud enough so I should hear—that we will soon be taken away. Perhaps it is their wishful thinking, and only said to tease me.

They take my grandfather away, and Grandfather Korek. Ten old men from our village and sixty from Nakovo are taken at night (March 14, 1944) and disappear. We grieve. We hope. We say: They have taken them somewhere else to work. Two weeks later, guards come to Elli's house. I see Elli's eyes reflecting terror. She did not mean it—she does not really want me to be taken away—I know. She watches, stunned, as we leave their house escorted by guards with guns.

I see the familiar scene of people and bundles littering the space in front of the municipal building. This time it is daylight. There are many of us. People from the surrounding villages and the entire German population of Nakovo are among us with their bundles. We find Grandmother in the crowd. We wait. We are counted off and herded into the building in small groups. We are afraid that the count may stop before all of our family members are included in the group going inside. We huddle closer. We see the people in front of us being separated, protesting in vain. Even though all enter by the same door, going through that door together with our family is important to us. We don't know what is waiting for us inside. The building swallows the crowd before us; those who enter don't come out.

Relieved by the count that keeps us together, we find ourselves in a rectangular room. I recognize some of the guards standing about—the one with the golden teeth and others from the sheep stall and Crna Bara. Some are women; some I do not know. The room is barren. The light enters, cautiously, through blinded windows as if to avoid the anticipated horror. Two blankets spread in the middle of the floor are littered with clothing. A long wooden bench looks isolated in the large room; it is its only furniture. This room reeks of deceit; it has the riggings of a trap. Caught in the horror of having to accept whatever it may hold, we wait. They first make us open our bundles. They take the few things we have; they pick and choose. Shoes, clothing—our meager belongings are picked over, with careless familiarity, and thrown on one of the waiting blankets in the middle of the floor. They joke among themselves and make offensive comments without looking at us. From some they take away everything without examining their bundles. Those finished leave through the door facing us; the embarrassed light recedes and the door shuts behind them. I see some guards gather one of the blankets and carry it out into another room. "Next!" We wait for the spreading blanket. The man with the golden teeth recognizes me. He flashes a scowling grin and commands me to sing. I see my mother approach the blanket to the left, opening our bundles. I start to sing. I touch the wooden bench beside me for reassurance. I hear my shaky voice rising, bumping into walls, trying to avoid the rampant shouts and orders tossed. Mutilated by the harsh sounds of raucous laughter and loud talk, my fragile song roams the room lost, unlistened to. Crazed, clinging to the ceiling, it flings its shadow on the noise below and, sucking the molten mass into the hollow cast, it makes an image of itself. Fool's gold!

While Grandmother is made to take off her clothes, and Seppi clings to her crying, I sing.

"Jewelry . . . take off the jewelry!" they shout at my mother. She—never thinking she had any jewelry—absently reaches for the bright coral earrings she has always worn, only because they point to them. But when they ask her to take off her ring, she protests. "This is not jewelry," she says, firmly and defiantly, while she weeps, "this is my wedding band!" They forcibly remove it from her finger. I start crying and continue crying while I sing.

My grandmother is standing in front of the other blanket in her long white petticoat. A slender white column, waiting. White . . . white robust laces, bedding and embroidered pillow cases . . . brides. The blur of white gives way to tall black boots crossing the room. My tearing voice collides with the other noises; the room spins into a jumble. The sounds coming from my mouth have a harsh accusing tone and the words taste bitter, tinged with reproach. The cacophony confuses. The guards tell us to go. We walk out with our ransacked bundles, keeping our downs. Grandmother in her petticoat, shawled with her *Umhängtiechl* (a large triangular wrap), carries the only thing left to her: her coat with the velvet collar that she brought from America.

The people outside huddle in groups around their diminished bundles. Some from our village come over to us. They ask about our downs. Theirs were taken away. We do not know why we were allowed to keep ours. They look at us suspiciously. Some, begrudging our fortune, question the fairness of it. My mother agrees, and pointing to Grandmother, asks why only she among us was undressed. Grandmother's shy, teary smile looks like an apology.

The waiting crowd grows. The enclosed yard fills to overflowing. And the macabre game continues. *Jedan, dva, tri . . . deset, jedanaest, dvanaest, trinaest*, they count us, as if they were telling our fortune, and decide our fate. They separate us. Women with babies have to take up to four small children with them. Grandmothers are frantic, placing their crying grandchildren with women they do not know. The sound of the crowd is subdued by the pain that spreads over it in steel sheets. My mother makes arrangements with Tanti Lisa to take Seppi; Seppi is crying and Johann cries sympathetically. Tanti Lisa is holding baby Anna. With a worried weepy look, her brown coat buttoned, surrounded by crying children, she looks isolated, abandoned like an altar in a darkened church. She listens as my mother tells her important things about Seppi—he has to be woken up at night, to pee. She gives Tanti Lisa a small bundle with his things. She tells Seppi to be brave. We try not to cry. Another Seppi is placed in Tanti Lisa's care by his grandmother. She does not know my aunt; she is from Nakovo.

The other children are segregated according to age; boys and girls are separated. I am with girls ages eight to twelve. We are placed, in groups of ten, under the care of one woman. I don't know the lady under whose care I am. My mother is among the working women and Grandmother is with the old. Our little group of four has been deleted. We stand divided by number and category in the yard of the municipal building at dusk. Waiting. We do not leave the village. It is the village, Elli's village, the elevated world of furniture, that suddenly fades out of existence. We will stay in a segregated part of town prepared for us. We walk by twos in long lines through moonlit streets, silently, without stepping on our shadows. We look at the stars. As the children in front disappear into houses, we know our turn will come.

Our room is empty. The straw on the wooden floor is divided by a wide walkway. Two bare windows face the street, mirroring our motions blindly. Completing the internal symmetry, we take our places in the straw, ten on each side of the room. The two ladies head up the lines, each with their own children next to them, taking their places under each window. We sleep in our coats. Later we sleep in our clothes and use our coats to cover up. We follow rules and mind the lady we call Tante. Our unit of ten is so focused on itself that after a while the ten children on the other side of the room, as well as their Tante, seem remote, as though they were in another room entirely. The notion of separate groups isolates us from one another. I know none of the children in the room except Anna, my best friend from home, but she is on the other side; there is no time together for us here.

There is another room in this house, with twenty children. I know that they exist because we take turns going to the outhouse; we get our ladle of soup, our evening meal, from a large container the ladies bring from the soup kitchen, taking turns eating it out of the same tin cups; we take turns washing our hands and faces, our feet, in cold water, in the chipped Lawor in the foyer.

We get up in the dark and go to sleep in the dark; the electricity is turned off in the streets where we live. Our room is unheated; it is April now and, with twenty-two of us in one room, we keep warm. We are up at four in the morning. We walk to the soup kitchen. We stand in long lines. We drink the *Einprennsupp* (a soup of roux) from tin cups. Guards with guns walk us out of the village and we follow them into the fields. We often walk for many hours. All day we weed the planted fields. Sometimes we weed vineyards and some of us are binding the vines. At lunch, the barrels with soup and water reach us. We know the sound of the rattling wagon. We drink the soup from tin cups. We crave water— we cannot ever get enough of it. When the sun shines on us all day, we remove some of our clothing and, encumbered by it, dragging it with us through the planted rows, trying not to lose it, we cautiously weed around the tender growths, row by row. We work in our own small group, watched by our own guard. He carries a gun. As we move from field to field, I see other children from our village. I see Hansi walking behind a plow—he is just seven but, tall for his age, he is made to work with the older boys. We see the women working in the fields; some of us see our mothers and grandmothers, but we are not allowed to mix or talk with them. We pass them silently. We rake the crowd, looking for familiar faces. They do the same. We stare at each other. We smile. Some quietly cry; I see some women wiping tears. The guards do not let us linger.

Our guard becomes aware that I speak his language when I ask a question. He has me tell the others what he wants us to know. He talks to me on our walks back to the village. I call him čika Dušan.

The room is always dark when we arrive. We eat our soup cold, by lantern light, in the foyer—a lucky find, the lantern, till the fuel in it burns out. We go to our places on the straw. Tante asks us to pray. We all know the prayer: "Our father, give us this day our daily bread. Deliver us from evil . . ." We ask it every day, but we have no bread. I think of the meaning of the words as I say them (I believe it will make the prayer more sincere and therefore more effective). I try to swallow the line about the daily bread to cause it to be overlooked, to minimize the transgression, to forgive the debt—God has only forgotten about our bread; I don't want him to be embarrassed by it. After our prayer, I always add my modified threefold plea. Silently, in our dialect, I ask for our health, an end to the war, and my father's and our own homecoming. Frieda, the girl next to me, sits up to pray. I see her delicate profile reflecting the moonlight framed in our window. Her long braided hair, wound wreathlike around her head, shimmers golden. I look at her while I pray and know what it would be like to be really good. Frieda has a hernia and wears a truss. She is often in pain after our long walks, but she does not complain. She lies quietly, crying without making a sound. Anni sleeps next to her. She never prays; even when Tante tells her to do so, she refuses. The thought would not occur to anyone that she does not know the prayer. Anni is stubborn and even mean. She hides the truss so that Frieda can't find it in the morning. She breaks the glasses of the girl who sleeps next to her and smiles her blue-eyed smile, her golden head shaking off all accusations. She admits to nothing. She shows no remorse.

We know our mothers, our grandmothers, our sisters and brothers are close by, but we are not allowed to visit them. Seppi is in the same street, a few houses from where we are, but I can't go to see him. My mother and my grandmother live in different sections of the street behind ours and are not to see each other and not to come to see us. We don't go to see them. Most of us don't know in which houses our mothers and grandmothers live. Everyone has to stay put. But my mother, like some, dares to find ways. She comes to tell me about the others; she shows me where she lives. Once I sneak over at night, but I stay too long. The guard who comes in the morning to take the women to work finds me there and gives my mother a lash of his whip. Sometimes our own people complain about such visits; some even inform on us. Terrorized into submission, we are watchful, afraid of anyone's transgressions. There is a kind of fear among us that is tinged with betrayal. We are learning to distinguish among many fears now. This particular fear has the smell and taste of something rancid.

I steal away to see Seppi. The room is overflowing with small children. Beside Tanti Lisa's four, there are four under the care of another young woman; she, too, has a baby. Seppi is glad to see me, but he cries when I leave. I always feel the deepest sorrow for Seppi; he does not have a mother. That there are many others like him is something I know, but I feel this sorrow most through him.

• • •

It is May and we are out in the fields barefoot, weeding vineyards. The guards shout to each other: "The war is over!" They shoot their rifles into the air and repeat their shouts, "The war is over!" We say it among ourselves, repeating it as if it should mean something. "The war is over." We pass it on to each other and the fields around us come alive with sound: "The war is over . . . the war is . . . over." It sounds like bells and the answer to my prayer: "Let the war be over, and let us all come safely home." I see the guards talk among themselves and leave each other again as we continue our work till dusk, as always. Back at the house, we wash our feet in the chipped Lawor. We eat our cold soup, potato soup, as always. We pray aloud. And, as always, I add my modified three-part prayer, asking for the war to be over. Next to me, Frieda still cries her silent tears and does not complain. The girl by the far wall has asthma and is gasping for air.

In the morning, before it gets light, we walk to the soup kitchen, stand in long lines, and wait to get our Einprennsupp. As always, we don't talk to the others there. Some hope to see their mothers. My mother works in the village, sewing for Serb children; I don't look for her here. A woman from the other line calls to me in rasping whispers: "You—are you the little girl that sings? We hear your songs in the fields," and nodding her head to some women behind her, she smiles a large approving smile.

We walk and walk. We walk for a very long time. Out in the fields, when no other guards are around, čika Dušan, unlike most guards, is kind to us. He does not hurry us while we work and lets us take breaks not just at noon. He lets Frieda rest in the shade and sometimes at dusk, on our long walk back, when Frieda cannot take another step, he carries her on his back. Though he knows only a few words in German, he attends to us individually in wordless ways. He likes children. He has three of his own—sons, he tells me. He often asks me to keep him company, to sit and talk with him in the tall grasses. Sometimes we sit in the shade of an acacia tree. He talks about his family. Čika Dušan, like all the other guards, is Serb, but he lives across the border in Romania. Sometimes he does not talk at all. Flat on his back, his shotgun to the side, his face covered with his hat, he is quiet. Perhaps he sleeps. I squat, picking at the grasses close by, thinking I should go back to the others. Not knowing what to do, I sing. I sing quietly at first and then louder. I sing with the breeze. It feels so easy and the sounds are so light. I feel alone, almost. Only field sounds, rustling greens that pick up the tune and hum with the sun-intensified smell of spring grasses, stay with me and my song. My voice becomes a tall tree, reaching into the landscape. I sing the same song many times just to follow my voice as it moves across the fields beyond. Čika Dušan moves only after I am still for a time. Very slowly, pushing his hat to one side, looking at me intently, he says, "I was dreaming just now and in my dream I heard—a little bird, singing. It must have been the bird with the golden voice," he teases, smiling.

The breaks with čika Dušan grow longer. Sometimes the other children sit with us. Listening to the same song must be tiring. I ask—could I sing a German song? I sing most every day now, and those who hear me know, and the whispering grasses intuit, that we have changed. Our work in the fields no longer has the sound of vespers. And I only sing laments.

One day, čika Dušan is very talkative. He has told his family about me. Would I like to go to live with them, if he can arrange it? I am very exited. I can hardly believe it. I don't think of anything else. That night, I steal away to see my mother; I am so glad to see her. We speak in whispers and it is not long before I feel disappointed; I know I am not going to Romania. She tells me what to say to čika Dušan. I am first to thank him. I am to make him understand; how would he feel in her position? How would he feel, giving one of his children away? I try to look proud when I tell this to čika Dušan, and I say it as if it is the right thing to say. To show my disappointment about not going with him to Romania would have been a better approach. What I tell him must sound ungrateful, and he does not ask me to keep him company for many days.

It is getting warmer now and I often feel tired and sleepy while working. Walking back in the evenings, I feel exhausted. I go to sleep without eating my soup, and one day, when it is time to get up, I don't move. All day I am alone in the room. I open my eyes only long enough to realize where I am and immediately fall asleep again. I sleep for days and days. All day and all night, I sleep. When someone rouses me, the empty room is filled with late morning light. I see čika Dušan leaning over me. He says something teasing that makes me smile. His voice is friendly and I drift back to sleep. He rouses me again—he looks concerned. He holds his hand to my forehead and says someone should notify my mother. I try to smile. It is the last time I see him.

CHAPTER 7

This Side of the Sugar-Crystal Window

I WAKE TO THE LIGHT of afternoon sun. For a moment I do not know where I am. Alone in a strawless room, I hear chirping birds and the chatter of children at play. Then I remember my mother coming to our room when no one was there, gathering my few belongings, saying only, "Do you think you can walk?" And we leave.

Out on the street we walk as if we belong and know where we are going, walking at a natural pace along main street. "It is less dangerous; if someone stops us, I will know what to say." She tells me this to give me reassurance. She does not look scared but I know she is. I am very tired and my walk is a bit shaky. She notices, and we walk more slowly. The fine houses on main street, linked like beads on a necklace, boast vaulted entries, massive doors, some replete with ornate carving. There is no time to admire them now. A line of children—disgorged two by two from one of the buildings ahead— is moving toward us. They cross the street in front of us to meet others like them on the other side. All are dressed in dark blue uniforms, boys and girls, look-alikes. "Children from the orphanage, going to lunch," my mother explains. I am so weak I have trouble standing up. "We are almost there," I hear her whisper, and almost immediately, we enter the vaulted entry of a stately house, which now is the sewing shop and the place where my mother works.

We walk over the cobblestone pavement to an entrance at the very end of the house. I have trouble climbing the steps that lead to the door. We enter a shallow room; only a built-in stove in the corner identifies it as a kitchen. The adjacent large room has two long windows embellished with decorative ironwork. A huge pile of rags lumbers in a corner below them and a wrought-iron bed clings to the wall on the other side. This is where my mother leaves me. I am to stay in this room, away from the windows; I am not to go outside. No one must know I am here, I remember . . .

I am eager to explore the new space. I examine the functional stove in the kitchen. The tin bucket, covered with a chipped enamel lid from an absent pot, is the chamber pot my mother has pointed out on the way in; I am to use it during the day. The door to the outside is half glass; a float of cherubs, caught in dense netting, fades against its panes—a reminder of a careless looting. Behind this fragile slackened shield protecting me from view, I see the expansive blind wall of the house next door—broken only by a slender window with frosted glass—throwing its dense shadow on the cobblestones between us.

The large room is bright with sunlight and the generous windows suggest French doors. The slated roof of the orphanage is obscured by the flood of sunlight that swells across the sills. The pile of rags, asoak with sun, is tepid to the touch, and I rest among scents of linen and wool tinged with dust: a profusion of bright gleaming whites, yellowing eggshell, blues, pale grays, atangle in differing textured weaves, luster buried in the meld. Rooting through the tangled heap makes the dust rise to float and speckle in shafts of sunshine coming through the windows.

I am to stay in this room. But I am curious. I open the door by which my mother left, slowly, only to discover a very short hallway leading to another door. Locked. And there, in the middle of the hall, is an unusually narrow door, waiting to be discovered! I lean on its metal handle. The door opens into a windowless space; a small square of wire meshing, just below the ceiling, is the only source of light and ventilation. Shelves line the walls in steplike fashion from a platform in the center, like bleachers around a soccer field. The misty light is directed, leaving the corners in the dark and the center dramatically lit. My own private stage! Once this may have been a pantry, a providing larder, but now it is the seamless space of imagination. Its stark white walls and empty shelving softened by the mist of light, giving the illusion of unlimited space, support the wisdom of its metamorphosis. Instead of the rich familiar fragrances of toiled-over provisions, it now has the dark, sweet scent of play. I imagine no one else knows of this place. Hidden in it, I make it my own. I come again and again, often just to convince myself it really exists. Sometimes its walls and the steps ascending blend into a fluid milky softness, dissolving all confinement, leaving a faint floral scent behind—perhaps the scent of dried white roses. At other times, falling shadows lead to a pantomime dance and I become a silhouette dancing mute motions, growing tall against the walls to reach the ceiling, sliding softly to the floor . . .

My mother returns in the evenings with enlarged bosoms, bringing food from the pantry of the orphanage. The cooks (Esti néni and others from our village) give her bread, salami, leftovers from the evening meal. I watch in amazement as the thinly sliced salami peels out of her opened blouse to make a stack, and pieces of bread appear, diminishing the size of her waist. She cautions me not to eat too much, since I am not used to eating so richly. But slice after slice I devour the unaccustomed fare, and days later, when I am covered with a rash, my mother's diagnosis leans toward an allergic reaction.

In the evenings, we go outside and breathe the air of summer dusk. The enclosed solitary yard seems almost too much space for the two of us. A scent of flowers—roses, perhaps dahlias, from somewhere the fragrance of a summer garden, *estike* (night-violet)—wafting on the evening air. A whiff enlightens: the smell of dampened sun-warmed soil—whispers of an anointed earth—envelopes like a familiar blessing. I think I hear the soft sound of bells. My mother tells me that the house next door is a convent and the small silver-bell sounds are calls to vespers. A convent, next door? The window with the textured glass suddenly has a sugar-crystal appearance.

In the back yard, three enormous barrels lumber belly-up, looking discarded. The familiar smell of wine inhabits them still. Open at one end, they become sheltering spheres in which to roll soundlessly on the soft ground, teaching me how to keep walking on a moving surface without falling down or getting dizzy, how to stop, and how to do all this without making a sound, without laughing. I imagine what it must look like observed from the outside, ghostly barrels moving on their own. There is a huge stable; I stand on mounds of straw and look to its eaves for swallows' nests.

The well in the yard we pump knowingly to avoid the squeaking noises it can make. Later, when my mother oils its hinges, a rush of cool water splashing is the only sound we hear.

We return to our room in the dark. We are not afraid in the dark, just cautious. We never talk about what we would do if anyone came into the house at night and we were discovered. Sometimes ominous noises wake us and make us listen.

Daily the chatter of children playing calls me to the window. Standing on top of the rag pile, looking down, I take part in the games they play, running, picking up the ball they toss. I am present in their most intimate exchanges, weighing their interactions, watching their expressions. I feel accepted by their gestures, accepting theirs as if they were my own. It is the noise of their play that excludes me; the collective sound of voices speaking simultaneously, laughing, chatting, belonging. They shout into the sunshine, throwing shadows, while I, locked in an empty room, afraid to show myself, watch the painted lines of shadows cast by iron bars growing longer on the wooden floor.

I like going into the quiet pantry, my own secluded space; it shows me new mysteries. I am lying on the floor, looking at the ceiling, when something glistening from a dark corner catches my eye. I imagine it to be the room's own sacred light. I am not surprised—like the light everlasting in church, it has a ruby glow. I climb up to the corner and, in a hidden nook, I see the crystalline spark of a miniature glass with a handle, and behind it the ruby glow of another similar glass. Removing them, I discover the cobalt blue so deep my eyes drown in it and I am blinded, momentarily, to the radiant amber, honeyed gold; sparkling crystals that cut the eye—deep, soothing blues, cool emerald greens, rich purple. Indigo. I line them up. I put them in rows. I try pairing them off, but they are singular, solitary, unpairable. Whole. I kneel in front of them, mesmerized, staring at the rich array in disbelief, then carefully ease them, one by one, back into the hiding nook and tell not even my mother about them. It is a secret so private it does not want telling.

I am noticeably more tired every day. And each day, when the sun shines into the room at a certain angle, I feel dizzy, nauseous. No matter how hard I try to dispel it—cracking the back door to get a breath of air, thinking of other things, talking fast—nothing helps; try as I may to avoid it, every day, midmorning, I have to vomit. I wretch and wretch over the unlidded bucket, closing my ears, trying to soften the noise I make. Bilious green transparent fluid floats in the water at the bottom of the bucket. When the spell is over, I am relieved but so weak I can barely reach the rag heap, crawling. I sleep the rest of the day. When I open my eyes, it is to the worried look on my mother's face, and I continue sleeping with minor interruptions. She washes me with vinegared water. I see her wiping tears. She talks to me. She heats water on the stove, heedless of the telling smoke from the chimney. She says it is too far to the back of the house to be noticed; it will get lost unseen. I smile, and with the hastened speech of high fever, I try to make her laugh by saying something frivolous: "If they see the smoke and trace it back to us, we will invite them to tea." Her smile looks like a lie on her face. She talks with a lot of enthusiasm, as if she wishes to infuse some of her vigor into my wilted frame. She asks me to sit up—"if you can," she adds— and leans me up against her. I smell the warm steam of chamomile tea she holds in a bowl under my face. She dips her hand, cupping some of it, raising it to my nose, and tells me, firmly, to sniff up the warm brew. "As hot as possible, the pharmacist said; sniff it up as hot as possible." And soon the most unpleasant happens. Large lumps of congealed blood come out of my nose and throat. I gag and choke. The largeness of the clots frightens me, but, relieved to get them out, I joke, calling them goose livers because of their size and to make my mother smile. She is relentless, making me go through the grueling procedure several times at night, and during the day she comes to repeat the same. I sleep. My mother's voice, our mutual ritual, and her quiet weeping defines my life for weeks.

Sometimes I see an unfamiliar face and I hear voices whispering. I recognize my mother's voice. No one will help her. The doctor for the orphanage told her she would like to help, but she is not allowed to do so. The pharmacist could not give her anything, not even aspirin. If she could get some chamomiles, a strong tea, sniffed and gargled, as hot as possible. No, he could not give her any chamomile tea. He should not even tell her what to do—he is only speculating, he is not giving advice. I hear consoling words offered in a voice I do not recognize. Later I know that the needed chamomiles are given to us by the nuns next door. Nightly the narrow sugar-crystal window opens to the healing help of small, delicately petaled white flowers with robust sun-colored centers, which come to breathe their strong fragrance into our room, filling it with hope while I sleep, bathed by the moist balm of promised health.

And one day I hear again the sound of children at play and wake to the sunlight painting intricate designs on the floor. Tears run warm into my pillow. I listen to the children and in their pealing laughter I hear my own. I am light as air. I float.

I am getting better every day. And one day I walk all the way to the back door with my mother and she opens it. The slender window in the convent wall is open too; I see the nuns looking at us, waving; they take turns coming to the window, smiling. My mother is blowing her nose; I know she is crying. She clasps her hands in a gesture of prayer and raises them in gratitude, pointing toward the open window. The nuns nod graciously, whispering something. "Yes . . . a miracle!" my mother says. And I, weak, breathe myself into a smile for them, trying to look miraculous. Six weeks I have been ill, my mother says.

It is Sunday. She gives me white stockings to wear, which I do not remember having. We are going through the grand gate. We are going to the apothecary, only blocks away. I get tired and I have to rest often. Squatting down, I admire my white stockings and my legs in them. We surprise the pharmacist. Distracted, inattentive, he talks to us reluctantly; he does not ask us in. I stand before him as proof that his advice helped to get me well. Our walk here is a pilgrimage to give thanks. He tries to hide his astonishment and, accepting our thanks, gives in to an uneasy civility. "A severe sinus infection could have affected the brain; could have been fatal," he mutters. Unaccustomed to using the word *miracle*, he says I am lucky, looking at me in disbelief, sounding more embarrassed than pleased. On our way back, I have to take many rests.

Perhaps this exposure after my long illness emboldens my mother to let me come out of hiding during the day; most likely she received permission from Sonja and Dafina, the Partisan bosses. I am introduced to the women in the sewing shop as the new helper. I am to bring them the threads and materials, sweep up the shop, and run errands. With a tape measure around my neck I feel officially initiated into the new order. The widow Hubert, who makes the most beautiful shirts, takes my apprenticeship seriously. She teaches me, among other things, how to make the double seams required in sewing men's shirts. I go scuttling about importantly, glancing now and then, at the tape measure falling in two straight lines down my chest; my new position makes me feel grown-up, proud, and very self-conscious.

When seamstress Annala and my mother deliver the finished clothes to a storage space near the kitchen of the orphanages, they bring back the emptied baskets filled and twice as heavy, with food hidden under clothes sent to be mended. On the street the heavy baskets have to appear light. "What things look like often depends on the way one carries them," Annala boasts, as if she were speaking about her own stately carriage. The ladies of the sewing shop eat well, supplementing the usual and only fare, the potato soup they receive from the communal kitchen. The women joke about this soup. When they get home, they say, potato soup will not be seen in any of their kitchens.

The women, going back and forth daily, inform us of events in the camp. Many people are dying. Gerold Hansi, Wagner Vedde Hans, and his wife Päsl Evi are dead. I listen. The scented air drifting through open windows conjures images of summers passed: a late afternoon stroll, going home from Grandfather's house; Vedde Hans teasing me and Päsl Evi asking me to sit with them on the bench in front of their house; a smiling Hansi in a long linen shirt; and Herta, sitting in the straw, watching, mutely assessing, her short life measured by a teaspoon of honey. Herta is dead. I say it to myself; I want it to mean something.

Johann is sick with scarlet fever and Tanti Lisa goes with him to the house where the sick are confined, taking baby Anna with her. Miller Päsl Nancsi brings this news one morning and by afternoon a new secret has to be kept from everyone. Seppi and Grandmother are hidden in the back room.

Grandmother's face has a way of telling the unspoken. Her smile showers gratitude and thanksgiving. Though we are in hiding, she feels safe again, she says. Sometimes, she has a cough and has to go into the kitchen to be farthest away from the front of the house. At night her cough makes her feel self-conscious; her attempts to squelch it are painful to hear and my mother urges her to cough. Grandmother goes outside instead, to get some air, she says.

The solace of being together makes us forget the nagging worry we always felt being apart. At night, with the quiet around us so immense even Grandmother's cough gets lost in it, we feel safe in the comfort of each other's presence. We belong. A light in the yard of the orphanage now softens the darkness to dusk in our room. Sometimes a bright moon tosses friendly shadows through the windows. Our breathing and the sound of our voices quietly talking lulls to a sweetness I had forgotten, almost.

I teach Seppi how to look down to where the children play, without being seen. When he wants to go out to play, I divert him with stories and remind him of the evening to come. In the evening, when everyone has left the sewing shop and the children are quiet inside the orphanage, Seppi and I play in the enclosed yard, chasing each other and making the barrels roll, all without laughing or talking above whispers. In the large stable filled with straw, we increase the volume of our whispers to span the immense space. We play hide-and-seek in its sheltering dusk while Grandmother's cough roams the yard, trying to sound faraway.

News from the others: Baby Anna dies of scarlet fever. The last time I saw her, months ago, she was sitting in the straw enjoying the attention of the older children; Seppi adored baby Anna. When my mother asks Sonja and Dafina for another seamstress, Tanti Lisa comes to work in the sewing shop, and Johann joins the others in hiding.

The room behind the locked door contains materials, the work in process, and the finished, undelivered garments; it is a kind of storage. Usually only my mother and Annala enter it, and sometimes the tailor, an elderly German man who does the cutting in the middle room; occasionally others come, bringing and picking up garments. This room is a kind of buffer between us and the two rooms more visited. When Partisan visitors come to the sewing shop, it is important to be absolutely quiet. Since we have no way of knowing who might be there, we are always cautious; when we hear noises in the storage room, we freeze.

Food is a problem now. When the women leave for the day, we cannot go for our rations to bring them back here. We depend on provisions hidden under the clothes brought back for mending and on food given to us by the ladies in the kitchen of the orphanage. In the evenings, when Frau

Kemper brings the milk for the children next door, she sometimes leaves an earthen pitcher hidden under the foliage of potato plants in a field behind the back yard. The orphanage used to be one of Frau Kemper's houses; she now works in the stables, milking cows. She tells my mother that the sewing shop—the Blasmann Haus, she calls it—was the house of the Bürgermeister of Nakovo. I now think of the crystal glasses as having belonged to someone.

While we, in the sewing shop, make disparaging remarks—proclaiming the potato's declining appeal, airing our discontent with the daily diet—in the back of the house, in our room, the discussion about potatoes takes a different turn. I hear my mother's voice arguing a point with Grandmother. It seems my mother has noticed, while looking for the crock of milk left for us, that the rows directly behind the house show many gaps of plants missing. She worries; this tell-tale sign, pointing straight to us, has dangerous implications. Grandmother admits it was her idea to take the potatoes, and with Tanti Lisa's help, they have accumulated quite a stash, which they now reluctantly retrieve from under the rag heap. They are preparing for times to come, they explain. "You know that it is dangerous to be stealing out in the open, but leaving a trail behind is reckless," my mother scolds. "And how are we to eat these potatoes, raw?" They have plans for that too. Later, when it is cold and the sewing shop is being heated, the smoke from the chimney will not be suspect. My mother is astonished. "The children are hungry," Grandmother says, smiling sheepishly, and she admits with a far-away look, she has a craving for diced potatoes baked crisp, dropped hot into cold milk, "like at home." My mother listens, shaking her head. Then, giving her approval, she says to Tanti Lisa, "If you decide to do this again, remove the potatoes carefully from below, taking care to leave the plant intact." I am surprised my mother knows how to steal potatoes.

A Serb woman called Sarka, a woman from our village, visits my mother in the sewing shop. She has come, she explains, to repay a kindness concerning an incident during the war, when clothing was unavailable and she, trading her chickens for clothes, was forced into an unfair trade. My mother, on hearing about this trade, gave Sarka some of her own clothes. The gesture of Sarka's visit is appreciated. Not knowing that we cannot buy things, Sarka gives my mother money. She says her son and another child from our village are here in one of the houses of the orphanage. We now realize that the orphanage is largely made up of disadvantaged children from all over Yugoslavia; some even come from Greece. The Dečji Dom is a home for children, not strictly an orphanage.

The tailor's apprentice, a boy from one of the houses of the Dečji Dom, is fourteen. He says he is from Macedonia. He has a German name, but when my mother points this out, he protests in an accusing, almost threatening tone. He, the only non-German working among us, has the power, at fourteen, to intimidate. His parents are still alive, he tells us, only because we ask him; he says he misses his home. Mostly he keeps to himself and hardly talks to anyone. He works with the tailor in the middle room away from the women. I see him walking about with a limp, looking sad. Sometimes I catch him looking at me and we smile shyly when we pass in the yard. I am almost ten now.

One day, the girl called Anni, from Tante's, comes to the sewing shop with her mother, accompanied by the *Upravitelj* (the superintendent). I am surprised to see her here, surprised to learn that her grandmother is one of the women working in the shop. Anni's mother is the Upravitelj's cook and housekeeper now, and Anni is allowed to stay with her mother at his house. Anni is even more obnoxious than I remembered. She immediately teases me about the boy apprentice. Quick, moving like a whirlwind, she has to be watched, kept away from the back rooms of the house. I divert her by showing her the trick with the barrels. She is not impressed. Instead, she suddenly wants to explore the stable again, and while we are there, she scans the space as if looking for something. Then, standing on a stack of straw, facing me, she abruptly lifts up her skirt, drops her panties, and asks me to sniff her as if we were dogs. Grown-ups do such things, she says, and I should be eager to learn. My jaw drops. I look at her in disbelief. Unperturbed, she instructs: I should drop my pants and she will demonstrate. She is up close now and I have my back against the straw. She is about as tall as I am; I could easily push her away. I think of it, but I don't do it. I am confused, embarrassed, curious. Not wanting to do what she says, and not knowing what to do, I start laughing instead. She looks demonic. Afraid to assert myself, I keep laughing with my eyes closed. She is goading me to do as she says. I freeze. Suddenly, she too starts laughing. I am relieved. It was only a joke, after all. I open my eyes. She keeps looking past me. I turn, and behind me, the apprentice is getting up from the straw, looking at us knowingly. She keeps her skirt raised. As he walks past us she whispers: "You think he likes you?" Now, when I pass the boy in the yard, I always look down. Inside, I never look at him at all.

I am often sent on errands. I cross the wide street to deliver messages and garments, walking down main street, past the church, where some of the teachers live. I always wear a tape measure around my neck, out of pride, and for identification and protection, to prove that I work in the sewing shop, if someone should stop me. Coming back from one of these errands, I see something flailing between the pavement and the road. I think it is a dying bird and I go to see, but it is only a rolled up piece of cloth, unfurling. Looking about me, I stoop to pick it up. Touching its silken surface, I know it is something important; it shimmers silvery in my hands. I shove it under my sweater and retrieve it only in the storage room of the sewing shop when I am alone. I unfold the finely woven cloth slowly: silvery white, slate gray, inky black silken threads, so fine one can barely see them, woven together into a letter-sized rectangle, framing a snugly fitting oval, and in it, the face of Christ with the crown of thorns. The delicately molded face seems painted rather than woven. The familiar image and the beauty of the cloth itself inspires reverence. I notice the eyes; they have the look and structure of my mother's eyes. When I show her the found treasure she says we must return it to the church. But the church, ravaged, plundered many times, is closed, we know, and no one is there to receive it. Perhaps it belongs to the nuns. She knows the convent has been pillaged once; it may be a lost remnant of that looting. My mother shows the cloth to Sister Kornelia, who examines it behind the textured window; we want the nuns to keep it. They refuse. We should have it and its blessings. My mother thinks finding it may be a good omen, and on the reverse side, in the margin under the oval, she writes with an indelible ink pencil: *Andenken aus Nakovo den 15. September 1945*; in remembrance. It is now our own protective charm.

• • •

It is my birthday. I am ten. I am surprised when out of the slender window of the convent three large dahlias appear; one of them is purple. I stand in front of the kitchen door, feeling awkward, shy, overwhelmed. Receiving gifts of flowers—just having one's birthday acknowledged—is something new, sophisticated, worldly. I am invited to tea.

Washed and combed, wearing the flowered dress that Annala has made for me, I enter the convent from the field at the back. I am greeted by Sister Kornelia; I am surprised how brilliantly blue her eyes sparkle close up. I am ushered into a room and introduced to the other nuns. I am too nervous to remember their names, and not knowing what to say or do, I smile. Gracious, smiling, they look at me admiringly, asking polite questions, inviting me to sit down. A strong smell of linden blossoms and honey fills the room, and soon Sister Kornelia's crisp white headdress, floating ahead of the others, leads us to tea. We enter a room with a large round table covered with white linen, set with silver spoons and white china plates, cups, and saucers showing a delicate gold rim. A glass bowl with yellow roses swells the center of the table. When they ask me to sit down I can barely move. The starched white headdresses span the periphery of the table, floating above it like huge, hovering, friendly birds, and below them benevolent smiling faces watch my every motion, so I think. I watch the tea being poured, the adding of sugar cubes to cups filled with steaming tea, the restrained, graceful gestures of the nuns raising them to drink, the giving hands passing the tray of cakes around the table. They make a wish for my birthday and we eat and drink and make pleasant conversation. I watch and do as they do, trying hard not to make a mistake. I divide my attention between observing and being self-conscious, uncomfortable about being observed. Some of the tea cakes have the familiar taste of anise; all are delicate and light as if they should be inhaled instead of swallowed. All are delicious. The tastes and smells complement the pleasant mix of sounds and motions, and all are presents wrapped for visual pleasure: a mix of crisp starched whites, soft white damask, delicate translucent china whites caught up in golden rings, a pluck of yellow roses, and the bright sparkle of cornflower blue eyes—all under the spell of powder-sugared pastry.

It seems I have hardly had time to get accustomed to visiting when it is time for me to go. They give me a present—colored pencils in a slender box. My mother has told them how well I can draw, they say graciously, smiling. Embarrassed, beside myself, I thank them. They wrap up the cakes for me to take along. Sister Kornelia is going to show me the chapel and the classroom before I leave.

I stand in the doorway of the chapel breathing scents of incense and roses. I am overwhelmed by the space before me; a space so serene, it has the power to hurt. I am suddenly sullen. I am confused. This tranquil space, so close to where I live, appears disturbingly discordant with the world out-side, the world which I inhabit. I feel betrayed, shamed, angered. Sister Kornelia, who seems to notice my discomfort, gives me a consoling smile and, with respectful distance, now leads me out by the front door.

I make a drawing of the dahlias with my colored pencils on brown paper the tailor has given me, and my mother proudly hands it to the nuns through the open window, asking them to keep it. They do.

The days are getting cooler and I am wearing a dark cherry-red turtle-neck sweater with rice-patterned texture. It is a hand-me-down from Annala, outgrown by her daughter Heli. I love the way it fits, smooth across my chest. I have outgrown my shoes. Anna, our best seamstress, has been mak-ing shoes for all the ladies and now she is making some for me. She makes the soles of cloth braids sewn together. The tops, made of durable dark blue material, lined, are topstitched in red and sewn onto the soles with heavy red thread. Laced with red cording, they look wide on my feet. Noticeable.

There is disturbing talk. We are going to be transported to another camp. The women in the sewing shop are worried; they fear having to leave. Some fear having to stay here without their families. Sonja and Dafina come to confirm the rumor; they choose the women who will stay. My mother is among them. I can stay with my mother, they tell her. She negotiates; she wants Seppi and Grandmother to stay as well. They draw the line. Seppi may stay, perhaps, but not Grandmother. Grandmother cries when my mother tells us the news. My mother decides: if one of us has to leave, all of us go. She does not waver.

The women are still doing the usual sewing, but now they are busy sewing rucksacks and other things for themselves. A stack of army blankets, intended for the orphanage, is steadily diminishing. We pack everything we have; things we have picked up along the way and those not taken away from us all get stuffed into our rucksacks. Grandmother has new skirts to wear. For all we know they will take everything away from us again, but we cannot think about that now.

Some women, told to stay, are not allowed to keep their children; they must choose. Some think by staying they will be able to help their children, their kin, with food (not thinking how). If all of them go, there may be no hope for any of them, they argue, confused. Annala is staying. She is allowed to keep Heli but not her son, Hansi. Choices are made. Past anxieties pale before the new.

I remember the hidden treasure. Their glow diminished in light of present apprehensions, the miniature glasses shine, knowingly, with distanced radiance. I restore them carefully to their hiding place and imagine they are safe, grateful being left behind.

The evening before we leave, one of the teachers from the Dečji Dom and his wife come to the room in the back of the house. His wife is slim, dark haired; her slender face has crisp angular features and dark piercing eyes that make her look intensely serious. His eyes, a rich velveted brown, give the appearance of relaxed composure. Our visitors excuse themselves at the door. Perhaps they are surprised to see the others in our room. My mother asks them in. They come in reluctantly; they wanted to see my mother only, the lady explains. We make room for them to sit, removing the rucksacks from the bed. The lady, hesitant at first, speaking softly, admits that she has come to ask my mother, to persuade her, not to leave. "Think of your children," she says in a tone meant for only my mother to hear. "The camp you are going to is an extermination camp!" She speaks in whispers; I hear her only because I cling to my mother. "We have been through much hardship," my mother interrupts in a subdued tone, accommodating her voice to the whispers, "but we want to stay together." Our visitor continues: "This is not a camp like the one you are in now. You are being put there deliberately, to die. Believe us," she looks to her husband as if she needs his consent to finish her sentence, "they intend to let you starve to death." And, as if she has anticipated our question—why, even now, after the war, are they doing this to us?—she explains in a hissed whisper, "It seems they have been given permission to do whatever they want with you. And they decided to give you five years . . . to die."

My mother appears distant, her face set in a look that I interpret to be a contradiction to what the lady is saying. In it I recognize my own stubborn refusal to believe what is being said; hearing it is so terrible it first has to be refused. Always, when I get sick, I first refuse to believe it; it is easier to accept that I am only make-believing. And I now think it must not be true, it cannot be true, what the lady is saying. I insist, assuming the same stubborn expression matching my mother's: *It is not true!* But my mother says, instead, "If this is true, then how can I stay, knowing my mother is going there to die?" "Think of your children," the lady repeats, whispering. "The children . . ." my mother says in a quiet but audible voice, looking at Johann as he sidles into his mother's lap (he and his mother will have to go regardless of what my mother decides). "How can I think of my children only—what about all the other children? In any case, I cannot, in good conscience, leave my mother alone in her condition. I have decided. I cannot do otherwise." For a time everyone is quiet.

My mother continues as if she were talking to herself and the dusk in the room: "I don't believe we can manipulate to escape our fate. I will do what I can for my family, my children, by going with them—I can only live with the choice I have made. I may regret it later, God forgive me, but I have to decide now." Our visitors listen, subdued. The man is quiet, looking down; the lady is persistent, and perhaps to shock my mother, to bring her to her senses, she repeats sharply: "You will regret it, I can assure you!" And, as if startled by her own pronouncement, she concludes in a pleading tone, "Think it over, gospodja, save your children." My mother thanks them for coming, walks them to the back door and they disappear behind impartial cherubs caught in dense netting, fading, their futile shielding gesture protecting us. Inside, Grandmother is quietly weeping and Tanti Lisa continues her vacant look. Seppi and Johann are still, vigilant. The darkening room enfolds us with consoling familiarity.

Early in the morning we are on our way. We walk openly on main street, passing the chain of stately houses, their closed facades and enormous gates shielding undiscovered treasures, while we are out in the open, exposed. Now we are fearless; we are not running to safety. We move within the allowance of our destiny.

We join the spread of people and bundles in front of the municipal building. The familiar steely reek of new separations emanates from the crowd. The losses of children, parents, and kin are mentioned to those who knew them and to strangers. "My child is dead," one woman says. "My son." She says it looking away, past other children, so that her covetous glances may not contaminate them. She weeps. The accusing tears fall everywhere. Feeling more fortunate, one cowers under them, afraid to offend. Behind the consoling gestures of grandmothers, of mothers surrounded by their children, hides not just the fear of envy but the dread of being next. Do they know about our destination? No one has cautioned them, behind lace netting, about an extermination camp!

We are in a sea of people in front of railroad tracks. The train comes. The doors to its cars are gaping. It has barely stopped when the guards urge us to hurry, driving us inside. The familiar anxiety spreads like poisonous vapors. The murmuring crowd adjusts to individual complaints. Some people have difficulties getting themselves into the freight cars. We help each other by making a step of clasped hands. There is the usual fear of being separated. Children are crying, being lifted into the enclosed space; they plead for their kin below to climb up. There is an array of guards with guns on the ground; I see them from my elevated position. Some shove and push those slow in climbing. Their shouts are heard above the throng. Finally, we are inside, crowded, standing, or sitting on our belongings. When they close the doors, bolting them from the outside, it is pitch dark and there is talk of not having enough air to breathe. I worry and move closer to my mother. She tells me not to listen and calls my attention to small slits in the side of the freight-car.

The train stops and slows down in places, and some strain to see the signs passing, to read the names of towns through the narrow breathing slits close to the top of the wagon. We stop somewhere for a long time and, jolted about, continue, the train now moving at a slower pace. Perhaps they have added more cars, some say. The doors are opened once only, somewhere in the fields, and people get down to relieve themselves. Some stay; they fear being unable to climb up again. Others anticipate atrocities and say so. Every time a shot is heard there is reason to fear that they have shot someone. If you don't see your kin in front of you, you fear them dead or taken away. I, too, worry when one of us is out of sight. Anxieties are rampant every time a change ensues. There is some relief when all are back again behind bolted doors. The train moves slowly and keeps moving.

• • •

We arrive in the dark. We sit in the unopened freight wagons for hours. We hear shouts and conversations, the familiar background noise, the distanced grumbling of the guards. The shouts come closer and the steely clatter of doors opens to a patch of darkness. Here and there a lantern glimmers faintly through the shapeless void. We are moving down a steep embankment. It seems we are descending into a hole. We move along slowly, making sure that those who came with us are beside us. The children are walking hanging onto adults, holding hands and clutching clothing. On the periphery of the crowd ahead, I see, in a lantern's gleam, that we are moving along a tall fence made of barbed wire. An open space in the fence, an invisible gate, lets the crowd pass and we gather behind it. The spreading crowd is divided arbitrarily and small groups of people are taken away by guards to vanish wordlessly into the eerie night. Our turn comes; no one tells us where we are being led. So far it is only the expected, the usual. Nothing has changed. We have done all this before. But each new beginning has its own special terror. We are never quite prepared for its coming.

There is an uninhabited stillness about, as if we were the first and only people here. This is the island beyond the edge of the world. Dim, vast, and silent, it absorbs the murmuring crowd; even the occasional cry of small children is lost in this empty, gravelike hollow. It is early October, and the damp night air adds its chill to the ominous impression. We move in ghostly pantomime, not hearing our footsteps, past the dark silhouettes of empty houses, their windows glaring hollow-eyed. This is a ghost town, remote from the living, unreachable even to the light of the moon.

A group of us is herded into a small house. Twenty people to a room. The rooms are empty, strawless. There is a clamoring for space. My mother is noticeably upset. I can tell by her demeanor that she will not get along with some of our immediate neighbors. Guards come in the morning. Some-one from each family has to go to bring the straw allotted to us. My mother and Tanti Lisa go. My mother comes back without the straw. She has found another place for us, she says. Johann, at first reluctant to go without his mother, is willing to walk with me; holding onto my hand, he toddles along. Seppi is clinging to Grandmother. We walk the wide empty street, meeting only people carrying straw. We pass the blind-eyed houses; their windows, not used to reflections of passers-by, look accusing, vacuous. We walk through neglected gardens; overgrown, unweeded, they must have been abandoned long ago. The pale October grasses give everything a sepia tone, reflecting an eerie light from the ground up. We walk through the back yard of a house. Its rooms are full, someone says as we approach, but my mother continues. Anna, our friend, the seamstress, comes to meet us, walking her cumbersome rotating walk. We thank her for finding us a place. Inside, Tanti Lisa is waiting with two mounds of straw that look huge in the small room. But the size of this room seems just right for us. We fill its width, comfortably, lying next to each other, and measure its length by Tanti Lisa's height—she being tallest among us—and the four feet left to move in when we are not lying down. At the head of our common bed there is one large, square window. To the side, and looking into the open hallway, is another, smaller, rectangular one. The door to the entry is half glass. This is our new place.

We share the house with forty people. It is not a large house. Facing sideways, it has two rooms to the street. Our friend Anna and her family live in the larger room with twenty people. The other room, somewhat smaller, also has twenty people. We share a common entry, the kitchen of the house, judging from the built-in stove in the corner. A narrow brick walk leads from the entry door along the stables and shed, far into the yard, to a weathered gray outhouse. Behind it, a broken-down lattice fence shows open grassland and what looks to be a neglected garden with tall grasses instead of vegetables. There is no well in the yard, only a cement cistern, containing rain water, to the right of the entry just below the slightly elevated floor of the hallway. Some think it is a blessing to have water so close to the door and count on the constancy of rainy weather.

There is nothing left in this house, nothing telling about its former inhabitants. Abandoned long ago, looted, picked clean like a bleached carcass, not a broken shard is left on the ground; not a scrap of cloth forgotten by careless looters, anywhere. Not even a shred of paper litters the tall grasses behind the treeless yard; in it only leaves of grass, from fields beyond, blow about. Not a rusting tool nor forgotten lantern in the stables, nor remnants of hay nor straw; not even a key or a meat hook left in the pantry; not a rope or speck of grain in the attic; nor a haystack or wagon or discarded plow about in shed or yard. Nothing. Left in the pigsty, below the empty Kotarka, corn kernels littering its floor, are two cement troughs. A treasure! Only the water in the cistern, showing the store of past rains, and here and there among tall grasses a show of domestic plants—the long stalk of a seeding onion, the withering greens of hidden roots, unharvested vegetables regrown—keep bringing up forgotten treasures; the last reminders of a cultivated past.

In accordance with an ancient curse, *"Das Gras soll Dir vor der Tür wachsen,"* the grass now grows in front of our doors. We live among the faded grasses of the damned.

The children are playing, turning somersaults and cartwheels on the spread of graying sod. They play ancient games, sing songs, chant and whistle. They laugh. And the faded grasses whisper with consoling gestures about the renewal of life, about life everlasting. I learn to turn cartwheels from the girls who live in the rooms next to ours. I fill with the pride of accomplishment. I am overwhelmed by my new ability. I test my power daily. These are the last days of October and the sun still shines warm on our play.

We are among the first to come to this village; those of us from Nakovo and those who came with us from Kathreinfeld are many, and still, daily more people come dragging their bundles past our houses; their crying children clinging to them, they fill up the streets with their grief. Twenty thousand—twenty-four thousand—hearts beat out a palpitating monotone, keeping time. Some people know this village by name. They call it Rudolfsgnad. The name invokes a sainted grace. It is its German name. This was an all-German village, they say. Most of its four thousand inhabitants fled a year ago (those who stayed met a fate like ours). Left behind, looted many times, emptied to its very bones, it bares its deceased image: a weathered monotone, the color of a clod of earth, a heap of dust, a grave. A stone. Its new name is Knićanin: a Partisan hero immortalized—by so many bones! We do not know.

The river is close, people say. A dam is visible if one looks over the gardens behind our houses. It seems almost as high as the one that bears the railroad tracks. The village and we in it are enclosed on two sides by these elevations—and by barbed wire. The other two sides, enclosed by barbed wire, fade into the fields beyond. The river behind the dam is the Theiss. Tisa, the same river, far upstream, a hundred kilometers north, flows by our village, our home. It is a thought that comforts, evoking feelings of familiarity. But this village, so unlike ours and no one's home, lends the river the look of treacherous muddy waters. Unrecognizable. Unapproachable. It is the river of sticks. A wash of bones.

Across the river is Titel, a town where people live in their houses among their furniture and stroll in their harvested gardens listening to the silvery sounds of autumnal grasses, perhaps collecting some to fill the vases ornamenting their homes. And some sit around small tables in outdoor restaurants sipping coffee and other aromatic waters, wearing tinted glasses, shielding their eyes from the sun, having pleasant conversations about things to come. Here, we hover over dried grasses, seeking those with roots, and worry over the diminishing level of cistern water measured out by a rusting cup. There is a bridge across the river we cannot cross. Walking across it, we could be in Titel within minutes. But people there would recognize us and say we do not exist.

CHAPTER 8

Rudolfsgnad
Iß Knićanin

SOON THE SEPIA TONE, the light from below, invades the internal spaces, making us part of the desolate landscape. My mother takes to sleeping all day. I sit beside her, watching, feeling my inadequacy. When she opens her eyes I ask her what I should do. When she does not answer, I massage her arms and her shoulders lightly, like I saw my father do when she was sick, and I concentrate on putting all my energy and affection into my touch. With it I try to bring her back out of her slumber of darkness, whose shadow has made a home in me long ago. The familiar anxiety makes the sunshine falling through the window and the sound of children playing outside seem remote, like some faded image remembered. I will stay all day and all night beside my mother and never tire till she gets well. I sit in the dark, listening to the quiet breathing of the others sleeping.

Three days and nights my mother sleeps and I, in the shadow of her darkness, only slumber lightly. When she wakes, she is gathered up, and with renewed energy she takes charge. I am amazed by this transformation. Relieved and happy, but very tired, I follow her about, attentive to her every wish. There is a bustle in the room. Blankets are being spread over the straw; the common bed is tidied. Our rucksacks become pillows and the downs are rolled up into a long cushion to soften our rest during the day. The room looks strawless now, and the remaining floor is scrubbed. A broom is made from tall dry grasses bound with twine. And then a larger construction: the rectangular window to the hall is bricked in behind the glass, making the room less light, though more private. I cannot avoid showing my displeasure and try to hide my sullen looks behind my irritability. With this transformation, the room has built-in shelving to store our food, when we get it.

No one has given us food. There is no one to ask about this oversight. Guards are seen all over the village, but they are unapproachable, unavailable for questions. They come into our rooms, our houses, and nothing is done without the dread of their appearance. If they catch us quietly sitting in our rooms, they have us scurrying out, cursing us for being lazy, picking us over and taking some of us for jobs they need done. When they find us outside, they chase us in and tell us not to leave our house, our yard, our street. They tell us what they do not want us to do. The restrictions are many and always changing. Even abiding by their changing rules, we cannot hope to please them. Though we know they cannot keep track of us all of the time, since there are too many of us, still, the terror of their presence is with us in everything we do. We do everything quickly, as if any minute could betray us, knowing what we do will incriminate us, what we accomplish will be held against us, what we make will be taken away from us. We are always watchful—even with their backs turned, they are in front of us. And when we sometimes manage to forget them, they have a way of showing up. We quickly learn this. Never forgetting it, we move accordingly, fending for ourselves.

Leaving the persistent to root through picked-over grasses, the more adventurous among the hungry explore the streets, looking for grain in attics of empty as well as inhabited houses. Evi, the woman from Crna Bara, who lives in the room next to ours, has a knack for such discoveries. Quick, matter of fact, she takes charge in her room, taking care of her own kin. She has a daughter of fifteen and a little boy four months old. A little Russian, people say. She says nothing. Evi now comes to our room to tell my mother about a nearby house where, in the attic, a mound of wheat lies waiting. They both leave with empty rucksacks. We worry. Others hear of the wheat and soon there is nothing left of the lucky find. Our stash is safely stored under the straw in our room. Some of it my mother gives to our friend, the seamstress Anna. The cement troughs from the pigsty are now put to good use: grinding grain into flour with the help of a large stone, dragging it the length of the trough, back and forth, back and forth across the grain. Grandmother and Tanti Lisa take turns milling, while my mother continues scouting. Others come to take their turn using the troughs; some come from neighboring houses. Some have corn to grind. The meager supply of grain, wherever found, is quickly exhausted, and soon the grinding, watched by others who have no grain, takes on an unpleasant aspect that requires a twofold watch: the ever present fear of being discovered by the guards, and the ever vigilant hungry eyes of the others looking on accusingly, betrayed by our having. These eyes are everywhere. The empty stares of children cling to the milling procedure, to the preparation of food, and remain fastened to every bite taken. Hungry, we swallow everything in haste, as if eating means eating it away from others, and everything we eat is seasoned with the taste of shame. Still, those who have food continue cooking their meager meals on the built-in stove in the entry. Smells invite and exclude at the same time. Every day assaults anew with countless separations. Though we share one house, one kitchen, one stove, one room, we are isolated, each in our own "family" unit.

For the first few weeks I move about freely, playing in yards and grassy gardens with the children from neighboring rooms and houses. Now we seldom play, and moving from house to house, walking on the street, is no longer undertaken lightly. When guards come to tell us we are not to leave our houses, our yards, we obey. We are used to such shows of power and move about, if we must, with caution. Things that need doing are done by twos. Someone always has to be the lookout while the other does the work. The lattice fence dividing the yard from the garden disappears first in increments, then altogether. The corn bin loses its floor first, to appear unchanged. Day by day its latticed siding shows larger gaps; the missing strips now hide under the straw in our rooms. I see my grandmother climbing about the floorless structure, whacking at remaining lattices with a brick, looking pleased as they fall, one by one. Whack by merciless whack she heaves her strength into every blow, balancing on the beams that held up the absent floor, making the lattices fall. She looks youthful and, as if she knows it, she smiles. I am her begrudging lookout. Even though I know that the wood is needed to cook our soup, I still have something against the changing appearance of the Kotarka. Its broken-down image, charged with a familiar anxiety, reflects unavoidable loss. I fret, complain, and with every lattice that falls, I secretly wish the Kotarka back whole again. Others take their turn, and soon the whole corn bin disappears, leaving an empty space above the brick pigpen; an invisible reminder of its former self.

Soon fences no longer exist. The suspended outside-door to our house disappears one night, and no one admits to having it. The doors to the stables follow suit. The front gate shows large gaps, where boards are missing, before it disappears altogether. People caught in such activities disappear themselves. There is a prison in the village, the *Bunker*, a basement where the light of day, coming through small windows secured with iron bars, is further obscured by bodies crowded into the dank space; where people are often forgotten without food, without water for days, for weeks.

Severely beaten, some die there. Once inside, for any offense, no one can be sure of ever coming out. Those who have been there fear it most. But not all who offend go there; some are shot on the spot. We hear of such shootings, some we see, but we continue foraging for food, gathering wood not out of defiance but out of necessity. If they should ask how the front gate disappeared, no one could say without incriminating themselves. But no one comes to hold us accountable for the destruction. They tolerate destruction; they are not irritated by it. Their violence is directed toward our daring to do. Nothing incites them as much as our assertion, our building, our doing, our will to live. They will not tolerate any action initiated by us, no matter how practical or unthreatening. It is clear now how much they want us not to be.

It is December and getting cold. The little food we find is depleted; our store of grain is diminishing. Other sources have to be found. We hear of people living in this village, Serbs. Some women have ventured there to trade their clothing for food. I see my mother taking a dark blue skirt and one of her pretty blouses she made in Nakovo, tucking them under her coat, leaving. She comes back with a small enameled cup filled with lard, a loaf of bread, some beans, some salt. She spreads the food before us, and we feel lucky. We know she cannot go back there again soon. There were others whose wares did not please, who were turned away, she says. There are not many with whom we can barter. Some say they had their clothes taken away, getting nothing for them. Such trading is soon prohibited and the added danger of severe punishment makes the risk of attempting a barter even greater. But my mother, like the others, will have to dare the same again.

The bleak December grasses shiver in the cold, making small silvery sounds. My little coat from home still fits. Its deep coral pink color, set off by the light brown fur collar, appears resplendent in the drab landscape. It was double breasted till my mother moved the buttons into a single row; its bodice still fits; tight. She has lengthened the sleeves, and with the hem let out, it almost covers my skirt and still twirls bell-like around me. The children of the house have been going begging for more than a week, bringing home pieces of bread, a potato, an onion, a pinch of salt wrapped in bits of newspaper. I have seen them. Now my mother tells me that I, too, must go begging. Children have a better chance of getting food—avoiding punishment. "I'll do anything, but please don't make me do that," I plead, but I know she is relentless, and her sullen looks convince me that there is nothing else left for me to do. The first day I miss the other children leaving the house and I saunter through endless open spaces, lost among graying grasses, looking for a house with a fence. But I see only gray sky spreading. I dream of finding an onion or potato hidden away and root among the tallest grass, believing I will be lucky and find something against all odds. I see the children coming back and, feeling shamed, I run to find the house with a fence around it. A large black dog appears from somewhere, barking ferociously, and with him, his shouting mistress, calling him to quiet, yelling at me, shooing me away. Before I can say anything, she scoffs she has nothing to give me. I cannot hear her clearly and suddenly I cannot see, tears blurring the view, and the harsh voice and the yelping dog make one foreboding barking sound. My rehearsed speech sticks in my throat and I turn away, walking slowly, trying not to run, fearing the dog behind me. I will not go begging again, I tell my mother. But next morning, I am among the children leaving.

I follow the others to houses they know. We make a small crowd in front of a door saying something unrehearsed, together. We stretch out our hands in front of us asking for bread in an accented Serbo-Croatian, betraying a hollow mime. But there is no doubt we mean what we say. Our eyes have a hollow look and our small hands, tugging gently at sleeves that pass us by, are pleading. No one cries. I feel ashamed that my chin wants to quiver and I am glad when we are on our way back. We compare what we have with others we meet. No one thinks of eating what they get.

The first time, I only get one onion. My mother says nothing. The next day, I get a piece of bread. I am so delighted, I cradle it in both my hands, taking a whiff of it now and then, floating home on the sweet familiar scent I had forgotten, almost. Proud of my achievement, taking pleasure in the bread I bring, I burst into the room, presenting the bread like an offering. I am caught by surprise. There are no cheers from anyone. The quiet in the room demands all my attention. Seppi and Johann sit, with their coats on, hollow eyed, motionless. Lately, they do not move much. Grandmother sits at the edge of the straw wrapped in her Umhängtiechl, her felted triangular shawl. Tanti Lisa is sitting, listless, in the corner. My mother is the only one standing up. She looks as if she has been waiting. I am confused. She takes the bread and, holding it in the palm of her hand, looks at it intently and says, mocking: "Now, let's see, how shall we divide this piece of bread—who might it satisfy?" And without directing her speech to anyone, she continues: "To which one of you should we give this pitiful piece of bread, you tell me." A raised arm, palm inverted, she throws the bread to the floor! Grandmother picks up the bread and, without saying anything, breaks it, and gives it to us children. The rest of the day no one in our room says anything at all. When the children leave in the morning, I am among them.

There is no electricity in our houses, nor on the streets. There is no heat. We use the wood we have hidden under the straw only to cook. Beyond the warmth such cooking generates, the house is cold. We keep warm by sleeping in our clothes, covered up with our blankets, our downs. Every night we talk in the dark, mostly about home, remembering our rooms and all our belongings as if everything still is in the same order it once was. We talk about our things, lovingly, as if we were still taking care of them. And, sometimes, we say: "When we're home again, we want only one room and very few things." Our nightly talks are comforting. We share our past adventures, we laugh, and sometimes we sing. We talk long into the night, and when my mother says, "Everything has a beginning and an end; let's not say another word," someone always has just one more word to say, and we hold our breath, trying not to be the last to talk, only to burst out laughing instead, and we laugh, provoking each other to continuous laughter till, exhausted, we finally stop.

At first, Tanti Lisa and I often visit the other rooms in the evenings, while Seppi and Johann sleep. The people in seamstress Anna's room know many songs, and we sing with them till late at night. A woman in the room next to ours knows how to tell stories. Sitting tall among us in the darkened room, wooing images into being with her voice, she tells stories about love, crimes of passion, mysteries, as we quietly attend, watching; everything around us disappears, and we live only in the ebb and flow of her voice. Mesmerized, we stay listening, and the impressions leave with us when we return, reluctantly, to our own rooms. But lately people there, ill, despondent with worry, are irritated by our diversion.

As time passes, we visit less. Quarrels about space, turns at the stove, the outhouse, and accusations about stealing, about spoiling the water in the cistern further divide us. In every room, aggressions are waiting to assert themselves. Some transgressions are worse than others. The women whose little boys are accused of urinating into the cistern are provoked, and a greater wrong is later attributed to them when floating excrement has to be fished out of the water that all of us drink.

We never change or wash our clothes now (they would take too long to dry in the cold). Saving water, we don't even wash ourselves. Some of us have lice. We have black fleas that jump about and drink our blood, causing us to wake at night, scratching. In the morning we take our blankets out into the cold, and when the bugs stop jumping, we take our revenge by crushing them between our thumbnails, leaving a bloody stain. This becomes part of our cleansing ritual. We comb our hair with a dense-toothed comb over a white handkerchief, looking for head lice. We examine the seams of our clothes for lice there. We groom ourselves.

Routinely the men with guns come to our rooms to select those needed to do various jobs. Tanti Lisa is almost always among the selected; tall and sturdy, she appears strong. Those taken to work stay out all day, often walking long distances. We see them carrying bundles of reed on their backs, coming back to the village at dusk. They bring the firewood to heat offices and Partisan housing, but they cannot bring back any for us to burn. Tanti Lisa's feet are badly frostbitten and her shoes have holes in their soles. I see her stuffing cardboard, from a box she found, into her shoes, hoping it will keep out the cold.

On one occasion, when guards come to select workers and before they get to our room, my mother quickly hides her shoes under the straw. She is not always among the selected, but a tall guard, holding a whip, points to her now. She shows him her bare feet; she has no shoes, she says: "If you expect us to work in the snow, give us shoes to wear!" I stand rooted to the floor. He orders her to step out, yelling: "If I tell you to go, you will go!" He hits her with his whip. I wince. Out in the hall, the women line up to leave, and he cracks his whip again, shooing my mother inside. When she retrieves her shoes, holding them up, triumphant, we laugh. But later I catch her quietly weeping. We allow ourselves such acts of defiance at our own risk, and sometimes such stunts even amuse us. When Tanti Lisa tells us the women had to plant onions all day long in snow and freezing cold, and realizing the futility of the job, to soothe their rage, some around her planted the onions upside down, we laugh, knowing that the determined onions, if they don't freeze, will find their way up. But Tanti Lisa, defiant still, retrieves a handful of tiny onions from the sleeve lining of her coat, gloating: "I made certain these won't grow for them!"

We begin and end each day being hungry. A certain numbness has set in, infusing the pain of hunger with lethargy. Even small children sit listless in their rooms. They seldom play. Most of the day is spent waiting—waiting out of habit. And our habit shows in our faces, our clothes, and everything about us takes on the look of waiting. And, whatever else we do has to be done in addition to this terrible demanding task. The days are long.

It is mid-December and still they give us no food. My mother goes to trade clothes without much luck. I still go begging. Tanti Lisa divides all we eat with exacting precision. She is sometimes caught giving most of her share to Johann, which irritates my mother. If she is concerned about Johann, she has to keep up her own strength, my mother tells her. Tanti Lisa smiles agreeably, but she has to be reminded about this often. Sometimes my mother loses her patience and I hear her say, "It isn't fair to the other children." Tanti Lisa looks surprised.

I come home bringing an extra large piece of bread. My mother and the two children are alone in the room. She looks as if she has a score to settle. I am uneasy. She asks me to take Johann outside to play. He, unaccustomed to such singular attention, is overwhelmed by the gesture. It is a mild day. The sunshine cools in gray shadows. We play in tall grasses, catching the sun. We run in small circles: I chasing him, pretending he is hard to catch and he trusting me, running ahead, his whole face beaming. I have an uneasy feeling about this game. Buffeted by apprehensions, intuiting the intent of my errand, I am preoccupied and suddenly stop. I look at Johann; the look in his eyes makes me reach for him and I catch him as he runs toward me. I hold him, and hold him. The wind on my face has the tepid touch of afternoon sun and I press Johann closer against the place in my chest where it feels heaviest. I hear him squeal and giggle and let him go, smiling, hiding my heaviness from him. I don't hear my mother when she calls us in.

Inside the truth is affirmed, the intuited confirmed, communicated without words. I understand it clearly when my mother shoves something under my arm and sends me out the door again, alone. I know without looking, and I press my upper arm ever tighter to my side, holding the wedge firm. I walk to the end of the open corridor and look away into the distance; I see only isolated houses and the large gaps between them where the missing fences used to be. I see the village: a gaping, hungry mouth, gaps between giant devouring teeth grinding down. I take the wedge from under my arm and stuff it into my mouth. I taste something familiar, moist and salty. I devour the bread my mother gave me; I swallow it for the sake of justice.

• • •

My chin still quivers every time I beg. I always stay well in the back, hiding my shame behind the tangle of outstretched hands. We beg in small groups. We move in the open spaces of yards and gardens, avoiding the street. The streets are used by men with guns; they do not like us to share the pavement with them. The houses we go to asking for bread are occupied by the free; we do not know who they are—perhaps they are the families of the guards we avoid on the streets. There are some things we do not need to understand; we only need to do our share. Some children tell of a house close to the dangerous Komandno Mesto, the Partisans' governing office, where a lady always gives bread. We enter the wooden gate of a large corner house; once it may have been the house of a storekeeper, judging by the shuttered door to the street. We follow the brick pavement to one of the doors in the back. The children are chanting in unison, asking the lady for bread: "*Tetka Mila molim parče hleba.*" It has an eerie ring, this rhythmic, hollow singsong. It sounds like a prayer asking for a blessing. The dissonant meld of voices reaches for it patiently; we understand that blessings are few. We want just one—for any one of us; our chanting asks for just one single blessing. It is not an individual plea; together we voice a singular hope. A lady appears holding a large round loaf of bread, cutting pieces from it against her chest, passing them out above our heads; she smiles in the giving. I reach for mine, and the liquid blue of her eyes alights like a blessing. I hold my piece of bread reverently, carrying the light on it to our room. I go to her house alone the next day and, reluctant to repeat the words, I wait for the children to come. After a while the lady comes to the door. My chin aquiver, at a loss for words, I repeat the chant to keep from crying. She says I should come tomorrow; she has given her bread away for today. She repeats this, saying the words *bread* and *tomorrow* in German, "*Brot...morgen,*" to make me understand. I tell her in a weepy voice, hiding my quivering chin, that I understand, and when I turn to go, she asks me to wait. She disappears behind the door and comes back with something wrapped in paper, saying softly, "biscuits." I take them from her hands, and her voice wraps around me like a warm blanket. We talk a while. She asks my name and compliments me on how well I speak the language. I am not sure I am hearing right—she is saying: "Come tomorrow, for lunch." I hear myself saying thank-you and repeat to myself all the way home: tomorrow, for lunch. I fill the room bringing my gift and my good news. Everyone listens.

Combed and tidied, I am wearing my best dress; the lengthened coat not quite covering it, its skirt peeks like a spring promise spreading flowers on the frozen ground before me. I stand at her door, my heart pounding. She asks me in. My dress spills its many flowers, and I can feel her eyes watching me as I fold my coat, placing it on a side chair. We are in the kitchen. Everything in it is white—the table and chairs, the credenza, and even the stove. A familiar, delicious smell fills the room. The table, covered with a white damask cloth, is set for one. She explains that her brother has been here earlier and they have eaten at noon. It is past one, I realize from the large clock on the wall. I apologize; we have no clock. She fills my plate with stuffed cabbage rolls and sauerkraut; she gives me a piece of bread and sits down, talking with me as if we had done this many times before. She lives with her youngest brother, she says; she has three brothers. I only have cousins; all boys, I tell her. Her father was a teacher in Perlez and one of her brothers is a professor there. Perlez is her home. She came only recently— to keep house for her brother, who works in the offices here; he is an accountant. She continues talking, now drawing me into conversation, now urging me to eat. The food is very tasty and I say so, but since I am unaccustomed to salted and sour food, my throat hurts eating it. I am too shy to ask for a glass of water and eat diligently, buffering the spicy fare with bread. I eat slowly. Looking at the huge mound of sauerkraut on my plate, I wonder if I can eat it all. I feel my tongue like a piece of raw meat, salted, swelling in my mouth. I listen to her talk. I am intrigued, bewildered by the attention she gives me. She treats me like an equal—like a person.

We are interrupted by an almost inaudible knock at the door. She excuses herself, saying, thoughtfully, "Ponkrac is bringing the water." She opens the door, and an old man, carrying two shiny tin buckets filled to the brim with water, comes in. Carefully putting the buckets down, he stands in front of the closed door looking awkward, making bowing motions, smiling toward the floor, rubbing his large gloved hands together to warm them. His hair, disheveled, peeks from under a dark blue stocking cap. He wears much-mended glasses. She now carries the buckets into what looks to be a pantry, while he stands still, his cap in hand, waiting. He glances in my direction only to let me know he knows I am here. She comes out of the pantry carrying something wrapped like a package; something for him, she says, and before she gives it to him, she asks if he would like to stay and get warm? Bowing several times, he declines in whispers. Placing the package in his hands, she smiles, and he, looking down, aware of her smile, takes both, adjusting his bowed body as if to a warm blanket, whispering thank-yous without raising his eyes, and leaves.

"Ponkrac," she says gravely, "is the famous clown," and she mentions his travels and the name of a famous circus. "He sleeps in the wash kitchen, here in the yard. He prefers it to sleeping in the camp. He does not mind the chickens; they keep him warm, he says. He feeds the animals, chops wood for me, and insists on bringing the drinking water from the pump, though I would really prefer fetching it myself." And, leaning toward me, she says, intimately, as if we have been friends for a very long time: "You must have noticed his nose, the strings of mucus hanging suspended, their fall pending . . ." Making a grimace, she adds, "I try not to think of it possibly falling into the open buckets—I don't have the heart to refuse him bringing the water." We smile at each other, sealing the secret. She suddenly remembers having to tell him something, and taking a woolen cape the color of her chestnut hair from a coat rack behind the door, she leaves the kitchen, leaving me to finish my food. I have managed to eat only half the food on my plate, and having been aware all along that I may not be able to eat it all, I have been uneasy, wondering what to do. It is important to eat it all, not only because it is polite, but for other more pressing reasons. Not eating it may give the impression that I am not hungry enough; that we don't need food. I can't bring myself to ask to take the food along; it would be rude and greedy. And I can't see myself explaining to her that my not eating it all has nothing to do with our not being hungry. Whatever I do, I must not jeopardize my coming here; those at home count on me. I must eat. But almost immediately after she leaves, I do something I cannot believe I am doing: I leave my place at the table, carry my plate to the credenza, open its doors, remove the lid of the covered dish, and with the spoon left in it, I carefully replace the untouched food from my plate, leaving some of the frayed edges my fork has touched on the plate. I cover the dish, close the credenza carefully, resume my place at the table, and cleaning my plate to the last morsel, I do not move till she returns. Seeing her makes me feel guilty about the deception, and I look at her apologetically without saying anything. She does not comment on the empty plate, and before I leave, she brings me something to take home. I put on my coat, and out of its pockets I retrieve the two small spools of thread I have brought with me. Hesitant, noticing the smallness of my present, I hand the threads to her, saying apologetically, "My mother thought, perhaps, you can use these." From the sudden change in her expression I surmise, startled, that she is displeased, offended. She hands the threads back to me, saying in a cool detached tone she does not really need any thread now. Accommodating the rejection, I have trouble making words, and I hear her saying, in an almost consoling tone, "If your mother has something to barter, she should come herself." I hope I can bring my voice to make audible sounds. "It is a present—a small present—for you." I can see her eyes brighten, filling the room with light. I leave with an invitation to come back every second day in the morning for breakfast. Walking back, holding my little package wrapped in paper, preoccupied with my new experience, I am being less careful on the street. But, by now, walking with awareness is second nature. For a brief moment I can afford the careless abandon of being caught in the past and looking forward to the future.

Everything is retold in our room. Everyone has questions about the smallest details. Were there pictures on the walls, Tanti Lisa asks? What is the pantry like, grandmother wants to know? That the stove is white enamel gets raving awe. They would have liked it if I had brought the food I could not eat—they cannot understand my not eating it. I open my mouth to show them my tongue. "Did you tell her I can sew for her?" my mother asks. "Did she like the thread?" I describe everything and tell all we did and said, again and again. And again, before we go to sleep, I tell, and they listen as if they needed to reconstruct the place, the experience for themselves. "Next time you go there, ask . . ." and everyone voices a modest request. And, as if they need to be convinced, they want me to say that I have been invited back.

Every second day I go to tetka Mila's house for a few hours, and I always bring back small amounts of food for the others, mostly bread. We ration it sparingly. Leftover provisions are kept, wrapped in cloth, in a knotted-rope satchel hung from the ceiling to keep it away from the mice. Yes, we have mice!

For Christmas Eve goodwill returns to our house. The corn swept up from the no longer existing corn bin floor turns up again, diminished but ample, with each room contributing their share. There is a fire burning under the kettle in the stable. A beam of the corn bin floor is sacrificed only because it is impossible to use it in the kitchen stove without a hatchet. Lighting the fire is an exacting craft and those who know it tend the flame, turning the rafter to keep it burning. The corn has been cooking since late afternoon. It has been soaking all day in the heavy iron kettle we borrowed from the house next door. A sweet smell settles in our house and yard, making our mouths water, waiting. Though we would like to contain this smell, fearing it will betray us, there is no stopping it from traveling to places it should not go. Someone thinks of hanging a blanket to cover the doorway, to muffle the smell and hide the fire.

In the evening we sit around the kettle enveloped by sweet smells and soft firelight, warming our hands on tin cups, dipping them into the savory juice as into holy water, retrieving moist kernels in sweet communion. Our voices, sweetened, ring silvery into the crisp night air. We sing, "*Stille Nacht, heilige Nacht . . .*" Children sit nestled in the crouching laps of their mothers, grandmothers. All is well in our stable. Outside, watching the street and the wide expanse of darkened gardens, the lookouts are eating their corn, warming their fingers in the sweet water; they come to the stable at intervals to reassure us and to fill their cups. Later, our singing is interrupted by their breathless voices announcing the coming of the guards. The fire is doused. Grabbing our belongings, our small children, we leave the stable in single file, as if rehearsed, moving mutely along the stable wall, our gaze fixed on lanterns cutting the dark some distance away, and disappear into the house without a sound. Inside, covered up, we listen to the loud voices of the men with guns—in front of our house—passing. When all is quiet, we retrieve our cups from under the blankets, singing softly, "Silent night, holy night . . ." to the familiar darkness of our room.

Days later they come to tell us, with the urgency of warnings, that we are to stay in our houses for three days; anyone seen outside will be shot. The men carrying guns say this looking at us as if they want to kill us all, outright, and only mean to devise this game to heighten their fervor by delay. Three days we stay inside; some dare quick runs to the outhouse. On the fourth day we go outside, not knowing what to expect. No one is there to notice us. No one shoots at us.

I make my cautious walk to tetka Mila's house; she knows nothing of the deadly game and I say nothing more about it. I meet her brother, whom I call čika Joca. He is charming, sophisticated, funny, always well dressed and on the way to somewhere in a hurry; he talks very fast and has a way of saying things that make me laugh. He teases, but in a preoccupied, detached way; sometimes he teases tetka Mila, saying there is a hair on his toast, when there is not, and performing a pantomime, pretending to re-move the imagined hair, making a disgusted grimace. She does not laugh. Sometimes I catch her crying and see him hastily leaving the house. At such times her eyes fade to their palest, and we say nothing. One day I hear an argument about the bread. She insists she needs extra bread. "To give away daily," he says accusingly, mocking the futility of it, and saying something unkind to her, using words I do not know, he leaves. She, looking self-assured, smiles knowingly; she will have her bread.

• • •

Someone in our house dies. A body shrouded in a blanket appears in the entry, and a continuous wailing, punctuated by loud shrieks, fills our house, making us listen. Grandmother says in her time there were professional wailers who, called to the house after someone had died, mourned with similar ritual. Though the woman wailing may be younger than Grand-mother, it is an old custom that some people still practice. Soon the pierc-ing shrieks increase, and the frenzied woman has to be forcibly separated from the bewailed corpse. Consoled by bystanders, she still shouts her ac-cusations to the unknown, to fate, to death—and beating her chest, she accuses herself. The way she tears at herself looks theatrical, almost. Her grief, overshadowed by the hysterical frenzy, appears false, unbelievable, unpleasant to witness. It seems the old custom has outgrown its usefulness here. This ritual is only for those who, parting from their dead, know they intend to go on living. We cannot boast of such assurance. Here, with our own death pending, such leave-taking is an empty lament. Its sound insults.

Anna dies. In spite of my mother giving her the last of our grain, in spite of our giving her some bread from tetka Mila, in spite of seeking advice from a man in camp whom people know to be a doctor but who has no medicine, our friend Anna, the seamstress, dies. Others die. Soon the many dead are visible wrappings littering the entry of our house, waiting for the wagon that comes already loaded with many corpses: some wrapped in cloth, some partly dressed, others, their skeletal bodies exposed to the cold, all piled on each other on the wagon. Together they make an almost inaudible acutely shrill sound that grates like chalk over slate, overriding the grinding sound of the wagon. The exposed faces, shadows of skulls atangle in with-ered hair, tinge the tune with the macabre. I always look with one eye only, keeping the other to the ground before me, trying to do both—accompany the dead on their way and not lose my own. A dense sepia tone, the color of old photographs, swallows everything around me with its terrible eerie light, and an endless space in which there is nothing but emptiness—with no room for anything, not even sorrow—takes me in as if I belonged to it. The eternal nothing occupies me, guiding my steps, hovering over me like a terrible jeering gargoyle. I see this wagon often stopped at our house, at the neighboring houses, and on my way to tetka Mila's. It never occurs to me that tetka Mila sees this wagon too—it can hardly be avoided. Even looking at it one-eyed, I know its image like my own face. We call it the death-wagon. It is a part of our existence and as usual as the setting sun; we look at sunsets less often now.

The wagon piled up with bodies moves always in the same direction: parallel to the river, away from the embankment of the railroad tracks. Every day, slowly, relentlessly, it moves the full length of the streets out of the village into the field beyond where the grasses grow, where we can't go. No one accompanies the dead; on their way from house to house, only the women who load the corpses follow the wagon's passage on the sidewalk down to the edge of the village. We hear from those who cover the dead that they are buried in long open trenches, dug ahead by people of the camp. Soon we learn that clothes and blankets are taken off the corpses by those who need them more, and the dead are covered with each other, and the ditches, filled, are covered over with earth. These common graves go unmarked; only the frozen ground keeps them distinguished from the graying grasses. We remember the dead in our prayers at night, saying: *"Das ewige Licht leuchte ihnen. Herr, lass sie ruhen in Frieden. Amen."* I think of the ruby glow of the everlasting light in our church at home shining for them (may they rest in peace). I still pray for the war to be over, and for everyone to come safely home, though I know the war ended long ago and only our talks, our yearnings, our wishes, and our dreams take us home. At night we pray for home, but during the day everyone knows where the wagon goes, and there is no day that we don't know where it will take us. It is a mesmerizing rhythm, this continuous going forth of the death-wagon by day and our relentless falling back at night, going home. The ebb and flow of our days and nights continues.

Seven thousand die in our camp this winter; some say more. It is the winter of 1946, and still more people come, brought here to die. They fill the houses, taking the places of those who have died before them; they pray at night, and the wagon keeps moving by day. People die of starvation, diseases; some are shot or beaten to death, caught begging for food, taking wood, fetching water, trying to escape. Others kill themselves. A young woman in the house in front of ours jumps into the well. I know her only by sight, by her doleful smile, having seen her in the gardens rooting for edible grasses, her two small children watching. She leaves a note—an apology, to her mother, her children. We hear this from the women who come asking to borrow a rope (which we don't have) to lower someone into the well to pull the body out. Helplessly we listen, and something within me trembles to sounds unheard, like distant gunfire, and the air chills to recall the stark white wall of Hallai's house—and the light hovers, bitter-gall green. An image clings to an insistence: the dismantled corn bin—I want it put back like it was! I want lattice by lattice back in place—I'll retrieve them myself, to make it whole again. A futile yearning for something lost overtakes the rage in me, trying to suppress it.

We are isolated, even in our houses. Only very rarely do people from other houses come to our rooms, even people from our own villages. There is one other family from our village living in our house. Kathi, a girl my age, her younger brother, their mother, and grandmother live in the largest room. Kathi and I played together outside when we first came. Now we seldom play. We don't know about each other's well-being. I only know when I see them they have not died. Dispersed among so many, seldom seeing each other, we have become estranged like relatives separated by long distances. Consumed by a singular concern, we are strangers among ourselves. We still recognize each other. Some of us know where our people live, and who has died; we keep each other informed. We keep track of our relatives, but we seldom see them. Päsl Leni comes to us when Vedde Niklos (Grandfather's brother) is sick. My mother gives her some of what we have, and Grandmother goes with Päsl Leni to see him. Later we hear they both died. Kodl Lisa and the twins and Anna and her mother live in the next side street—I can see the house, looking across open gardens—but we seldom see them. Gathered here to die, we have become remote.

More than three months have passed without rations. Now, late in January, they open soup kitchens. We stand in long lines. They give us one ration daily: soup, consisting of corn meal and water, often unsalted. Much later we get bread made of coarsely ground cornmeal; often we find chunks of corncobs in it. These loaves are about a foot long, looking like domed bricks, and are quite as heavy. We get a loaf for the six of us. Its thick crust is impenetrable, hard to cut even with a knife, and we hack away at it or break it by hitting it against something harder still, to get to the rough inner core. We continue hacking at it with our jaws; our gums bleed; remaining bites are colored pink. I have blisters in my cheeks and on the roof of my mouth, and my jaws feel dislocated. The bread we get from tetka Mila we save for Seppi and Johann, and Grandmother, who has no teeth. The routine of getting something to eat is not to be taken for granted; for just as we get used to going for our rations, they suddenly stop, and after a time, they resume, and we get only ounces of uncooked cornmeal. As if to set us up for punishment, they give us no wood to cook it with. But we take everything without question, knowing that in this system there is one constant: nothing can be counted on. Engaged in the business of dying, we live from day to day, breathing, moving, expecting nothing, accepting everything with increasing impartiality. Waiting.

Among so much patience my own irritability, my petty conceits are disgusting, even to me, but they well up from somewhere within me to shame me. Grandmother is patient when I complain: "I can't go to tetka Mila's house with a hole in my stocking where it shows." I expect her to have fixed it. I am disgruntled, irritating, mean. She is consoling and kind. Only when I pout does she remind me how much she loves me, and did I not know, the first cherries, the first watermelon, the loveliest smelling grapes, which I liked so much, all the first fruits were mine, were picked for me—every year she brought them to see me smile. I remember. I hang my head, grumbling, looking cross, to hide my shame. And I feel very unlikable. I am sorry for being mean to Grandmother, but I can't bring myself to say it. She smiles as if she knows. Her cough is getting worse now, and a foul-smelling fluid stains her handkerchief brown when she blows her nose. My mother scolds, seeing Grandmother wipe Seppi's nose with the same handkerchief. She will be more careful, she then says, smiling sheepishly, indicating she forgot. My grandmother is patient and kinder than anyone I know.

Tetka Mila needs someone to help with the large wash, the ironing. My mother now works there when she is needed. This gives us a decided advantage. Such jobs are coveted among us for obvious reasons. And they are legal. The Serb families living here are allowed to avail themselves of such labor. They pay to the management, nothing to us. Since my mother is working, things in our room have changed. We have a built-in stove! My mother finds a piece of cast iron in tetka Mila's yard and brings it back to build a stove around it, using bricks from the corn-bin-less pigpen and mortar she makes herself. Carried away by her ardor as she is, a third of the large window at the head of our common bed is bricked up behind the glass, to keep the cold from blowing in on us. No one seems concerned that our room is much darker, and my mentioning it is ignored.

We now have a real broom, though somewhat worn, and an old enameled *Weidling* (a large bowl-like container) with a tin bottom that we use as a washbasin. All this my mother finds at tetka Mila's in stables and attics as things discarded. In our room, exalted for their usefulness, they are restored to their former selves and become treasures. A much chipped blue-enameled water can, with mended bottom, stands in the corner now, holding water. We brought it here carrying wheat that my mother found in the attic of a stable there. Tanti Lisa and I made several trips transporting the newfound treasure concealed under Grandmother's Umhängtiechl. I, showing the way, only provided the courage of shared company. "The closer to our room we get, the lighter our load," Tanti Lisa says, looking about; we have become experts at carrying things under the Umhängtiechl. Even some of the wood that Ponkrac chops comes home with us under its protection, with tetka Mila's blessings.

There is talk of a flood. It has been raining for days without stop, and though we cannot see it, the river is rising. I hear tetka Mila talking about it with friends who come to see her. There is rumor of an evacuation of the "free." One is led to assume that the rest of us will be left here to drown. We talk about it in our room. The cistern in front of our entry is overflowing, transforming the yard into a mud puddle with ever widening ripples. The water level is steadily rising; Grandmother says the ground is beginning to liquefy. There is talk of the dead being disgorged from the graves, of countless bodies floating into the rising river. This time it is Grandmother who is most concerned. I try to console her with fanciful tales of rescue in which I, stranded by the rising waters at tetka Mila's and evacuated with her, return with a boat, which I row myself, to take Grandmother and all to higher ground. Grandmother, lost in thought, listens without her usual smile.

But it suddenly stops raining, and the swollen ground slowly swallows all excesses, draining yards and gardens, mud puddle by muddy puddle, finally to lie down again, regaining its former firmness. Our cistern is holding its water. Framed in the square opening, it flashes its silvery surface, glistening like a mirror, reflecting clear skies.

Saved from the flood, without evacuation and rescue needs, we are affected by another natural disaster that has the potential of driving us from our houses. Walking home from tetka Mila's, I see women coming through the gardens carrying large pieces of red meat in their hands. In our house, I hear a terrible quarrel going on in the entry. The women are accusing each other of greed and wrongdoing; holding knives and defending their right, they use their sharp tongues to lash at one another. They are fighting over a dead horse, Grandmother explains: a horse died somewhere in the village, and the women who heard about it ran to cut pieces off the carcass. She too went, Grandmother admits, but the throng of women climbing over each other, fighting to get a piece of the dead animal, slashing away at it with knives, kept her away. She, with her crippled hands, is no match for their quick-wielding blades and agile fingers. Not being able to participate, having to watch the unattractive sight, dampens the desire, Grandmother argues apologetically. Soon the stench of the meat cooking floods the house, assaulting our senses, forcing us out of our rooms. There is no stench to compare it with. It has some of us making rash promises; even under pain of death, we will not eat such meat. Others eat it to avoid pains of hunger.

There is an epidemic spreading among the animals in Serb households. They discard the dead carcasses on their dung heaps and watch us fight over them, without interference. As more animals die, a variety of meats makes an appearance at the stove in the entry. We see piglets, days old, their pink skin blistered with disease, being cooked without the adding of salt or spices. The diseased flesh, cooking, spreads the stench of death among us.

• • •

Grandmother is sick. At first I don't notice. She hides it behind her touching smile. She wants me, when I go to tetka Mila's, to ask for some tomato juice. I look at her surprised, not taking her seriously; I say I will, but like putting off the wishes of an unreasonable child, I know I will not. I know I can't bring myself to ask tetka Mila to give us things that to her may seem unnecessary. My mother asks for honey to soothe Grandmother's cough, and vinegar—I see Grandmother sipping it from a bottle. Knowing that she has given us these things, how can I ask her to give us more? When I come back from tetka Mila's, Grandmother is waiting for the tomato juice, which I do not have. I say I forgot to ask, but I will—after tomorrow. But after tomorrow, I do the same. I feel bad about not bringing Grandmother what she asks for and worse about having to ask tetka Mila. Grandmother always smiles and says consolingly, "Next time you will ask."

We ask Nina néni to take care of Grandmother during the day. At night my mother takes care of her. Tanti Lisa works in the fields. Sometimes she stays in the village, carrying the ill to houses where they are gathered. She comes home late, exhausted, and when she sleeps, not even Johann's cries can wake her. He has nasty scabs all over his skin that keep him awake, scratching. I hear his adenoidal cries, periodically, throughout the night. Both Seppi and Johann have whooping cough, and the whooping noises vibrate into our sleep. Seppi's rectum protrudes when he coughs, and he calls for my mother with frightful shrieks, "Kodl, it's coming out, it's coming out." My mother sits him on her knee, pushing on the protrusion, and keeping him there for a while, she talks to him in quiet, soothing tones, consoling him—putting me to sleep.

Grandmother is getting worse. Her pleading for light pierces the darkness of our room, and my mother comes the next day with an oil lamp from tetka Mila. The oil has to last, she tells Grandmother and we burn it only when Grandmother calls for it and blow it out when she sleeps. We have matches. Grandmother's groans stretch into mournful moaning and pleading cries for my mother: "Wawi, Wawi," calling for light all through the night. All through the night my mother gets up to light the lamp she blows out when Grandmother's moans fade into sleep. When my mother goes to work, Tanti Lisa is away at work already and we are alone with Grandmother.

Nina néni comes. The Steins lived across the street from Grandmother's house, and Nina néni is also our relative. She is glad to come. And in return, we share our food with her.

Looking at the many bottles of tomato juice in her pantry, I approach tetka Mila obliquely, making comments on the many bottles, hinting that my grandmother likes nothing more than tomato soup. Without understanding what I really mean, she pleasantly replies, "Next time I cook it, I will send her some." "She even loves drinking it right out of the bottle," I say, feigning amusement. She is amused; not hearing my plea, she smiles. The bottles of juice, preserved long ago by the people who owned this house, line the shelves, waiting. But I can't bring myself to say: "Please, give me some tomato juice for my Grandmother."

Grandmother has been very sick for more than a week. And now we keep the light burning even though it is getting low on oil; my mother frets about how she will get more when it is gone. Grandmother has taken to calling my mother's name continuously between moans, and the room resounds with her pain and her modest wants. Nina néni, who is sleeping here now, helps my mother lift Grandmother. They sit her into the Weidling because she requests it; its tin bottom is cooling, she says, making grateful groaning sounds of relief as if, just for a moment, she finds the right place to be—without pain. And then the moans continue and she wants to be laid back down again. Wracked with pain, she now calls for light even when it is on. Nina néni is patient. In quiet whispers and soothing sounds, she adds her reassurance, giving moist rags soaked in vinegared water for Grandmother to suck on, to hold. And Grandmother's moans, subsiding for moments, lull to fragmented sleep.

It must be close to morning. The light is flickering, about to go out. Except for our breathing the room is quiet. Nina néni stirs beside me. She is sitting up, reaching over me; I feel her arm tugging at my mother. "Wawi—wake up. Your mother is dead." She says it quietly and as calmly as if she were announcing the time. I see my mother rising out of the covers, stepping over me, crouching down beside Nina néni, talking in whispers. "The last thing she said was Hans—three times she called out your father's name. She died, just now . . ." I hear the soft whispers of my mother's weepy voice tinge with regret, "Why didn't you call me?" Nina néni says only consoling words, and making room for my mother, she gets up and leaves the room. My mother sits silently next to Grandmother, and I hear her softly blowing her nose. I can't move. I don't make a sound, but I hear everything. I am wide awake. The words keep repeating from somewhere in the room—somewhere in my head. I keep very quiet as if to negate having heard them. And, smiling within me, the quiet says: it isn't so, it's nothing. Nina néni has returned, and I hear her saying to my mother they need to straighten Grandmother before she is cold. I am afraid to turn and remain motionless, waiting. I hear them working around Grandmother. My mother wants to undress her, down to her petticoat . . . her long white petticoat . . . so no one will maul her corpse for her clothes. I hear them struggling, moving and removing. Even with my eyes closed, I can tell it is already light outside. The lamp has stopped flickering. The light has gone out.

When I finally turn to sit up, Grandmother's body is covered up with a blanket. My mother tells me calmly what I already know. I say nothing. I can't even cry. My mother looks composed (she stopped crying some time ago) and quietly tells the others. Only Seppi cries. He cries so bitterly I feel the pain in my own heart. I hear my mother consoling him: "Don't cry, my boy, don't cry—Grandmother is in heaven now, where nothing can harm her." His large eyes widen to accommodate the notion of heaven. He holds onto my mother tightly, and his crying subsides to quiet sobbing. No one else makes a sound. Tanti Lisa, shrunk into herself, looking helpless, looks to my mother, and the somber tone of her voice is gonglike when she says: "It's April the second," as if to give Grandmother's death some significance, and as an afterthought, as if reminded of something important, she adds, apologetically, in quiet whispers, "It's Johann's birthday." Johann looks at her with questioning eyes; she leaves for work.

My mother is rooting through the straw at the head of our bed, pulling out a gunny sack. Nina néni is taking the two boys to the room where she lives, some houses down the street, to gather her few belongings. She is now moving in with us. I am to go to tetka Mila and tell her my mother will be late. I walk through the fallow gardens. I walk there and back. I pass the stable. I look to its floor—we now place the dead there for the waiting wagon. The floor is bare.

I enter our room. Quiet, like in a church, my mother is kneeling bent over Grandmother's shrouded body. She is sewing her into the gunny sack. With her back toward me, she does not move, she does not acknowledge my presence. Only her hands move, gliding rhythmically, breathing their way over the open seam. Standing to the side of the closed door, holding my fists to my chin, I see her pale profile, marble-like, eye downcast, lips thin, chin firmly set, her gaze fixed to her moving hands, as if her hands and eyes, engaged in holy covenant, cannot be parted. Tears flow down her face uninterrupted by any sound and fall into the sack below. Motionless, I stand in awe before the silent image too private to witness, too large to behold. Empty of all else, I stare. The image takes me in and breathes within me. I tremble with reverence. I am a large cathedral . . . a vaulted dome . . . a sacred offering . . . a silent requiem.

CHAPTER 9

The Death-Wagon Moves

SEPPI'S DOLEFUL EYES search the room for the familiar smile and doting eyes; Grandmother's. Playing with other children in the stable, crouching around the tightly wrapped body shrouded in a burlap sack, he does not recognize the familiar outlines. Except for the children playing, who notice the dead as things among others there—the empty kettle housing, the earthen walls, a singular brick—no one comes, not even the wagon to take her away. I see her straightened body wrapped in the familiar texture, cocoonlike, lying on the floor, alone. No one else has died in our house for days. I pass the stable, peering in detached. One day I see that the floor is bare.

Nina néni's intense black eyes pierce the room. She is quick moving, lively. Her presence in our room brings an unaccustomed restlessness. A feeling of separateness has to be accommodated and reconciled with loss of familial privacy. Nina néni is caring and kind, but we are only her distant kin. She is Altkroßmotter's youngest sister, but I think of her only as Grandmother's neighbor. Now she sleeps next to me in Grandmother's place. Often she does not talk for long hours; she is praying, using the rosary she keeps in the pocket of her long skirt, fingering it, lips moving in a ruminating fashion, making soundless words. She likes talking about her children and grandchildren who live in America. She, too, has been there several times. I like the stories about her childhood adventures best. And the warmth we miss getting during the day, we get from her generous storytelling at night.

In conversations about home, airing our hopes and wishes, Nina néni's wants are modest, well reasoned, practical. When we talk about home, about what we will do when we are free, we know we are only imagining—when we are free, I want to live in the woods where there are no people, I always say, and I imagine how peaceful it would be. She does not imagine; she is planning. When she goes home she will tell the Partisans they can keep her house and all that is in it; she wants only to live in her wash-kitchen, in the yard, where she will be trouble to no one. She has it all worked out and tells us the intricate details of the arrangement in nightly increments—the furnishings she will use, the utensils, the linens, all limited to basic needs, all modest requests, and since they have the use of her house with all its contents, she is sure that whoever may now live there will honor her bid. She even specifies the time of day she will be seen outside; all calculated to minimize her being trouble to anyone. As for money—her children, Katherine and Peter, will send her some from America; or she will earn her keep, and there are many versions of how she will do that. We listen to these stories; they interest as well as amuse us; they pave the way of our nightly trips home. Because Nina néni's stories are so well thought out, it occurs to me that behind those soundless words during her many hours of praying, she is busy making plans. I think this only because I am not pious myself and because it helps me reconcile her mercurial nature with the devout, prayerful image she projects.

The room without Grandmother is no longer the same. I don't think about it much. I don't fret. It is almost as if I don't miss her, as if I don't feel the loss of her presence. I don't feel anything. Except at night. At night I dream of Grandmother. I am looking for her; I have to tell her about the tomato juice, to say how sorry I am, to ask her forgiveness. I cry in my sleep, waking the others. I wake up screaming. And soon it is a nightly occurrence and always the same dream, till one night, I wake up in a dream crying, dreaming on.

I am in a desolate landscape; earth colors, sepia tones predominate. The expansive plain is empty, treeless. I am alone. I am walking against strong winds blowing. I lean into the wind to keep going. I am barefoot; I can see my feet touching the ground, walking. I know I am dreaming but I am aware that I am moving in real space just as I would if I were awake; I have control over my movement. I keep walking against the storm; I feel the increasing resistance of the wind. I squint to keep out the blowing dust; the grit is pelting me, stinging my skin. I hold my open face against the raging power of the storm. It keeps blowing. I keep leaning into it, feeling it restrict my motion. Suddenly, wordless commands charge the void, expressing annoyance: I should not be here; this is no place for me; I should go back. But I go on. And, abruptly, the wind subsides, the dust settles. I can see the ground beneath my feet littered with debris, bits of rags on sandy soil, and in front of me three large crosses rising, elevating the crucified over rolling hills, over steeples and towers, into the ominous turbulence of dark skies. I can see far into the distance where the horizon curves. I stand small against the scope of my view. At the foot of the center cross, at eye level, close up, I see crossed feet pierced by a large spike, pinned against the wood. A white tablet with an inscription—I do not look up, but I sense the presence of the central figure, teaching me by showing, making clear that the cross on the right has someone impaled on it who is faithful, obedient, acquiescing. On the cross to the left, I sense a willful, defiant, unpenitent self. Facing them I understand: to my left is the good, to my right the bad. But a benevolence from the middle smiles down on me as if to say I have it wrong. Instead of understanding, I feel relieved. I gaze at the view beyond. The mountains purple, and the sky grows azure blue. As I turn to go, I hear the same wordless command, meaning clearly: "Your Grandmother has forgiven you long ago . . . You will not need to look for her again." I remember this dream; the power of its landscape fills me with vitality for days. And, as predicted, I stop having the recurring dream.

• • •

Entering tetka Mila's house, I am startled to see her packing. I often have apprehensions about her moving away. They are going to visit their brother Sava and his family in Perlez, she explains. She pauses. They are thinking of taking me along, she says. I choke with surprise. I cannot contain my excitement; I radiate joy in all directions. I can't believe I will be allowed to go. "Čika Joca is making arrangements," she says, convincingly, as if she knows what I am thinking. "And tomorrow, we're off to Perlez," she says with theatrical gesture, adding in whispers, "in a carriage pulled by two white horses." I run all the way to our room. Breathless, I can't say a word. The all too quick transition from one world to the other is jarring. My mother has nothing against my going. With so much joy it is difficult to sleep.

The wagon, not quite a carriage, is a buggy of sorts pulled by two handsome horses. Čika Joca prods me to climb up. "Take care you don't fall and break your cup," he warns, making me laugh. "For precaution's sake, perhaps Lujza should sit in the back, keeping low—just while we are riding through the village, of course, to avoid meddlesome inquiries that may cause us delay." He says this to tetka Mila with patronizing assertiveness as the man in charge of our well-being. She, keeping her composure, looks at him with astonished liquid eyes of lightest blue and, as if his shortcomings still take her by surprise, diminishes her disappointment with an accepting smile. I climb over the seat and, crouching down behind it, discover the place under it. The seat being high and covered by a blanket makes the enclosed space below it a perfect hiding place. "May I sit under the seat?" I ask him. "If you like. Perfect!" he says, beaming.

The buggy rumbles along. The quiet muffle of voices seeping into the cozy space blankets my excitement, transforming it into tranquility. Lulled by the continuous movement, I make small sounds, listening to the vibration of my voice, and almost feel interrupted when čika Joca lifts the blanket, asking me to come out. The spread of fields and sky pierces my eyes, and my chest expands to accommodate the stretch of magnificent view. I smile, my face wide open, inviting the breeze to blow on it. Squinting into the sun, inhaling the smell of hay and horses, I am part of the eternal presence of the land.

Perlez is not far; our trip is shorter than I thought it would be. We arrive in a place with real houses with curtained windows, fenced-in yards; with people walking on the streets, greeting each other. And later there is light—electric light. I see it looking down the street, its orange glow framed by windows dotting the street like gleaming beacons, beaming invitations to come inside. Though I am used to seeing a furnished house, being at tetka Mila's, here everything makes a new impression. The house is filled with books, and the library has a large desk. Tetka Mila tells me it belonged to their father. Rugs and ćilims, patterned walls and cushioned couches, plants on window ledges, paintings, give the place a layered look, an easy elegance. While my senses glut, taking in everything, a self-imposed restriction governs every move I make. Just allowing me to be here is generous enough; I want to minimize my presence by wanting nothing more. I am even reluctant to ask about going to the outhouse and don't, till tetka Mila offers to take me. And, later, sleeping beside her, I try to make myself as small as possible, taking hardly any space, lying on my side close to the edge of the bed.

In the morning I wake alone, on fat white pillows, under a yellow satin comforter enveloped in buttoned-down white linen. A friendly chatter from somewhere inside, and the chirping of birds and sounds of domestic fowl outside, make the room seem even more private. I scurry to dress. Everyone is gathered around the table, having breakfast. They smile, making room for me. Tetka Mila's older brother Sava is easygoing, soft-spoken, assured in an understated way, and seems more akin to tetka Mila than to the mercurial, quick-moving čika Joca. His son, Duško, has inherited his fair complexion and is tall and lean at fifteen. There is an inherent alertness about Duško. His eagerness to know everything is expressed by a certain scrutinizing gaze. He looks at me as if he means to extract an essential essence. His mother, tetka Olga, is slender, dark-haired, plain. Her eyes have an underlying look of concern, lighting up only doting on Duško, on whom they look worshiping, as on a god. Only Duško asks me about the concentration camp and only when no one is present. He says he has seen women hiding about their village, begging, peddling clothes for food. Yes, some steal away in the dead of night, I tell him; some, caught on their way back, get punished, and their food is taken away. Some are shot. Only those who are lucky bring the food back. My Kodl Lisa has done it several times. She will probably do it again. Duško is quiet when I tell him these things, and I notice his sensitive long-fingered hands.

We are surprised by an overnight snow almost a foot deep. Because of my cloth shoes, I am told I will not be going along with tetka Mila to help with her errands in the village. Čika Sava and I are left alone in the house; he in his library and I in the sitting room. I am a little disappointed; I would have liked seeing the village. Looking past the red geraniums in the window, down the snow-blanketed street, its sounds muffled against the crisp stillness, I recall the familiar quiet of a time remembered. I am glad to be alone, without the nagging constraint I impose on myself in the presence of others, and I look at everything, taking the largest possible view, enjoying it without apologies.

A knock at the front door startles. I stand rooted to the floor. Čika Sava enters the room, bringing someone with him. He looks at me surprised, as if he had forgotten about me, and with an apologetic "Oh," continues looking for something, talking with the girl behind him. A familiar image stands framed in the doorway dressed in a dark blue coat, a knitted shawl slipping from a haloed head, blond hair, braided, framing a pale face with freckles, light eyes and, though I cannot see them from this distance, I know these eyes have pink eyelashes. The girl comes closer. Noticing me, she stops, her eyes riveted on me, and finishes her sentence, stammering. Her face, not able to bring itself to fading beyond its usual pale, blushes to express shock, and the fringes around her eyes embellish, sparkling like old gold. I want to greet her and almost do, when čika Sava's voice interrupts saying something to her, handing her a paper. She now talks excitedly, hiding her confusion, trying to retrieve her composure. Čika Sava accompanies her to the front door, saying he expected her to have gone home during break. She gives an explanation, which I cannot hear, and when the door closes, čika Sava returns to his study.

At dinner I mention our visitor for the sake of conversation and because I am curious. Čika Joca teases Duško about not having been here when the girls come calling, and the jovial banter has Duško blushing, enjoying the attention. I interrupt, asking if the girl's name is Manji. Surprised looks circle the table. Čika Sava's eyes rest on me, endowing me with oracular power. I explain. The girl I have seen here today is from my village. Her father is the principal of schools there. I know Manji. Čika Joca looks wordless accusations toward tetka Mila. I realize, with embarrassment, my admission is causing concern, and when I apologize, the good-natured čika Sava says, consoling me, that I did the right thing not saying anything to Manji. Not having my identity confirmed, she cannot possibly be sure who it was she saw. And he tells the others, as if I am not present, that most students have gone home on break, and gossip about the professor harboring Germans in his house will not get out of hand. He laughs an uneasy laugh. Tetka Olga's concerned look proliferates warnings. A discussion follows, and words like *suspicion, zealous fervor, entrapment* are bandied about. I feel I have poisoned the space, the air we breathe, with my presence. At night I cannot sleep. In the morning, tetka Mila informs me our visit will be shorter than she intended; čika Joca has to leave on business.

The April snow has melted. Someone is moving in next door to tetka Mila's. I see them bringing furniture, boxes. A tall young woman with dark hair and eyes, beautiful, with regal bearing, barely smiles talking with tetka Mila. Everything about her—her appearance, her posture and demeanor, her clothes, everything—shows self-assurance, breeding. Her name is Zoraida. She has a job here, working in the offices of Land Management where čika Joca works. She explains about needing someone to keep house; she has two children, boys, ages six and two. Tetka Mila recommends my mother.

Working for Zoraida has special advantages. My mother now buys the bread for Zoraida's family in the bakery for Serbs, and the first thing she does is buy bread for us, on the side, with the money Sarka gave her in Nakovo. She does this only a few times till the money is gone: a third of the money buys bread for Lisa Kodl and the twins; two thirds is spent buying bread for the six of us. And, since my mother has no need of her own meager ration, she tells Tanti Lisa and Lisa Kodl to share it, each getting it on alternate days. She is at Zoraida's all day long and comes home only to sleep. Tanti Lisa often sews for Zoraida's family, and Lisa Kodl comes to do the wash. Our benefits multiply.

I still go to tetka Mila's as always. When I am there I sometimes go to see my mother, but only for a few minutes. The high wooden fence divides the two abutting houses and its narrow gate is latched between us. Gospodja, Zoraida's mother, is always there—tall, dark, stately, her expression austere. Compared to her, Zoraida gushes friendliness. Proud, giving her discriminating look to everything around her, she gives new meaning to selectivity.

Very private and distant, she is used to having servants. Though my mother cooks, does all the work, Gospodja, who manages all, is in charge of the children. Saša is six, tall for his age, green-eyed, sassy. Caco, not quite two, is plump, with enormous black eyes; he waddles when he walks. Gospodja treats them both like little princes. Later, when Gospodja breaks her icy silence, we learn more about the family. Gospodja is from Crnagora and related to the royal family of Montenegro; Gospodja's mother and the last queen of Montenegro were sisters (making Zoraida a second cousin to King Alexander of Yugoslavia). She has three other daughters, younger than Zoraida. They are away, studying at universities. Her husband, abducted during the war by people they knew, Partisans, was killed because he refused to support them. He was loyal to our king. Gospodja tells my mother in confidence that she knows those responsible and that if she had the power she would, and when she gets the opportunity she will, kill them. My mother believes her. I only intuit that she could do what she intends; Gospodja's presence banishes all frailties. She tells my mother that Zoraida's husband, a prominent businessman in Crvenka, was shot by the Partisans only a year and a half ago. To express her anger to my mother, even in private, is truly bold. It is dangerous to talk about such things to anyone, even in whispers. But Gospodja does not hide her feelings. The scrutinizing looks she gives the men and women Partisans who, on occasion, visit Zoraida, express her feelings with absolute clarity. To some who address her as *drugarica* (a common address among them, meaning friend, comrade, implying equality) she is quick to reply: "I have never been nor will I ever be your friend." Proud, severe, always dressed in black, her image personifies open defiance. Later, when I hear Saša sing salutations to the king in tetka Mila's yard, I am not surprised; it is a song his grandmother taught him. Not heeding my quieting, he continues repeating the refrain, hailing: "*Kralju Pero, diko naša, pozdravlja te mali Saša*" (King Peter, our pride, you are greeted by little Saša).

• • •

"*Tetka Mila molim parče hleba.*" The chant in front of the kitchen window continues. There is the usual throng of children begging for bread. Edi and Franzi are always there. They are both twelve but Edi is taller. They seem inseparable and I never see one without the other. They stay waiting for tetka Mila to give them a job and often they just play in the yard, making mischief. They set up traps for birds and check them periodically. I think the traps are a clever device, not thinking of the plight of the birds. It is exciting to watch the entrapment work, to see the birds close up, to stroke them. Holding one, feeling its heart beat against my palm, I somehow miss the larger purpose of this game; not having stayed to the very end in the past, it takes me by surprise. I am shocked to see the boys ring the necks of these birds, twisting them like a wet cloth. I see the birds limp in their hands; I am too horrified to scream, too late in protesting. They laugh at my faintheartedness, and my futile attempt to convey my disgust they ignore. They explain, whispering as if it was a secret, that they are catching the birds to take to their mothers to cook. I quiet. But I no longer take part in their game. And when I see Ponkrac disarranging the unattended traps when the boys are elsewhere, I feel as if I am taking part in a betrayal, being glad for the birds. I watch the boys make slingshots, shooting at the birds with stones, missing. After one of their stones cracks a small window pane across the yard in the *menza* (the eating place for Serb men who work for Land Management, managing the vast confiscated farmland of the German minority in the vicinity), čika Joca talks to them. They listen, looking contrite.

One day I hear the most horrible caterwauling outside the window. I cannot imagine anything capable of such hideous wailing. I rush out. Edi and Franzi are gathered around the rain barrel, looking down, poking at something. The noise that fills the yard has others running out of the menza to see. The boys, too busy to notice, are holding a wire-mesh doormat over the barrel. I approach the barrel carefully. It is a cat, paddling frantically, trying to claw the wire mesh, spitting and screeching, looking half drowned. I stand terrified, my fists under my chin, shrieking: "Don't—don't! Please, let her out!" I pull on the wire mesh, but they push me away, shooing me to quiet, calling me stupid. Suddenly, two large arms arching over me grab Edi and Franzi by the scruff of their necks, pulling them away from the barrel, and the cat, clinging to the lifted wire mat, now streaks through the yard quick as lightning. Edi and Franzi have run away as well. Days later they come back, sullen. They tell me my stupidity cost them the loss of a perfectly fine find of food. Or did I not know, was I that dumb, that cats are rare? People have eaten most of them already, and now when they find one ... they are convinced that my screams, not the cat's wailing, brought about their loss. I don't say anything. I know about the rarity of cats. I have seen one skinned and cooked in our house. But hearing those screams, seeing the frantic cat in the shaft of the barrel trying to keep from going under, holding on, I forgot the larger purpose; a bitter-gall green drowned out everything. But I say nothing to the boys about that.

Arriving at tetka Mila's on my usual day, I am surprised to see Lisa, the little girl I have seen in the menza, where I go to get the milk for tetka Mila. They have already fetched the milk, tetka Mila informs me as she speaks to Lisa with animated gestures, interspersing the few German words she knows, entertaining Lisa, observing her, taking pleasure in her company. Lisa does not speak Serbo-Croatian. I try to fit in as interpreter. She stays for lunch. Čika Joca, too, seems taken by the petite little girl. I hear them talking to each other above our heads. While Lisa understands nothing they say, I listen. They talk to each other as if we both did not understand: what an unusual little girl Lisa is—how quick and clever when she works; there is an unmistakable ethnicity about her appearance and demeanor, and she is the image of innocence, of the truly good. Listening to these words, I feel awkward, apprehensive, afraid. I try to smile, nodding my head in agreement, though no one is looking at me. I glance at Lisa sideways. She looks like she always does, gathered into herself. I am not surprised that tetka Mila sees Lisa's goodness. Hearing her talk about it, I am only concerned about my lack of goodness. I have never heard anyone praising me other than my mother on occasions when she wanted me to do the things I did not like doing. But such praise was more of a game than a genuine assessment. Lisa does not understand what they are saying about her, but I do, and something about hearing it makes me feel anxious.

The thought occurs to me that tetka Mila may not always want me to come. I think of it now that she seems to have developed such a fondness for Lisa. I feel left out of their communication even when I have to interpret for them. And their relating without words leaves me out entirely. Soon I become irritated with all of Lisa's goodness. Just how good is she, I think, being curious?

In the wash-kitchen, where the chickens have taken to laying their eggs, the ambiguous curiosity persists, tempting me to tempt her. One of the nests is in a tight nook behind some crates. Crouching down, I see and count the eggs. Seven. I call out to Lisa, "There are only six eggs today." I get back, letting Lisa have a look. She counts seven. I try to confuse her: "Six, seven—what difference does it make? No one would miss just one egg. I think there are only six eggs. Let me get the basket, and you put in however many there are." I say all this in a matter of fact voice, but I am nervous, knowing I am trying to make her steal an egg. She does not even think of it. I feel worse having proved her truly good. I become more persuasive; I do all but tell her to steal it. "Edi and Franzi sometimes take eggs. No one minds," I say. I want her to steal this egg. I can see by her wide open eyes when she gets the idea. "While I check the nest in the stable, you get these." Back from my errand, I see only six eggs in the basket. I say nothing. I expected to feel better having seen that she, too, can do something that is not good. But now I feel truly bad. We take the basket in to tetka Mila. We are standing in front of her. The door is open behind us. I hear birds chirping, and as if to affirm my own wickedness, I do something that surprises even me. I look down at Lisa and see the bulge in her apron pocket. Touching the egg I say, "You forgot to put this egg in the basket." The look on her face distills shame; it wakes me as if out of a bad dream. Lisa takes the egg, puts it into the basket, and runs out of the kitchen, crying. For a moment I stand rooted to the ground, saying nothing. I don't answer tetka Mila's puzzled look. I run after Lisa, calling her back, "Please wait, please don't go." Instead of her running into the menza, I am surprised to see her clearing the gate, and as I stand on the street watching her run away, I say to myself, meaning her to hear it, "Please come back. I am sorry," and I fear I have been the cause of an irrevocable disaster. I loiter in the yard clutching my hands; my fingers digging into my palm. When tetka Mila asks why Lisa ran away, I can't bring myself to tell, and shrugging my shoulders, I say nothing.

A new boy comes to the window; I see him towering above the crowd, pale, thin-faced, gaunt. He stays after the others have gone. He did not come for bread, he says, though he keeps it. He came to ask for paper. He needs it to draw and paint. She asks him in. I am very quiet as she chats with him. He speaks perfect Serbo-Croatian. He has learned it at school. He speaks like a poet, I hear tetka Mila saying. I notice his expressive delicate hands. He is fifteen—Duško's age, she says—and after he leaves she still talks about him. It is obvious he is a genius, she says. When he comes again, she takes him past the kitchen to the parlor. There is a piano. He knows how to play. We listen, mesmerized. Tetka Mila's face is transfixed and her eyes gaze their faraway look. It is true. He is a genius. I watch him intently. He is golden-haired, blue-eyed, but it is difficult to fix on his physical appearance; even his features are fluid, as if his spirit, inhabiting his every gesture, plays his body like a song. Seeing him, we listen. I cannot tell if I like this boy. I am awed by his presence.

He comes again, bringing presents. Two paintings; one for tetka Mila, and a beautiful rooster with brilliant plumage painted on light green paper, for me. He makes both paint and brushes himself. He explains the preparation of various pigments from plants, minerals, using bird eggs as binder. His paintings are detailed, delicate; I am afraid to hold mine in my hands. He knows we appreciate his work; he has no need of appearing modest. He bears all compliments with an impartial grace, as if his gifts were not his own and are here for everyone. But there are days when he does not come . . .

• • •

Suddenly they let us have visitors. We see them through the barbed wire. We speak to them in single words, from a distance. We shout to be heard above the others. They shout back: "For the children . . ." We know their meaning. The visitors stand in long lines delivering their food to the authorities. We wait till the authorities call us to take our packages from them, seeing our visitors close up only in passing. We exchange whispers, passing messages, crying mostly, all under the prying eyes of the guards. Even those who have no reason to expect visitors still go to see, in hopes they will recognize someone, believing someone will remember them. It is a crying crowd, clamoring for recognition. Urgent pleas, important messages get lost before they reach those for whom they were intended. There is a patient insistence, a straining-to-see among the skeletal throng on this side of the barbed wire, and a tearful quiet gazing, a helpless amazed observing, on the other side, all amid obeying rules, waving handkerchiefs, wiping tears, speaking singular words, calling out names. Bearing witness. Faces fixed on each other, dissolving the barbed wire between them, confirm the exchange, the connection, the affirmation. We look to our visitors and in their consoling eyes we recognize our former selves and weep.

Such visits, not frequent enough to sustain us, make us feel remembered, giving us hope. Our relatives from Sajan come twice. Kodl and Tanti Lisa see them. Sometimes visitors are turned away and have to take the food back home with them. Sometimes they leave it with the authorities who keep it for themselves. But whether the visitors come or not, the crowd gathers this side of the barbed wire, waiting, even when visitations stop altogether.

It is warm now, and the wild clover and dandelion greens supplement our daily diet, our rations of corn meal afloat on tepid water. Fewer people die than in the winter months, but the death-wagon still makes its rounds daily, gathering the many dead. The children whose mothers and grandparents have died and who have no other kin are gathered in houses they now call the orphanage. Workers, women of the camp, are assigned to take care of them. Without the affection, without the supplements that the resourcefulness of kin may have provided, and with their meager rations diminished by the hunger of those now caring for them, these children are truly abandoned; the orphanage distills the very worst of bad conditions and the many children there die of hunger, disease, neglect. Aware of their plight, the older children whose immediate relations die approach distant relatives to take them into their family unit. The last of what we have is kin; without them we are truly discarded.

• • •

Soon the worst happens. They take away the children from their grandmothers, aunts, cousins. They take away the children from their kin. They simply come and take them from us. While my mother is at work and I am at tetka Mila's, guards with guns come and take Seppi from our room. "How could you let them take him!" I scream at Nina néni. My mother is beside herself. She speaks to no one. No one dares to make a sound in our room.

Later we hear that someone from our village, in an attempt to save her nephew and niece from being taken, told the authorities about my mother keeping Seppi. It takes two days and Zoraida's persuasive negotiation to get Seppi out of the orphanage. Now he and my mother sleep at Zoraida's, in the iron bed in their wash-kitchen. Does Zoraida know we will keep Seppi only weeks? Why doesn't she tell us? Had we known, would we have done as one grandmother did? Clutching her grandchildren, she walked into the river.

They come before noon. I see the two guards with guns walk past the kitchen window of tetka Mila's house. I see them go through the narrow gate into Zoraida's yard and immediately intuit the terror of their intent. I run. My mother is standing in front of the wash-kitchen. I hear the words the guards are saying. I understand their meaning. I see their mouths moving, making words. Nothing else moves. The summer sun is beating down. Frozen in time, we will stand like this forever: Gospodja, standing on the raised floor of the shaded foyer holding a glass pitcher with lemonade, her gazing grandchildren at her side; my mother, in full sun below, standing barefoot facing the guards. Behind her a white sheet, suspended, hangs slack. Somewhere behind that curtained door, swallowed by the darkened room, the little boy intuits the meaning of the ominous stillness. He darts out of the darkness like a flash of light. The air tears with shrieks of terror. Like an animal marked for the kill, he runs the length of the garden up to the tall fence, and stretching his arms up, he screams. Somewhere glass shatters. I see the guards moving in slow motion, my mother following with arms outstretched toward the screaming child. This image makes a home within me. And I know all that is deemed stable, sensible, and safe will be measured against this image from this day forward and forever.

My mother is sweeping up the broken glass in the foyer, quietly weeping. I hear Gospodja's voice inside. The tone is solemn. She is talking with Zoraida: ". . . rooted to the ground. I literally could not move. The pitcher sliding out of my hand . . . still, I could not move. And the children, horrified, looking on . . ."

My mother and I sit in the darkened wash-kitchen without saying anything, not knowing what to do.

Two days later someone comes running, calling for my mother: "They're taking the children out of the village." I hear the women in the menza screaming. My mother is beside herself. "You must come quickly—they are holding the children in the Komandno Mesto. They are taking the children . . ." Looking away, absently, my mother does not move. She cannot endure, she mutters. She cannot endure it, she repeats. Suddenly I feel invincible, convinced I can do anything; I am going to bring him back! I start running.

Within seconds I am across the street climbing the wall of the Komandno Mesto, looking over a throng of children. I see guards milling about, children standing in groups. I see Seppi squatting on the ground among the smaller children. I call to him, "Seppili, Seppili!" When he sees me he starts crying. I am coming in to see him, I yell, and to avoid the barbed wire I slide back down. I approach some guards at the gate. I only want to say good-bye to my brother, I tell them. One of them lets me in.

I kneel down to hold Seppi. "Don't cry," I hear myself saying. "You are going to a better place. You are going to your mother." I don't know why I am saying this. I don't know where they are taking him; I only know I want to say something to make this parting reasonable, to give him something to be happy about. You won't forget, I say, pleading. You won't forget me. He nods. He is four and a half.

There is movement within the crowd; the children are being organized. Six abreast are going through the gate in long lines. I stay with the younger children. I hold Seppi's hand going through the gate. Guards with guns are flanking the troop of children on both sides. We are walking in the middle of the street. In front, the older children are singing. The sound of their voices singing Partisan songs cuts through the haze of heat and churned up dust. *"Druže Tito kad ćeš u Rusiju . . . Druže Tito"*—there is a noise growing ever louder, making the sung words sound far away—*pozdravi mi Crvenu Armiju . . . Smrt fašizmu . . . jedan, dwa . . . Crvenu Armiju."* They sing the vacant words, heavily accented, about comrade Tito going to Russia, greetings sent to the Red Army, all under the seal of promise: Death to Fascism! The charged air chills the summer sun. Soon we are in a funnel of people, and the noise from the sidewalk swallows the singing sound entirely and turns it into something else. The mangled melody wails into a raging lament—past terror and sorrow, past eyes blind with weeping. Sounds that down heaven. Our street is a funnel to hell. The guards make sure that there is distance between the crowd and the children, that no one comes close to the children. Grandmothers and relatives weep their good-byes, waving their despairing hands, shouting the names of their children. And the children echo the anguished gestures, weeping. The torrent of grief whips the line into a tangle and the guards urge the children to a faster pace. I feel unusually tall, conspicuous; I feel like an impostor. Looking into the grieving faces from the center of the street, I see something not meant for me. I have no response to give back. Misplaced among the children, witnessing, not fully participating, still holding Seppi's hand while they, kept away, are out of reach of their children. I think of staying with Seppi, leaving with him. My mother always said if she had to let one of us go it would be me. I was old enough; I would remember.

Transcending the meld of voices, the sound of the crowd metamorphoses into a full-bodied droning. Bells. Bells. Thousands of bells. Ringing. Droning. The lifting up and pulling down of thousands and thousands of bells, ringing . . .

I see the embankment of the railroad tracks. Trucks. They are loading the children on trucks! I look at Seppi. I hold him. The children are going on. He is going with them. He looks back at me and his face disappears among the throng of children crowding into my view. The image clouds. A guard interrupts, urging me on. "I am going back," I say, "I am not one of the children leaving." He yells something unintelligible. I think of my mother. "I am not one of them," I hear myself repeating. The guard who knows tells me to get lost.

Back through the street with the roar of the crowd behind me, I walk slowly, looking to the ground. Like after a flood, the ground looks violated, as if littered with debris of once alive things now dead. In the dim light of the wash-kitchen in Zoraida's house, my mother is sitting on the iron bed, quietly weeping. I sit beside her, motionless, for a long time, watching the afternoon breeze move the white sheet over the door ever so slightly, back and forth, cutting the light. Intermittently, flies are buzzing. The dry somber sounds of my mother's voice grope the stillness: "Did you hear the ringing of the bells?" I nod.

• • •

A typhus epidemic has broken out in camp. I hear some anxious talk at tetka Mila's, and my mother says Gospodja is worried about the two children. But to us the added anxiety is just one more above the level of tolerance. The new threat to our mortality registers. It only means that among the many dying, some die of typhus now. There is no cause for panic; the new threat requires nothing more of us. Before we die of hunger, we are driven to exhaust all possibilities of getting food. The new threat requires no preventive measures. There are no practicing doctors here, no medicine. Patiently we yield to the new threat, waiting; its essence lingers. If we do not die, we go on waiting.

Another threat is more pressing. There is a drought. The wells are dry. Several people are caught fetching water from the river. The offense is rationalized: the river is low and our taking water from it will further deplete it, causing the grounding of boats, preventing their trafficking, harming the economy. Sabotage. We are not to go to the river, we are told. And when they catch a few people disobeying the warning, they resort to severe punishment.

Some are shot: a young boy, perhaps fifteen—face down in the dust, merged with the ground. The blood-encrusted dust around him, leatherlike, maroon, cracked by the heat, is curled up in patches. Sounds of buzzing flies. His body remains there for days. They want us to see it. We do. And still others are punished for getting water. Some are beaten and put into the cellar, in attics. Now that it is hot, attics, veritable furnaces, are chosen as preferred places of confinement, and there are others. The image of a priest confined in a pit, an enclosure too small to stand up or lie down in, imposes its horror in secret whispers.

Guards do the shootings. Though spontaneous beatings are done by the guards, official beatings are prescribed by those in charge. Meting out the punishment is a German man in his fifties. People call him Schtecke Pede. Robust, red-faced, sturdy, he walks with a limp and carries a big stick. He does his job well. His beatings are merciless. He is well known, feared as much as he is hated. I hear an impassioned Gospodja tell my mother, "When you are free again, you must kill this man!"

It is getting hot. I am on my way to tetka Mila's house about to pass the dreaded cellar; I forgot to cross the street as I usually do to avoid it. I notice a disembodied shriveled arm sticking through the iron bars of the low window. The darkness gathered behind it has swallowed the person, and the arm lying on the ground, looking discarded, acquires a macabre animated presence. I pass it cautiously, avoiding its reach. I hear a graveled voice sounding out swollen-tongued, "Wasser," as if in a foreign language. Rasping whispers, verging on the inhuman, echo from below. I walk faster, crossing the wide street on a diagonal. I cannot forget the sound; its memory distills horror. I tell tetka Mila. Later, when the sun is still high, I go with her, carrying an enameled cup. We cross the wide street on a diagonal, and putting the buckets down in front of the window, she submerges the cup in the cool water, and the reaching hands grasp it, one by one, while she assures she will not leave till everyone gets some water. We don't talk, walking to fill our buckets, crossing the wide street to the artesian well, off limits to us in the camp. We pump the water without saying a word. We walk with intent, without thought of avoiding anyone. Back at the window, we take turns dipping and handing down the cup. The hollowed-out whispers are pouring out thanks from below. Tetka Mila's eyes fade to their palest blue.

Tetka Mila takes me with her to the river, sunbathing. It is a short walk: past Zoraida's, the baker's, and two other houses in which Serb families live. Standing on top of the dam, I see the river, receded. Tetka Mila spreads a blanket some distance away from the muddy shore. I see others on the beach, adults, wearing skimpy bathing suits, straw hats, and dark glasses; children are tossing bright balls and building moats around islands of mud. Some are swimming. There is a dog. He, too, can swim; the bigger boys are tossing sticks into the river for him to fetch. Out of the water, he keeps close to his mistress. By now dogs are rare in the village. The people are Serb; the dog, a German Shepherd. Beside the small gathering of people and half a dozen playful pigs herded here to drink, the shore on this side of the river is empty as far as one can see. Across the river, the beach is dotted with bathers. I sit in the sun with tetka Mila, watching the children swim. I like the water and once in it, I stay. Squatting in the shallows, I move my arms, miming the breaststroke to give the impression I too can swim. But mostly I just jump about churning up mud and come out only when tetka Mila calls for me. I am turning blue, she says.

Once, we go across the river to visit tetka Mila's friend. She is a midwife. Her house is dark and cool, with wicker furniture and potted ferns. She serves us drinks in tall glasses. She has a white angora cat called Mici. She treats Mici as if she were a person. I am puzzled. Later the three of us go to a coffeehouse. We sit at small tables, eating ice cream with silver spoons from fluted glasses, sipping water. I sip the water slowly, knowing it is rare.

• • •

Standing in the doorway of the entry to our house, overlooking the desolate view—parched earth and dried grasses—I stare into the void. It is hot and the shadows from the stable walls are shallow. There is no breeze blowing. Suddenly, screams tear the air, matching the landscape timbre to hue. I see Anna running toward me. *"Päsl Nina! Päsl Nina—mei Motter is tot . . ."* She rushes past me sobbing, blind terror in her eyes, mouthing, "My mother is dead. My mother is dead." There is a void in my chest with Anna's cries echoing. There is nothing else. Hollowed out, numb, helpless horror glowering from the empty space within me, I want to laugh; I hear the crazed cackle within.

I am in the land of the lost . . .

• • •

The corn in front of the menza in tetka Mila's yard has grown tall. I can see it looking over the small crowd of children in front of the kitchen window. There, tall, towering above the crowd, I recognize the boy, looking pale, almost skeletal, bald. His face has the appearance of a skull with eyes. There is a change more disturbing, betrayed at first glance by a chilling giggle; on closer contact the change is devastating. To all our questions he responds with the same frustrated giggle that shatters the poetry of his former appearance. He is with a small, nervous woman. His mother. She clutches his wilted wrists, staying the erratic movements of his hands. Her wounded eyes peer into our faces. He had typhus; she saved him from dying, she explains, searching his face lovingly as if to assure herself he is really here, with her. A large pain pushes from within; I look to his knowing eyes. The smirk lurking within confuses. I search his face, waiting. I ask him about his paintings. Unwilling to accept the chilling giggle, his only response, I ask again. When they turn to go, I stand motionless, watching how tenderly the smaller figure tilts, holding to the slender tall one as they both disappear in a shaft of light through the narrow door in the gate. The shattering blow falls. I recognize its steely reek. I run into the tall corn. I gag and cannot stop gagging. I bite the earth in desperation, trying to swallow the ground, grinding my teeth on the grit, spitting. What have they done, I weep, what have they done? Soft sounds rustle through the corn. The silken tassels are tuning brown.

It is mid-August and very hot. The sun shines circles in my face. I try to squint. I see nothing any more but a soft white haze, a spreading web of circles and under it, sounds of children whimpering and occasional moaning close by. Everything spreads into sound, and seeing nothing, I hear all around me. A swell of buzzing encompasses the earth. I try to stand very still and look into the sun, as they tell us. The earth is swaying beneath me; I am like a tall tree, rooted, swaying with it. We are standing in close proximity on a grassy plain. I have lost the direction from where we came. They herded us out of our houses in the morning, driving us through the streets into this field. They did not say why. Päsl Nina and Johann are near me. My mother and Tanti Lisa were at work when they came. I don't know if they, too, are here. They may be somewhere in the crowd of thousands. I can't go looking for them. We are not to move about; we are not to leave our places. We are here to stand in place and look into the sun. I was afraid when they came that they were taking us away. Perhaps they are going to shoot us, I heard some say, but they only want us to stand here and look into the sun. I trust them. All of us, fifteen thousand—twenty thousand people are here to confirm it—all they want us to do for the rest of the day is stand here turning toward, looking into the sun. At first I take it very seriously. I try not to look away, not to move, but I get dizzy, and glancing at the others around me, I see their sweat-drenched faces, bodies slack, arms raised shielding their eyes, some looking down. Eventually some sit on the ground. Within the standing crowd, they become invisible. They sit till whispers warn of the coming of the guards. I start relaxing my gaze, looking at the faces around me. These faces are no strangers to the sun. The furrows in them, earthen, sun-baked, are an expression of the land. The land and the sun know the owners of these faces. Days spent under high skies in the treeless landscape, harvesting and planting, these faces have mapped the passage of many suns. And still they hearken, open to the moving sounds over endless fields. There is no talk even in close proximity, only the smell of grasses and ground, the scent of soil and sweat, the noise of buzzing flies, isolated moans and whisperings. Heat and endurance meld into metallic smells, tin and brass. The living field fuses into a receptacle of time: a live sun dial, a living clock. Sweat runs through my hair, over my face, and drips to stain my dress at the neck. I lick my lips; I finger my eyebrows for salt. When a breeze gets lost among us, we try to prolong its stay, rolling our head from side to side, turning our cheeks, cooling our faces. I move the skirt of my dress back and forth, fanning my thighs and letting the air billow up against my chest, cooling my neck. Flies settle on sweaty places. Some sting. We hope for rain. But there is not a cloud hiding the sun from us, and we keep following orders, turning our faces to the sun. I see the guards with guns on the periphery. They wander into the crowd occasionally. We stand still. I see Johann tilting his head up, trying to squint into the sun, his long lashes making a tangled brush over his dark eyes, his mouth contorted into an awkward grimace. I ask him to sit in my shadow, and when the fanning skirt cools, he tilts his head up to smile at me. When guards come, I pull him to his feet. I think of Seppi. Nina néni has abandoned her prayer. Her mouth is slack. Her long dark skirts stand in billows touching the ground. Without moving, I make trips back through the soundless village to the empty house, where it is cool and dark and I can smell the straw in our rough horse-blanketed bed. When the guards are in the vicinity, I am back with the others, tilting my face up. We listen to the guards taunting us. They have water. "*Oćeš, Švabo, 'oćeš vode?*"—You want water, do you, Švabo, they insult. Somewhere in the periphery of my vision, I see them offering water to an old man who is kneeling on the ground, exhausted, trying to get up. He does not reach for the flask they offer. They do not intend to give it to him. He knows. No one approaches the guards asking for water.

The sun turns slowly in the sky, and we follow it standing on the ground. A yellow haze is hanging low. I cannot remember what a cool breeze feels like, and suddenly in close proximity, I hear a small voice sing: "*Ich stell mich Ihnen vor, als Tänzerin vom corps, als Tänzerin vom Stern; ein jeder hat mich gern*" (I introduce myself to you, as dancer of renown, as dancer of celebrity; everybody likes me.) At first I think it is an apparition. I see a girl, smaller than I, with a head full of dark curls, large dark eyes, in a little summer dress so delicate it seems woven out of gossamer. Her skin looks pale. She stands before us, gesturing as she sings: "*Ich trag ein seiden Kleid, den Federhut so breit, die Handschuh aus Glace, ein volles Portemonnaie!*" (I wear a silken gown, a wide-rimmed, grand, plumed hat, fine kid-leather gloves, and carry a full purse!) She is aware of the impression she is making, and looking flirtatious, smiling affectedly, she continues gesturing as she sings: "*Oh, Glorie das Ballett! Ich schwärme für Ballett, die Augen so braun wie Natur, die reizende Lockenfrisur, die Füsse so zierlich und nett—ja, so ist das Wiener Ballett*" (Oh, glorious ballet! I am smitten with ballet, the eyes of Nature's brown, the charming coiffure of locks, the feet so neat and fay—yes, such is the Vienna Ballet.) Still I can't believe my eyes. She looks as if she has sprung from the ground. She says she is from the Untersteiermark and was brought here recently from a camp close to the Austrian border. She speaks with a city accent. She is very pretty, and even though she is small, she is convincingly affecting the gestures and mannerisms of a grown-up girl. Capriciously, with quicksilver movements and the agility of a jester, she disappears. Later I hear her entertaining the guards. Their laughter, full of the shade from trees beyond, and her small singing voice drift our way, bringing diversion to our difficult endeavor. Squinting into the sun, I visualize her gestures and repeat the words of her song to myself till they say themselves quietly within me. Someone close by says, "I want to go home—why can't we go home?" Is it Johann? I hear faraway sounds like wind blowing through hollow reeds. But there is no wind.

When the sun is low, we are herded back to the village. We only see those who do not move when we stumble over them. Two small children sit crying next to their grandmother, who does not move. Someone will recognize them and take them back to their mother, I think as we keep moving, being carried along by the flow of the crowd. Some ask for help carrying their sick kin. The isolated laments reach us in passing, and the throng of people, the undulating sea of thousands, moves with a continuous sound like low-flying migrating birds, hovering; a sound informed with ominous portent, and I worry that the flow of the current will carry us past our houses, our rooms, and we, an inseparable meld, will forever drift through the wide streets of the village.

Our small dark room embraces us like a comforting mother. My mother comes home later. The guards came to Zoraida's looking for her, she tells us, but Gospodja had locked her in a wardrobe, telling them nothing. Gospodja knows how to lie without saying anything. Tanti Lisa comes back late from faraway fields. It seems that only those left in the village, mostly the old, the sick, the children, were on this outing. This punishment, Tanti Lisa tells us, may have something to do with a letter smuggled out, sent to important places to inform about our continued bad treatment more than a year after the war has ended. But we are too tired to listen; too exhausted to talk.

• • •

It is a time of changes. Ponkrac has to leave. The new Komandant wants everyone accounted for and living in their camp housing at all times. Zoraida is transferred. The family leaves. My mother no longer has a job. Čika Joca already works in Novi Sad. Soon tetka Mila will follow him there. I can't bear to think about it. When Ponkrac leaves, I see him doubled over, his face in his hands, weeping inconsolably. He comes back a few times to visit. When he no longer does, we know he is dead. "Lisa is dead," the women in the menza tell me, weeping. Lisa is dead! And when I look as if I did not hear them, they say it again. "Lisa, you remember Lisa?" As if I could forget. "Our Lisa, is dead."

The chanting in the yard continues: *"Tetka Mila molim parče hleba . . ."* The outstretched hands persist, and still their patient gestures look less like pleas and seem an offering.

CHAPTER 10

Land of the Lost

THE SUMMER LIGHT LINGERS in warm nostalgic leave-taking. Crisp shadows fall to the yielding ground. The air, informed with scents of faraway harvests, enlightens every breath. Faded grasses whisper in the wind. Is it fall? Tanti Lisa looks to the pages of the little black notebook she keeps hidden. She says it is my birthday. I am eleven. I am greeted with smiles. I have grown up, they say. Johann looks at them puzzled. Like me, he knows I am still the same.

Tanti Lisa is mending her coat, getting it ready for another winter. The rich, dark-brown wool, worn in places, showing some patches and mended tears, withstood the ravages of nasty weather; it survived the long treks from dawn to dusk, under the tangle of sharp-twigged branches she carried on her back, walking through rain and blowing snow. This coat is part of her identity now. With her always, it witnessed her endurance; its hem touched all the obstacles on the way. There from the very beginning, in the first horrible days of freezing cold, in the sheep stall, it gave shelter to her infant. And in the yard of the municipal building in Nakovo, surrounded by crying children, it was the munificent mantle of motherhood. It was her comfort at night, when she wept; in it the tears for her dead child lay gathered. Through all hardship it was there. Lying across her lap, now, it does not belie the life it has led; shabby and worn, it looks more enduring. I watch as she carefully rips a part of its hem—I am puzzled. Groping for something, she extracts first one and then another golden earring. A ruby glow, mellow red-faceted reverberations multiply and spread, sparkling, over our room and into the dismal landscape outside. Jewels. A miracle! And all this time the coat secreted the treasure. Hidden, it became part of the sheltering dark, forgetting its light and the thousand reflections in mirrors, the admiring glances it only dreamed about, floating above the dismal landscape. And the coat carried the treasure patiently, while it grew ripening into the miracle it now is. Glowing before me, the ruby light reminds me of sour cherries. Tanti Lisa says, "A present, for you," giving me one of her soulful looks. She wants me to wear the jewels. I am overwhelmed. The holes in my ears accommodate the precious metal only by force. I gladly endure the pain. I wear the present like a prize, holding my head very still, mindful of the glowing radiance about me. I show my earrings to the girls in the yard. My shoulder-length hair keeps them discreetly out of view. I feel adorned even when no one sees them. I never take them off. When, days later, somewhere in the yard among other children, I hear, "Luisa, you lost one of your earrings," I stand startled. Touching my ears, I finger the loss. Unmoved, I hear myself saying, "Oh." And time stops as I look to the ground; but instead of looking for the earring, I am really groping for a feeling—a feeling among the many I have known—but nothing comes to the fore. I think of the loss. I think of the beautiful treasure. Looking around mindlessly, I go on puzzling my emptiness. When feelings are lost, all is spent; there is nothing. A curious accusation, feigning guilt, follows; guilt for not having any feelings about the loss, for feeling nothing about it at all.

Tetka Mila is leaving. Even though čika Joca is marrying, tetka Mila is moving with him to Novi Sad. How can she go away and leave us? I am haughty, trying to conceal my resentment. I do not tell her how I dread her leaving; I act as though it does not matter to me and go to the rubble of the church across the street and search the remaining walls for prayers. The details of our leave-taking are shrouded in a deliberate distancing, which I devise to deny my affection for her. She promises to come to visit; she has friends here, she says. Nelli. I should go to see Nelli, to keep informed. I stop listening . . .

It is late October, and the dead grasses in the desolate gardens look their most abandoned.

In the house where Zoraida used to live, there now lives a doctor, who befriended tetka Mila before she left, and as a favor to her, he gives my mother a job. She works in a small room near the orphanage, mending clothes. The doctor has come here to help, he says. Setting up the mending shop is part of the help he offers. He carries a black bag when visiting the sick, but he gives no medicine; he has no medicine to give. He mostly observes, looking wistful, assessing the suffering, puffing smoke from his pipe; saying a few words in German, he makes diagnoses and gives advice. The children are suffering from malnutrition and neglect; they need to be kept clean, he says. But his advice is wrongly interpreted, and daily, even when the weather is freezing, the children are taken outside under Partisan supervision, dowsed with cold water and swept off with brooms. My mother cries when she tells us about it. She cannot bear to watch it, she says. How the women working there can bear to do it, we cannot comprehend. My mother has seen the sparsely clad children lying in squalor on strawless floors, ten, twenty in a room, abandoned. Their skeletal bodies too frail to carry their large heads and swollen bellies, they sit and lie listlessly about, their vacant eyes staring, the fruit of their death waiting within, bearing all patiently, making a gift of themselves. Watching them wilts hearts, she says. We listen in the dark, not making a sound.

• • •

It is freezing cold. We have no access to wood now that tetka Mila is gone. Unless we find ways to remove the rafters in the stables and those under the roof of our house, there is no wood, no tree to be found. But hatchets and saws are not something we own or would be allowed to keep; the knives we have don't cut that deep. Our keepers are not afraid of us having tools such as hatchets. They do not fear us. They just don't like us having what we need. Without wood the stove in the corner of the room is useless. Our meager rations—soup, consisting of coarsely ground cornmeal afloat in warm water, now with salt, now without, and the coarser corn bread that tears at our gums—we fetch once a day, standing in long lines. When they don't give out rations, there is nothing to eat. Johann is beginning to look like a skeleton. His skin is acrust with rashes. Like many children, he has the *Krätz* (the scab) and suffers unbearable itching. My gums are always bleeding and I can do a trick with my teeth. Holding my lower teeth, I can move my jaw inches back and forth, stretching it like a rubber band. We all have trouble with our bowels. Dysentery. Cramps. Bowels grinding glass, sputtering blood. In the yard, along the stable walls and all along the open hallway, our bloody excrement stains the ground. There is something about emitting red blood that immediately frightens. The messenger of mortality, the angel of death, is bloody red.

We sit with our coats on, bundled. My mother cannot bring us the wood or extend the warmth of the fire she has at work; when she takes me with her, the women there complain. There is not room enough, they say; their kin, too, sit in the cold, they reason. I cannot stay.

Nineteen forty-six, the year of uncountable losses, has no Christmas.

The snow has covered the grasses. I am standing at the end of the open hallway, looking past houses, across the dusky landscape. Along the horizon, stretching far into the distance, moving single file in one continuous line—giant birds, thousands, walking storklike on long spindly legs, carrying their own cages on their backs—gliding on the edge of the earth, defining its arc darkly, their stark silhouettes held against the frozen silence. Mesmerized, I float with the cage-carrying birds dancing on the edge of the world in the deepening dusk—I know the familiar image, I remind myself; the women are coming home from faraway woods, branches stacked on their backs, towering over their heads. It will be dark before Tanti Lisa gets to our cold room, freezing and empty-handed. She brings no wood for us.

There is no escape from the cold. We shiver under our covers day and night. There must be some way to get warm, some way to get wood. My mother comes up with an idea. She says, boldly, as if there were nothing to it, addressing me, "Tomorrow, I want you to go to the Komandant. Tell him you are cold. Tell him you want a job, inside, where it is warm!" First I think it is a joke, pointing out the ridiculous, and I laugh. When I see that she is not amused, I shiver. Looking around the room, I can tell it is not a joke to the others either. Tanti Lisa brings wood from faraway forests to cook our common rations, to heat Partisan kitchens, offices, and housing; she knows that somewhere in the village warm places exist. She now gives me one of her doleful looks, as if to say I must do my share. "Wherever there is a warm place there is food," Nina néni says, nodding her head in approval. Johann is wistful, wearing his lost look. It seems only I realize how outrageous this proposal is, and it becomes all the more disturbing because I know I will have to do the unavoidable.

I have seen the new Komandant. He is taller than anyone I have ever known and he is known for his cruelty. The stories about the severity of his punishments are legion. One of them has him hanging people in wells, not to drown but to torture them. I have seen him looking fierce, walking alone, carrying a shotgun. He does not live in the village. His entrance each morning marks time. We take care to avoid him. I have seen him once at tetka Mila's house playing cards with other guests. I did not know who he was then. "Dour, hard to look at and harder still to like," I remember hearing tetka Mila say, expressing her dislike for him. *Sly, sadistic, mean* are words she used talking about him, čika Joca shooing her to quiet, even though no one but I was there to hear them. And when the Komandant proved as despicable as tetka Mila judged him to be, sending orders to dismiss her help, she called him a monster. Because of him Ponkrac had to leave. I had to be hidden. And now my mother wants me to approach this man whom everyone fears, with an obviously ridiculous request! I am to tell him, I am cold—of course I am cold, and so is everyone else in camp. Is this to be a complaint? Am I to face the Komandant with an accusation? I turn and twist, examining the preposterous notion, looking for clues how to approach the unavoidable encounter. I know, once my mother has fixed on a course of action, no one can persuade her to reconsider.

I am worried about what I will have to do; I don't sleep. I decide to approach the Komandant on the street. I will wait for him and ask him in passing, casually. I don't have the courage to go to the Komandno Mesto to ask to see him. I do not believe they would let me in.

In the morning, I walk through the gardens to the street behind us and wait. My feet are frozen; my hands, hidden under my arm pits, ache. I am too frightened to cry. I stand, moving my feet in place, up and down, up and down, crunching the frozen snow. The shawl covering my nose and mouth is showing a large patch of frost. An occasional gust of wind blows the snow in circles before me, making it hard to see. I must have missed the Komandant's entrance, I surmise, after having waited what seems to me a very long time. Almost relieved, I return to a much warmer room. My hands and feet keep aching and the thought of having to go out again tomorrow sickens me with anxiety.

The next day I wait in the same place. I see the Komandant coming. Instead of crossing the street to approach him, I freeze. I stand looking on as the tall image gets smaller farther down the street. When I am aware of moving, I am crossing the snowy space of the gardens, looking down at my much-mended cloth shoes. I tell no one the truth; I say the Komandant did not come again today. And the day after, I wait again in my spot in the snow, rehearsing my request. He comes. I can see him from afar. The tall man with a shotgun; a solitary figure in the street. I look to my frozen footsteps from days before and a surge of fear fills me to forgetting. My arms, my legs are numb. My heart is pounding. The tall image is coming closer. I start crossing the wide empty street at an angle, away from the approaching fig- ure, to avoid walking toward it. I hear the crunching long strides eating the path behind me, and suddenly he is in the periphery of my vision. Before I reach the sidewalk he is there and I walk faster, trying to catch up. I start speaking immediately, addressing him, *"Druže komandante,"* trying not to sound breathless, telling him I would like to have a job somewhere inside, where it is warm. I buffer the lack of response with subtle variations of the request, taking care not to sound as if I am pleading. In the shadow of his image, in close proximity, I feel the power of his presence and know that showing any weakness would be a mistake. My chin does not quiver when I speak, and I hear myself calmly voicing my request in rational variations. His response is silence. I hear only the sound of his long measured strides, his falling footsteps crushing the frozen snow coalescing with my many soft crunching steps, nothing else. I follow silently, steps behind him. Still, no response. I turn to cross the street. He stops, and with his back toward me, he shouts, "Halt! Who goes there?" I try for the right response, but I hear my voice interrupted. "You are coming with me! Now!" he bellows, looking over his shoulder.

I walk beside him, doubling my steps to keep up with his long strides. I talk about the weather, the snow, to keep my fear in check, but I soon realize that being quiet, saying nothing, is what the occasion calls for, and I bridle my fear, concentrating on running in tune with the sound of his steps. He, saying nothing, does not even glance my way. It seems a long walk to the Komandno Mesto. I follow him through the guarded gate to the building in the center of the yard.

Ascending the narrow cement stairs, we enter a large room, an office: men and women sitting at desks, quick-clicking sounds of typewriters, a meld of voices and metallic sounds. No one looks up from their work to greet us, though they seem to notice our entrance. The Komandant sits down at a desk facing the others. Laying his shotgun down in front of him, he looks about him. I am standing to his left, facing the room. I feel his glance resting on me. I try to remain very still. "Quiet!" He bellows, stilling the room, and as if to soften the blow of his fist on the table, he says calmly, "Look what I have brought with me!" Every eye is upon me. I try to smile. "Take a good look. Where do you think I found this?" The tone of his voice implies it is not a question needing an answer. The hush in the room amplifies the sound of his words. "I caught her," he points at me shouting, looking at them, "trying to escape!" I want to laugh at first; I want to think it must be a joke, but the tone of his voice, so utterly threatening, stills all to a pitiless void. Echoes of horror reflected in the mute faces before me confirm, this is not a joke. The walls tilt, trembling. I hear a roaring in my ears like rushing waves breaking, drowning me in my own surprise. I think of running—how far could I get? I see myself rushing toward the door, hurling myself down the steep cement steps, lying dead on the ground. I am in a chamber of horror! I know about rooms into which Partisans took men and women and where, amid celebration, music, drinking, and laughter, they dismembered them with knives, hatchets, saws. People now in our camp—ladies from Ruskodorf/Ruskoselo; cooks in the menza—who had to clean up after the blood feasts, picking up bits of flesh in baskets, discarding them on dumps, know to tell about the carnage they saw. I search the faces before me for help, but they are closed against me. I hear the shouted accusations directed toward me like so many hatchets falling. The bellowing voice is disembodied and the room is askew; the ceiling tilts in tune with the startling vibrations. "We know what to do with her—make an example of her," I hear, over the roar in my ears. The meaning of words floats away from me as if I am dead already. Suddenly, I hear my own voice protesting: "No! No! It isn't true! It is not true." Like a slap in the face, a shout cuts the air, "Quiet!" The stern voice belongs to the face, the golden-haired man whose mouth is moving. His look spitting nails at me, he screams, "You dare to call the Komandant a liar!" I hear my voice, as if from afar, making words slowly, deliberately, carefully: "No—he is just not telling the truth now." I would go on, but searching the faces before me, I know there is no hope, no reason to believe they want me to explain. I know I am trapped. I make no sound. My helplessness is no longer reaching out; turning inward, it tames the roar in my ears.

A sudden jolt; a sound almost inhuman, a ghoulish laughter, shatters the space. Horror has a voice! Behind it, echoing cold, the unsounded lament of a thousand mouths is roaring. Vengeance is laughing, shaking the room to sobriety. The laughter stops, abruptly. The voice of the Komandant is calm. He says, almost wistfully, "You were fooled. Admit it! You all believed me! And what of truth? You don't need truth when you have power. Power makes truth useless . . ." A soliloquy follows. The crazed laughter lingers; I see it, recoiled, in the eyes of those before me, reflecting an impenetrable darkness. The call to blood feasts present, passes, receding deep into that darkness, sheltered by it, hidden, like an ancient heirloom under closed lids. I listen to the spoken words, letting their sound flood me with relief. I am aware of my shaking knees. I feel glad to be alive; glad to be allowed to live. My gratitude spreads like a blessing over the room. The clicking of typewriters resumes, binding time. The Komandant dismisses me without looking at me and, as an afterthought, he charges someone to take me down to the kitchen, to introduce me to the cook as her new helper. My legs are so rubbery I cannot trust them to make steps as I descend the stairs, defying the pull of gravity.

The Partisans around the long table number seven. Sometimes there are visitors. They all have a distanced expression; some look sullen, angry; all are young. The women, especially, are tough looking, self-absorbed, un-approachable; their every gesture negates our presence, mine as well as the cook's. The only thing I admire about them is their splendid tall black boots. I notice that the Komandant, though seated among them, keeps to himself. Surrounded by relaxed conversation he sits, stiff, his gun at his side, often saying nothing at all. When he is finished eating, he leaves without a look, without a gesture to anyone. They do not appear to be afraid of him; they look self-assured, aware of their own power. Nevertheless, their conversations are always livelier after he leaves. Sometimes, seeing him bent awk-wardly over his plate, I offer more food. He does not acknowledge the ges-ture. I am all the more surprised when, one day, he asks me to meet him outside. I put my coat on trembling; he is outside waiting for me. He wants me to take a walk with him around the grounds. We walk in silence, circling the yard. I try to keep in step with his strolling strides. I am so uncomfortable I have to talk. He says nothing for what seems to me a long time, and when he does speak, he says, looking down at me, "You don't have to talk on my account; we are just taking a walk together, to enjoy the winter air." I startle; taking his remarks as consideration, I find it even harder to relax. Not knowing what to do, I endure the discomfort.

My presence here promises little of warmth and food for the others in our room. When I ask the cook for wood, food, for anything being discarded, she grudgingly gives me some potato peelings, letting me know, without incriminating herself, that she has others to think about.

Someone takes notice of me. It is the wife of the Intendant, the sullen young man with golden hair who accused me of calling the Komandant a liar. She is dark-haired, very young, chubby; pregnant. Like the other Partisan women, she wears tall black boots. Though she can look stern, like the others, there is a softness about her, perhaps because everything about her is round. The frowns on her plump face seem more like affectations, and her most sullen looks are unconvincing grimaces. Even when she does not talk to me, I can tell she is the most approachable, the least threatening of the group. The way she seeks the attention of her husband, wooing him with words and gestures, makes her seem more exposed, needy. Because her continuous show of affection has the power to embarrass him, he sometimes leaves, with her in tow. She does not work in this office, but she comes to eat here every day. Often she stays after lunch and it is then, when no one is present, that she talks to me. She is just eighteen. Her name is Smiljka. She has a younger sister at home in Sombor, she says as if she missed her. Talking with me she forgets to attempt her stern look, and at times during our conversations, I feel as if we were the same age. She sometimes asks me to go on errands with her. The cook is only too glad to be rid of me. I follow Smiljka as she makes her rounds to offices in the village. She, like the other Partisan women, carries a shotgun.

It is very cold and we are walking out of the managing office of the orphanage; Smiljka is walking ahead of me. I am watching her tall black boots crunching snow. We are crossing the yard when, there, behind the building, in a two-wheeled wagon of weathered wood, I see something clearly, which I am immediately compelled not to recognize. Piled up on each other, unclad small skeletal bodies with large shaven heads and bloated bellies, skin stretched over bones, leatherlike, asprawl, entangled—discarded dead children. I hear the familiar rattle of bones, the high pitch of frozen skin cutting the cold. The sharp sounds keep me looking to the ground.

Smiljka calls my name. *"Lujza; gledaj!"* she says pointing. I don't turn my head. "Look!" she shouts, impatiently. I see her face contorted into a scowl and I look to see the horror she points to. I don't know which is the more terrible, the ghoulish smirk on the pitiless face of the figure before me or the gesturing horror in the wagon of bones. She spits toward the site, clearing the rounding bulge protruding from under her coat. A feeling of revulsion grips me. The grit of rage crunching sounds of snow follows me as I walk beside her, silently, on empty streets. I want nothing of hers to touch me. Nothing can bridge the space between us. She makes conversation. I don't listen.

When she needs someone to keep house, to help her get ready for the baby, I volunteer my mother. Smiljka lives on the other side of the wrecked church, facing its spacious grounds, next to the Blees's house, sharing its yard; the two old people to whom it belonged, still live in their summer kitchen. They are German. My mother and I talk to them often. Though their house has been taken away from them, they were not put in the camp. Their son works in the offices of Land Management. We don't understand, but we don't ask questions. Blees is not a German name, my mother says, trying for reason. There are fruit trees in the orchard in front of their summer kitchen. Plums, apples, sour cherries. Päsl Zilli, Mrs. Blees, points them out to us proudly. Trees. A rarity.

Going to Smiljka's house we walk down our street; I never go through the gardens anymore, to avoid passing the house where tetka Mila used to live. The street is empty. A solitary figure is walking toward us. It is a familiar image—shaven head, face large-eyed, skull-like. The skeletal body moves slowly, limping. It is a girl, my height. Her knobby knees stick out from under a coat too small, pulled together by only one button, sleeves too short, showing lumpish wrists, hands dangling. I walk briskly, trying to keep up with my mother. We greet in passing. "Wawi néni, don't you know me?" her voice pleads for recognition. "It is me, Else," she demands. "Else, Else," we repeat warmly, embracing her. Else, my classmate, from our village. Else, whom my mother praised, and whom she most wanted me to be like. "Else!" Her grandmother has died, she tells us; now she is alone. She has to report to the orphanage, to the doctor there. She has an open sore that will not heal. My mother makes consoling talk. Feeling more fortunate, being with my mother, I dare not mention hers. But Else does. She is still in Nakovo, she thinks. I talk, trying to avoid my feelings, fleeing her gaze; I try to quell the horror that wants to express itself in laughter. Pity? I can't even feel sad. I chatter nervously. I don't want to feel the pain of her envy. I want to hide it from her that I am better off, but I know I can't. Why is it not me who bears that fate? What did I do to deserve better? And then these questions condense into one assertion: whatever I did, my being better off wronged her. I stand before her in my shame.

• • •

In spring, our relatives from Sajan come again bringing food. Hidden in the opened parcel we find a letter from my father. He is a prisoner of war in Jablanica, Bosnia. He asks our relatives to write to him, to send him news about us—he is allowed to receive letters. My father is alive! The thought alone is powerful enough to conjure up his presence, and the letter, though smelling of flour, still has a faint scent reminiscent of my father. With my face in the paper, I inhale.

A woman from our village leaves a parcel for us. Soft sweaters in pastel colors brighten our room. Tin cans with foreign labels, opened, their contents replaced by more familiar fare, intrigue us. A hidden note explains: packages from our relatives in America are being sent to her; she will come again. There is something revolutionary about this news. Though we do not discuss it, the idea that as far away as America people know about our plight distills assurance, affirmation. We now look at each other differently, and our room fills with assertion, even defiance. Tanti Lisa takes out the knitting needles—the remaining spokes from an old bicycle wheel she found in Nakovo—and having unraveled the sweaters that fit none of us, she starts knitting with a vengeance, to give the event symbolic expression. A delicate lacy pattern of light blue grows; she asks me to stand while she measures for length. A yoke of darker blue, puffed sleeves, all come together in a dress, for me. She works with fervor, in a frenzy, knitting even when there is hardly light enough to see. "For Easter," she says. "It must be finished by Easter!" Her doleful look is charged with defiance. It is cold on Easter Sunday, raining. I wear my lacy dress inside, shivering. Johann has a new blue sweater and matching short-legged pants.

The weather is getting warmer; the orchard at Smiljka's house is showing first fruits. The sour cherries have ripened. Plums are still green; the few I steal taste sour.

Smiljka's mother comes to visit, and in her presence the image Smiljka projects, that of a ardent Partisan, acquires a measure of modesty. She still shows herself stern and tough, walking about the village self-importantly, but around her mother she is almost docile, smiling a lot. When Smiljka is not at home, her mother talks about the misfortune that befell the ethnic Germans of our country. She speaks openly of Partisan atrocities and expresses her regret about her daughter's involvement through her unfortunate marriage to the Intendant. "Gospodja," she says to my mother, "I fear the wrath of God. Such deeds will not go unpunished!" I listen. Unencumbered by my presence, she confides in my mother, and their intimacy reminds me of our village at home. I am startled when Smiljka's mother comments on conditions in the camp, in the Intendant's presence, asking him about the veracity of the beatings and torture she hears about. Unflinching, he tells her, "We don't beat anyone." He mentions the man we call Schtecke Pede, who doles out punishment. "Generally, we just watch, while they do it themselves." Smiljka's mother looks at her son-in-law with the same quiet loathing that is part of her expression whenever he is around.

When Smiljka's mother leaves, she reminds her daughter in parting, "Be good to gospodja and her people. Remember, you have a personal debt to repay." Smiljka knows the debt she owes. Her father's life was saved by German neighbors during the Razzia, the massacre of Serbs by Hungarians during the war. She looks confirming smiles at my mother. But with her mother gone, Smiljka's fervor to be a good Partisan returns.

Every morning, peering out of the kitchen window, she scans the yard of the menza for guards, looking for the two little boys who come to scavenge food from a slop barrel into which the cooks dump leftovers. She waits behind the curtain, and as the boys get their hands into the watery slosh, she yells her threats, sending them running. Her mother once caught her at this and stopped her by a scolding: "Why begrudge the children the fermented food they fish out of the pig-feed, when you know it keeps them from starving? Since you don't have the courage to give them food outright, have the humility to let them be." Smiljka, unable to resist a contradiction, scoffed, "Just look how chubby they are!" Now she continues her ugly habit, using small stones to throw at the boys. When my mother looks at her questioning, she mumbles grudgingly, "I know I shouldn't do it . . ." But the next day she does it again. That Smiljka could shoot at the boys, we dare not think. If the Intendant were at the window, there would be cause to fear.

There is something Smiljka wants to hide, something she is ashamed of. A large spot on the wall next to their bed; she wants it to go unnoticed. Deep gouges, plaster chipped away in patches, scratches mutilate the stenciled pattern. Its mysterious appearance is shrouded in secrecy; Smiljka says nothing about it. The spot grows. Later, the bed is moved away from the wall, the gouged wall mended, the scratches hidden under a cover of paint. But soon, the same pattern of scratches appears above the headboard. I look at the spot with curiosity; its mysterious reappearance gives it a ghostly cast. I am shocked when Smiljka tries to deny seeing it. She keeps the shades pulled, and in the darkened room, the spot acquires a sheltered look and seems less obtrusive. She worries that the marred wall will annoy the Intendant. Since he hardly ever speaks in our presence, we don't know what he thinks. I can't imagine him being concerned. For the rest of us, the spot has a larger presence; it occupies the room, the house, our imagination. Burdened by its insistence to be noticed, Smiljka confesses to my mother that she has recurring nightmares during which she scratches at the wall. She shows her worn-down nails. But she does not tell what these nightmares are about. It is only through her mother that we later learn Smiljka was present during a massacre where German people, men and women, even children, were shot into an open pit. She now nightly digs at the memory. My imagination presents startling images, and the spot on the wall peoples the house with complaints. Smiljka's mother blames the Intendant.

When the time comes for the baby to be born, my mother and I stay with Smiljka in the front room. A midwife, a German woman from the camp, is called. The Intendant is pacing in the kitchen, behind closed doors, peering over the half-curtains, watching. My mother and the midwife attend to Smiljka, who shrieks and screams intermittently, now calling for her mother, now calling on the Mother of God. "*Sveta Majko Božija, pomozi!*" she pleads between piercing shrieks. My mother grips her hand tightly, giving encouragement, and when the screams subside, I am startled to hear my mother say, in a reprimanding but positive tone, loud enough for all to hear, "So, now we are calling on the Mother of God! It might be good to remember this when all is over." The midwife, who does not speak Serbo-Croatian, is unaware of the barb; the prickly remark goes unnoticed. It will be some time before the baby comes, the midwife says. My mother stays. I am sent home.

Smiljka's baby is a boy. They name him Slobodan. Freedom asserted by name, born in a concentration camp, he starts life with a contradiction. My mother is at Smiljka's house every day, and sometimes she stays overnight. The benefits of her job are many. She now goes to the market in Titel weekly. With a note from the Intendant she can go there alone. They don't know she brings salt for people in the camp. She even brings such fragile luxuries as eggs, three at a time, for Nina néni, whose children send money from America to Hungarian relatives; she finds it hidden in food they bring. We always share the food my mother brings from Smiljka's house: leftovers, stale bread, and all the potato peelings Nina néni would want, even a potato or two on occasion, and we share the food we occasionally get from our relatives, but Nina néni keeps her eggs to herself. We don't mind. Johann and I watch her sucking the slimy content through a small hole in the shell, agog with amazement, admiration, disgust.

My mother's trips to Titel bring with them a contraband commodity: access to the world outside by mail. People like my mother, who are allowed to go out of the camp because their work requires it, carry letters hidden on their person. My mother carries not only the letters we write but other people's as well. She knows it is dangerous. Caught, she risks the loss of her job, severe beatings, the cellar—the guards usually search the people going out. On one occasion, a guard approaches my mother accusing, "We hear you are carrying letters!" She, putting on a bold face, quips, "Who . . . me?" and adds, bluffing, "Please, have a look!" She starts unbuttoning her blouse. If he calls her bluff, she knows she is done for; there is a stash of letters on her. He yells to button up and get going. She noticed, she tells us, how unsteady the bridge seemed that day, crossing it with her knees shaking. We laugh. We dare not flirt with the thought that someday she might be caught.

Slobodan grows. Tallow-haired, blue-eyed, cheerful. Everyone's darling.

On one of my visits, I people the yard with large images, faces mostly; Smiljka refuses to believe I drew them. She will not allow me to erase them; she wants to show them to the Intendant. Coming back with her mother from Titel one day, she brings me a box of watercolors and a drawing pad. I am overwhelmed by the gesture. Smiljka shines in front of her mother.

The purple plums are ripening and Päsl Zilli asks me into the fenced in orchard to pick some. "They taste much better ripe, don't they?" she says, winking into my face. I squint into the sun to avoid her eyes.

I am not always at Smiljka's house; I am most often home with Nina néni and Johann. New people have come to the camp recently. I notice a girl in the yard next door. She looks out of place. Her clothes, her complexion, her bearing, all seem new, untainted by the desolate sepia tone of our landscape. Small, delicately built, graceful, she has black hair and eyes, a slender face, porcelain-white skin. Self-assured, aloof; when I speak to her she is reluctant to reply to my questions. Her name is Helga. Both her parents are here. Captured in transit, they were brought here from somewhere near the Austrian border. They have never been in a camp before; she does not explain. She is only ten years old, but her serious demeanor, her manners, make her seem older. She wears leather shoes. I am barefoot. Later, when we know each other better and she takes her shoes off to go barefoot (it seems a treat for her), I am amazed how narrow and white her feet are. She speaks beautiful German and uses many foreign words. She is educated. I admire everything about her: her serious, expressive face, her graceful bearing, her sensitive long-fingered hands; everything, down to her narrow, elite feet. We occasionally play in our yard, squatting on the ground, using sticks to draw rooms, which we furnish with bricks, and we cook make-believe dishes using real grasses. She is a bit awkward at play; she does not often play, she says. She reads a lot. They have books. I am amazed. When she invites me to their room to meet her parents, I am even more surprised. They have made a corner of the room into a private place by cordoning it off from the others, using blankets; this corner is filled with their things. So many books! I am baffled; they were allowed to keep them? Her parents are both small, her mother especially; she has a curved spine. Polite, affectionate with each other, they speak with Helga as with a grown-up. They receive me like a guest. I am confused. Their attitude, their assumption, even their being together seems out of place here. Helga's father complains openly, talking about the terrible conditions in camp as if they were something to have an opinion about instead of something to be endured. They are concerned about Helga's education, and, it seems, in the short time they have been here, they have already managed to find a tutor.

Coming home to our room, I see Nina néni wielding a knife, stabbing away at the walls. Without a rational explanation, it is hard to imagine what she is up to. She is not the kind of person one would expect suddenly to go mad. "Ah," she says, "it got away!" "What got away?" I ask, testing for sanity. "Why, a mouse," she says, scolding. "The nasty, greedy little pests— they eat all and everything we have. *Az ördög bújjon bele!*" she curses in Hungarian, sending the devil after it. I laugh and cannot stop laughing. She looks annoyed. Suppressing my laughter, I ask seriously, "You were going after a mouse with this long knife? Did you really expect to get it?" She looks peeved, at first, and then her dark, piercing eyes flash triumphant. "Of course," she says proudly, "I got one yesterday." I imagine the knife-wielding image I just saw, modified by the telling detail, a little mouse impaled on the huge blade, bleeding. Sickened, I try to reconcile it with the more familiar image, Nina néni mouthing words, fingering the rosary. Watching the two images collide, I recoil with helpless laughter.

The civility in our room confines itself to our nightly talks; visits to other rooms for singing and storytelling have stopped long ago. I talk about my visit at Helga's. Her parents seem not to realize where they are, my mother says, but she is very interested in the notion of a tutor, and the next evening we call on Helga's parents uninvited. My mother is not intimidated by those more educated; everyone is an equal in her eyes; status does not confuse her. I am a bit embarrassed by her lack of humility. Helga's parents are accommodating; they will arrange for a meeting with the teacher, whom they met on the transport to this camp.

• • •

Fräulein Gebauer is slim, well groomed, looking prim wearing a vest and skirt of hunter green with a cream-colored, long-sleeved blouse tied in a bow at the neck. She seems older than my mother. Her short hair, looking more blond than gray, falls softly curled, rounding a handsome rectangular face with creamy clear complexion, pink cheeks, and sparkling blue eyes. She has a soft melodic voice, a lilting speech pattern. I immediately like her.

Smitten by her gentility, her graceful bearing, I watch her every move and listen. She was born and educated in Vienna, she tells us, but she has been away from home for quite some time, living in Graz, and most recently living in Bulgaria, employed as governess to the children of the royal house. Such credentials intimidate, but I admire her even more.

Two boys, brothers, Peter and Nikolaus, are part of our small school of four. The weather is warm and we have our lessons outside, writing them on the ground, perfecting a lyrical script, erasing everything when we are finished. When it rains, we meet in the shed attached to the house. Fräulein Gebauer entertains us with stories from history: the First World War, the Battle of Verdun, replete with details about the personalities of generals, their strategies, their character flaws. Dismantling historic events, reducing them to personal gossip, to secrets whispered, is power demystified. And all this is done with careful attention to detail, as if what we learn, being of utmost importance, needs our exclusive care, and as if we were the only remaining keepers of knowledge, lovers of wisdom. We learn not only about incidental world events but about astronomic concerns. The names of planets, their size, position, and relation to the sun are known to us. We make drawings of them on the ground. We recite poetry we learn by heart. Fräulein Gebauer tells fascinating stories, some about her personal experiences, all to point out good behavior and strength of character, teaching morals and manners. And she tells us stories about her royal charges. About the princess, Maria Luisa—about one of her parties. The vivid descriptions challenge; I strain to accommodate some of the imagery. A large pavilion, the place of the party, mushrooms into existence without the slightest point of reference; I do not know what a pavilion is. In it, a huge canopy, clusters of violets hung from invisible threads make a ceiling of delicate fragrance. I imagine white silken tents billowing in fields of roses (why roses?), fragrant breezes wafting through sheets of silken softness. Billowing whites, clusters of indigo, violets, laced with verdant green, undulate, their delicate fragrance suspended amid music and laughter, satins and laces, elegant ladies, gowned and sashed, dancing with handsome men in white, gold-buttoned uniforms. Outside, an exaltation of doves pierces the crystal sky. Somewhere in the distance, silver stallions wait late into the moonlit night . . .

The younger of the royal children is Fräulein Gebauer's favorite. Precocious, eloquent, well-mannered, perfect in every way, a genius, is the exemplar against which all of us are measured. Simeon—the way she says it sounds like a song. I understand it as Simone, a girl, a princess. Assessing all my shortcomings, I jealously yield my quest for Fräulein Gebauer's affection to this Simeon, a superior self. Helga quickly tires of Fräulein Gebauer's stories. Within a week, she no longer comes. Her father deems it a waste of time. He tells my mother Helga is bored; she already knows much more than the teacher. His daughter needs a challenge. When they get out of this camp, they plan to go to Germany, but they will not stay there. Germany, at this time, is not the appropriate environment for his daughter. Her superior intellect demands that they go elsewhere. I am impressed, confounded, abashed. Helga's father speaks with such certainty about his plans for the future that it makes him look foolish, and Nina néni's plan, to live in her summer kitchen, acquires a tone of humility by comparison.

In time the boys and I are invited into Fräulein Gebauer's room. It is a long narrow room; it may have been a pantry. Of the dozen or more people living there, I get to know two better than the others: a man, whose place in the straw is immediately next to Fräulein Gebauer's, and a woman they call Karola, who sleeps at the very end of the room, under the window. I am surprised to see a man in the room. Only women, girls, and small boys live in our house. The people in this room have only recently arrived. Like Fräulein Gebauer, most of them are citizens of Austria captured on their way home. Unlike us, they have been allowed to keep some of their possessions; luckier than we, they were spared the earlier terrible years here.

The man living in Fräulein Gebauer's room has many drawing pencils, a compass he keeps in a small leather case, pens, and—it seems unbelievable—he has small bottles of colored ink. "Herr Böhm is not fond of children," I hear Fräulein Gebauer say in his defense when he seems particularly rude to us, and she adds, kindly, "but he is a gentleman; an architect." He usually sits on his place in the straw, looking pale; he seems sickly. Peter tells about seeing him do something disgusting using a rubber tube, trying to urinate, sucking on it to get the flow going. The boys recall this image with snickering whispers, miming behind his back. I don't like hearing about it; it embarrasses me and it also makes me feel like a traitor to the boys, since secretly I feel sorry for the architect.

Karola is a woman about Fräulein Gebauer's age. Her face, in spite of well-shaped features, looks coarse; her skin, an opaque yellow, has the appearance of worn leather. Her large hands, fingers showing dark brown stains, betray an old habit. She has a nasty cough and, according to what others say, a disposition to match. Her habitual expression is sullen; her eyes, under heavy brows, alert, watchful; their direct glance sharpened by a slight squint, she can look unfriendly. Fräulein Gebauer makes little eye contact with her, even when she greets her. I know she has opinions about her; I hear them aired in talks with the architect. I surmise they don't think much of her. She is a lady of questionable morals; her way of life caught up with her. Although I don't understand most of what is said about her—it being said in whispers, not intended for anyone else to hear—I know they don't like her because of who she is. I see Karola keeping to herself. I always greet her when I see her in the yard. I mispronounce her name; she corrects me, saying it does not matter. Looking sullen as she usually does, never saying a word, I am surprised that she speaks to me at all. She thinks well of me, she says. She has been watching me, she adds, wistfully. Her voice resonates like a bass. She has a lot of faith in my spirit—"They won't be able to rob you of that," she says prophetically. "Don't let them fill your head with the pallid bloodless notions that govern their lives. It may make life more manageable, but it kills the spirit. Don't let anyone kill your spirit." She says this gravely, looking intent, as if she were seeking the great darkness, the source of life. I must look as if I understand, for she continues: "Look at them—they are like reeds that bore even the wind blowing through them. They have made ghosts of themselves, and still, even in the face of death, they cling to their ideas—denying death! I love life. I lived it. I am not afraid to die." She looks at me, and in the timbre of her voice, I feel the earth tremble. She repeats, "I am not afraid of death," and adds in whispers, "I am not ashamed of my life." I feel almost as if I am only overhearing her talking to herself. But I know she is aware that I am listening intently. "I have faith in your robust little spirit." She touches her fingers awkwardly to my cheek, as if to remind herself that I am really there. One day, much later, when I come to the house, I see her corpse lying in the yard, fully clad, facing the wall. I walk by slowly, not looking away. Letting the dark timbre of her voice resonate within me, I say her name.

There is a peculiar pain I am aware of, being here among the watching, the waiting to die. The educated, like finely wrought ornamental objects, quickly pale in the dusky sepia light that reduces everything to ground. The grace expressed in elegant manners gives way in appreciable increments to the color of dust. Such changes disturb. The people from the village, having never been far from the ground, retain their earthen tone and stay the same. While our common destiny reduces us, bringing us to equal perfection, eventually, it is the changes that are ominous, difficult, painful to witness. Sometimes, I seem to be a pair of eyes, watching.

I don't talk about my taking lessons with Fräulein Gebauer; I never mention it at Smiljka's house. Education is forbidden. Any social activity, even communal prayer led by a priest, is forbidden. If it occurs, even in secret, the priest risks punishment; if he is not caught outright, he may be reported by informers. When some months ago my mother approached a priest about lessons in religion, he scolded curtly, "In a place where thousands of children receive no religious instruction, it hardly matters if one child does." My mother agrees; she is never put off by bad manners when it concerns justice.

Fräulein Gebauer knows about the danger she courts by teaching. She must be brave. She talks to us about courage. She asks us to tell her what we most fear. We whisper it in her ear and she gives us each private counsel, to help us face our fear courageously in the future. I am afraid of the dark, I tell her. On dark nights when I have to go to the outhouse, groping my way through the entry, the back yard, I lose all points of reference and, about to lose my mind, I think of terrible things. Going to the outhouse is fraught with temptation as well; you may avoid the hazardous path by squatting down anywhere. Piles of excrement keep cropping up nightly all over the yard; transgressions that bear witness to a fear in common. As an act of courage, I am to offer up my trips to the outhouse, showing my love of God. Though Fräulein Gebauer is not religious in the conventional sense, she aims for moral character as service to God.

The boys don't tell me what their fears are. Peter hardly talks to me at all. In spite of the manners Fräulein Gebauer teaches, he is boorish, rude, and nothing like his brother, Nikolaus, who is sensitive, polite, and who talks to me.

A summer storm comes up suddenly. An ominous darkness threatens night at midday. Voluminous clouds unfurl low to the ground. A strong wind whips the grasses, tossing everything loose before it. We are ready to leave when we hear the first thunderclap close by. The boys decide to brave the storm. Fräulein Gebauer urges me to stay; the boys will run faster without me. When I too want to go, Peter makes a face, forcing a quick decision. The boys take hold of my hands and we start running, the wind pushing us from behind. They laugh, their legs flying under them. Mine are completely off the ground. I am plucked up; wind pushing through me, my breath is somewhere before me. Thunderclaps and brilliant lightning follow each other with hardly an interval between. The earth loosens; churned-up dust from miles around swallows the houses before us. The air, quickened, pelts us with needles of dust. Large singular drops fall, popping, uncorking the smell of loam; a heavy rain ensues with quick pelting pummels, and then water falls in solid sheets, soaking us to the bone, weighing us down, dissolving us. The boys shout to each other but their voices shatter in pieces. They run, driven. My arms seem destined to go with them; I feel them pulling out of joint. Their hands clasped firmly around mine, there is no letting go. Our clothes clinging to us like a second skin, we run, slicing sheets of water.

We reach the still, dry inside of a house. I see the familiar loaves being stacked, like bricks, by sepia-clad women, their shadows, enlarged, licking the walls like dark flames, the diffuse light transforming the stacks of our bread rations into golden pyramids. The boys' mother, who manages the proceedings, takes us closer to the ovens; we stand in front of the radiant embers, drying our clothes, quickened.

The storm and the experiences in Fräulein Gebauer's yard are isolated incidents that have the power to lift us out of the confinement of our everyday, into the world outside.

Fräulein Gebauer teaches about morality. Having always wanted to be good, I am interested. We learn long poems that exemplify goodness, rightness in conduct, character. The boys and I each memorize one to recite. Mine is about the valiant deeds of Saint Elizabeth: feeding the poor, defying her husband's will, and about the grace of her gifts turned miracle, the evidence of her transgressions turning into roses. Fräulein Gebauer also asks each of us to think of the worst thing we have ever done. We are to tell her in private. It is important to know, admit, and face one's transgressions, she says. We must not manipulate to avoid the shame. Wrongdoing, unattested, leaves permanent scars, damages character, and darkens the spirit, harming the soul. I listen. I remember the egg and Lisa's face, and the dark feeling within me surfaces, weighing me down. I have trouble telling Fräulein Gebauer. With long hesitations and deep breath taking, I get it said. Relieved, watching her face I see nothing of reprimand or disapproval. She speaks softly. The tone of her voice is reassuring but the words startle. She wants me to go to the house where Lisa lived, to find her mother, to ask her forgiveness. I am panicked, shocked, and something within me is repelled by the suggestion. The wrong of which I accuse myself is grave. Measured against the offense, the proposed gesture seems inappropriate, theatrical, irreverent. Stunned, I say nothing. Days later I find myself at Lisa's house, in a large room, whispering. The woman who says she is her mother is expressionless. Looking detached, she listens to what I have to say. An older woman, dressed in black, sits close by. I tell the story about the egg as well as I can, covering up my quivering chin with one hand, talking into their faces. Suddenly the younger woman's expression changes. Something like an affront comes over her face. I ask her to forgive me. I think she says, "Is this a joke?" I cannot look fast enough to read the changing expressions moving across her face. I think it is rage that sends her running past me, into the yard outside. Feeling helpless, ashamed, I look to the door, unable to leave the room. The older woman gets up and, speaking to me kindly, leads me out. Her somber voice comforts; I no longer listen to the words. Outside, in the distant grasses, a solitary figure, her back toward us, is silhouetted darkly against gray skies.

• • •

Nothing here has changed. We still get the same rations with the same erratic frequency. Escorted by armed guards, thousands continue their treks to faraway fields, working long hours. People are still dying of hunger and disease. Many are being beaten, tortured; some are killed. The oppressive uncertainty that tinges our every day is with us always, like the color of the landscape. It is 1947. We are still not allowed to write or receive letters. News of our kin comes secreted in food brought to us on rare occasions. Those who come leave their small parcels for inspection at the camp's entrance and wave to us across barbed wire. We call them our visitors. Sometimes people brought here from other camps bring news of our kin. These connections to the world outside are incidental, spurious.

Our waiting to go home is only a habit—we don't trust. No one believes. We who have always been here have grown weary. Numb. Unaccustomed to hope, for us waiting is a reminder of something forgotten.

CHAPTER 11

A New Identity

I N LATE SUMMER, packages from relatives in America arrive in camp; we receive them already opened. We finger the wrappings, reading the addresses, pronouncing every letter of the meaningless words; Gift Package, we read, crying jubilations. Cincinnati, Cincinnati, we say in recognition, and the sound itself conjures exotic images of a faraway land. Cincinnati, city of the fair, we cheer! My mother smiles. She was born there. Only Nina néni knows this city and we see nothing in her cunning eyes to dispel the illusion of the magic city of our dreams.

We hover over the open packages in anticipation. A foreign fragrance transforms our room. Each article emerges, miraculous. A red tin with the words "Baking Powder" over the profile of an Indian, in full headdress, gives no clue about the caramel-colored paste stored in it; it smells like nothing we know. We like its taste. Tanti Lisa doles it out sparingly each evening, a teaspoonful for each of us, till it is gone. Years later, a taste of peanut butter recalls the precious substance of our communal ritual. Round, striped candies, wrapped in cellophane, receive immediate recognition. Unopened tins keep their surprises. We examine clothes and shoes, giving them each our undivided attention. Some dresses have words written on them; some with large floral patterns have ruffles; still others have pleats and decorative embroideries; most fit none of us. The shoes, bright reds, brilliant blues, all showing impeccable detail, are small, narrow, high-heeled; we cannot imagine the person who wore them. We divide everything, usually with only minor disputes. Tanti Lisa is so docile, accepting anything, it irritates my mother having to speak up for her when Lisa Kodl stubbornly continues taking first choice. Nina néni always sides with Kodl, against my mother. Pious as she is, you would expect her to stay out of such arguments. Depending on my mother as she does, you would expect some gratuitous abstention. But, I have noticed, people do not like being indebted to others. It irritates them to acknowledge, and they try to avoid their debts at all costs. Why else would we have to pray to God—to forgive us our debts? I am embarrassed. Even so, each time packages arrive, forgetting the previous row, I go running to fetch Kodl. There I see Anna, wearing a wraparound much like mine; we smile. I see the twins shyly tugging at her; they are almost four now and hardly know me.

In the room next to ours, Theres, the quiet woman with the curved spine, receives many packages from her kin in America; beautiful things— elegant clothes, scarves and coats, leather purses, sensible shoes. Even fur stoles, jewelry, and watches were sent to her, according to the list of contents, but these are missing. Still, she is the envy of everyone. Soon some of her things disappear from her room. No one admits to having taken them. The woman from Crna Bara accuses Theres of never having had such items, of being delusional. Later, when on a quiet day in winter Theres disappears as well, they find her in the attic. Hanged. The woman from Crna Bara cuts her down. With help from others, the small corpse is lowered, sliding stiffly, bumping, making muted wood sounds against the ladder. People whisper; some accuse. Having survived the worst of times, why does she, more fortunate than others, now hang herself? She was despondent, ill, some say. Others say she was harassed and blame her envy-provoking gifts.

When my mother is sick with a fever, I take Tanti Lisa to work in her place. I walk beside her quietly; I can see she is disgruntled even before she says: "I would rather you lead me into the Theiss!" I take it she does not want to go to the Intendant's house. Is she afraid? She knows I have been going there all this time, and I am just a little girl. Was she not afraid for me? I remember her approving my approaching the Komandant. I feel disappointed, annoyed. Working outside in bad weather, exposed to the cruelty of guards, she has been working for the Partisans all along; why is working for them inside, in a warm room, suddenly worse than death by drowning? And all this time my mother's working there benefiting all of us—I ponder, disgusted, saying nothing.

• • •

We no longer meet at Fräulein Gebauer's house; we no longer have lessons, for Nikolaus and Peter have disappeared. Escaped? Fräulein Gebauer now comes to our room. It is more convenient and she likes the walk, she says. She and my mother use the familiar *Du*, you, and call each other by first names; and I call Fräulein Gebauer Tante Gebauer now. Always cheerful, looking prim in her Loden coat, cheeks glowing pink, eyes sparkling, she comes bringing smiles. Wrapped in the lilting sound of her voice, sitting beside her on the straw, I feel among the privileged few, the pampered by fate.

Wearing her fingerless gloves, Tante Gebauer is supervising a water-color I am painting, a night scene in winter: the moon—our own village moon—fixed, full, garlanded by softly frayed clouds scrubbed clean, its lambent light lulling snow banks sleeping below. The trees and houses hearken, reverent, still. In the foreground, where the road makes a sharp bend into the village, a small roadside shrine, its roof heavily laden with snow, stops a solitary passer-by; a woman, facing the dimly lit view of the open shrine, her long skirts against the snow, stands wrapped in solemn contemplation before the sheltered Madonna and Child. The road, iced, showing blues, ochers fused into tracks and shadows cast, curves around the image and passes. The large brown house in the foreground, its roof and ledges weighted, squats in mute observation—its windows flickering yellow-orange—amid mounds of snow delicately laced with lattice fencing and lacy shrubs. Tall brown-trunked trees confine themselves to the edge of the painting, losing their shadows, letting them fall outside the picture. Their bristling branches and frozen twigs, snow laden—around which the dark blue sky has to dance carefully so as not to spoil the pristine white lines they hold so still—raise their precarious offering to the moon. Up the road, a gather of houses hover, towered over by the sharp steeple of the village church; a beacon, windows framing orange beckoning light; a signal, a sign of life inside. Outside, serene evergreens echo verdant greening. Behind the village, dark purple, rumpled mountains lumber, dreaming . . .

Johann sits, his coat buttoned, quietly watching. Nina néni sends furtive glances toward me now and then. "Na, are you finished yet?" she says in a tone betraying impatience for a chore to be done. Finished, we send the painting to my father, folded. By now my mother is an expert at mail smuggling; we don't think about it not getting there.

Christmas Eve. Tante Gebauer is in our room. We have a small fire smoldering in the stove; we got the wood from Blees's yard without anyone's permission. The smell of cornmeal mush has me wishing we had milk; it tastes best spooned into cold milk, I remember, but instead a dusting of sugar and cocoa powder, from America, covers the mush on my plate, steaming chocolate. Hushed by the soft light from the glowing embers, we sit bowed over our plates, inhaling the scented warmth, listening to spoons touching tin. A delicate whiff of pine, faint as if remembered, reminds us we have a tree. A small mangled branch of evergreen (a clip from the Blees's shrub that survived the tuck under Tanti Lisa's coat), now ribboned with pastel strands of wool to remind us of tasseled sweets, stands on the ledge of the partially bricked-in window, looking tall. The shadowy light veils our faces and our voices, subtle with nuances, become a malleable probing, a tender touching, and our words, caressing the darkness between us, fade to delicate whispers. The space in our room trembles, reaching for faraway sounds.

Absorbed in our feast, we barely hear the soft knocking at the door, and only when it is repeated do we know we heard it before. Thoughts of hiding our tree, the glowing embers of the fire, the warmth in our room, our food, our company; all our transgressions tumble over each other in fright. My mother jumps up, and the door opens to something hardly believable—candles on a pine branch with—could it be?—real *Salonzucker* foiled and tasseled, the smell of Christmas at home, and behind the branch, a smiling Smiljka and her pretty sister, looking like angels. The splendid image has no voice. In the miraculous light our tasseled twig looks for an apology. I am hoping it goes unnoticed only because a gesture so grand should not be diminished by our having any tree at all. We grope about for the appropriate words. We don't know what to say or do. Only my mother stands calm, unruffled.

Candlelight on silver-foiled sweets sparks familiar scents; the taste, remembered, buds memories that grow into full-blown sugary pleasures. Dense with memories, layered with incongruities, the event struggles to pass from a moment of grace to a simple exchange, an offering and a receiving. We are touched by the moment, giver and taker alike; our awkwardness hovers to shield it, for safekeeping. I hear Tanti Lisa's sibilant whispers directed toward Johann, whose eyes glow, big as saucers, reflecting the miraculous. Soft laughter tinged with humility, lit faces, gold-haloed hair, a willowy figure aflicker in candlelight. Smiljka's gracious sister reminds her they have to go; her fiancé is waiting outside. I have not had time to adjust to the surprise. I repeat thank-yous, feeling inadequate. My mother walks them out the door. She returns disgruntled; she has to take care of the baby for the night and for days after. I try to soften her mood, expressing appreciation for the wonderful surprise, hoping she will curb her temper in front of Tante Gebauer, knowing that nothing can placate my mother at such times. She leaves without saying goodnight, leaving a familiar worry behind.

The candles flicker. No one says a word. The moment collapses on itself. Tante Gebauer tries to rescue the mood with Christmas stories. Johann's stares have outlasted the disruption; rapt in attention, caressed by flickering lights, his face glows angelic. Later, Tanti Lisa blows out the candles, "to save them for tomorrow," she says. We sing Christmas songs; I worry about my mother, thinking she is unhappy.

Smiljka, the Intendant's wife, and myself, in their front room in Rudolfsgnad/Knićanin. Photograph sent to us at Bor, May 4, 1948.

• • •

The yard of the Komandno Mesto is thronged with people. We see foreign dignitaries sitting behind long tables, among them ladies with painted fingernails; all are well groomed, worldly, some speak a foreign language. They take note of us: our names and dates and places of birth. No one asks about our missing family members, those taken from us, those who are dead. Their names, their dates and places of birth are not noted. No one is asked to give account of them. I watch the peaceable hands, weighted with rings, move over the white sheets of paper, leaving laced letters behind, writing us into existence, asserting our right to be; this seems a revolutionary act charged with intent to right a wrong. No incriminating looks rake us, only impartial glances, sometimes smiles, graze our faces. Among the pertinent questions asked, explanations and even advice are given. My mother gets interested looks. Born in America? Does she know she may have a chance to return there? The American Consulate should be informed. Who are these strangers? As guests of the Partisans, they cannot be trusted.

While the taking-note continues, more people arrive from other camps. Brestovac. Gakovo. Molidorf. Mramorak. Nameless faces come to claim their identity, leaving behind the thousands discarded, lost in tall grasses. Our camp is flooded with people, all anxious, searching for kin. Despair in not finding them, knowing them dead, and disbelief, seeing them alive, now find expression in tears. Reunited, we affirm to each other all that has happened to us; it now is the essential aspect of our identity. While the visiting dignitaries are busy with our names, our dates and places of birth, our former selves, we, informed with a new identity, know ourselves.

Loch Vedde Sepp comes to our room. He stayed in Nakovo with his wife. Päsl Nani was a cook in the Partisans' kitchen. He was hidden. All this time? Hidden! I can almost imagine what it must have been like, hidden from the sun for more than two years. I notice he is not pale. His face is a ruddy color that on closer look seems brownish blue, like a bruise healing. The eyes, puffy, edged with red, tearing, look beaten. He holds a handkerchief in the only hand he has, raising it now and then to wipe his face. He is a big man of burly build, tall even sitting down. Crouched low, perched on the board at the edge of our bed, he makes a bulky heap. He weeps softly. Speaking slowly, his voice weighted with grief is so gentle the air in our room, touched, trembles with reciprocity. His wife is dead, he tells us. Killed. To avoid being brought here, she joined him in hiding. He stops talking for a while, looking at us, smiling at me and asking Johann how old he now is. My mother offers something to eat. He puts down his handkerchief to hold the bread she gives him. He has massive bruises on his arm; his hand is swollen, blue. The handkerchief rests rumpled on his knees. He does not eat.

His eyes glaze over with a faraway look, looking toward my mother, looking through her to a dark distant place unreachable to us, straining to find it, tears running down his cheeks unattended. The words come slowly, grouping the sorrow, holding back an inward push, stalling, damming the flow that wants out. The flow of tears continues. The Partisans found them in hiding, took them to a room. They beat them. They tortured her—he looks at me and then at Johann; his face, helpless, is consoled by a gesture of his arm, hiding it momentarily, wiping tears. With my knees drawn close to my chin, I press my legs into my chest so hard that I feel a hole where my heart should be. My eyes riveted on his face, I give room to his sorrow, lending my face to his pain. "They beat us, and beat us, mercilessly. I did not mind for myself, but watching her suffer, seeing how they went at her . . . merciless . . . God . . . They threw her down from the couch; using it to stand on, they jumped on her belly booted, bouncing, making frolicking sounds, laughing. Her eyes popped out, *her eyes.* The terrible shrieks, the groaning and I, there, could not go to her, and she—only a reach away." All is quiet in our room. No one takes a breath. We make room for his sobs only; they shake the room to his bent body's quivering. Tall black boots, trampling geraniums fallen from a window sill—my mind tilts, straining to cover up the image of horror. Eyes, detached from their sockets, bouncing eyeballs, like soft eggs encased in a membrane; eggs without shells, an oddity I have seen harvested from butchered chickens lying on a kitchen table. Unfinished eggs, my mother called them. Put them back, put them back, please . . . I want to run, to press back the sightless eyes. My mother is using her handkerchief. My eyes cannot find the walls that enclose our room.

I see the anguished purple face, the movements baring arms, chest, ankles, showing black and blue, as if to prove it really happened; to expose it; to have it verified; to give it credence. Because there are not words enough to say it, we must see. His baring, wordless gestures are simple, full of grace. And all are like the showing of a finger that got pinched in a door, a knee that was scraped by a fall at play, a hurt for a mother to see and say the appropriate healing words to make it better; a hurt looking for affirmation; a complaint looking for understanding. "See," he says. "See!" And deeper, a groan, a guttural gargle in the throat dredges wordless accusations. Against whom? Is it God? Or is God being asked to console? No. No. Some things are inconsolable; we know. No one could—not even God would be so irreverent. We sit silently, welded solid in his pain. No one notices time passing. No one thinks of moving; when he moves, we are awakened into ourselves, slowly. He apologizes to my mother, looking at all of us. "The children—they should not have had to hear this," he says and his voice sounds like a caress. "Yes, Vedde Sepp," my mother says, softly, "you are right. But these children have seen the bottom of hell; they have witnessed things they should not have had to see when their lives were just beginning. As it is, they know about such things all too well already." She coaxes him to eat but he only raises his hand to his mouth as if to be polite and asks, apologetically, if he could have some water. Everyone moves at once, but my mother, being closest, stands up to get it for him. He says he has not eaten for quite some time and, though he should be hungry, he cannot seem to eat. My mother gathers some food (from America) for him to take along. Days later, we hear he has died.

The Austrian citizens are leaving. Tante Gebauer hopes she will be going home to Vienna. Saying good-bye, her blue eyes spill their sparkle and pale. I walk back to our room brokenhearted. I do not want to believe I will never see her again.

Freight trains come bringing more people. Johann's grandmother comes. My Kodl Leni and cousin Jozsi appear in our room; we thought they had fled, left with the covered wagons in the fall of 1944, and all this time they have been in Gakovo, a camp like ours. Jozsi's father was taken to Russia, they tell us. Their story is told later, in the dark, how Partisans captured them, how they beat Jozsi. He was only thirteen then. Changing his shirt in the morning, he shows me the indentations on his bony rib cage. "Kicked in," he says, sliding his hand over the spot where the ribs seem to undulate.

They summon us to the Komandno Mesto. The working force is sorted out, selected for work in the mines of Serbia. Others are chosen for field work, here, in Vojvodina. The old and sick, who have no kin, are grouped together. No one wants to be classified among the sick. What they really intend to do with us none of us knows. My mother thinks the threat of mines is a hoax and volunteers. Lisa Kodl and her father are in the group of field workers and glad about it. Nina néni still has faith in her long standing plan to go back to our village, to live in her summer kitchen.

A miracle. Grandfather arrives in our room. His presence instantly revives feelings of home. He was "bought out"—sold to a Serb farmer of Stari Bečej, on the second of April, 1946, to work as a hired hand; it saved his life.

Grandfather tells his story. The men taken from Nakovo were put to work in the forest in Deliblato. Each day, after their ration of cornmeal soup, they walked ten kilometers to work all day with nothing to eat but a slice of corn bread, coming back at dusk to a cup of unsalted pea soup. At work they were harassed, beaten. There were some men, eighty and older, who could not make the long trek; they died on the way. Others died at work. Some were beaten to death. The Komandant, armed with a rifle, wielding an acacia club, hitting indiscriminately into the crowd, greeted them on their return, shouting: *Evo ide moja stoka!*—Here come my livestock!

"On Palm Sunday, in the evening, they drove us into the yard; we had to get down on our knees and bark like dogs, then get up, wave our hands and hum like bees, get down again to hop like frogs. Those who fell were beaten mercilessly. They finally told us to lie on the ground to rest, and then took to running over us, stomping and kicking with their boots, making a game of it. I was lucky; I only had a shoulder dislocated and the small finger of my left hand broken. Some died of their injuries. One of our men hanged himself that night."

They were shuttled about now to Franzfeld (Kraljevićevo), to Pančevo, on to Mitrovica to work on the railroad, and later to build bridges at Petrovaradin and Novi Sad. Grandfather tells about the men from our village who died on the way. I hear Tanti Lisa weeping beside me. In June, 1945, the men were put in the camp at Bački Jarek. "It was a camp with twenty thousand people. A young woman, no older than twenty, was the Komandant. Cruel and terrible, fond of riding her horse through the streets, she would attack anyone she saw, driving them down like prey, making a game of it; especially cruel to women, she would pull them up by their hair, cursing them, calling them *švapske kurve*. Whores. She insisted on daily reports of the dead, cursing our God, complaining they were too few; we were too slow to die. She often took to shooting people on the street . . ." Grandfather continues to describe the peculiarities of the camp in Jarek. There must be an unwritten manual, retrieved from an ancestral chest, consulted with unfailing regularity, since all we experienced as random acts of cruelty here was done to others miles away.

Grandfather Korek died in Jarek. Tanti Lisa asks, in weeping whispers, for the date. Grandfather tells only what he knows. There is no interrupting Grandfather. He has to tell us everything, as if all the wrongs had to be counted up, to be accounted for, and all of his telling is like a road map, showing us where we have been.

• • •

It is the third of March, 1948, early in the morning. A milky light fills our room. My mother is rolling up and tying the downs, fastening them to her rucksack. The room looks bare; the straw, pulverized, worn to a slivery chaff, covers the floor sparsely. The patched up windows look blinded; the shelves askew, emptied of our few possessions, lament their uselessness. The stove hugs the wall as if to seek succor. We leave nothing behind; even our broom is going with us. We close the door, shutting in the abandoned walls. My mother is wiping tears. I know she is thinking of Grandmother. The wind is howling around the house, whipping the dry grasses in the distance. Tall reedlike sticks tremble in place, stunned. We leave without looking back, bundled up against the chill, carrying our bundles, leaning into the wind. The familiar anxiety hovers over the crowd waiting for the train. We climb the embankment and glance at the huddle of houses from crowded freight cars, looking at each other puzzled. We are surprised when the train starts moving with doors left unlatched.

Belgrade, the mutter is passed among us. Someone gets the idea to open the door a crack, and the city falls in on us in strips of light with clicking metal sounds. Giant girders caught in steel netting glide past us close enough to touch. We are crossing the Danube. Yes, it is true, we are going to Serbia. We realize they were telling us the truth. It is their first time of truth telling, we jest disheartened—how could they expect to be convincing at it? "What kind of mines are in Serbia?" I ask Grandfather. "Coal," he says, "copper, even gold mines." Gold. Will we have to live underground? I want to ask, but I am ashamed to admit my ignorance in front of Jozsi.

We have picked up speed, and the rhythmic sound of the moving train settles in among us. Outside, a shimmering silvery surface, shifting swiftly through red clay, threads itself like a ribbon through the sliver of light at the door, rushing past, unraveled, changing with the angle of light, now looking red, now glistening transparent. A river! We open the door of the wagon wide: the smell of steam and coal on spicy air, so crisp, it hurts to breathe. Sunlit hills apatch with meadows, densely dotted with scraggly dwarfish trees. We recognize them from afar. Plum trees. A flock of sheep grazing on steep slopes. "Mountains," we say, "beautiful mountains!" The red earth wraps the glistening stream in burnt umber. Billowing waves rise, folding in on themselves, brimming pleats of burnt sienna gathering close. "Beautiful! Beautiful," we repeat. Some of us cry. I rub my eyes in disbelief. It is as if, for the first time, I see color.

We cannot get enough of the unwinding view; image starved, we gorge on it, and the train, biting steel, hissing steam, puffing smoke, cradles our view in perpetual motion. Soon evergreen-tree-clad mountains rise and the river sinks to steep and stony shores. A long whistle greets its departure; the engine is climbing. Suddenly, it is pitch dark, smoke eating our throats. "Close the door," I scream, startled. "Please, someone close the door," I correct myself. People shoo me to quiet. I am ashamed of myself, but my panic talks by itself. "Please close the door," I whimper with my eyes closed tightly, my mouth against my sleeve. It seems the dark lasts forever. Soon we catch on; when the whistle blows, darkness swiftly follows. Please let someone close the door, I think to myself each time the whistle blows. Nothing but the clear blue of Grandfather's eyes conveys understanding. Then all is pitch black again. I screw my eyes shut and try not to breathe. I hear sliding metal sounds; someone is closing the door, and the familiar odor passes our car like the angel of death. I feel safe leaning against my mother.

We keep traveling, day and night, wrapped in the doleful churn of the winding train groping its way, tearing the air with shrill whistles. Other trains pass us, swallowing sound. We keep moving for days; I hear the whistle in my sleep and smell the acrid air, dreaming. Niš. Borski Rudnik. We disembark. Sensations of the moving train circulating through my blood, it is difficult to walk with the ground unsteady beneath me. Somewhere in the distance a terraced mountain is glowing orange. A field of red embers lights the night sky.

CHAPTER 12

Freed to Consigned Labor

ELEVATED TO THE TOP of the world, we now live among furniture; we sleep on straw-filled mattresses in wooden beds made of two-by-fours. Our extended family of eight has a room to itself with five beds. Raised from the floor, divided from each other, we have to get used to our separate lives together. We are free now, they tell us. We believe them. But what it means to be free takes time to bring to cognition. Occupied by our past conditioning, we continue our old ways. Waiting.

No one comes to goad us, to fetch us for work. No one goes to work in groups escorted by guards with guns. All who work are responsible to get to their places of work on their own and on time. Suddenly there is a need for clocks and calendars. Our days are divided into schedules to follow, night shifts and day shifts and in betweens. My mother works the night shift. Alone at her post, switching tracks, she fears most walking the mountain in the dark. Grandfather often meets her to walk her home before he goes to work himself. He works where they smelt the ore.

Tanti Lisa needs to take a letter to the post office; would I walk to town with her, she asks sheepishly? We expect to be questioned by guards; we are baffled—no one stops us leaving the barracks or on the way. Still we walk cautiously, looking to the ground, trusting that the road will lead us to town. In town the feeling of uneasiness is compounded by a perplexing bustle, bombarding us with sights and sounds. Unable to focus in all directions, our only defense, intense awareness, is rendered ineffective. Occupied with insecurity, our perception turned inward, we are disarmed, and the world falls in on us from all angles.

We enter a book store to little bell sounds and stand by the door bewildered. A book for school, in Cyrillic, I stammer. The clerk shows me a book on mathematics. I think I cannot refuse to buy once I have asked for it; hearing its price, I look to Tanti Lisa for confirmation. She shrugs her shoulders, looking helpless. She wants to buy stationery—envelopes and a note pad, she whispers apologetically. The smell of print on crisp new paper follows us to stay a first reminder of our transaction with the world.

We walk silently past stores and houses. Suddenly, a piercing shout from across the street welds us together and to the ground. Without looking at each other, eyes cast down, we stand stock still, barely breathing, lame. There is no measure of time where we stand; we stand forever. Loud voices—an interchange of words spanning the road, punctuated by small sounds of laughter in the give and take of conversation—collapse and revive and eventually break our vacant stare to the ground. We look at each other informed, decoding, delayed: a shout not meant for us. Our surprise turns into smiles and we walk away without looking back.

A large feeling suddenly expands the panoramic view before me. I want to say something about this feeling but we only chatter aimlessly; we laugh, and our laughter takes wing like so many birds flying. At the overpass, the

Kodl Leni, Magdalena Marschang (second from right), on the collective farm of Borski Rudnik, Bor, 1949.

rushing stream below us, I break into singing shouts. We are free! We are free! Tanti Lisa smiles, looking about shyly, and her silvery whispers, scolding me to contain myself, sound insincere. I feel like running; my impatience spanning spaces before me, I think I can fly. Tanti Lisa's smile turns to shouts of her own, surprising us both. The excess of our exuberance has us whirling about giddy with power.

Within weeks of our arrival, my mother makes inquiries to find Seppi; an official notification informs us that Seppi is in the orphanage in Uzdin. With a permit to travel, she now leaves Bor with the intent to bring Seppi back to us.

Deliriously happy, I take courage and face the frightening task of placing myself in school. Sitting among the boys and girls, I realize how painfully shy and self-conscious I am. The dark-haired girl they call Radka, whose father is a Partisan hero, says her parents are upset knowing there is a German going to school with her. But none of the children taunt me; they look at me with assessing distance and let me be. I am most embarrassed during reading. The book is passed from hand to hand; as it comes closer, I panic. Sometimes I can't see the letters in front of me, I am so uncertain. The room turns quiet with attention. All ears are cocked as I grope to sight the eluding letters. My voice cracks, groaning out sounds, slowly linking them into words. I expect someone to laugh. I strain to listen, to discern the hissing whispers around me. At any moment, I expect to give in to the dizzying frustration. "I can't any more," I want to say, but I go on. Once, when someone snickers during my reading, saying the word before I groan it out, I look up surprised to hear Jelena, the best reader in class, say sharply, "Let her be; she can do it on her own. Don't you see how she suffers, trying?" And her dark eyes look respectfully into mine.

My mother comes back without Seppi. The initial disappointment gives way listening to the many stories about her trip. She visits Lisi néni in Betschkerek, now Zrenjanin; everything in her cousin's house is unchanged, as if nothing had happened. And she goes home to our village. I have a thousand questions, at least; I want to know everything all at once.

She recognizes Seppi immediately; still, she looks for the pockmark on his forehead, to make sure. He is not the same, she says, evasively; he is six years old now, she gropes to explain. At first he seems distant, but later, as they talk, he appears glad to be with her, and when she leaves, he asks, shyly, if she will come again.

And at home? No one treats her return as if it were the slightest bit unusual. No one talks about our absence. The Hallais give her the photographs they salvaged from the streets when our houses were ransacked, cleared of their contents. I think of our house empty, its windows shuttered, looking dark and abandoned. New settlers from Bosnia are now living in our houses, my mother tells us. Strangers to the village, they bring their habits, their way of life with them; some bring their goats into our rooms and take to cooking on open hearths in the middle of the floor. Even as gifts our houses seem inadequate, ill suited to the needs of the new settlers. The neighbors lament the intrusion, citing the carelessness with which property is treated, calling the broken image of the village to witness. But the village, not hiding its brokenness, adjusts to the recent betrayal. Bereft of its sainted name, gifted to strangers, it continues under its new name, Ostojićevo, to honor a Partisan hero.

I have news of my own to tell; I am going to school. My mother is pleased but immediately finds fault with my being placed in third grade. I wanted her to be glad, but instead she is disappointed.

• • •

Nothing but the arrangement of the sturdy beds is stable in our room. The changing shifts that govern our sleeping and waking, the variety of personalities among us, determine the limitless irritants of our every day. I am convinced my cousin just likes provoking me. He wants me to quit sweeping; it is raising dust. I keep doing it. He looks at me with a smile askew, and I know he is about to irritate me. "Well," he says, glancing at the disarray of papers spread on our bed, "aren't we the good little girl, doing our homework. You had better clean up that mess before your mother gets home. Sweeping up, are we? Leaving it to the last minute?" I continue sweeping, taking even strides, trying to keep from laughing because his attempt to provoke is so obvious and because his words, like tickling fingers, irritate to laughter. I say nothing. "Always trying to be good, are we? Pleasing mother! So serious and studious, so anxious about keeping everyone happy." He makes a face. I can feel myself getting riled. "Why don't you hurry putting yourself together; you'll be late," I say with even intonation. He is changing his shirt. "Don't worry about me," he says sarcastically, "you are the one who is missing everything. Instead of poring over those books, hanging about pleasing mother, you should be with boys and girls your own age, learning about the important things in life." He is close to me now, buttoning his shirt. "I know enough of life already," I say controlling my anger. He smirks. "Some one should tell you about growing up, about important things—here you are, almost thirteen, and as dumb as the day you were born." "I don't want to listen to you," I say, raising my broom as if to hit him. He grabs it and I continue holding on with both hands. He pins me to the wall and smirks into my face: "What can a little girl like you do to me now? You will kindly listen till I am finished." He blows hissed laughter down my face. "Get away from me, you fool," I say. He just laughs and holds me pinned. I see the white flesh of the inside of his arms close up; I wriggle closer, reaching for a spot, and take a bite. All the anger teased out of me locks my jaws to the bite. I taste blood but I don't let go. "The beast bites!" he screams, half laughing, attempting to squelch a groan, and the pressure on the broom handle gives way. "Let go!" he says, trying to shake me off. I feel the flesh in my mouth; I am sure I could bite it off, but I let go. He holds up his wrist, looking at the damage. "You drew blood," he says, astonished. "It will probably get infected—we will have to watch you closely," he says, cringing, not taking his eyes off his wrist. "If you start foaming at the mouth, I would not be surprised. You should be chained up like a mad dog," he continues grumbling, tying his handkerchief around the injured wrist. Let me see it—does it really hurt, I want to ask. I am sorry, I did not mean to hurt you, I try to say, but I stand mesmerized and finally say instead, "Oh, stop whining, you overgrown little boy; you got what you asked for." He buttons his sleeve, hiding his injury. As he turns to leave, he smirks into my face, "As far as I am concerned, you deserve to stay as stupid as you are."

There is a place where one can go to be alone. The gorge. I like going down its stony steeps and often use it as a shortcut to school. The stream below rushes transparent, threading its sibilant sounds through pebbles, lapping its fluted edges over the jumble of rocks, bedding down its waters, if just for a fleeting second, pushing on, cold as ice, crystal clear, moving like quicksilver, cradling rocks that seem to undulate under its slippery surface. I measure its speed against my bare feet. Shallow, barely covering my ankles, it betrays a secreted force; a spring of latent power. During heavy rains the rushing stream metamorphoses into a raging river, boiling up murky swells of deep umber to rise and fall, filling the gorge with its power.

• • •

Rushing to school, I fall and skin my knee. I don't have time to go down to the stream to wash it. Reaching the top of the gorge, I examine my wound; I blow on it and look self-consciously about, realizing I am near the railroad station where there are always people waiting. And there, on the open platform, in alarming proximity, I see a tall man carrying a shotgun, standing still, his gaze fixed to the tracks, looking as if he were made of wood. I recognize the figure, the profile; it is the Komandant from Knićanin. I hope he does not notice me; I would rather not greet him. But suppose he did see me? I can always pretend I had not noticed him. I get up and, deliberately looking in the other direction, hasten to cross the street. I have taken only a few steps when suddenly I stop. I feel ashamed. I turn and walk toward the figure standing, stiff as before, facing the tracks. I greet the Komandant. He turns his head and, without looking surprised, greets me in recognition.

Cousin Jozsi, Josef Marschang (far right), with friends from the copper mines, Bor, 1948.

Facing each other mutely, consciousness snapping back and forth—"Here we are," he says as if we had come to the end of the earth to discover each other being there. I nod. My knee is throbbing and I hold my skirt away to keep the hem from touching it. I tell him I am on my way to school. "What is the matter?" He points to my gripping hand. "Oh, it's nothing," I say, "only a scraped knee. I fell, there," I point, "coming through the gorge. It will heal—I fall often," I say, and show him the scab on my other knee. He shakes his head; he wants to see the knee I have just hurt. I raise the hem of my skirt slightly and, to keep from seeing it myself, I don't look down. "This knee needs immediate care," he says lowering his head to take a closer look. "Come," he says, "we will go across the street to the first-aid station to have it cleaned and bandaged." I look up in horror. "No," I say, "I'll be late for school. I'll be late, and you will miss your train," I stammer insistent.

He is already crossing the street and I am following. Why did I stop to greet him, I reproach myself. The nurse has me sit on a table, my legs dangling. I can see from the expression on her face that she thinks it is a trivial wound, unworthy of her care. She is used to treating injuries from the foundry and the mines. Brushing his concern aside, she gives in to his

Nora and I, 1941. *Courtesy* Elisabeth Martin

insistence with an air of impatient resignation. I notice that the Komandant does not have any power here; he is just a person, like any other, made to look eccentric by his exaggerated concern over a scraped knee. Iodine! I dig my fingers into my skirt, gripping my thigh to keep myself from wincing. The Komandant watches. A hint of concern has displaced the familiar sullen look, putting his usual expression askew, giving him a certain look of instability. His face strains to accommodate the look of concern; it seems his face and his concern, strangers to each other, have to get accustomed to their coexistence. Somehow I am not surprised by the jarring look, not put off by its startling awkwardness. Perhaps I always expected it to be there.

Bandaged, I slide off the table. "Now I am really late for school," I say, as a way of parting. Would I like him to give me a note or go with me to explain? Surely he jests, I think, and I shake my head, smiling. An awkward silence, a mute exchange, consciousness snapping back and forth between us. "Take care of yourself," he says, calling me by my name, his face broken by a smile, mouthing words that sound raw, untried. "You are the only one among them I could not manage to hate." I nod, forgiving, as one would accepting an apology. We turn and walk in opposite directions. Before I enter the school yard, I look down the long street, back toward the railroad station. There, like a wooden cutout, the still image of a man shouldering a shotgun looms darkly silhouetted against hazed-over skies. "I saw the Komandant from Knićanin today," I announce in our room for all to hear; no one is interested.

• • •

Lisi néni and Jani bácsi, with their son, Ervin, are coming to visit, my mother tells me; they want to take me home with them to Zrenjanin, to live and go to school there. I am stunned. It will be better for me living with a family in a more favorable environment, going to school in the city, she coaxes, and while I am there, I would have the opportunity to see Seppi every Sunday. Suddenly I want to go. And long before their arrival, I am packed and ready. My traveling papers are in process. The picture of me with my beautiful doll Nora, marred by water stains and curled edges, signs of its trashing and its survival, now has to be sacrificed, my head severed, cropped to the appropriate square. It is the one picture we have large enough for identification. Even though I was not quite six when this picture was taken, it is accepted by the authorities; I look the same, they say.

We raise the window in our compartment for the last clutching of hands, the last words of parting, shouts and whispers jolted by the moving train. I feel a tinge of sorrow looking at Grandfather below, and long after the platform fades, I see the marble pallor of my mother's face.

CHAPTER 13

Lisi Néni's Garden

LISI NÉNI'S HOUSE is quiet and serene. A soft breeze wafting through billowing linen hung over the entry brings the smell of flowers, the faint scent of wild carnations, pansies, and dahlias inside. The fragrance of the garden, displaced at times by the inviting smell of Lisi néni's cooking, returns poignantly in the evening with the scent of night-violet, *estike*. Everything in this house distills familiarity; all things in it are precious, blessed with the promise of being everlasting. There is a sour cherry tree in Lisi néni's garden and everything about her house is grounded, and though I am miles from our village, I am reclaimed by the anointed earth, the sacred garden. Home.

Lisi néni starts her day early. She approaches her work like a prayer of praise, as if she wakes to work and goes to sleep with the promise that she may rise to work again. Work is not a job to be done, not a chore. Work and life are integral, seamlessly united in Lisi néni's days. She lives in a paradisal garden in which nothing has the power to seduce, to provoke to expulsion. Everything she does is part of a blessing that continues throughout the day. She seems to sleep this blessing, unaware, leaving no room for anything superfluous to the joy of being.

I am introduced to the neighbors. Soso néni, as Lisi néni calls her, is middle aged, tall, plain looking. Everything she says has the tone of complaint, and her facial expressions aim for a suitable accompaniment. She wails her words with a country accent, stating the obvious. *"Evo, došla sam da ti vidim priju"*—I have come to see your guest, she says, peering at me with shifting hazel eyes, trying to see me from all sides. *"Zar govori srpski?"* Appraising my looks, she asks Lisi néni if I speak Serbian.

The Kis family: Ervin, Lisi néni, and Jani bácsi in Lisi néni's garden, Zrenjanin, 1958.

Bakos néni speaks only Hungarian. She understands Serbo-Croatian, but she makes a point of never speaking it. She is large, robust, pleasant looking, oracular. Her speech is fluent like a brook over stones, warbling, reading the wrongs of the world. There is something benevolent in her pronouncements, as if, dredging among ancient curses, she aims to bring up one lesser than all the others, expressing the inevitable futility, stating with confidence and without exasperation that all and everything turns to shit: *"Minden szarba mén!"*

I have been waiting to see Seppi, looking forward to visiting him on Sundays, and now Lisi néni tells me the relatives from Sajan are coming to take me to stay with them for the summer. Stunned, unable to control my disappointment, I say reproachfully, "It was promised me—this is why I came. And now . . ."

• • •

We are on our way to Sajan, waiting for the bus in Kikinda. It is early afternoon and hot. Katica is chatting with people she knows; she introduces me as her cousin. Katica is very pretty; with her dark hair fashionably styled, she looks grown-up. She must be twenty. The *kamion* comes. It is really a truck; an olive-green remnant from the war. Someone disembarking shouts, calling for Katica. A woman close to us repeats the message not to board the truck; Tamás bácsi is coming for us with the surrey. While others clamber up the kamion, we stand in the shade drinking cool sparkling water, eyeing our lunch.

We wait. Katica removes a bottle from her traveling bag, fills it with water from the pump, and quietly says we may as well start walking to meet her father on the way. We walk the dust-covered road, the sun melting us into light. High skies dwarf appearances of solitary trees far off, enticing us to cooling shade. But we don't leave the road, and our eyes keep scanning the distance ahead. A wagon coming toward us appears like a speck in the eye, coming closer only to disappoint. Now, without hope of being picked up, we tackle the task of getting home more seriously. We take off our shoes.

We have abandoned the road, crossing the fields, dragging the sun behind us. Field fragrances penetrate my thoughts. I am mute with the sound of birds calling, the quieted buzz of insects bedding down, the hiss of grasses brushed in passing. Alone in the center of the world, with the universe fixed on us, we, moving through an unchanging space, seem to be standing still. A peculiar sensation—as if my leg bones, cut above my ankles, were grinding bone to bone—reminds I am taking steps and soon may take no others.

The sun has gone down behind us; a soft light tinges the haze to a purple shade. A thicket of houses, dots of lights flickering in the distance, and suddenly a terrible clatter—noises from afar shatter the dusk. Isolated dogs bark, adding their complaints to the vociferous intrusion: a woman's voice, scolding, shouting insults, accusations; coming closer, curses hurled into the diminishing light frighten with their clarity, and I hasten to catch up with Katica. "It's my mother," she says quietly; "she is upset with my father for having come back without us."

The fields turn into a garden. We walk a well-trodden path, past the scent of hay and fresh milk, toward a large house and the cool fragrance of quieted dust. Flowers. When I ask if this is her house, she shakes her head. "The people living here don't mind?" I whisper. "No," she says. "This used to be Great Grandfather Lang's house, where your grandfather and my grandmother were born." I look to the house in reverence, awaiting its blessing. A small woman dressed in black, looking grandmotherly, comes to greet us. It is obvious that she is well informed about the cause of our delayed arrival.

We approach the house directly facing the ancestral home. The dog barks and the noisy chatter stops as we pull the latch at the gate. I enter hesitant; afraid of dogs, I stay close to Katica. A tall, lean woman silhouetted against a softly lit doorway, her head covered by a kerchief, her skirt not quite meeting the ground, comes toward us with quick agile gait, a reprimand to the dog (putting me at ease), taking my suitcase and parcel, talking all the while, leading us toward the light. Under the flickering lamplight, a spread of blue-and-white checks, the familiar ironstone plates, set, the towering round of bread, its subtle smell discernible, await like a blessing. The stocky man sitting behind the table rises, his shadow playing against the wall, his round face aglow, clear blue eyes beaming. Tamás bácsi! I greet him, smiling. I had seen him last at Elli's house in Nakovo. His smile widens in recognition. Vera néni's eyes flash electric, defusing his smile to a sheepish grin. Though her demeanor is caustic, a glint in her eye betrays that she is somewhat amused by her husband's childlike simplicity. "Imagine," she says to all of us, looking at her daughter, "someone waves at him from the kamion and he, what does he do, the big ox? He promptly turns around and comes home, thinking it must be you who waved at him. With half the village on that bus, the thought that it could have been anyone never occurs to him." Katica says nothing. Tamás only smiles, seeming impervious to his wife's scorn.

I sleep with Vera néni in the open hallway. Under its protective ceiling we sleep as if under the stars, breathing the night air, cheating the rain. The noisy racket before dawn, the clucking and quacking of chickens and ducks assures an early rising. When Vera néni gets up, I slip deeper under the downs to muffle the cackle and gabble and slumber to the muted creak of wagons leaving for distant fields. I rouse again to the quieted morning hum of the awakened day: the sing-song of birds, the temporal lay of domestic fowl, the buzzing of flies, and the sweet smell of bread baking. The dog, sleeping in the sun, looks up through squinting eyes and deems it unnecessary to follow me to the shed where Vera néni and Katica are bustling about, cleaning the utensils and the huge wooden tub they use for making bread. The bread is baking in an outside oven, to keep the house cool. "Can I help?" I ask. "Next time," they say, taking no time from their tasks for idle chatter. I should help myself to breakfast, Vera néni says. The *lángos* (a flame-baked flat bread), wrapped in a checkered cloth, is on the table in the summer kitchen and the milk is cooling in the well.

I love going to the artesian well to fetch water and feel important being seen on the street. "*A Lang Kati unokája,*" people call me, and I am proud having no other name but "the granddaughter." And the life of our every day, like a favorite summer dress forgotten over the long winter, gladdens by its perfect fit.

Every day after lunch, everyone in the house takes a mandatory nap. I ask Vera néni's permission to use this time to draw and paint. A pale Mary hooded under layered veils, Saint Theresa with an armful of roses, the curly-haired Saint Apollonia (copies from an ancestral missal) all appear, enlarged, with watercolored translucence here in the summer kitchen.

When I don't paint, I play in the barn in the back yard. Its huge floor, earthen, dark, is covered by a mound of grain after threshing, its space transformed into a magic landscape. Behind its mountain of gold I play with ears of corn, which Vera néni has allowed me to pick for just that purpose. My dolls, I call them, and I give them names to suit their appearance. Sometimes I feel ashamed that I still like playing with dolls, but it is only a passing thought and I go on playing undisturbed. The soundless motion of swallows nesting in the high eaves captivates me, momentarily, and now and then a neighbor's cat startles me, moving stealthily about, making me think of mice. But sometimes all of a sudden and without reason, triggered only by a dull awareness, the changes of fresh green corn—the opulent silks brought to wilting, the fraying dry husks—become reminders of betrayal, of the inevitable unraveling, and the dried corn silks turn to wilted hair atangle on the death-wagon. A look to the heap of wheat becomes an ache in my belly, an unredeemable regret. I immediately stop playing and leave the cool shaded seclusion to face the light of day. I sit in the searing sun, alone, against a shadowless wall, my arms about my legs, pressing against my chest, feeling the emptiness enlarge inside me, making room for the terror of death.

Tamás bácsi brings home a lamb! Vera néni uses her scolding voice to fend off its charm, telling Tamás bácsi why it cannot stay. He wants me to have something all my own, he says. "That it will be hard for her to part with—that, I suppose, you didn't think about," she shrills. But she gives me the chaff to feed it, and smiles to see it nuzzle, eating from the palm of my hand. A sweet surprise. A lamb.

Most evenings we sit on the narrow bench in front of the house till dark. The neighbors gather, their voices tuned to the deepening dusk. From across the street, the tall house with the open gable, our ancestral home, looms like a benevolent ghost. Children asleep in their grandmothers' arms are carried home and we, too, go inside. Vera néni lights the lamp and I watch her unwind the braid wreathed around her head, letting it fall. "May God bless us," she says and blows out the light. We huddle together under the cover. "Where is Tamás bácsi sleeping tonight?" I whisper. "In the pantry," she says. "We are lucky to be out of hearing range of his snoring." Sometimes in the dead of night I wake, as if to a sudden noise, only to discover absolute stillness, a silence so deep, as if the world had emptied.

• • •

It is Sunday afternoon and I am painting my saints in the summer kitchen. Everyone else is taking a nap. The linen sheet at the door is gently undulating, guiding a telling breeze. A painted saint levitates above a rotating sphere, awaiting completion. Suddenly, I am aware of a peculiar stillness. A parting of the linen sheet startles me. Vera néni motions for me to come outside. There, in the middle of the yard, a slender figure, a man, wearing a light gray suit with pleated pockets, a white shirt, its collar unbuttoned, the tanned skin with the familiar scent—I scream, *Tati! Tati!* I fling my arms about him; we hold to each other, floating in the sun. Our shadows gather, making a circle with those about us, and together we lift an image of our reunion into the sky. I look at my father, inhaling the scent of his skin, taking in the measureless kindness of his soft brown eyes, and I renounce my disbelief. I really do have a father!

Tamás bácsi readies to leave to report my father's presence to the authorities in the municipal building, as required by law. Watching him take to the fields, aiming for a shortcut, Vera néni scolds, "Tamás, *de az anyád Ur Istenit, le ne feküdj az úton!*" (defiled be your mother's God, don't you lie down on the way!). Tamás turns his smile toward us and goes on wordless, as he usually does when she scolds, adding nothing to the noisy world in which she batters about, confident that no matter how much noise she makes, his silence is there to absorb it. Turning to my father, Vera néni says, "You cannot trust this man; on a fine day like today he may lie down, the lazy fellow, forget his intent, and sleep past dark." And she tells my father the story I already know, how Tamás, summoned to the municipal building on some important business, took the shortcut across the fields to save time, but since it was such a fine summer day he stopped to rest in the shade of a wayside tree, lay down and slept, leaving his errand unattended, coming home way past sundown. Since then, whenever he leaves on foot, sharp warnings and loud invocations are necessary to remind him not to give in to his urge to lie down on the way. My father laughs; he likes the story.

He has come on a bicycle that someone from our village lent him—he went there to get the appropriate papers to apply for my mother's transfer to Osijek—and he now tells us about his reception in the village. Veljko, one of his former apprentices, being at the courthouse, getting married, invited him to the celebration. Complaints about Zuska's brother having the tools from our blacksmith shop were aired. "They're no longer my tools, things being as they are, but I would rather you had them," my father tells Veljko. Others inquired if we had given some of our things to our neighbors, and had he now come to get them back? My father's reply: "Since the things we once had are no longer ours, no one has anything of mine; no one owes me anything." Later, walking down our street, čika Milan came running to meet him, crying, "Komšija, komšija," calling him neighbor, embracing him teary-eyed. Some, like Ilija, glowered behind closed doors. Dušan Markov (Ilija's uncle, once a rich farmer), driving his horse home from the artesian well, called across the street voicing complaint, pointing accusations, perhaps as an apology, lamenting: "Majstore, vidi šta Tito radi s nama!"— Master (blacksmith), look what Tito is doing with us! My father only shrugged his shoulders. Just to imagine my father walking through the streets of our village dressed as he is in his suit from America, looking grand, kindles an audacious feeling of pride in me. Defiance.

In the evening, my father tells his story to a gathering of relatives.

He was lucky during the war, being away from the front, shoeing horses. Never far from danger, still he was lucky. He tells of the time when, separated from his company, exhausted, he dozed off outside a small Bosnian village and woke to find all his tools missing; how he walked into the village, apprehensive, telling the people there of his plight. "What do you think the German officer will do to me when he finds out?" And he returned to find the tools back on the wagon. He tells how once, encircled by Partisans, his company met up with troops led by General Phleps, himself an ethnic German from Romania, who promised to lead them to safety "without a shot," and how Schadi Jani, a seventeen-year-old boy from our village, instead of following the general, walked off on his own toward enemy lines. "I am tired, Johann bácsi, I am going to give myself up. You know how we are treated; they're only using us as cannon fodder. I don't believe any of them, not even our own," and he walked on, my father calling after him, "Come back, Jani, you know they don't take prisoners..." An image of the slow stagger of a solitary soldier, a white handkerchief suspended from a shotgun, flickers in the lamplight around our table. "He was just a boy, a child almost."

In October, 1944, retreating with the German troops, his company crossed the Austrian border. Captured by the English, transported to Rimini, they lazed about with nothing to harm them, getting their rations, going swimming, watching movies. For them the war was over, and they were glad for it. "After the war ended many of us wanted to return home, to our families. Amazed at the simple-mindedness of our intent, our captors advised us to reconsider before going into 'living hell,' but they later relented, and in October, 1946, those wanting to go were transported back to Yugoslavia. We realized our mistake immediately. 'Izlazi Švabo!' they shou)ted abuses, roughing us up, taking everything the English had given us—extra clothing, shoes, blankets, food—and they even took the shoes from our feet. Within minutes of our arrival, we were left with nothing but regret. In Zagreb we were fed. Hamhocks and beans! We consoled ourselves with the familiar fare, still hoping we had made the right decision. Transported to Slavonski Brod, to work on railroad repair, we slept on the floor of a vacant warehouse, in freezing cold, bedded on paper sacks we salvaged at work, using them for cover as well. Other men were brought to join us. Captured by the Americans, they were transported here without their consent. Hearing our story, they thought us fools.

In spring we were taken to work in the mountains of Bosnia, clearing forests; we worked and slept outdoors. Though we were worked hard and fed poorly, no one starved to death. In fall the skilled laborers were taken to Jablanica to rebuild bridges. It was there that I met others from our village and learned about my brother's fate. He and old man Herzog deserted outside Beodra, where they were guarding horses. Partisans caught them. Tied by their feet to a wagon, they were dragged through the center of the village—as spectacle, as amusement." The quiet in the room gives way to my father's alarmed look; I can tell he had forgotten I was listening, and he continues in a consoling tone, "My brother should never have been drafted; he was severely asthmatic, couldn't run or walk fast without gasping for air . . ." I cannot bring myself to imagine the horror; memories of my Pat called to rescue collide with galloping horses, the Intendant (he being from Beodra), Smiljka in tall boots, skeletal remains of children—all coalesce with a faceless mass of exposed flesh. I try hard to hold onto my father's voice.

"In Jablanica we were confined to a fort on top of a mountain, escorted daily to our work in town. The food was better; they even gave us white bread to eat. As professionals, we were treated with respect; we had apprentices, young men from Bosnia who came to learn the trade. The hardest part of our imprisonment was being away from our families, fearing them dead, and later, knowing about their plight, not being able to help them." There is a hush in the summer kitchen. "This June our men were offered freedom, working under consignment for two years. There were some who thought it a ploy; they expected to be freed without such binding conditions. Because we were promised our family would be allowed to join us at our place of work, many of us were eager to accept. I now work for a construction firm in Osijek, and we may soon be together, at long last."

On our trip to Zrenjanin, my look attached to my father, I see little of anything else. Catching my eye, he winks at me, and the underlying smile reveals the familiar goodness. I hear him whistle softly through his teeth, as he used to at times when his shyness showed.

The fragrance of the flower garden at Lisi néni's house greets us at the gate; her voice showers blessings. My father stays only a day. When I accompany him to the station, I already imagine myself going with him.

• • •

I can't believe I am on the train to visit Seppi. I sit on the edge of my seat, afraid we will miss our stop. Uzdin. The sound melts into scorching sun. I feel my legs turn rubbery, walking down the well-tended streets. Uzdin, a predominantly Slovak village, is in pristine order. The few people we see are dressed in their Sunday best. Floral kerchiefs tied at the back, colorful skirts distended by funneled layers of stiffly starched pleated petticoats, gaily embroidered velvet slippers tantalize the noonday sun. We greet people in passing, "*Dobar dan.*" They return our greeting in Slovak, bidding us good day. We walk, my anticipation rushing ahead. Lisi néni's quieting voice grates against my impatience. Why is she slowing so, I think, listening past the lilting sounds, unwilling to decipher her words.

A young woman at the orphanage leads us toward the increase of voices, out to a spacious enclosure. A boy standing close by is dispatched to find Seppi: his sister has come to see him. My heart pounding, I scan the face of the child brought before me. I melt into the familiar appearance. Seppi! I kneel down and put my arms around him; feeling him stiff under my embrace, I try not to frighten him with my grasp, holding him gently, giving room to his arms dangling limp about him. My gaze trembles over his face, searching for the pockmark, and the familiar dark eyes light a landscape where I go unrecognized. I scream, voiceless, into that vastness; my pain rebounds through the measureless space, echoing. "I am your sister," I say softly, holding onto my voice; surprised by its presence, I repeat, "I am your sister." Trying not to confuse him, I don't explain. I tell him my name. His face opens to take me in. My heart breaking, I try making conversation. A gather of children has formed a ring around us; looking at the faces before me, I ask Seppi, "Are these your friends?" He nods, hesitant. "We brought a sweet for all of you," I say, watching my words light their eyes. Lisi néni gropes through the cloth bag for the promised treat and carries it to the attending ladies to divide among the gathering throng. I am left alone with Seppi. His face lights up opening the paper bag I give him, and he picks a candy with great care, looking at it for a long time before he puts it to his mouth. Pushed by the desire to give back what is his, I tell him the names of his mother and father, our grandfather, our village. I ask, does he understand German? I tell him he spoke it when he was little, and I say a few words, trying to make him laugh. Does he know we are German? I ask this, I don't quite know why; I did not come intending to instruct. "No," he says, looking perplexed, rolling the candy in his mouth. A few children have come back to gather around us. I ask their names. All are German names. Do any of them speak German? Only Josef; they point to a boy looking at us from a distance. I beckon him to come but he stays away, not altering his sullen expression. "Do I have a sister?" a voice asks shyly; the question echoes through the small crowd.

"I'll soon come again," I tell Seppi. He smiles.

The afternoon sun accompanies us on our way back to the railroad station. The wide street gapes, empty. I walk mutely, my eyes cast to the ground. The brick pavement undulates, uncoiling under my gaze. Brick by brick rises, dislodged, disgorging pain; I tread firmly, my rage pushing them into place. My steps, weighted, measure an unreasoned desolation. The brick pavement bulges like a river, raging. Dark umber, burnt sienna liquefy with gathering urgency to swell under my feet. I walk on water. The power of my rage, building, surges; I cannot stop it. I stop instead. I scream! Lisi néni's face pales into the sun. "I curse them a thousand times! I curse them!" The familiar dust in the empty street, knowing our dialect, absorbs my intent. "The curse of thousands upon them!" I scream, my rage raising me up to the mouth of the oracle. "Let them be cursed!" I shout, merciless, my fury spreading like a nasty wind, sucking the dust into the sky. "Luisa, *mei Madl*"—Lisi néni's voice pleading to quiet down, warning that people will hear me, reaches my height like a speck of dust. "Let them hear; I am not afraid of them; they know what they have done." My voice, rasping, calls on the only evil large enough to wish upon them, the one I only know about but did not suffer by their hands, the dreaded unknown, the bomb. With my arms wrapped about me, my pain soaring like a pointed missile, I shriek, "I want the bombs to come! I want them dead!" And, drawing in a gasping breath, I say, "Even if I, too, should die among them." "Lujzikám, Lujzikám, you don't know what you're saying," Lisi néni's voice pleads reason. "Even if you're not scared of them, you should fear God, saying such things." Turning on her words, whirling, my fury flung into her face, I scream, "You think I am afraid of God? What can God do that they have not done already, the grand butchers?" Lisi néni's face fades, voiceless. My voice wails a repeat: "Grand butchers, they, God and all!" With this last indictment the spirit leaves me. I am a hollow reed, an open receptacle, a look to the ground. The pavement bricks into me. A red embroidered slipper slides into my view. Sounds mutter through me—"Dobar dan." The soft shuffle of feet vibrates within me. The smell of dust makes room for itself. A hollow reed.

I sit on the train, my vacant gaze fixed, taking in all images before me, letting them fall. I am tired. Broken. Like after an illness, the fever breaking, I am ready for the long sleep. My chest feels hollowed out. My heart is silent within me. I do not look at Lisi néni; I know she is somewhere beside me.

• • •

At Lisi néni's house everything is as always. The neighbors come to visit. Soso néni talks about her garden; about the trouble she has with the rabbits and birds. Bakos néni never speaks of having to work in her garden, and even when she hacks into her hand with a hoe and has to wear her arm in a sling for months, she does not complain. She just curses the day she did it and goes on telling her stories. It seems she recently visited her son and daughter-in-law in their apartment in town. Her daughter-in-law is Croat. I have seen her walking past the house, looking handsome, august, sullen. Bakos néni now tells us, playfully, of the lady's quirky little habit. "Being Croat, living among Serbs, she has developed the unfortunate delusion that she is better than they are; poor misguided creature. She doesn't talk with her neighbors; she is too exclusive for that. She tolerates them. But, if there is an opportunity to annoy them, she is quick to do all she can. Let one of their holidays come, and her clever antics would drive a saint to exasperation. At Christmas, New Year, Orthodox-anything, she will find a way to tell the world it is not her holiday. This year, on their Easter, she washed everything she owned, hanging it out, slowly, humming hymns, the devil in her pedigreed Croat gut, and looking so innocent butter wouldn't melt in her mouth. So, on Orthodox Easter Sunday, in front of their terraces, flung into their faces, fluttered sheets and shirts and aberrant undergarments, beckoning like the proverbial red cloth. Bull! Even having been purged of religion, freed of God, people still remember their holidays, I tell you. When I ask her about these maneuvers, she feigns innocence. When I tell her that her tricks might just seem the slightest bit offensive to her Serb neighbors and that one of them may be provoked enough to cause trouble, report her, or worse, she balks. 'They would not dare! After all, we are Communists now, and such holidays are of no consequence,' she quips, tossing her head, all her little blond locks falling into place, looking prim; the devil take her brazen hide, the blue-eyed little darling of a Croat liar that she is. Why does she do it, I ask you? Why?" We laugh; there is nothing left for us to say.

I now visit Seppi on Sundays, alone. The children greet my coming, shouting, "*Sepina sestra, Sepina sestra!*" Seppi's sister, they call me. I have learned to pick him out of the crowd. Our being together consists of quiet talks and smiles. When they move him to Bačka Palanka, I see him less often. We talk about how it will be when he comes to live with us, but mostly I watch, gripping the iron railing around the playground, while he plays with the other children. Sometimes we take a walk together, around the grounds. He tells me they take hikes in the country, walking two by two, singing songs. Memory snaps back to a fated sound—*Druže Tito*, obliterated by pealing bells . . .

The first day of school. Ervin is ready, waiting for me. I am still fussing with my hair. "*Gyere mán, Lujza, ne cifrálkodj,*" he calls to me impatiently, shifting his weight from one foot to the other, telling me to stop fussing. He goes the Hungarian school. All the children in my school are Serb. I am introduced as the new student from Bor, Serbia, the place of copper and gold mines. Attached to this introduction is the tutorial aside about the plunder of our mines by the Germans. Though the children in my class know I am German—I tell them so myself—they never call me *Švabica;* they simply ignore what I tell them and say I am Hungarian, perhaps because they hear me speak it with Ervin on our way home. One of the girls blatantly asserts that I would not be here if I were German; I would be dead.

Amid the stale smell of chalk and scholastic dust, the rancid reek of Partisan fervor is present here. All instruction is spiced with it, exuding the familiar gore. The hatred that kills is alive. The mouth that aimed the spittle's fall at the skeletal heap of dead children is fixed, ready.

I will be leaving this school, I console myself. When I find out that the alphabet is different in Croatia, I am upset. Remembering past humiliations, I tell Lisi néni I cannot accommodate another alphabet. Jani bácsi offers consolation: "If she doesn't want to go she can stay with us, we will keep her, *ugye mama?*"—isn't it so? Lisi néni smiles.

On crisp autumn evenings we sit in the warm entry room, Ervin and I doing our homework, Lisi néni tending her mending, Jani bácsi soaking his feet in hot water, looking tall. I take out the ribbons my mother sent for my thirteenth birthday—a profusion of colors, two of each, for my braided hair—and Ervin and I, with Jani bácsi's indulgence, explore his sovereign

Lisi Néni's Garden   253

potential, creating ribboned transformations: The Gypsy King; The Mongol Lord; The Majestic Monarch—all in quick succession. Jani bácsi collaborates, adding the appropriate demeanor, entertaining an appreciative audience represented by Lisi néni.

My father comes a week before Christmas to take me to Osijek. Our leave-taking is preempted by excitement and anticipation, there is only just room enough for gratitude. We say our last farewell to the noise of the arriving train. I wave behind closed windows; closed into themselves, they wave back, making a small unit against the dusk.

CHAPTER 14

A Place of Light and Reunion

OSIJEK. Out of the darkness lights, like sparkling showers, rain against the window pane. Magic. My father sits across from me, behind and all around him a crystal dazzle, luminous siftings, windows shifting to a satiny glide aslide on steel; mirrors, reflecting, giving back what fell into them, multiplied. Lights. Thousands and thousands of lights. Glass panes glisten crystalline, weighted; my father's voice becomes a silvery chime, ringing. A scatter of bells, a silky slide of opening doors, a gauge of steps descending coalesce with the even cadence of gongs outside.

The air is crisp and my breath, vaporized, floats before me. I look about. "The *trg*, the city square," my father says, pointing to the round of buildings edging a spread of paved triangulation. A kiosk with placards posted, peeling: Opera. Ballet. Jazz. Latin letters! I can read, my gratitude affirms, aiming my sight to the sky. And there, piercing the stars, a pointed steeple captures my gaze, intercepts my gratitude, grounding them both before a massive facade. A church. A cathedral!

Gornja Dravska Obala 25. A dog barks within the distant dark. "He is chained," my father says, knowingly, and we walk deep into the yard toward lit windows. We are home! Grandfather grins, his blue eyes paling, their look inclined to a distant sorrow. My mother cries. She shows me around the kitchen, taking me to every object as if to introduce us. "The stove," she says, "a charm; cooks well and heats the whole place." The sturdy rectangular table, two backless chairs, a long wooden bench, "all homemade," she boasts. The wrought-iron bed behind the table flaunts its conversion into a couch, its long round cushion leaning against the wall; at night this sofa becomes Grandfather's bed.

She opens the door to the pantry, showing off a shelf for dishes, and there, glowing into itself, the familiar floral fullness of our china pattern—our plates from home. I gasp.

She shows me our room. A flip of the switch reveals gleaming white walls, a large cardboard construction, curtained by a gray army blanket, housing our clothes. "It's here for practical purpose only," she says, assessing my disapproval. Two wrought-iron beds, joined, their length extended by a divan, jut out to the middle of the room; a gather of black and green stripes (I recognize the former flounced skirt, a gifted remnant from the days of packages from America) covers the iron bars, and a matching valance anchors the beds to the floor, making a decorative garland against a spread of gray, hiding more storage under the bed. Everything is my mother's handiwork. She is especially proud of the divan, filled with straw, upholstered in army-blanket gray; my bed. Two cardboard boxes, standing on end, painted to look like night stands replete with fake doors, try to conceal their emptiness from both sides of the bed. She eyes my critical look. I like everything, I tell her, looking to the green and black striped valances atop the two unevenly sized sheeted windows. "Tetka Katica gave us back some of our sheets and pillowcases with the embroidered monogram ripped out, the needle holes showing, like accusing stains. She gave us back three soup and three flat plates of our set of twenty-four, saying the rest had broken. We are grateful. The Lakatóses gave no excuses, they simply did not give back anything, not even the money Grandfather gave them." She smiles; she has one more surprise.

We take a lantern outside. The wooden door to a small shed falls open, creaking. My eyes widen—there, in the corner, a gleam of white feathers shrinking from the light, making small hissing sounds—a goose! "For Christmas," my mother says, "for homecoming."

By morning the amorphous yard is transformed into a spacious plane with tall stacks of lumber looming like square mountains, surrounded by stretches of two-tiered sheds, their sheltered stacks of timber, their nooks and spaces, inviting me to explore. A large rectangular pit of undetermined depth, storing jelled whitewash, is only yards away from our door. The familiar sounds of the blacksmith shop, from the distant corner of the yard, extend the feeling of home. A red-haired dog, chained to a run, is far enough away and rendered harmless, protecting the yard only with a ferocious bark. The dog belongs to Ignac, one of the bosses here. "A real Partisan, fought in the woods with Tito himself," my father says, adding importantly, "but he is the most good-natured man you would ever want to meet."

I meet all our neighbors. The Schehrs live in the dwelling next to ours. Frau Schehr survived the concentration camps of Jarek and Gakovo. Her husband was a prisoner of war with my father in Jablanica. Their only daughter was taken to Russia at eighteen.

Separated from us by the considerable length of a two-story shed, in an addition to the main house, lives a Croat family. My father says gospodin Blažević, once an officer in the king's army, now playing the Communist, still insists on being addressed formally as gospodin. His wife, always dressed in a long cobalt blue robe, hardly ever leaves the darkened rooms of their apartment. Their nine-year-old daughter Vikica, unnaturally pale, showing the constraint of days spent in confinement with her mother, soon regains color playing with me outdoors.

Ignac and his family occupy the main house. Tall, blond, quiet, Ignac is Slovene. His wife is Serb. Their two daughters Maca and Vesna, both shy, only seldom play outside. Their son, Zvonko, often comes to our door alone, calling to my mother, *"Teta, imaš žgance?"*—asking for a remembered treat, cornmeal mush.

The sun shines into our enclosed world. The lumber yard is spacious enough to accommodate our diversity. The river flows in front of our door. With the giant steeple of the Gothic cathedral hovering over us, its pleasant gong measuring time, all is well in the lumber yard, our new home.

Except for my natural shyness, I feel comfortable in the new school from the very first day. I am seated next to Zdenka, the best student in class. Self-possessed, helpful, she explains assignments, offers advice, acting as if she had been put in charge of my well-being. We eye each other cautiously and soon become best friends. Our class is a mix of students from all over the country; some are Serb, some Slovene, most are Croat, and it seems not to matter to anyone that I am the only German in class. Our teacher treats us with equal attention and has something good to say about each of us. While most of us call her drugarica, I hear Zdenka and Nevenka call her gospodja Gavrilović, and soon I too call her the same.

On my way home from school I see Melita, a girl from class, coming through the grand cathedral doors. I am astonished. It is allowed, she says, and if I like, I could go to church with her on Sunday. A subtle floral fragrance, a scent of holy water, a fleeting glimpse of dusky calm filtered through heaving doors closing, hint to a translucent light the color of sour cherries. Osijek has the grace and flavor of forgetting.

Zdenka asks me to come home with her after school. She lives at Štrosmayerova 105. Her house is serene, elegantly furnished; they have a piano. Her mother, a beautiful dark-haired woman, speaks in hushed tones. Her father is Professor Heil of the Gymnasium for Boys and teaches art. I am overwhelmed by their hospitality. Her father plays the violin for us; they show me his paintings. I can barely survive the attention, the responsibility, and feel relieved when Zdenka takes me aside to shows me her books and dolls. I tell her about the dolls I had at home. I can tell by the look in her eyes that she feels sad about my no longer having them. And later, at tea, when Zdenka mentions our having had to leave our home and all our things, her concerned look seeking an explanation, I can tell by the exchange of knowing glances sliding by that I am not to mention the concentration camps, and we go on to talk about other things.

• • •

I like doing my homework on the floor, sitting on my knees, doubled over, but because my father does not like me to give in to old habits, I now sit on the sofa bed in the kitchen doing my homework at the table. There is a loud altercation going on in the yard, voices coming closer; accusations are bandied about, now seemingly in front of our door, and before I can go to see, the door opens. Instead of entering, the two men stand preoccupied, one still scolding, expressing disappointment, asserting demands, all in an accusing tone, and the other, Comrade Flec, the boss here, motioning the enraged man to step inside, muttering unintelligible responses. I do not know the man who speaks with such abrasive flurry. He is well dressed, handsome. But what I notice most is the change in his demeanor when he steps inside. His voice, abruptly subdued, takes on a halting, mellow tone and his countenance assumes a surprised serenity, as if the low ceiling of our dwelling has blunted his rage to a mute apology. He stares at me as if I were a specter manifest. My mother emerges from our room carrying a basket with neatly folded linen she mended, washed, and ironed days ago. Introductions, explanations, apologies follow. The man's name is Berger; he is one of five recently released prisoners of war who have just arrived from Jablanica to work here as carpenters. They were promised lodging, and it now turns out they have to sleep in an unfinished building, in a room without heat, on beds without mattresses or linen. When Herr Berger hears that my father came here from Jablanica, he beams smiles of recognition; he knows my father.

The men from Jablanica soon come to visit. My father addresses them by their last names. I preface their names, calling each of them uncle. They talk about their families; most fled to Germany and Austria in 1944. We each tell our own story, authenticating our shared destiny. Kin in a common experience, we listen to each other with mutual respect. Sometimes the men take turns entertaining, telling funny stories and jokes. And when Onkel Berger brings a borrowed guitar (he knows where to borrow things), our small kitchen bulges with song and laughter late into the night.

It is spring. The river, a silvery ribbon reflecting rippling skies, slides past the slender rowboats that skim its slippery surface soundlessly, swift as arrows cast, their piercing oars gleaming in unison, giving new meaning to precision and grace. I have seen the bronze-skinned young men, now rowing, vault into the freezing water since early March, their lithe bodies in scant bikinis glistening in the sun, the splash of their fall sending shivers down my spine.

Onkel Berger takes me fishing across the river. Caught up by the play of chance, I wait, impatient to recognize a nibble; seeing the bobbing cork radiate rings around the line, feeling the tug of the catch has me excited. The fish I catch are small and we toss them back; I am glad to see them swim away. But the boredom of the wait outlasts the anticipation of a catch and I soon tire of the sport. Onkel Berger seems to know this just by watching me, and taking the pole from me, he says, "This is not for you, this fishing, is it?" And I play alone on the loamy shore, running and skipping along the water's edge. I wade in shallows. Sometimes we gather pebbles and he shows me how to skip them across the surface of the water. We walk home, our shadows loping along, fish splashing, making tin sounds about us. Later, a hearty fish soup cooking in our kitchen becomes the fare for another gathering.

When my mother expresses an interest in having me take piano lessons, as Zdenka does, Onkel Berger takes me to the conservatory. I really don't want to go; there are tests to pass, sounds to repeat, Zdenka has told me, none of which I believe I can do. "If you can't do this, I'll eat a broom," he says, to make me laugh. I reward his absolute faith in me with achievement. And a rented baby grand is now moved into our room, nestled snugly under the two uneven windows laced with chicken wire mesh. Finding itself in such elegant company, the furniture in our room absorbs the rich tones with perplexed astonishment.

My mother has been making visits to the orphanage. These trips are always coupled with futile transactions, excitement and hope, disappointment and despair. On one of these visits she is led into an unheated back room filled with narrow iron beds each sleeping two boys, toe to toe, covered by unsheathed downs. The stench of piss, the frigid air, has my mother questioning. "These children are bed-wetters," she is told, "they sleep naked and without bed linen. The wet downs, though aired by day, are still damp; it can't be helped in this weather." At night the children are to pee into tin buckets kept in front of the door outside, and it is not surprising, my mother tells us, that no one is using them. The windows to the back of the room are broken and a large dog from the neighboring yard barks ferociously and sticks its snout through missing panes. Finding Seppi, she wakes him, gently—"Seppili, *mei scheene Puu*," my lovely boy, she calls him—and he, half awake, smiles dreamily, calling out, "*Kodluka, došla si, došla si!*" (Kodl, you came!). With her coat wrapped about him, he slumbers cradled in her arms while she quietly rocks him. "Seppili, *mei scheene Puu.*"

• • •

Summer is coming to an end. Days are languid, quiet. A brisk breeze blowing scented air, a scatter of clouds against pale skies. Across the river vibrant greens are paling; hints of autumn in the light. The girls and I are chasing Vikica's yellow ball, scattering effervescence across the yard. The yellow ball is rolling toward the open pit of whitewash. Shrieks and clamor. Saved! Onkel Berger throws it back to us. Stunned by the magical rescue, glad to see him, I hurl myself at him, throwing my arms about him. He picks me up and whirls me about. I screech and giggle and slip to the ground. The girls are getting in on the act. Vikica yells, "Me too, me too!" We giggle and plead till he swings us each to whirl about him, our legs dangling. "Enough," he says, laughing, shaking his head, "enough." Our noisy clamor continues till Onkel Berger retreats to the safety of our kitchen. We stay out playing till dusk.

My mother has something to tell me. I follow her to the offices of the lumber yard. She does not start cleaning; she sits down, instead, as if to indicate what she has to say may take some time. But what she says is quick, cutting: my father thinks my behavior toward Onkel Berger needs changing. I am no longer a little girl and Onkel Berger may not think me a child. I hear other things said, but absorbed by the shock, I no longer listen— something has been taken from me in a blink of an eye, and what is left me of innocence I lose irrevocably, heeding my mother's cautioning words.

I mourn my loss, my friend, in three days of crying, without interference from my mother. I assimilate my altered perception. I show my resentment later: to my mother in random acts of defiance, to my father in acts of cold obedience, to Onkel Berger in ways more subtle—imposing distance tinged with coyness; mistrust.

It is my birthday. I am fourteen. I have invited Smilja, Melita, and Zdenka. Onkel Berger has borrowed a camera from somewhere and we take a picture. After the celebration, the four of us go to the movies. "Your uncle is terribly doting," Smilja remarks in snickering whispers. "Don't you find it annoying?" She has older brothers and uncles who dote on her, but they live in Opatija, which used to be her home, and only visit occasionally. "They're all alike. They coddle and indulge, now treating you as if you were a child, now teasing you about growing up, even holding it against you. It is embarrassing, disgusting. Don't you just hate it!" Zdenka objects. She would like to have an uncle who adores her. Melita is quiet. One of her uncles is a priest, she once told me. Melita is the most grown-up among us; she is growing breasts and is not shy nor indifferent to being noticed by boys.

Celebrating my fourteenth birthday. My mother, Grandfather, my father, Onkel Berger, and my school friends Zdenka (front left), Melita, and Smilja (right) in the lumber yard at Osijek, 1949.

We are practically grown-ups; we attend the Gymnasium for Girls in the old part of town, downstream. The various professors come to give readings, and since we have no books, at the end of each lecture one of us is called on to recite what we have just heard, giving all a chance to hear it again. I am often called on for such recitations; I can repeat lectures, hardly forgetting a word.

Zdenka and I walk home, loitering, looking in shop windows, speaking our own made-up language, giving it a nasal twang, pretending we speak English to impress passers-by. (In school we have only Russian as a foreign language.) Fluent in our deception, in demeanor and gesture, we flaunt our invention, hoping to look subversive, courting intrigue.

As first student, I am chosen to be Pioneer Leader of our class. One of my responsibilities, opening our weekly meetings, is the only thing I don't like about school. In light of my personal history, my ethnicity, and given the common association of German with Fascist, it is humiliating for me to stand in front of the class with my arm up, elbow bent, fist to my head, saying, *"Smrt fašizmu—Sloboda narodu!"* This is our official greeting: Death to Fascism, freedom to the nation! It brings back memories of greetings past, feelings of reluctance to raise my hand, and still distills the same shame—only now, the greeting is at the same time an indictment. With my fist to my head it seems a promise fulfilled, symbolizing my intended death. I carry the shame of that intention with me always. I am a witness to the deed done. The survivor. It is difficult not to be humbled by this symbolic gesture, knowing that a long line of children killed in the name of this ideology is represented with me. I stand before my class in humility and shame, concealing from them the pain that is mine alone. In the seconds that it takes to perform this greeting, I fake a kind of arrogance to keep that which is my own, bearing witness to the larger experience in the privacy of my heart.

Our history lectures are interspersed with contemporary events. National heroes visit our class to tell us about their own experiences during the war. A woman on crutches, a member of the Communist Party, visits our class. She was a Partisan and a spy during the war. Caught by the Germans, interrogated, tortured, she kept her secrets in spite of everything they did to her. She describes her torture in detail. Sexual assaults with billy clubs graphically depicted have us listening. She shows the tools with which they tortured her. We cast down our eyes to avoid looking in the direction of our professor, the only man in the room. And I, the only German here, listen mutely to the anger in her voice, feeling the discomfort of accusations, shamed in front of my classmates. At first I listen in disbelief, wanting to deny the allegations. No! My father could not have done these things, I know. No German soldier I know would have done them, I think, defiant. It must be some mistake, propaganda, hate. I sense the familiar flesh-grinding grist. I smell its rancid malevolence. I listen with eyes downcast, dodging the rancor unleashed. And to dispel the hint of blood-feasts present, I focus my gaze on the polished calm of wood, the smooth curves of aging initials cut across the grain of my desk. I recognize the blunt texture of pain, the bleeding fingers scratching to find the fiber of truth. My gaze, informed, lets go of the carved markings (the claim to identity) and gropes the space across the room to find the face, the eyes, belonging to the voice of pain. Yes. Yes, I know, it is true! I was there. I have seen what they can do! Germans, Partisans, Fascists, Communists, Croats, Serbs, Russians. Names. Initials. All. I have seen the stark agony reflected on the faces of the living waiting to die, waiting for the death-wagon to collect them as if they were nothing but a debt to pay. I, watching, saw the mounds they made. I know where they are buried. Denying the pain I now hear, grief capable of making the walls about us listen, would be denying our pain, our dead, our existence. This pain is large. Grown past the smallness of name calling, it looks down on the clamor of clenched fists and the futility of pointing fingers; accusing by name is to it nothing—a clinging to denial; an evasion. Our pain rises to where none of our pallid reasoning, our scorn, our good intentions can touch it and upholds an image of us that none can belie. I keep looking into her eyes to make room for our pain. I no longer feel separated from her. There is nothing left to defend between us.

• • •

Seppi is released to us. We cannot believe our good fortune. We stumble over each other's words, not really caring what we say. Grandfather cautions, "He is not here yet." I ignore his comment, whirling about, hugging and kissing him in spite of his protests. "I have always loved you best, Grandfather," I say, reminding him, playfully, that he used to say this to each of us, his grandchildren, and he shakes his head as if to scold, but I recognize the smile hidden under his mustache and say again, meaning what I say, "I have always loved you best."

Seppi's arrival changes our life. Now there is nothing to wait for, nothing to harm us. An easy tranquility settles among us. We speak only Serbo-Croatian now. For us this seems a small adjustment. "We don't need a language separating us," my mother says, and we waste no time teaching him German.

It is Sunday and my mother has us dress in our Sunday best. I wear my red dress with ribbon appliqué and Seppi wears the new clothes my mother has made for him: a dark blue suit, a white shirt with pale gray pinstripes, a gray silk tie with diagonal striping. He looks splendid, adorable! We tell him how handsome he is; he likes the attention. "The two of you are going to church," my mother tells us. "It is a mission of gratitude. Our prayers have been answered, and you are our emissaries to a public thanksgiving."

Walking together, holding hands, we ascend the steps to the *trg*. As we near the cathedral Seppi loosens his grip and, without explanation, starts running away from me. I am stunned still; it takes some time until I start running after him, calling him back, pleading for him to stop. He keeps running; I can hardly keep up, sprinting down the incline of Ribarska. Is he running to the river? Running away? I don't let him out of my sight. As he turns the corner, I am relieved; he is going back home, I think. But why? He hides around stacked lumber in the shed near our stable, waiting. "What is the matter with you? Why did you run away?" He does not answer, squeezing himself into a corner, looking at me with frightened eyes. "Don't you want to go to church?" I prod. He says nothing. "Why don't you want to go with me?" I repeat. And after a long silence he says, determined, cold, as if pronouncing an indictment: *"Nema Boga!"* My eyes widen in recognition, and I let the words slide over my mouth, repeating the pronouncement: There is no God. He starts to cry only when my mother comes to take him inside. The

With Seppi in Osijek, 1950.

delicious smell of Sunday cooking consoles, and my mother's voice, words velveted, reassuring, laud the goodness of God—how good it is that we found each other, how good to be together again, all this is like the goodness of God. And all is said not as an argument to convince but is, instead, a tender declaration of her love, punctuated only by his muted, involuntary sobbing.

We celebrate Christmas Eve with all the uncles present. The door to the front room opens on a lighted Christmas tree hung with fringed candy, nuts, and apples. A gift from the Christ child, my mother tells Seppi. The tree is actually a steal from the nearby park, cut down by Onkel Berger. There are presents for the two of us; a sled for Seppi and a writing desk for me, both made by Onkel Berger. Grandfather and I put on our coats and take a bundled Seppi through the snow-dusted yard, pulling and pushing, trying to bring the new sled to a glide. Inside, we resume the celebration, eating *Maaknudl* (sugared poppy-seed noodles), singing *"Tiha Noć"* and *"Stille Nacht"* alternately. Seppi recites the poem he learned in the orphanage— *"Veje, veje sneg. Peć puckara i bubnjara pa se slatko spi, a kad svane, sunce grane, uzmi sanke tociljalke, pa na breg! Veje, veje sneg"*—which, coincidentally, is about comfort and joy: "Sounds of a wood-fire burning on a snowy evening lull to sweet sleep, and at dawn, when the sun has risen, take sleds and skates, and up the hill we'll go! Blowing, blowing snow."

Early in March my parents are summoned by the authorities to appear at the municipal building. They, like all other ethnic Germans, are offered citizenship; they have only to sign for it. While my father is ready to sign without argument, my mother refuses. "I have always been a citizen of this country, till you took it away from me. I will not sign to get back what was mine to begin with. I don't want your citizenship." My father pales. The man in charge stares at her. "What do you mean, we took away—nothing was taken from you. Are you accusing us?" he blares at her red-faced. "You must excuse my choice of words, perhaps I did not express myself well in Serbo-Croatian. My intent was not to insult. Since I have been deprived of this citizenship without having had anything to say about it, given a choice now, I want nothing further to do with it. I choose not to sign for it; I was born in America and have other options." The man stares at her, speechless. For days after, my father walks about pale and preoccupied; he is worried, afraid.

When Onkel Berger comes to tell us, months later, that he and the other men have just received their papers to leave, I am stunned. Within a week they will be gone. My parents are glad; they say our turn will come. It is a gray afternoon, a Sunday. We watch the train pull out of the station. People wave from windows and platforms. We ride the streetcar home, taking the emptiness with us.

• • •

I am going to visit our village, to stay a week with tetka Mara. I am so excited I can't sleep. I fantasize about how it will be walking down the streets, seeing the houses and the people I know; showing myself to the village. Alone on the train, going home, I feel grown-up.

It is early afternoon when the train arrives. I step into the sweltering heat to the smell of coal smoke on hot powdery dust. I walk through the shaded station, the buzz of flies following me out. I am walking down the street, ribbons in my hair, my heart pounding, my white city sandals covered with finest powdered dust. I am home, I think, passing houses that know me. I am home.

The water offered from familiar cans is as cool and sweet as I remembered, and later, we eat *kiselo mleko* (yogurt of sheep's milk), which tetka Mara draws up from the well. I can't stop grinning. In the evening I go to the artesian well to fetch water, hoping someone will recognize me. I think of making drawings of the village, I tell tetka Mara. She disapproves. My going about the village drawing might cause trouble. The people from Bosnia are very defensive, possessive about their houses; they may get suspicious, angry . . .

I cannot bear to look at our house; I pretend I do not care, and pass it trying for distance. I flaunt my fluent city accent talking with neighbors. Čika Trandafir, the dead Jelena's father, shakes his head, giving me appraising looks. "Lujza forgot how to speak our language," he says, his voice tinged with reproach. I am stunned. I now speak Serbo-Croatian better than ever, I tell him. "That's just it; you have picked up a foreign accent," he quips, accusing. "You used to speak just like us," he says, his words weighted with disapproval.

I don't really know why I brought my music—to prepare for my recital or perhaps to show off. I ask tetka Mara whether there is a piano somewhere in a public place. She does not know of any, but she thinks the Lázárs may have one. I remember the house on the corner opposite the Catholic church and the handsome woman who lives there. Her seventeen-year-old daughter was, for a short time, in camp with my mother in Čoka. Irén néni, remarried to a Hungarian, was allowed to stay at home. The Lázárs now have three small boys, tetka Mara tells me.

The low pitched reed roof of Esti néni's father's house still has a stork's nest on its chimney. The Lázárs' house facing it is wrapped around the corner, its windows shuttered against the afternoon sun. By the time I greet the people inside, tell them who I am and why I have come, I am beside myself; I am someone else. Could I come to practice the piano once or twice during my stay? It will help—I have an exam, I hear myself saying. The children are sleeping; I should come back tomorrow, in the late afternoon, and of course, I can practice as often as I like. They show me the piano. The room is dark and richly decorated, the wood floor covered with Persian rugs. My glance picks up a motif of roses. A sweet smell cools, intoxicating. I leave, ashamed. I walk the wide street, the sun beating down on me. The tranquility of the room I just saw torments me. I feel like crying. But why? Considering my rudeness, the people were nice to me. Why do I feel disappointment—defeat—or perhaps it is only shame? I wanted to flaunt my survival, my well-being. But why to them? They could have been among us, among the discarded, among those who did not survive. Why do I have such aggressive feelings, and why such arrogance now? And how could the appearance of that room subvert my arrogance, turn it to defeat? I ponder, looking at my feet wading in the warm powdered dust. That room did not just survive; it stayed unchanged. The life taken from us, our life, is in that room. I recognize my childhood in it, my youth, and even my old age. Something within me wants to rage against that room. Rage! Measured against this rage, I feel small walking the wide dust-covered streets past both churches to tetka Mara's house. I think of not going back tomorrow.

Before I leave the village, I visit the family graves as my mother has asked me to do; I pick the crosses out of the weeds, pulling the grasses reverently, claiming that which still belongs to us.

• • •

Early in August Grandfather and Seppi have permission to leave. Though we have talked often about their leaving, Seppi does not want to go. Letters with pictures of his father and mother and of his little brother, Emil, and all our talks about the trip are to no avail. He likes it here; the lumber yard, the city, the school—all are too fine to leave. We entertain him with thoughts of things available in Germany. The possibility of having a bicycle works magic, and my mother writes to his parents of the wished for bike, thinking they can surprise him on his arrival. Seppi and Grandfather leave Osijek accompanied by my father, who goes with them to Belgrade to make sure that they get on the right train. Our house is empty without them and no longer feels like home.

We hope to leave as soon as my father's obligation here is finished; we have made applications months ago. Those who have accepted the imposed citizenship are not eligible. (It will take both my Kodls' and Tanti Lisa's family years and two thousand dinars per person; some people leave as late as 1956.) While we go about our work as if we intend to stay forever, we make preparations to leave as well. I tell no one, not even Zdenka.

I turn fifteen without anyone's notice; the excitement of receiving our papers has us scurrying about. By the seventh of October we have to be out of the country.

Johann on horseback, 1951, on the collective farm near Kikinda where his parents worked until 1954.

Kodl Lisa with Werner and Walter, her sister Anna, and her father Anton Gross, fall, 1948, on the collective farm near Kikinda where they worked under consignment until 1954.

Our train leaves after midnight. Zdenka and her father have come to our house to see us off. Professor Heil helps carry our suitcases. While he and my parents are talking in hushed tones, Zdenka and I are quiet, watching, waiting for the tram. The square looks abandoned. Steel rails glisten silvery into the distance. The cathedral gong marks time. My parents talk about the concentration camps, about our suffering; things we have talked about only among ourselves are aired now, for the first time, here below the gong of the cathedral, perhaps to explain our willing departure, as a last admission of our love for our home. Zdenka's father is gracious; he acknowledges having been aware of our plight. "It is finished now," I hear my father say, "but I still can't believe they will allow us to leave the country. I won't believe it till we are safely across the border." Hushed, I try to comprehend the reality of our leaving our home forever. I look into Zdenka's face; her large, understanding eyes fill with compassion.

The glass panes of the *tramvaj* windows catch the passing lights; the glide of steel beneath us, the tin-sound of bells, eyes trying to find a place to rest frame the reflections mirrored by the dark outside. Osijek.

CHAPTER 15

Germany, a Window View

HOVERED OVER BY A standing crowd, we sit, our gaze fixed, taken in by the view of endless fields, villages with whitewashed houses, wide dusty streets, a flock of geese on a parched meadow, all stilled, flattened under glass for easy distancing. The steady clacking of rails mesmerizes and the friendly visions gathered for our leave-taking wave by, while we, preoccupied, look on transfixed, bypassing the sorrow of our parting. Names of villages, cities cling to us in passing and the sights grow less familiar, more distanced, as time passes. The setting sun surprises us with mountains, and we reach the border at Jesenice late at night.

The train has stopped for more than an hour. Men in uniform, shouldering guns, come to examine our papers. They take our traveling pass with them. My father is eyeing his watch, convinced they will not return the papers; they will not let us leave. It is an hour after midnight already; it is the seventh of October now and our visa is valid only until the seventh—or is it including the seventh?—he fusses quietly. My mother, wearing her pensive look, says nothing. But our papers are returned and we are told to move to another car. The new compartment has plush seats and only a few passengers. My father motions through the open window to a vendor peddling šljivovica and shyly stores the slender bottles in one of our bags, his face still showing signs of worry.

The push and pull of wagons disengaging, and soon the even glide, the hum of rails speeds us into the night. In time the darkness is replaced by lights, windows garnished with flowers—Villach. The sound of words surprises us, announcing an enlargement of the world to include us; announcements spoken in our mother tongue! Is it possible? We have become public.

Traveling pass with photograph, Osijek, 1950.

We look at each other, not needing to say a word, beside ourselves, re-deemed. When the conductor comes lilting a friendly greeting in an Austrian accent, asking for our tickets, our papers, we feel personally addressed. We are propelled past the fear of uniforms, the silent acquiescing, the acute vigilance, past our subservient, anxious, inhibited selves. "Are we really in

Austria?" my father asks, just to make sure, and after a playful reassurance, he falls backward across the empty seats, his up-stretched legs aiming for the ceiling, shouting joyously: "We are free! We are free—free!" He is laughing, treading toward the ceiling, transcending his timidity, and so unlike my undemonstrative father. I watch in astonishment. Compared to this display, my mother's sanguine glances look almost shy. He now jumps to his feet, retrieves the small bottles of šljivovica, and offers them to the conductor, to the astonished others in our car; rounds for all.

Villach, Rosenbach, Salzburg, and still my father is talking, beaming glee. The smell of fine coffee, an array of bottled drinks, soda water, chocolates neatly packaged in wrappers with images of alpine flowers—Edelweiss and blue Gentian—pass on carts and through open windows. We must change our money to buy; perhaps at the next station. It does not matter; just seeing these things, experiencing the pleasant atmosphere, makes us believe we have returned to a civilized world. In time our exhilaration subsides and we settle into an easy bliss. Exhausted. Unwilling to sleep, we look out on soaring snow-covered mountains catching the dawn. We watch the early morning light crisp villages nestled in mountain deeps, dazzle autumnal foliage, spark rivers to an emerald green, as shifting shadows slide out of the morning mist. Voices sing by—soft laughter, sounds that tell our mother tongue, mulled by the silken hum of gliding steel, propelled, speed us into existence, giving proof that we are allowed to be. We listen, smiling.

The new authorities, German, inspect our luggage, check our papers, tickets. The mood changes. The man asking for our papers is gruff. We notice his uniform. We assume our apologetic stance to accommodate the tone of his voice. "Date of return?" he says, making it sound like a command. "As soon as you arrive in Stuttgart you must consult the authorities. This pass is invalid as a permanent stay." The tone unsettles, throwing us into confusion. Suddenly my father regains his voice to protest: "As far as we are concerned, we are never going back. Never . . . not even dead!" The face that stares at us stays unmoved. My mother looks inaccessible, staring her defiant look into the distance. Our first experience in Germany, our new home.

• • •

Our reunion with Seppi is sweetened with chocolates bought on the train. I am astonished at how quickly he learned to speak German. When I speak to him in Serbo-Croatian, he does not answer. "He no longer speaks it," his mother says. Speaking German makes him appear distant, estranged. He has grown some and seems more serious. Emil's affectionate disposition captivates us and we dote on him immediately. We celebrate our reunion with a feast and stay around the table till dark. My mother contributes a treat, offering grapes she has bought in town. "You should see the stores here; unbelievable," she says, arranging the grapes in a bowl. The children reach for them eagerly. Seppi's grasp is interrupted by a curt reprimand: "Not you, you aren't eating any." Tanti Rosi's pithy remark is followed with an aside for all to hear: "He will piss in his bed if he has anything this late at night." The abrasive tone rebuffs; an old sorrow shocks itself into existence. I cannot bear to look at Seppi's face; I look at my mother's instead. Her expression, impenetrable, slides past what is being said; the unworthiness of the remark being clear to her, she goes on talking about the store, the things she saw there—and all the time her look is like a steady spot in an eddy, a place to hold onto, a hand across the chasm, a bridge. I want to weep.

Later, when Seppi and Emil are put to bed, talk continues in hushed tones. My mother tells about Seppi, how they took him away. "We had a few problems at first," Tanti Rosi tells us. "He expected a bicycle—imagine, a bicycle—but things are fine now. He is doing well in school," she says sweetly. Seppi Onkl interjects, suppressing a chuckle, "After the first week here, he told Grandfather, 'We have seen everything now; it's time we went home.'" "All kinds of adjustments," Tanti Rosi continues, endearing, trying to keep the tone of the conversation light. "Life changed after they arrived. To my surprise the cake that I baked on weekends, which usually lasted all week, would only last two days." Grandfather yawns and leaves to go to bed. We stay up talking.

Tanti Rosi tells about the convoy to Russia and the camps there. How they were herded by the thousands into cattle cars; forty-eight and more crammed in a car, from the last days of December to the beginning of February, eating only food they had brought from home. "The cold made us forget we were hungry and our hunger was not easy to forget. We consoled ourselves with the thought that such a long journey indicated they didn't intend to shoot us." She pauses, keeping thoughts of her parents—shot into a common grave with the people of Sanad—safely at bay. "When the transport arrived at Krivoy Rog, we thought we had come to the end of the world. Food once a day; cabbage soup and a piece of dense dark bread, our only provisions, we walked two hours and worked all day breaking and cutting stones. Those too weak to walk the long distances, too weak to work, if they did not die, were transferred; they simply disappeared, like the dead, while we were at work. It never got better—except for the last winter, when they had glass installed in the windows of our building. Cut off from everything, it was as if the world had disappeared and nothing but that place existed. You did not want to talk about home, it only made you feel worse. Being a fast worker, well liked by supervisors, I was lucky . . ." It is always the end of our story. Surviving, it seems, is a game the lucky won, deserving of their luck because they were clever or good at something. The tone is familiar. We have to rationalize our survival, somehow, making a place for ourselves among the living. It was August, 1948, when Tanti Rosi arrived in Germany. The part about her coming here, finding her husband living with another woman, having a child, is told speaking haltingly, looking at my mother.

The lights are out now. A spray of street light falls in on things abandoned; the table and its chairs hover mutely. I think of Emil, the little boy I have just met, my cousin, not remembering his own mother, his sister. But it is Seppi I feel sad about most.

The morning sun reflects in tin sheets on patched roofs of slouching barracks asprawl on the treeless meadow. Sparse autumnal flowers float their gilded colors across tiny garden plots, flaunting their riches against the drab surroundings. To the many people (perhaps a thousand) living in the Schlotwiese, who fled their home in the fall of 1944, their well-tended patch of garden is the only thing that has the power to bring them closer to home. They work in factories now, but here, among their own, an aspect of the village continues. The way of life they brought with them—their customs, their cooking, their dialect—is trying to survive. Seppi Onkl feels at home in the little house he built himself, he says, except for autumn days, when the light is just right, the smell of summer's passing haunts him with a terrible longing for home, our only home, our village.

In less than a week, we leave my uncle's house for a displaced persons' camp only a station away by train; our parting does not require long goodbyes.

The camp in Kornwestheim is a civilized place on the outskirts of town, a twenty-minute walk from the railroad station. Our fourth-floor room is occupied by four families, one family to each corner. Each family has four wrought-iron beds, two stacked on each other in bunk-bed fashion. We fence off our spaces with gray army blankets fastened to the periphery of our beds, to clotheslines strung, and inadvertently create a hallway through the middle of the room of soft blanketed walls, responsive to a flick of a finger. These fragile physical boundaries metamorphose, intending a private space; one has to maintain the proper distance to keep up the illusion. The realization that a flick of a wrist could raise doubts about our blanketed privacy would lower the curtain and bring down the house.

The corners by the windows are the most coveted, and as people move out, such places pass on to families with seniority. Through the good fortune of others, it takes us only two months to land a place by the window. Our space is enlarged by the window's outside ledge, our pantry and refrigerator, and by a stretch of clothesline strung, our opportunity for sun-dried

Leaving the *Durchgangslager*, the refuge transit camp, to come to America (left to right): my father, Emil and Tanti Rosi, Seppi Onkl, Grandfather with my arm in his, my mother, Seppi, and Frau Rehm, Kornwestheim, 1951.

clothes close at hand. The virtual space is extended by a view to fields and sky, which makes us one of the privileged few among the many inhabitants of the *Durchgangslager*, the refugee transit camp.

Outside, the paved world is full of new visions. Fruit stalls tantalize: the exotic yellow of bananas peering out from purple tissues to pierce the eye; oranges in crates, beaming pampered from rustling hulls of white gossamer, their fragrance weaving a web of finest mist, jolting Christmas images out of the past; foil-wrapped chocolates, boughs of hazelnuts popping off their encasements. Rings of figs. Marzipan. Everything is wrapped, cellophaned, all enveloped in a delicate communal fragrance tinged with pristine clean, with not a hint of the ground, the earth I know present. The dust here, if there is any, is only dust and not the fine of a conversant earth. Even the scents at the railroad station seem cleansed, routinely civilized. Though the farmhouses here have the dunghill in front of their doors, with the smells of stable and hay keeping their distance, it only reeks, bypassing its origin. I realize, with quiet acceptance, that I am far from home.

Pastry shops with sweets, bakeries with varieties of dark and light breads, salted pretzels in rows all waft their marvelous fragrances to the sound of bells. In shops where my mother buys knitting needles and woolen yarns, as elsewhere, the world is attractively packaged, neatly ribboned, its scents confined, conveying the added aftertaste of indigenous air. Touching things is not encouraged, though everything beams invitations. And everywhere one enters, little bell sounds announce the comings and goings so as not to shock the fragile sensibilities of merchandise readied for the asking. One can spend hours viewing things through plate glass windows, but once inside, one must know what one wants, ask for it, buy it, and leave. With so many things to see, one is frustrated leaving them unexplored, and the little bell sounds tinge with regret on the way out.

While nothing reminds us of home, nothing here is threatening. Having escaped the place of danger, we assume that in this civilized world, now, there is no place for the kind of horror we have witnessed. We feel safe. Till one day, in the railroad station, my eyes fix on a flyer under glass: murder, rape, showing the mutilated victim in tall grasses, the name and face of a man at large, all in a sickly sepia tone, shocking anxieties out of the past, mocking the feeling of safety. Why did I look? I accuse myself as if I were responsible for the betrayal. The reality of murder seems incongruous with the feeling of safety, with our trust in the new environment. But here it is, the bleating, bleeding, fleshy reality. And the deed seems uglier for being secretive, personal. I am used to brutality on a large scale, in the open, for everyone present to see, and the perpetrators are many and have the power and approval of many more. The grotesque images, the acts of mass murder are public, executed on selected victims by the select in power. Blood-feasts are events. Celebrations. Invitations are offered to executions. The horror is publicly shared, the terror inescapable. Mass murder—brutality exposed, clear at its source, untainted even by hate—seeks no redemption, while homicide, brutality less candid, hides behind deceit, trying to redeem itself. The pitiful placard shows a private indulgence, dark and secret, to be despised all the more for betraying a peculiar fear, charging the environment with hidden danger. The blemish of civilized life discovered, its dark cord weaves itself into my perception, distilling revulsion. And the revulsion persists on seeing the bombed-out buildings in Stuttgart, whole blocks of rubble, here and there a remnant, an arch, a pillar of a palace, standing, bearing witness to the destruction of a beautiful thing; I gag looking on the gorge of power. I cast my eyes to the ground to keep from throwing up. What have they done, what have they done, I moan. I want it put back stone by stone; I want it whole again, I insist, to evade the pain.

• • •

In school I am apprehensive, lost, and the only refugee in class. The rigor and speed with which everything is attacked here makes me aware of my slowness. Drills in math class have the girls waxing enthusiastic, tossing their arms up in flailing flutters, impatient to be chosen for the answer. Barely is "seventy-eight times twenty-seven" uttered and the hands go into action. I am impressed, distressed, mortified. I notice the teacher often calls on those whose hands do not show, and while the person called on strains to answer, the others interfere with groans and gesticulations. It is humiliating to watch, but it seems to be a game that no one minds. The subject that surprises me most is history. The history lessons in Yugoslavia were focused on events, some augmented by personal accounts. Here we discuss the heroic tales of Siegfried, adventures involving dragons, magic swords, itinerant swans. I listen in disbelief; it must be another game to mystify. And I, once the best of students, am now among the ones lagging behind. But, in art, I far surpass everyone in class.

A realistic Rübezahl (a legendary giant) on large manila paper fills the space to loom over mountains, his long beard trailing charcoal. I am an instant success, rewarded with the respect allotted to those who excel. I have status. The art teacher, on the other hand, a pallid young woman, gets no respect at all and is often made fun of behind her back. I am surprised by the attitude the students have, by the lack of regard for their teachers. In Osijek we respected our professors in a spirit of fellowship. Here the students are staunch observers, finding fault, judging all as if everyone and everything depended on their approval. And all this is like a mental fencing, a show of wit. Only Ute Grözinger, a serious redheaded girl with freckles, the best student in class, delivered from all judgment, enjoys a place of neutrality; status is important. The peer-approved mode of conduct for the rest of the students is to excel without effort. To appear zealous, to strive, is low on the scale of esteem. To compete without struggle, to have strong opinions and stand by them regardless of the consequence or the teacher's approval, earns a better endorsement. Above all, one must be strong; showing weakness invites disdain; ninnies are scorned. Those who are sensitive had better be clever at hiding their sensibilities. The girls here are sharp; nothing escapes their scrutiny. Hanna Schiller is the most assertive girl in our class. She seems mature at thirteen, fiercely independent, knowledgeable, grounded. Since Hanna is fastidious about her friends (a group of five girls), I am surprised to find myself among them. Hanna thinks I am funny. The way I blunder into the obvious as if it were an undiscovered room makes what I say funny, she says. Clustered around Hanna, concerted, anonymous, we communicate as a group with signing looks in class, strolling about

Germany, A Window View   277

during recess, and walking to the train. We loiter around shop windows, talking of Christmas wishes. I don't tell the girls that all I want is this doll that looks like Nora; they don't even look at dolls.

We have drawn names and each of us is to bring a Christmas present to one girl in class. I go to the store with my mother to buy chocolates, marzipan, tangerines, figs and nuts, wrapped candies, everything I would like to have and would not buy for myself. The brown paper bag is tied with a ribbon; the little card inside says "For Gudrun," the girl whose name I pulled out of a paper sack. We exchange presents, giving our gift when our name is called. I receive mine from Ute Grözinger. Wrapped neatly in a box, a red apple with cloves outlining eyes and other features, cotton fluff for hair and beard, a red paper cap with cotton trim, the decapitated Saint Nicholas looks out at me boastful and polished. I hear the admiring *aahs*, but I am too busy trying to hide my disappointment. I smile only to keep my chin from quivering. I know Ute is smart enough to tell that I am not impressed with her artistic achievement. She looks confused by my expression, disappointed. It was her best intention to give me something artful, made by herself; it was a compliment to me, a sign of admiration for my talent. I understand all this. But after choosing the best of everything I liked to put in my gift, eating none of it myself, I feel cheated. Sorry for myself, I feel ashamed. No one, not even I, could have predicted this. I try to hide my feelings behind forced gratitude and, preoccupied, almost miss my name when it is called to give my present to Gudrun. No one was ready for this present; too generous, the girls hiss. Fräulein Thüringer, who is usually so tactful and understanding, makes an example of my gift with a comment that those who have least to give often give most, which only exacerbates my feeling of embarrassment, shame. I feel misunderstood, lacking in etiquette, socially inadequate. Selfish.

On Christmas Eve a life-sized Saint Nicholas comes to the Durchgangslager. I open my present. Nora—in a floral dress.

· · ·

Whether anyone likes it or not I am grown-up, I think, looking down my undershirt to pear-shaped protrusions that appear boil-like, knotted, disfiguring. At first I view them with disgust; feeling the discomfort, annoyed by the change, I want to disown the awkward mounds. But something about the mystery emboldens; I claim the power as if I owned it and pride myself in growing something all on my own. So approved, the twin protrusions round out slowly to become part of me. And one day, in early spring, on my way home from the station, without thinking about anything, without first looking, I know, and later, when I see my bloody bloomers, there is no doubt about it, I have grown up. My mother makes some flat flannel pads, pink sausages I call them, and I wash them in private and we hang them out to dry in the window, just like my mother's, taking care to remove them when we expect company.

It is early May and warm. The fields beyond our sun-filled window show delicate greening. I have seen the flowers growing in the park. This Saturday, like any other, is astir with its usual pace. When Frau Rehm, from the window space across, calls to my mother in passing that someone is at the door asking for us, winking at me, teasing, "Someone to see you," I am not even curious. I hear voices at the door, but my mother returns alone. "Guess who has come to see us," she says, pausing, her look priming me for a great surprise. She motions me to come out as if our crowded corner hadn't room enough to hold what I am about to see. Two young men greet me standing at a distance. One of them is dark-haired; I look at him first, and as if the anticipation of looking at the other were too much for me, knowing already who he is, I fasten my eyes to an uncertain smile and say, "Arnold—" "Baunoch," he adds, looking pleased. "And do you know who this is?" he says, guiding my look to the other man. My eyes widen to behold the gilded image. A tremor, somewhere inside me, and something shatters bell-like to sounds of lilting laughter; my whole body smiles. My lips don't move. My eyes slide to the floor; I have trouble lifting my gaze to the light. The feeling from long ago, nurtured by dreams and rememberings, sleeping sheltered, waiting for its time, now trembles into existence, given, like flowers growing, offered without choice. "Horst," I stammer, startled by my voice. The distance between us is filled; sounds well to flesh out a familiar voice, a smile flashes. My mother invites the young men into our corner; we shuffle to sit, making small talk. I mostly listen, blissful, suspended, unfocused, daring a glance now and then to the curling light hair, the sharp well-shaped nose, the sky-blue eyes, the mouth, the smile, as if to check each, weighing its value in the play of light. A tinge of arrogance gathered in a gaze looks almost apologetic in these smiling eyes. Our laughter spills and mingles, and when my father comes in to add his surprise to our happy gathering, our little corner grows crowded. The reshuffling of seats has the young men sitting on the bed facing the window. Suddenly, my blood rushes through me with the thunder of speeding trains and I realize, without looking, and with my eyes cast down I see the string of little flesh-colored flannel napkins grinning a slackened ark across the window. I hear the guffaw in the grimace over my heart's pounding, drowning out the conversation. A glance to confirm what I hope is not there. I talk louder to distract but it is no use; the visit is spoiled, marred by the unfortunate sight, the source of my shame. After our visitors leave, I cry. They say they will come back, but I know they will not. I still catch myself looking at the window, hoping nothing is there. My mother consoles me, saying the boys probably thought the napkins were hers. It does not help. I keep recalling the unfortunate event, imagining it differently, wishing I could change it. When, weeks later, our window sparkles with sunshine as if to assert that nothing there was ever amiss, Horst and Arnold come to visit!

• • •

The surprise of all surprises. We receive a letter regarding my mother's inquiry about the status of her citizenship. Though she was born in America, the authorities regret to inform her, she is no longer a citizen of the United States, and they give complicated reasons we do not understand. However, we read on carefully, I, her daughter, am eligible for citizenship and can be sworn in immediately. The conditions are specified: I must spend five years living in America before I am twenty-one. Since I will be sixteen in September, I must be in the United States on or before my birthday so as not to forfeit this opportunity. We understand only that this may be a chance for us to go to America; once I am there, my parents will soon be allowed to follow, everyone concerned assures us. And my father writes to Aunt and Uncle Stocker in Cincinnati explaining it all, asking whether I could stay with them till he and my mother get their visas. My mother adds her own concern: I would have to be given the opportunity to go to school, for which she and my father promise to provide; they both have jobs and will have money. An immediate response by telegram assures my parents, and the letter that follows explains, that not only will our relatives have me come— they will pay for my fare. As for going to school, it is mandatory in America for everyone under eighteen. My parents are pleased; they accept the cost of the fare as a loan. It seems the decision is made. Enchanted by the proposed adventure, I think of nothing else. Everybody would want to go to America! At school I am an instant celebrity. Soon I am sworn in by the consul general at the American Embassy in Stuttgart in a short ceremony with only my parents and a deputy present. The thing I do not like is having to raise my hand, an old aversion, swearing loyalty to country—I show my dissension by mouthing the hollow words, scowling in defiance. The authorities don't notice and congratulate me.

I take my American passport to school. Hanna immediately finds fault: "They changed your name; you signed it Louise; why did you do that?" "They told me to sign it exactly as it was typed," I say in my defense. Ingrid scolds, "You should have had them change it; you should not have let them change your name instead." I don't tell them that I know how trivial, how troublesome, names, initials, claims to identity are. I say instead, "What does it matter?" They look at me perplexed.

My mother takes me shopping in fancy stores in Stuttgart. I try on beautiful dresses in front of long mirrors, ladies fussing over me. They are all too long, too grown-up for me, my mother insists. The salesperson disagrees. We pick out a white pique with bright flowers, a sun dress with a bolero, matching shorts and halter—to wear on the boat—a suit, some blouses, a pleated skirt and dress. My mother will shorten them, she says. "It will ruin the line," the lady protests, "the fashion is long this year." "She is only a little girl," my mother asserts, "she will wear them short." I say nothing. We buy beautiful white suede shoes and fancy red wedge-heeled sandals. It is quite an expense. I did not know we had so much money.

The fifteenth of July arrives, chilled and overcast; an all-night rain left the road to the station showing puddles. I leave the Durchgangslager with an entourage of family and friends. We take the train to Stuttgart together; Arnold meets us at the Hauptbahnhof, bringing greetings from Horst. Past the repeated embraces, tears, well wishing, cautions and directives, promises to write, past my mother's concerned looks, there is my anticipation. I am not leaving; I am going on a journey, on an adventure of my own, sent off with blessings. I beam my good fortune and everyone cooperates, telling me I am right.

• • •

The *S. S. Washington* is planked for boarding. Giant cranes lift the cargo onto its decks. The ship is larger than I could have imagined. On board it seems larger still. It is a city afloat with all kinds of amenities: stores, restaurants, bars, movies, board games. I am free to explore. The overwhelming view of sea and sky, the pleasant atmosphere on deck, the congeniality in the dining room, the exotic food, and the presence of a real captain, entice.

A stop near the coast of Ireland. Hills of lush green wedged between sea and sky; bright whites flicker, reflecting the sun. Seagulls. Small boats come to greet us, selling their wares.

Not being responsible to anyone is restful. Now and then I catch myself being self-conscious, thinking I am noticed, perhaps wishing that someone would notice me—anyone—but this feeling never occupies me for very long, and it never makes me think I might be lonely; it just makes me feel awkward, restless.

We see the hazy skyline of New York rising from the water, the torch of liberty raised for our arrival. So greeted, a wave of appreciation sweeps the decks in floods of cheers and clapping. Announcements inform us U.S. citizens are first to debark.

The captain and his staff, lined up for leave-taking, chat with passengers leaving. Shaking my hand, the captain says something I do not understand.

CHAPTER 16

America,
a New Beginning

I AM LOST IN A SEA of people, scanning the exotic faces of velveted brown. The waiting crowd, those seated and standing, those passing through, all in continuous flux, gives the enormous space in which we wait the appearance of being ungrounded, floating. Announcements on the loudspeaker pitch their echoing beacons to guide our way. I only hear the cadence of speech; I cannot single out any words. With help from others, I am on the train to Cincinnati.

The train moves out of the station; long stretches of industrial landscape present a dismal view. Soon this will change, I think, but I tire before it does, and my shifting glances brush the passengers sitting before me. Their faces, their clothes, their bearing seem unfamiliar and a thought surprises: I am among strangers now. The man across the aisle is languorously leafing through a large book aspread on his lap. A glimpse of pastel colors— paintings. Nudes. He catches my gaze and smiles. I look down, blushing, and try not to look his way again. Later, with my eyes cast down, I see the book closed; I read the bold letters. Renoir.

I stare, vacant, listening to the sound of the speeding train, and suddenly a disturbing feeling emerges full-blown, insistent, racing to a startling realization: I am here alone, without my family; I am going to live with people I have never met, and I will have to stay. Thoughts so urgent and disturbing leave no room for me to breathe. I keep staring into the void, trying to avoid panic. I feel like throwing up. A sense of finality, an indictment, a long sentence charged with feelings of regret. Trapped. It is all a terrible mistake; I must be rescued! I look to the book. The man holding it has his eyes closed.

Cincinnati! I recognize Tanti Stocker among the waiting crowd from pictures they sent. Her white hair and handsome black eyebrows make her distinguished, easy to notice from afar. Onkl Stocker is the small man with the flat haircut standing beside her. We greet each other with kisses. Onkl Stocker drives a large powder blue car, a Chrysler. *"So wie in Klan-Niklos,"* just like in our village, he means, pointing out sights on our way through the city. The long ride ends with a turn into a gravel driveway; I recognize the familiar birdhouse perched on a pillar where the drive forks around the brick house with the many windows. Behind the house a sizable shop of cement blocks boasts the sign: Stocker and Sons Roofers. Several trucks are parked near a dump of rusting metal.

I don't know why nothing here surprises me. I am shown everything with such pride, and the only expectation is that I be duly impressed. I don't want to disappoint, and to show my gratitude, my respect, I feel obliged to fake the desired response. "This is America," they say, showing me its wonders, and to make the distinction clear, Onkl Stocker scoffs, "just like in Klan-Niklos." I smile to show appreciation for his humor.

There is always a sizable crowd gathered around the dining room table on weekends. The young people speak English only; the aunts and uncles talk to me, speaking the dialect of our village interspersed with English words. Only Onkl Nick still talks about the village, introducing me to some of my father's childhood adventures. I like Onkl Nick's sad, soulful eyes.

The first week the Stockers take me sightseeing. The imposition of my motion sickness has me feeling apologetic wherever we go. To my surprise, Onkl Stocker regards the malady as a symptom of my backward attitude and something I should be able to control. I am bewildered that a spontaneous sensation that can lead to the guileless act of throwing up should be suspect, relegated to willful fabrication. But my dubious maladjustment does not stop us from going places, and I am expected to participate in everything the Stockers do with their friends. On long nights of bowling, my lack of interest showing, I smile a lot. When the ball betrays my aim, rolling into the gutter, I am accused of not trying. I quickly get used to such criticism; it only registers as a difference in Onkl Stocker's mood and my aunt's hovering concern about him.

I am learning things about myself and my new home. I now call Tanti and Onkl Stocker Mom and Pop. This is what they call each other and what the crowd around the dinner table calls them, except for their friends, who call them Anna and Joe. Around the table, as everywhere else, Pop dominates the conversation even when he says very little. Things said by others are listened to with his approval in mind. He has strong opinions about everything and his pronouncements color the conversation and tend to obliterate any opposing views. One knows how to slant one's comments to please him. There is a tendency on Mom's part to slant everything, even the food, to his preference, serving special foods only for him. It seems everyone around the table is here to please, to gain his acceptance. This is painfully clear with his sons. Johnny, mild-mannered, shy, is always talkative around his father, cautiously seeking his approval. His efforts are all the more pitiable as they seem futile. Joe is sullen, says very little. His wife Marylee, gently coaxing him with smiles, playfully voices opinions to which he only grunts his agreement or disapproval, and she continues curbing her play around his grunts. He rarely says anything in this crowd, and when he does speak, his are unslanted remarks inviting no reply.

I am not encouraged to talk much about my parents, about the past in general. To me, it is important. When I talk about the concentration camp, acknowledging their packages, telling them what a difference they made, I expect them to be interested, since they had so generously responded to our need. "It was Mom who did all the work. You can thank her," Pop says curtly. "Regin gathered clothes from her neighbors, but the rest was all Mom's doing, preparing the packages, taking care that they were mailed." She spent days wrapping packages, Mom admits, looking grateful, appreciating his acknowledgment. But when I talk about events that happened in the camp, the conversation is discounted with a wave of a hand. Granted, things were bad, but how bad could they have been, for here I am. In any case, there is no point in talking about unpleasant things; there is life to be lived. Yes—theirs, I think to myself, feeling dismissed. At such times it is difficult to believe that their help had anything to do with understanding our plight. It occurs to me that helping us may have been just coincidental, the thing to do at the time. That I am here at all suddenly takes on the significance of whim, and a chance at survival has the value of a missed outing to the amusement park. Thinking like this makes me feel ungrateful, ashamed. Sometimes my talk about the camp is cut off abruptly by a reprimand from Pop made to sound like concern, done in the interest of that all-important undertaking, that deliberate construction, the remaking of oneself. "We are the master of our own destiny." It is the amen in the invocation to reason, and I soon learn to say nothing about my experiences.

I used to be just myself, and now, it seems, I have become a problem. Everything about me is perceived as needing change. My name is changed, my beautiful new clothes are relegated to the storage closet, and I, wearing other people's clothes measuring the appropriate length, down to my ankles, still don't measure up. My name, my clothing, even my identity is in question.

Everyone here calls me Lucy. Everyone but Tanti Regin, who calls me Lewis (which she pronounces Le-vis). "My neighbors' name is Lewis," she explains, giving her approval, proudly adding, "Mr. and Mrs. Lewis are real Americans." Tanti Regin lives in Norwood, on the first floor of a two-story frame house next to a gas station. Her kitchen smells of herbal teas, reminding me of Altkroßmotter's house; I tell her, but she doesn't respond to my talking about her mother and never talks about the village, her childhood, her home. Only the familiar pictures of her son Albert, dressed in white, playing the accordion, confirm the relationship.

· · ·

I am disappointed. In my first test, in general science, the questions are true and false and multiple choice. My grade, 92, is an A. The initial excitement of this achievement soon wears off when I consider that I know nothing of the content, having memorized the assignments in the text without understanding what I read. I can only conclude that the grade proves I can match words. Relying on my memory, I can tell if the words are in the right order, or if a word is missing, I can find it on the list provided. What about the content studied? I know nothing about that, and no one is able to tell from this test that I have not learned anything. It seems only I find this devastating, for when I try to tell others, no one seems to care, no one listens, no one understands what I mean. The only condition my mother made for my coming here, to continue my education, is now betrayed by a single test.

Though I understand little of what is being said, I pick up the general attitude of the students. Many are disinterested; going to school seems an imposition, not a privilege. The love of learning, the desire to know, is not evident in the classes I attend. It may be an individual pursuit, but it is not the aspiration of the school; here the approach seems to be a matter of good-natured putting up with instruction. Students are more interested in being popular, being accepted. A definite concept of the "good life" and a strong desire to make oneself into the thing to be, I later learn, takes precedence over learning. And the aim of education is primarily to perpetuate the existing social values, to meet the status quo. That one can succeed without being educated is what makes this country so great, I hear my relatives boast, reflecting a general opinion.

The lack of importance given to an education and the lack of respect for the educated is new to me. Even the Partisans singled out the *inteligencija*. Professors, teachers, priests, the educated of our ethnic group, were killed first. They were the bearers of our culture, and their death conveyed the ultimate aim, the death of our culture. Here the educated do not seem important enough to cause much concern. Such are my opinions at sixteen and, having no place to air them, I keep them to myself.

On the bus coming home from school, the noisy chatter yields a single phrase: "He said," and then, in alternation, "he said, she said," fall out of conversations. Words, words. The noise unravels into fluid speech, sentences, words. I understand. I want to shout, but restraining my inclination, I grin into the sky. "He said, she said," I skip up the drive, singing. "The sky is especially blue today," I write to my parents, "and today, for the first time, I understand what people are saying when they speak to each other; I am so relieved." I do not tell them how I feel about school and about other things— I do not want them to worry.

Only the sky, with its intense crystal blues, invites participation; everything else is poised for admiration. Even the landscape is distant and detached; the earth itself seems indifferent, removed, unresponsive to affection, as if to deny us. Fruits I taste—peaches, apricots, plums, grapes—betray this misfortune. All look luscious, but their individual taste is tinged with a flat, undistinguished generality. At first the distance between their good looks and the expected savor shocks me and I spit out the tasted morsel involuntarily. In disbelief, I taste each again and again, trying to eke out their essential flavor; nothing but flat pulp. I mourn the loss. "Haven't you missed the flavor of grapes?" I ask Mom while eating the opulent berries. She looks at me bewildered.

I allow myself comments about food. The taste of potato chips is unpleasant to me; my relatives seem disbelieving. I excuse my undeveloped palate, referring to the salty delicacy as the crunchy host-wafer of satanic rituals. Pop, who does not like potato chips, enjoys the comment. Cocacola, with its medicinal taste, is reduced to something that should be taken in teaspoons for indigestion only. That, too, gets a laugh. They think I am trying to be funny; they cannot imagine I might be serious. Though there is an abundant variety of food, all is seasoned to an obtuse uniformity, tasting tinny. Canned. Only the bricks of ice cream Grandfather told me about are as good as or better than I imagined; something to write home about. I can always count on Grandfather not to disappoint.

All this unloved food takes its revenge. When I get one boil after another, "It's the rich food," Mom says, "You're not used to it." The boils multiply, hurting like the abscesses they are, and remain unresponsive to the poultice of home remedies. Marylee takes me to the doctor. Dr. Frieden looks at me with kind, brown eyes. "I bet they hurt like hell; why didn't you come sooner?" Lancing the boils, he scolds, accusing "old-country" modesty, backward attitudes responsible for letting things get out of hand, causing a lot of unnecessary suffering. I don't feel accused. I grit my teeth against the pain and puzzle over his notion of old-country, backward attitudes as a diversion.

• • •

"So this is the little girl who came from Germany, all by herself," the man delivering groceries says, being friendly. His mother's people originally came from Frankfurt. My parents live near Stuttgart, I offer in reply. "Her mother was born in Cincinnati," Pop interjects grudgingly, sparing his words, flitting by. It is obvious he does not like this grocer.

The subject of my origin reappears mysteriously at a gathering around the dining-room table with the usual crowd and one added guest, Joe's friend, Professor Nosow. Preoccupied, chatting, I miss the gist of the conversation initiated by Pop from the far end of the table; I recognize the tone as the onset of a tongue-lashing and sense the cringe of discomfort bracing for it. I am especially embarrassed for our guest, who may not be used to such fare. The topic this time is deceit. The tone of the talk is provoking, but the accused are not yet named. I deliberately ignore the harangue (perhaps to conceal my embarrassment) and it takes some time before I notice that I am being set up. Shocked into acknowledgment, I first try to ignore the accusation; if I just say nothing, it might pass. But Pop is resolute and continues increasing his insults. It is obvious to everyone, I can tell from the covering looks around me, that I am the target of these charges.

Shamed, I confront the assault, asking almost casually, "Are you directing these accusations at me?" "If the shoe fits," Pop retorts, without looking up from his plate, and continues: "Some people pride themselves, putting on airs, saying they come from Germany, lying about their origin, as if being German were something to be proud of." I am reluctant to answer; I don't know where to begin. "I don't understand your point?" I interject. "Ever since I came here I have been introduced as the girl who came from Germany; I never thought much about it. Germany, the place I left to come here, seems an appropriate reference." "You are from Klan-Niklos, a village in Yugoslavia," Pop interrupts. "You are a Yugoslav, a *Schwop* from Yugoslavia; you are not German." I can feel myself getting angry even though the argument seems ridiculous. "Like you, I am Swabian and from Yugoslavia," I continue firmly, taming my anger. "Though you and I were born in the same village, you were born in Austro-Hungary, but since you came here in 1920, you came from Yugoslavia. Are you Austrian, Hungarian, Yugoslavian?" He ignores my argument and says sharply, "I am an American." Johnny, eager to please his father, offers a plum: "I would not want to be German, if I were you; I would be ashamed of it." And seeing me look surprised, he buffers the comment, smiling, "You don't want to be on the losers' side, do you? Why would you want to be one of them?" "I don't want to be anything; I can only be who I am," I interrupt. Others have picked up the argument, but I cannot listen to everyone. "Since I was put in a concentration camp at nine and a half, left there to starve to death only because we were *Nemci, Švabe*, it seems ridiculous for me to deny being German now. Having been where others lost their lives for it, my being German is not a matter of patriotism, fashion, or pride. Even those who thought to kill us never accused us of wanting to be German; they never asked us to be anything other than German. They insisted on us being German; their fervor to kill us demanded it. They did not make us feel guilty for who we were," I say, directing blaming looks at Pop. "They only wanted us dead! Forged by their fervor and our endurance, my ethnicity is in no danger of ever being denied, no matter by what name you call it; it makes no difference— I am among the intended not to be; this is my origin, my identity—and it is you who are asking me to deny it, to do the very thing you say you find deceitful!" By now my voice has taken on a harsh accusing tone and people are looking to their plates to avoid getting involved.

"It could be said that there were good reasons for you being put in concentration camps, that you deserved it because you fought against your country." I can't believe I am hearing right. "Who fought against their country? Those who were starved to death were women, children, and old people, none of whom fought anywhere, and some, like Nina néni, never had anyone in any of the wars—even priests were put in concentration camps, tortured, killed. They certainly did not fight against their country." "But some would argue differently," he interrupts, asking for the butter. "It may take being in a concentration camp to realize that no reason good enough could ever exist to justify people being persecuted, made to suffer and starve to death." Livid, I become prophetic, speaking in tongues: "It would seem reasonable to consider that the deliberate extermination of a people is always unjustified, undeserved. It is a crime; a crime that cannot be excused as deserved, as revenge, without condoning all such crimes." There is quiet around the table. Pop reaches for his prune juice, satisfied with the entertainment. It seems I just sang for my supper. Feeling appreciative for all that was done for us is harder to accomplish. I recall how grateful we were, how remembered, how understood we felt when packages arrived from America—and the spoonful of peanut butter doled out in the dark, luminous like a sacrament, pales here in the light of the laden table.

I carry my home with me like a cradle. Here among strangers there is no feeling of belonging, no trace of the integrity of the village. Here I have no identity. Cut off from everything, unrelated, undefined, unintelligible to others, alone, I lose meaning.

Since I am nothing, I could become anything, I think, searching my face in the mirror. I am seventeen. I watch the image slide off the slick surface, the mirror giving it back, shallow, tinlike, reflecting a vacuous assurance behind which a feeling of despair lies waiting to be exposed. Who am I? The image consoles, affirming: it is the image most fit for the new environment, the new image for the place to be. It has arrived. That which the new environment is incapable of holding, the mirror takes in, keeping it from being abandoned like the winter clothes of travelers to the tropics. Everything is as it should be, the image approves. I cultivate this image with defiance and wear it like a mask, like tribal markings, proudly. People around me notice I have changed. And I, the hidden witness, grounded in alien experiences, continue waiting to be recognized. Mute among the conversant, my experiences and I hover inferior, looking insecure. And the deception of our disguise becomes a cover, a hiding place where our riches hold their breath in shame.

• • •

Coming home from school, hanging my clothes in my closet, I find the storage showing a noticeable order and immediately feel accused for not having thought of doing it myself. I notice that my clothes from Germany, my beautiful clothes, are no longer where I am used to seeing them. A vague apprehension sickens, and I hurry to ask Mom about the change in the closet, the whereabouts of my things. She has given my clothes to the Salvation Army, she says curtly. My dresses, skirts, blouses, coats, my sweaters that my mother knitted, all flash before me one by one with the distress of leave-taking. My clothes—gone. I stare at her stunned. She says something about needing the space, but I do not hear her; I only see her smile. I cannot let her see me cry. I run out of the house, not knowing where to go. Past the shop, down the cement steps to the stable, I want to keep running but the fence, its gate bolted, stops me. I look to the hill, thinking of a road beyond it and where it would take me. Fumbling with the tangle of chains, I wail to the rusty rattle, looking to the silvery line describing the crest of the hill against the sky. The barren fruit tree, alone in the shallow of the hill, its branches drooping to touch the tall grasses—"never bears any decent fruit," I recall Mom's scolding voice, "cherries sour like poison, only fit for the birds." Sparrows chirp in the empty stable. The horses have been sold long ago. The scraggly spotted pony that replaced them looks at me from behind the fence, its tousled mane and long tail a gather of burrs and thistles, and goes on grazing. The smell of the stable comforts me. I sit down on the cement steps and concentrate, insistent: there must be a way out. I cannot bear to stay here any longer. I must find a way to earn money, to pay for my trip home. I fantasize about a job, the trip, crying quietly. But my parents—they want to come here. I do not want to ruin their chance. I continue weeping. I see my mother's face, her marble profile of endurance, and my father's kind eyes looking helpless. The sour cherry tree in the distance undulates, blurred by my tears. I stare into the emptiness, turned in on myself, sitting very still, unaware of time passing. A sudden soft flutter, a heavy hum, sparkles iridescence into my face. I startle into a shriek, lurching back against the stable wall, watching the darting transparent flutter of crystalline green retreat: a hummingbird. I burst out crying. A hummingbird, I say consoling. A hummingbird.

• • •

Pop buys a piano. Standing upright against the wall of the living room, it surprises everyone. I am to take lessons with Mrs. Kennedy who lives up the road. I am stunned.

Lessons with Mrs. Kennedy are pleasant, engaging. But on a day when I feel especially discouraged, and perhaps only to cover for a week of neglected practice, I break down sobbing, telling Mrs. Kennedy how I miss my parents. She, always in control, suggests I write to Senator Taft. It takes a week, a whole notebook of paper wasted, and seems like writing a letter to God. In it I tell about having been in concentration camps in Yugoslavia, about the reason for my coming here, about being separated from my parents for almost two years now, about my no longer wishing to stay here without them, even if it means losing my citizenship. It is a long letter, written in secret and in my best script, asking for help.

"A letter to Washington. She wrote it herself and got a reply from the Senator—imagine, a letter from Senator Taft," Mom tells Regin on the telephone. I count on the Senator's promises and immediately write to my parents.

I now have a part-time job at Kroger's. I work in the back of the store slicing and wrapping cheese. I stamp the egg and milk cartons, replenish the stock in the dairy case, and give refunds for pop bottles, stacking them in wooden crates, with leftover bottles crowding my dreams. I make mistakes on prices, inverting numbers, usually to the customer's advantage. Luckily such mistakes are discovered in time, thanks to Mabel, the lady in charge, who covers for me with sullen looks. Tough, outspoken, not given to friendly chatter, she allows no one to cross her. I see her eyeing me distrustfully, as she does everyone, but I can tell she likes me. Jack, a tall, blue-eyed stock boy, who now takes me home from work—since it is on his way, he says—asks, would I like to go to a movie sometime? I say yes, not thinking much about it.

A letter from Senator Taft's office! I am beside myself with joy. My parents are coming! The air is charged with anticipation; my excitement spills over everything. I now go to movies with Jack and his friends. I am introduced to Frisch's, french fries, chocolate malts, and banana splits, and within a month I become a "real American teenager." I am interested in and agree with everything around the dinner table, and when someone remarks carelessly, "You might soon be sorry; when your parents come, you will be poor again, you know," I only cringe, excusing the callous remark, thinking they say it only to remind me that I look insultingly happy to be leaving; showing so much happiness may seem impolite.

I cannot realize the truth of the coming event even now. Waiting for the train, I feel a dizzying excitement teasing me with the impossible realization, boosting my anticipation to float among the mosaic patterns of muraled walls . . . the echoing sounds of voices floating by . . . footsteps tapping the floor like hammers in juxtaposition to the imperceptible movement of the giant wall clock, its impartial bold face watching.

Everything slows into existence with my mother's face, pale and marble-like, looking straight ahead, her slender body slicing the space, looking smaller then I remembered, and my father, looking splendid in his gray suit with the pleated pockets, his fine eyes searching the room, walking weighted carrying suitcases. Seeing them, I am shocked into realization of the great loss having been away from them. This awareness could only be realized in their presence; without them here, it could not have been endured. I read this gift of grace from my parents' eyes groping for mine. The loudspeaker rasps, imposing on our embraces. Nothing can intrude on the space between us—on the warm, wide plain of home.

Epilogue

When friends would say on occasion, "You had a terrible child-hood," I was always surprised, and a bit disappointed. What were they thinking? It was my childhood, the only one I had, as remembered and as dear to me as theirs was to them. How could they equate childhood, the beginning of things, when all is new and eternal, with *terrible*. Growing up seemed less integrated, more alienating; as a teenager, especially, I felt foreign, socially inept. The idealistic notions, dreams, and aspirations of others my age—being popular, getting married—seemed make-believe, a game, its only meaning being that I was expected to play it. I wanted to belong.

The feeling of home brought about by the reunion with my parents extended only to our family; the world around us seemed pleasant, but we were strangers in it. Norwood High School was a much better school than the one I left. Though I did not have any close friends, I achieved some recognition with my talent in art. And when the art teacher, Mr. Olmes, and his young wife took me to weekly evening classes at the Art Academy and, on their way home, to visit other artists, their friends, I saw the possi-bility of a more attractive world. Later, as a student on a scholarship at the Art Academy, I felt among my own. It was a small school and afforded the feeling of belonging. Being singled out for intense work, surrounded by the individuality of intent students (Tom Wesselmann among them) made for an appealing atmosphere, a place of escape from conformity. The sheltered environment offered fellowship, identity. Languorous strolls through the museum, lingering around favorite works of art, transported me into a world to which I liked belonging. I wanted to stay in that world. And when a graduating student, admired for his talent, asked me to marry him, it seemed the best of two worlds—the dream world of the good life and the reality of art united.

Interrupting my studies would be throwing away my talent, my teachers were concerned enough to mention, perhaps only because they were recommending me for a scholarship. I was twenty and insisted I could do both, go to school and be married. They must have known it was not so. The connection to that world to which I wanted to belong would be maintained through my husband, Glenn Owen, who continued to paint; I worked in an office. I would go to classes at night, but it was not the same. I missed the continuous work, the community of students; the space to belong.

I often wondered how my parents had the energy, the faith, to start anew with such enthusiasm and untiring vigor. In a new country, without knowing the language, they had jobs the third day they were here. Others from our village, refugees who came here before us—Wagner Vedde Hans, who still teased me, mimicking my gestures, *"gaće gore, gaće dole,"* and his wife, Margit néni—helped my parents get jobs. My mother worked in a sweatshop, downtown, sewing piecework. It took three buses to get to the machine and tool shop where my father worked. He did all the shopping on his way home and knew where to get the best of things in different stores. We lived in the apartment on the second floor of Aunt Regin's house. My parents spent their weekends working at Stocker's, and my mother dazzled them with her Schtrudl and other pastries; masterpieces, Pop called them. Though my parents paid off the loan for my trip immediately, they felt they had to repay in work for the two years of my stay. When, after five years, my father finally stopped going, and Aunt Regin aired a complaint in his presence, Pop scolded: "If truth be told, making an account of it all, we'd be surprised as to who would be owing whom."

Within two years of their arrival, and just after I got married, my parents bought a house, astonishing the relatives. It would take a lot longer for my father to buy a car; he waited till they had the money saved to pay for it outright. My parents took such pride in their work, their house, their yard and garden, and everything they did was measured by principles that governed life in the village at home. They had little time to socialize, but the village was there for them in people they knew from home, who, like them, were living the "good life," isolated.

The birth of our son Erik was the fulfillment of my parents' dreams.

In 1959 my husband and I attended the Art Students League summer session in Woodstock, New York; I studied drawing with Arnold Blanch. Working among an array of colorful, energetic students—seeing some slashing away at huge canvases (action painters), looking glorious, important—

being invited to the house of Arnold Blanch and Doris Lee, meeting other artists, I felt intimidated, unworthy. Washing diapers on a washboard and taking care of Erik kept me grounded, observing the tantalizing fringe of the art world.

When my husband decided to get his degree in education, we moved in with my parents. I now worked for an advertising agency (from four to twelve at night), feeding cards into noisy machines, sorting them alphabetically, producing mailing lists. It was boring manual labor in a factory environment. The agency looked down over the Taft Museum gardens, where a lush evergreen ivy had a way of reminding me of home. I spent my breaks at that window; it offered a connection to a former self.

Longings for the past would often emerge unexpectedly. On weekend rides in the country, for instance, I would want us to stop at a farmhouse; I wanted to meet "real" people, and I was convinced they would have sheep cheese and yogurt for sale. On late autumn days, the crisp air would conjure familiar scents, the excitement of a disznótor. Though such memories were comforting, invigorating, they informed, at the same time, that the feeling of home was elsewhere and far away.

In 1962 we moved from my parents house to Yellow Springs, a village near Dayton, Ohio, where my husband had a job teaching art in high school. He had befriended one of his professors at the university, Dr. Duke Madenfort, who now taught at Antioch College. Our long intense talks, discussions of books he recommended, reminded me of the privileged tutorials with Tante Gebauer and was the education I craved. Through this friendship I developed insights about art and aesthetics, a way of viewing the world that enlarged and supported my own perception. My interest in teaching came about because of this association, but the decision to go back to school was sudden, unrelated, and followed a trip home in 1967.

Exhausted after the long train ride, I am walking down Vinogradska toward Lisi néni's house, carrying a heavy suitcase. No one knows of my coming. In talks about home, those who did not know would say I have idealized it; one visit would cure that. But that is not why I have come. Down the dusky road, a lone bike rider is coming closer; it is a young man, and without a trace of surprise in his voice, he calls to me, *"Te vagy, Lujza?"*— is it you, he asks, calling my name. Ervin and I have not seen each other since 1950, and here we are in mutual recognition at dusk. The fragrance of *estike*, as poignant as always, in Lisi néni's summer garden convinces me all is exactly as I remembered. And as if by some design, I have come just in time for Ervin's wedding; he and his bride, Eta, will soon move in with plans to change the house. Everything embraces, comforts, and reassures; all is as remembered. Tantalizing scents and tastes entice. A wedding feast.

At home in Yellow Springs, Ohio, 1962, photographed by my son Erik when he was four years old.

A blessing. I have come home! And soon an insight gifted with candid simplicity reveals: *All is as it was, only I have changed.* The question as to where I belong is moot; the decision has been made without my knowing it.

Returning from my trip, I tackle the job of going to school seriously, preparing to be independent, making decisions on my own.

Some of the old experiences continue to surface; I am never far away from them, it seems. I see a film in sociology class—a Jewish ghetto, some newsreel footage; a little boy dancing, begging for food; the familiar vacant look, the staring eyes of children in a concentration camp. The commentator has things to say. The class is taking notes for discussion. But the images I see are a reality to me; I cannot bear them to be used as teaching tools.

This is not an experience to distance, to have opinions about, not an occasion for sentiment or for imparting notions of social justice. When the first paltry statements by the class are uttered, I unglue myself from my seat and quietly leave. I have so much rage; I wish I could vomit, but I only hold my face and sob.

Sometimes I wake to the sound of chanting, *"Tetka Mila molim parče hleba."* I tell my stories to friends, on occasion—I do not really know why; when I start, I am unable to stop. And at times a chance conversation—others airing concerns about discrimination they have observed in a restaurant, and a callous remark about my being European, never having been discriminated against, I would not understand—can enrage to laughter. I say nothing at such times; revealing any of my experiences would be a betrayal.

But memories of the past do not govern my life. They are an integral part of it; the past is something I do not keep at bay, nor do I dwell on it. Particular experiences surface at times, bringing the attending feelings with them, but these are isolated incidents. Life with family and friends in the attractive environment of a most unique village is pleasant, favorable. It is the physical village, its natural charm, the ground itself, it seems, that recalls the integral unity I had known only at home.

Continuing my education at Wright State University, getting a masters degree and a job teaching in the College of Education, and earning a Ph.D. from Ohio State University brings new experiences—confidence. During this time Erik and I are alone; his father and I are divorced.

In 1984 my son and his wife, Deirdre, go with me to Europe; we visit our village as guests of the priest. Except for some isolated houses that still reflect the old order, the village looks desolate: its houses in disrepair, grass growing in front of their doors, here and there newer additions (imports from Germany) disrupting its structural unity. Driving through the empty streets—it is too hot to walk on a sweltering midafternoon—we scan the distanced view. We stop at our house. The gate is open. I go inside alone. Doves that still live in the attic of what once was the blacksmith shop flutter above me. Three little girls, about nine years old, are playing in the shade by the climbing ivy. A small woman, her hair tied back with a floral kerchief, steps down from the shaded entry, eyeing me with a scrutinizing look. I explain the intrusion, speaking in Hungarian, giving credentials, cautiously offering proof: "I think this may have been our house once—does one of the rooms have a floor of yellow hexagonal tile?" She asks me in. Crossing the threshold of the back room, I look to the window, checking for height (it seems much lower since I last saw it, nearly forty years ago), and follow her through the rooms. The front room is dark, the shutters closed. Sudden and unexpected, an overwhelming surge of grief gathers; I strain to squelch the impending scream, tears rolling down my cheeks before I can think, before I can feel embarrassed. I see my fingers making a gesture, touching the shutter to gently stroke it. A look to the woman; she, too, is crying. We stand wordless, looking at each other, embraced by the dusky light. She asks softly, would I like to see the room that once was the blacksmith shop? I shake my head. No. We walk back silently, and on the way out, below the cupboard with the glass doors, in a narrow bed, a beautiful man with curly black hair is sleeping. "He won't believe . . ." she whispers. Out in the yard, the children are crouching on the ground, quietly playing, remote like an image from the past, not noticing my passing. I turn to the woman to thank her; she does not follow me to the gate. The doves are cooing above me; all else is stilled as if in a dream. A gift, only for me, Erik says when I tell him I wish he had been there.

• • •

My father claims never to have been homesick; to him everything in the United States is an extension of home. My mother will occasionally lament about this and that—the lack of community, identity: "At home we were somebody; here, among strangers, we don't know who we are." And the Schtrudl, the dobos she continues to offer as presents for the kindness of others, are also, I think, telling about home, about who we are. Yet my father surprises me, expressing his feelings obliquely: I watch him looking at a feather I had picked up in our churchyard, a slender pigeon feather I had brought back from our trip. He takes it and gently strokes both his cheeks with it; seeing me, he whispers, shyly, "from home." In 1997 I put this feather in his coffin.

During years of teaching, teaching art, teaching aesthetics, drawing attention to the subtle communion (exemplified by the arts) that transcends all our divisions, pointing to an awareness that integrates, that does not divide, I was never far from home. While my teaching did not approach the excellence of a work of art, it did avoid the proliferation of just another ideology, I hope. If I gave anything, I gave encouragement to my students to trust this integral awareness; to develop and express their perception; to question their preconceptions and prejudices. In this quest for awareness, integrity, I gave the establishment only what it required, and I always knew that nothing it had to offer was mine.

Living this awareness in community with others continues to confirm my trust. Seeing my son grow, being with my grandchildren, reaffirms the joy of being. Life is good.

• • •

It is a privilege to start life anew in a country with wonderful opportunities, it is true, but one's past cannot be forgotten; only laid aside. As survivors, we offer the new world—a world of belonging—to our children, our grand-children, and whisper our secrets to the dark.

Still, an irrevocable loss needs confirmation, needs community, needs commemoration; we know. An ethnic cleansing, given no acknowledgment, necessitates no denial; its victims, banished from ever having been, excluded from all community, require no mourning. The oppression continues. At least for the survivor, such oppression tinges the values of society with dis-gust. It takes courage for the survivor to be a member of society. Silence about the unspeakable may be the wisest when beginning life anew in an undiscerning society. But survivors are subversive even in their silence, and their choice to play the social game, for what it is worth, is itself an act of defiance.

One hopes for a bit of grace.

The birth of my granddaughter Marina, my first grandchild, brings about the grace required. Being with my grandchildren, Marina and Oona, ex-tends that grace to speak for those who did not live.

The forever remaining
cradled in the lap of the land,
the open portals to our being,
heirs to our endurance,
messengers of our faithfulness.

ISBN 1-58544-212-7